WILLIAM GOLDING: A CRITICAL STUDY OF THE NOVELS

also by Mark Kinkead-Weekes

SAMUEL RICHARDSON: DRAMATIC NOVELIST
D. H. LAWRENCE: TRIUMPH TO EXILE 1912–22

also by Ian Gregor

THE MORAL AND THE STORY (with Brian Nicholas)
THE GREAT WEB: THE FORM OF HARDY'S MAJOR FICTION

WILLIAM GOLDING
A Critical Study of the Novels

IAN GREGOR
and
MARK KINKEAD-WEEKES

*with a Biographical Sketch
by Judy Carver*

ff

faber and faber

First published in 1967
by Faber and Faber Limited
3 Queen Square, London WC1N 3AU
Published in paperback 1970
Second edition, revised, 1984
Third edition, revised and reset, 2002

Photoset by Wilmaset Ltd, Wirral
Printed in England by Clays Ltd, St Ives plc

© 1967, 1984 by Mark Kinkead-Weekes and Ian Gregor
New text and revisions © Mark Kinkead-Weekes, 2002
Bibliographical Sketch © William Golding Limited, 2002

ISBN 0–571–21564–5

2 4 6 8 10 9 7 5 3 1

CONTENTS

vii

PREFACE

This new book incorporates an older one. In 1967 the late Ian Gregor and I published a study of Golding's fiction up to and including *The Spire*. We thought of this as having a double purpose: to provide detailed readings of the five novels; and to describe the evolving nature of Golding's imagination as it revealed itself step by step in the process of their composition. Our treatment was more exploratory than judicial; more concerned (with an author in mid-career) to trace the changing nature of the fiction than to attempt conclusive judgements of strengths and weaknesses (though we had something to say about these in particular cases), or to 'place' the work in the context of contemporary literature. In 1983 we were asked to provide an additional essay on three more novels, which had appeared in the interim. These seemed to us to have an interesting relationship which we were mainly concerned to bring out, through readings somewhat less detailed than before. By then, too, Ian was far from well.

Golding's work is now, alas, complete, after four more novels and the award of the Nobel Prize. Suddenly, he belongs to the past; and we shall no longer be surprised by a new book whose nature could not possibly have been predicted. The time for conclusive judgement is not quite yet: Golding's letters and his Journal are being prepared for publication; and these will tell us a great deal more about the genesis and the problems of writing the novels than we can know at present. Time also needs to pass before we can tell how the fiction will last and come home to a new generation.

There may be readers in the meantime, however, who would welcome an account of all the novels, together with some interim consideration of the nature of Golding's imagination, on the evidence purely of the books themselves. Asked to provide such an account on the same lines as before, I have thought it best to leave our original book to stand, as a tribute to my good friend and colleague, and to keep his work current. It has a self-contained argument, and it allows the new book to be seen as the record of half a century's reading of a contemporary. I have however expanded our 1983 essay on the three books which followed *The Spire* into separate chapters, to match their predecessors, and have found – as one does – that time and the final works have altered the light somewhat, particularly in the case of *The Pyramid*, though our sense of the connections among the three books still seems sound. Unfortunately I have, now, to take sole responsibility for the readings of the four final novels, in a way that sharpens a sense of loss.

The final chapter is an attempt to approximate something of the process of mutual criticism between friends that produced the original book. For the volume which celebrated Golding's seventy-fifth birthday, Ian Gregor and I wrote essays which we deliberately never discussed until they had been sent away; only to find that, from different angles – Ian on what we might mean by calling Golding 'religious', I on the relation between the visual and the visionary – we had chosen many of the same examples and found ourselves making many of the same kinds of point. In order to balance the 'structural' chapter which had concluded our original book, I have made my essay the basis of a 'textural' chapter to conclude the whole; but have used Ian's as an equivalent of the kind of critique we used to make of one another's drafts; modifying a reading here, or adding a useful comparison there. What is missing, of course, and greatly missed, is the last stage after draft, commentary, and re-drafting: Ian's final comments.

I would like the book to be a tribute not only to him but also the friendship we were lucky enough to enjoy with the Goldings. (I am particularly happy that Judy Carver has encouraged me to write about her father again, and has provided a biographical sketch.) Our work was never in any sense an authorized account. Indeed our relationship had the self-imposed condition that we would never talk about Golding's writings unless he himself began. There was no lack of other subjects; or of laughter, beginning at our first meeting when he had been expecting 'two Scotch moralists', or so he said. It was a friendship more occasional than close, but it meant a great deal to us, and in its spirit I would like to dedicate the book

TO IAN, AND BILL, AND ANN

Mark Kinkead-Weekes
Ramsgate, 2002

LORD OF THE FLIES

(1954)

I

Lord of the Flies has become a compulsory stop on the route of any surveyor of the English novel after the Second World War, an addition to the canon of writings prescribed by school examination boards and even to kings, as one remarked before handing its author a Nobel Prize. It has been the subject of at least two volumes of critical essays published in the USA, and an award-winning film directed by Peter Brook. Such popular success has eluded the four novels which followed. They have received wide and sometimes generous notice, but it is the earlier work that has guaranteed them their respect. They have achieved virtue by association. Yet Golding's novels are unmistakably all of a piece. Among themselves they reveal a family resemblance, a unity even, that gives the phrase 'a Golding novel' a readily understood meaning. Why does the first occupy so unique a position?

What distinguishes *Lord of the Flies* is its powerful and exciting qualities as narrative, and its appearance of extreme clarity of meaning; the later works are more difficult both to read and to understand. *Lord of the Flies* fulfils most effectively the novelist's basic task of telling a good story. It also meets Conrad's pre-scription: 'by the power of the written word to make you hear, to make you feel ... before all, to make you *see*'. It was not surprising that it should have attracted the attention of the film director, providing him with an unwavering narrative drive, and also with an unbroken series of intensely visualized scenes. On the other hand, at every point and with a kind of inevitability that is as impressive as the story itself, we are made aware that much more than this story is being told; indeed a clearly focused and coherent body of meaning appears to be crystallizing out of every episode. A reader can feel that he possesses this novel in an unusually comprehensive way, and that he could give a lucid, even con-ceptual account of it. The book has high polish, and seems to present itself for our contemplation as a remarkably complete and solid structure. This of course may not always be regarded as a strength. Many readers may feel the book to be too crystalline, too insistent, too manipulated to be acceptable, but it seems likely that it is this combination of narrative momentum and thematic clarity that explains the popular success, which greater Golding novels have failed to achieve. Whether the art *is* so clear and crystalline, however, is perhaps open to question.

Let us consider the finding of the shell, which provides the title for the opening chapter. We watch the conch, we might say, liberated from ordinariness, grasped, filled with meaning:

'What's that?'

Ralph had stopped smiling and was pointing into the lagoon. Something creamy lay among the ferny weeds.

'A stone.'

'No. A shell.'

Suddenly Piggy was a-bubble with decorous excitement.

'
'Sright. It's a shell! I seen one like that before. On someone's back wall. A conch he called it. He used to blow it and then his mum would come. It's ever so valuable –'

Near to Ralph's elbow, a palm sapling leaned out over the lagoon. Indeed, the weight was already pulling a lump from the poor soil and soon it would fall. He tore out the stem and began to poke about in the water, while the brilliant fish flicked away on this side and that. Piggy leaned dangerously.

'Careful! You'll break it –'

'Shut up.'

Ralph spoke absently. The shell was interesting and pretty and a worthy plaything: but the vivid phantoms of his day-dream still interposed between him and Piggy, who in this context was an irrelevance. The palm sapling, bending, pushed the shell across the weeds. Ralph used one hand as a fulcrum and pressed down with the other till the shell rose, dripping, and Piggy could make a grab.

Now the shell was no longer a thing seen but not to be touched, Ralph too became excited. Piggy babbled:

'– a conch; ever so expensive. I bet if you wanted to buy one, you'd have to pay pounds and pounds and pounds – he had it on his garden wall, and my auntie –'

Ralph took the shell from Piggy and a little water ran down his arm. In colour the shell was deep cream, touched here and there with fading pink. Between the point, worn away into a little hole, and the pink lips of the mouth, lay eighteen inches of shell with a slight spiral twist and covered with a delicate, embossed pattern. Ralph shook sand out of the deep tube.

'– moo-ed like a cow,' he said. 'He had some white stones too, an' a bird cage with a green parrot. He didn't blow the white stones of course, an' he said –'

Piggy paused for breath and stroked the glistening thing that lay in Ralph's hands.

'Ralph!'

Ralph looked up.

'We can use this to call the others. Have a meeting. They'll come when they hear us –'

He beamed at Ralph.

'That was what you meant, didn't you? That's why you got the conch out of the water?'

Ralph pushed back his fair hair.

'How did your friend blow the conch?'

'He kind of spat,' said Piggy. 'My auntie wouldn't let me blow on account of my asthma. He said you blew from down here.' Piggy laid a hand on his jutting abdomen. 'You try, Ralph. You'll call the others.'

Doubtfully, Ralph laid the small end of the shell against his mouth and blew. There came a rushing sound from its mouth but nothing more. Ralph wiped the salt water off his lips and tried again, but the shell remained silent.

'He kind of spat.'

Ralph pursed his lips and squirted air into the shell, which emitted a low, farting noise. This amused both boys so much that Ralph went on squirting for some minutes, between bouts of laughter.

'He blew from down here.'

Ralph grasped the idea and hit the shell with air from his diaphragm. Immediately the thing sounded. A deep, harsh note boomed under the palms, spread through the intricacies of the forest and echoed back from the pink granite of the mountain. Clouds of birds rose from the treetops, and something squealed and ran in the undergrowth.

Ralph took the shell away from his lips.

'Gosh!'

The whole rhythm of this seems one of transformation – the unliving thing is disentangled and given a new social purpose. It announces man and summons men together, this 'Sound of the Shell'. As the novel proceeds this meaning becomes more and more sharply defined. 'We can use this to call the others. Have a meeting . . .' It is his association with the shell rather than his size or attractiveness that makes the children choose Ralph as their leader; and having been established as the symbol of assembly, the conch becomes identified with its procedure, with democracy and the right to free speech. It becomes a symbol of immense suggestiveness. Every time a boy cries 'I've got the conch', he is drawing on the funds of order and democratic security. We take the point when Jack blows it 'inexpertly', and when he lays it at his feet in rejection. The conch helps both to trace the trajectory of plot, and to establish character. Nowhere does Piggy's role seem more economically and poignantly expressed than when he prepares to confront the Tribe and its Chief with 'the one thing he hasn't got'. Then the conch in Piggy's hands becomes no less than the basic challenge to the Tribe to choose between democracy and anarchy, civilization and savagery. The answer comes in unequivocal terms: 'The rock struck Piggy a glancing blow from chin to knee; the conch exploded into a thousand white fragments and ceased to exist.' The shell, whose sound began as a summons to society, ends as a murderous explosion on the rocks. It traces out for us the swift tragic progress of the tale, and condenses its meaning – or so it seems.

But will this kind of reading satisfy, when we stop talking about the book from a distance and really look at the texture of the writing and the kind of experience it proffers? What will strike us most immediately is surely that the episode is far too long and circumstantial for any purely symbolic purpose. When we investigate the nature of that circumstantiality, what it reveals is Golding's concern to hold back rather than encourage the conceptualizing or interpretative intelligence. The counterpointing of the two boys shows this very clearly.

It is Piggy who is first excited by the shell, but only as a curio. It is Ralph's consciousness we live in, and he hardly listens to Piggy. Not one of the fat boy's sentences is heard to a conclusion. What is important about Ralph's 'day-dream', moreover, is that intelligence and social memory are laid asleep, while the physical senses, alone, remain sharply aware. Hence the description of fulcrum and lever, weight and resistance; the interest in how the shell is physically disentangled from the weeds. In fact the 'civilizing' intelligence is kept at bay while the actual conch in its strangeness and beauty is made real to the senses. Suddenly Piggy's babble stops, while he too strokes 'the glistening thing that lay in Ralph's hands', wet, reflecting light, strangely beautiful.

The second half of the scene elaborates the contrast. Now Piggy invents the idea of the meeting, giving the shell a social purpose; but again the life of the passage comes from Ralph, and he is only interested, as any schoolboy would be, in finding out how to blow it. Again Piggy moves into unison, the shell is primarily an object of play for both of them, and the simple vulgarity of the farting noises fills them with equal delight. The imagination at work is profoundly physical, and what it seizes is, precisely, the *sound* of the shell. It is made real to us in its context of salt water, brilliant fish, green weed; then in its own strange cream and rose spiral, embossed by an art other than the human; finally in the harsh otherness of the noise which shatters the peace of the island and terrifies bird and beast.

Physical realities come first for Golding and should stay first for his readers. Other meanings are found in and through them, as the man-breath passes through the shell's spiral to emerge as signal. But we must not translate the shell into the signal. What comes out is far from simple; and the human beings will be as taken aback as the animals and for the same reason. If we really look and listen, what we shall see and hear will be the harshness of human self-assertion as well as the signal of human sociability; will be the sound of irresponsibility and childishness as well as of forethought and intelligence; will be the fragility of order as well as the impulse towards it. As the sound penetrates the densest thickets, while clouds of birds fly and 'something squealed and ran in the under-growth', man-sound prefigures stuck pig and stuck Ralph squealing and running for their life, as well as the assembly and the rules. Golding's symbols are not in fact clear, or wholly articulate, they are always an incarnation of more than can be extracted or trans-lated from them. Even at this early stage, when the fiction seems to offer itself so alluringly for conceptual analysis, it is always richer and more profound than the thesis we may be tempted to substitute for the experience.

It is not a question of rejecting such meanings, so much as developing a delicacy and tact in handling them; a sense of how limited they are in themselves and how far they fall short of accounting for the density of the fiction. We need similar tact with the characters. Even from the finding of the shell, for example, it is easy to see how one could extend Piggy's point of view until he came to stand for something like 'rational humanism'; and many of his physical deficiencies might seem to express Golding's critique of the humanist. We certainly cannot see him as simply a fat boy. Yet he is much more complex than such a formulation could account for, and often inconsistent with it; we would have to mutilate Golding's boy to fit him to so Procrustean a bed. If we respond to what is on the page we shall find in the novel less the pummelling of humanism than the growth in stature, in credibly boyish terms, of the 'true wise friend' who on the last page is almost the tragic hero. Like the other characters Piggy does embody meaning of various kinds, so that we become aware through our imaginative response to the boy of wider horizons and deeper problems beyond him. On the other hand, he is too diminutive to support an acceptable representative significance, just as Jack cannot be Satan or the Power Urge, though he may reveal truths about both to us, and Simon is both less and more than the Saint. Indeed, if we became less eager to confine Golding's creations to a crystalline structure of meaning, we might be rather less worried about the ability of the island and the boys to sustain the weight of a full statement about 'the human condition'. We ought to admit more readily the limitations of the insights Golding can legitimately embody in so select a situation, while at the same time pointing to the fact that his fiction is far richer and more ambiguous, even in *Lord of the Flies*, than it looks. Both too much and too little has been claimed for Golding's first novel. That is why it is often so difficult to be fair to it.

Finally, and on the deepest level, it is now possible to see that there is a sharp irony in the temptation to translate the fiction into an unambiguous emblem: this does worse than simplify, it subverts. It is exactly the tendency to convert and reduce complexity into simplicity which Golding sees as the root of evil. This was not perhaps easy to see when the novel appeared, though it was always there, and there is no missing it now. For in novel after novel Golding has attacked on the same front: the way that 'homo sapiens' makes Neanderthal man the image of his own evil; the way that Christopher Martin and Sammy Mountjoy recreate real people into the shapes of their own need and lust; the set of emblems that must be cleared from Jocelin's mind at the moment of death and replaced by the vivid and complex physical truth of the Spire itself. For Golding, the Evil Tree grows in the human brain, in human consciousness, and emblematic and conceptual reduction are dangerous manifestations of the Fall. So, in *Lord of the Flies*, it is the way in which the children look for an external manifestation of what is really in themselves that releases the sin of Cain. Evil exists, but not as a Beast. There is an analogous truth about the conch. What the Sound of the Shell really is ... is a sound. Like the whole island, the shell is a unique, physical existence whose being is its meaning. Yet it can reveal man, as the shell shows forth all the implications for good or evil of the human breath that resounds through it. Only it is fatal to forget, as the children and many readers do, that the meaning is in the boys, not the shell. The conch's symbolic meaning depends on the state of the children's minds. Once power becomes more real to Jack than the rules, the conch is meaningless; but when he raids the camp for fire, Piggy thinks he has come for the shell. Though Piggy reaches his greatest stature at the moment of his death, it is also the moment of his greatest blindness, rendered for us at a level far deeper than his lost spectacles. For he holds out as a magic talisman what is, literally, an empty shell. It had a more inclusive sound, which the boys tragically could not hear or understand.

II

The island gives the children freedom to reveal themselves. We listen with increasing attention to what it is that the Sound of the Shell announces about these human beings. Golding re-occupies R. M. Ballantyne's *Coral Island* and declares its portrayal of those idealized British boys, Jack, Ralph and Peterkin in their tropical paradise, to be a fake, since boys are human beings, and human beings are not like that. Or, rather, he does not 'declare', he shows the falsehood by producing an island and boys that are more convincing than Ballantyne's, and then gradually revealing what the difference implies. The structure and technique of *Lord of the Flies* is one of revelation.

At the beginning the most obvious element of the Shell, its strangeness, its glamour, its beauty, parallels the first response to the island itself. Disaster has brought the children there: an atomic explosion, an evacuation by air via Gibraltar and Addis Ababa. Their aircraft has been attacked, probably over the Sunda Sea, and has released its detachable passenger tube to crash-land in the jungle of a convenient island while the plane itself flies off in flames. There is a great storm, the jungle is loud with crashing trees, and the tube, with some children still in it, is dragged out to sea by wind and wave, while the rest scatter into the thickets. It is a terrible experience; but it is not one we share. Indeed, that story has to be pieced together from scattered hints in the boys' conversation. For, once they have slept an exhausted sleep well into the day, the experience has left virtually no scars on their consciousness, though they may have nightmares later. What Ralph is conscious of, and what occupies our delighted attention too, is the *Coral Island* glamour, the unspoilt beauty and excitement of trees, rock and beach. The fact that there are no grown-ups is primarily 'the delight of a realized ambition'. And as Ralph takes in the marvels of the island: the strange green shadows crawling over his body under the coconut palms, the surf breaking on the coral reef across the peacock-blue lagoon, the incredible beach-pool with its ready-made diving ledge, 'here at last was the imagined but never fully realized place leaping into real life'; the perennial boys' dream of which the worlds of *Coral Island* and *Treasure Island*, and the lake islands of *Swallows and Amazons*, are only shadows.

The first chapter resounds with 'the deep bass strings of delight'. The children gather to the casual summons of the conch, they elect their leader, draw up laws, divide out function and prerogative; but we ought to be sharply aware of the inappropriateness of this kind of terminology. It is a wonderful game played under perfect conditions in perfect surroundings; and though it acts out memories of grown-up order, it can go on all day with no interference from grown-ups. There are the tensions that there are bound to be in any game, between Ralph and Jack and Piggy, but they are containable because the game is large and splendid enough to have acceptable parts for everyone.

There is not only 'government' but 'exploration'. A specific reminiscence of *Coral Island* occurs as Ralph and Jack, talking over the top of Simon's head, set off to explore their domain, and the aura of glamour is strong.

They turned to each other, laughing excitedly, talking, not listening. The air was bright. Ralph, faced by the task of translating all this into an explanation, stood on his head and fell over.

There is also something of the fairy-tale: 'The coral was scribbled in the sea as though a giant had bent down to reproduce the shape of the island in a flowing chalk line ...', but, best of all, there is no giant, no ogre, it all belongs to them.

The 'glamour' is set, however, as it was not in *Coral Island*, against a real jungle, dense, damply hot, scratching. This is not a stroll through a nineteenth-century English wood with different trees. Demonstrably, discomfort and joy authenticate each other:

Here, the roots and stems of creepers were in such tangles that the boys had to thread through them like pliant needles. Their only guide, apart from the brown ground and occasional flashes of light through the foliage, was the tendency of slope: whether this hole, laced as it was with cables of creeper, stood higher than that.

Somehow, they moved up.

Immured in these tangles, at perhaps their most difficult moment, Ralph turned with shining eyes to the others.

'Wacco.'

'Wizard.'

'Smashing.'

The cause of their pleasure was not obvious. All three were hot, dirty and exhausted. Ralph was badly scratched. The creepers were as thick as their thighs and left little but tunnels for further penetration. Ralph shouted experimentally and they listened to the muted echoes.

'This is real exploring,' said Jack. 'I bet nobody's been here before.'

It is the same with the rock-rolling, which is a specific comment on the scene in *Coral Island* where the boys are taken aback as a huge rock thunders down the mountain side. We are convinced that boys, faced by poised rocks like this, would behave as Golding's do, and there is a realistic sense of mass and force. The boyish argot and happy wrestling, the sweat and dirt and scratches, the shining eyes, all act with one another to make a world that is both solid and boyishly glamorous.

On the other hand, the darker elements we heard in the Sound of the Shell are not forgotten, though they are for the moment submerged. When we look more closely, we can see that the glamour is shot through with more sinister suggestions. Mirages are created for us as one of the physical realities of the South Seas; but we can never be unaware of the deceptiveness of appearances afterwards. The marching choir, and the way Jack treats it, recalls an army world of authority, arrogance and callousness, rather than the holy singing their uniform suggests. Jack's angry blue eyes and his habit of driving his sheath-knife into a tree-trunk hint at a capacity for dangerous violence. Hidden in the games there might also be an irresponsibility which has wider reverberations. When Ralph 'machine-guns' Piggy, or the 'enraged monster' of a rock crashes down 'like a bomb', we are perhaps primarily aware of a kind of innocence. This is obvious in the episode of the piglet, where even Jack cannot kill 'because of the enormity of the knife descending and cutting into living flesh; because of the unbearable blood'. Gun and bomb are only a game, or a schoolboy phrase. But as soon as we replace game and cliché within the context of the situation that brought the children to the island, we may feel less assured; there is certainly blindness, perhaps something worse. The glamour of the 'natural' is also ambiguous. On the one hand there is pleasure in ripping off the clothes that speak of discipline and regimentation at school, the pleasure of nakedness in sun and water. On the other, it needs only a little of Piggy's 'ill-omened talk' about the realities of the situation to make a school shirt 'strangely pleasing' to put on again.

It is however worth pointing out that Golding in his opening chapter is seeking to re-imagine the Coral Island more truly. To imagine fully is, for him, to reveal indications like this existing naturally within the glamour; they are not simply put in like sign-posts pointing out a fore-ordained road. In retrospect, Ralph's standing on his head can be seen as a warning signal, but it is doubtful if any reader has ever taken it as other than a lifelike movement of joy at the time. It is perfectly ambiguous; that is its success. The diarrhoea might seem to invite allegorical translation – the body of man is no longer fit for Eden – but it is, no less, a realistic comment on the effects of eating nothing but fruit. The snake-clasp speaks of Eden too, but, more than any other detail, it is also eloquent of British schoolboy uniform.

In the first chapter, then, the *Coral Island* glamour is the domin-ant note in the Sound of the Shell, but there are one or two more sinister undertones if we really listen. The second chapter reverses the over- and undertones of the same concert. Glamour and game are still strongly present in the second Assembly, as rules are made up and Ralph's simple confidence in rescue outweighs Piggy's fear.

'This is our island. It's a good island. Until the grown-ups come to fetch us we'll have fun.'
Jack held out his hand for the conch.
'There's pigs,' he said. 'There's food; and bathing water in that little stream along there – and everything.'

But 'everything' means more than glamour. When the idea of making a fire as a rescue signal takes hold, the *Coral Island* element of fun and adventure is still high, and one notices particularly what a sense of community it gives the boys. In this there is irony for the future.

Ralph found himself alone on a limb with Jack and they grinned at each other, sharing this burden. Once more, amid the breeze, the shouting, the slanting sunlight on the high mountain, was shed that glamour, that strange invisible light of friendship, adventure, and content.
'Almost too heavy.'
Jack grinned back.
'Not for the two of us.'

Very soon, however, the harsher Sound of the Shell drowns the delight. It is clear that the making of rules may have as much to do with the desire to inflict punishment as the desire for order, for that, too, figures large in boyish games. The profound difference between the second assembly and the first is that the dark side of boys' psychology unmistakably makes its presence felt. The 'littlun' with the strawberry mark, describing his terrifying night-time vision of a 'snake-thing' or 'beastie', is voicing that part of the child's psyche that is beset with terror of the unknown in himself or his environment. That this is widespread among the children is shown by the intent eyes which fail to respond to Ralph's reassurances, and by the unexpectedly passionate reaction to his promise of rescue. There is nightmare as well as delight on this island. And finally, with the lighting of the fire, the note of irresponsibility in the Sound of the Shell reaches its full resonance.
We may feel impatient with Piggy's premature middle age: 'I bet it's gone tea-time.... What do they think they're going to do on that mountain'; and with the 'martyred expression of a parent who

has to keep up with the senseless ebullience of the children'. But if we do, we soon learn the implications of acting 'like a crowd of kids'. We are made aware that innocence which consists largely of ignorance and irresponsibility may be far from harmless. Jack's arrogant chauvinism may find it easy to contrast English boys with savages, as Ballantyne complacently does. But as the fire spreads into the jungle because nobody looks further than keeping 'a clean flag of flame flying', we get a deeper insight.

Small flames stirred at the bole of a tree and crawled away through leaves and brushwood, dividing and increasing. One patch touched a tree trunk and scrambled up like a bright squirrel.... . The squirrel leapt on the wings of the wind and clung to another standing tree, eating downwards. Beneath the dark canopy of leaves and smoke the fire laid hold on the forest and began to gnaw.... . The flames, as though they were a kind of wild life, crept as a jaguar creeps on his belly.... . They flapped at the first of the trees, and the branches grew a brief foliage of fire. The heart of flame leapt nimbly across the gap between the trees and then went swinging and flaring along the whole row of them. Beneath the capering boys a quarter of a mile square of forest was savage with smoke and flame. The separate noises of the fire merged into a drum-roll that seemed to shake the mountain.... . Startled, Ralph realized that the boys were falling still and silent, feeling the beginnings of awe at the power set free below them. The knowledge and the awe made him savage ...

Irresponsibility and ignorance liberate a power that is more and more 'savage', the 'squirrel' turns into a 'jaguar', and that power appeals to something 'savage' in the boys themselves. There were good reasons for bird and beast to be terrified by the harsh sound of the conch as it 'spread through the intricacies of the forest'. And not only bird and beast:

'That little 'un –' gasped Piggy – 'him with the mark on his face, I don't see him. Where is he now?'
    The crowd was as silent as death.
    'Him that talked about the snakes. He was down there –'
    A tree exploded in the fire like a bomb. Tall swathes of creepers rose for a moment into view, agonized, and went down again. The little boys screamed at them.
    'Snakes! Snakes! Look at the snakes!'

'Like a bomb' isn't such a cliché now, nor is 'silent as death'. And if it is rather over-emphatic for Piggy to look 'into hell', since there is no real evil here, nevertheless we could say that if this was Eden, it has been destroyed; and there has been a 'snake-thing' manifest, not the creepers, but the children's own irresponsibility. The 'drum-roll' of the fire will remind us not only of savage tom-toms, but of the ceremony of execution. What the Sound of the Shell announced was also the coming of Death into the Garden.

As the second chapter focuses on the irresponsibility that had lurked largely undetected in the first, the third proceeds to explore the differences between the boys, present obliquely in the first expedition to the mountain:

Here they paused and examined the bushes round them curiously.
Simon spoke first.
'Like candles. Candle bushes. Candle buds.'
The bushes were dark evergreen and aromatic and the many buds were waxen green and folded up against the light. Jack slashed at one with his knife and the scent spilled over them.
'Candle buds.'
'You couldn't light them,' said Ralph. 'They just look like candles.'
'Green candles,' said Jack contemptuously, 'we can't eat them. Come on.'

Now however we begin to see below mere difference to division and antagonism. Ralph is trying desperately not only to build shelters, but a sense of 'home'; his instincts are to domesticate, to ward off terror by social community, to civilize, to provide against the littluns' nightmares the security of 'home'. Jack on the other hand rediscovers in himself the instincts and compulsions of the hunter that lie buried in every man. On all fours like an animal, he learns to flare his nostrils and assess the air, to cast across the ground for spoor. But the rediscovery is deeper than that, deeper even than 'the compulsion to track down and kill that was swallowing him up'. It is another dimension of awareness:

The silence of the forest was more oppressive than the heat, and at this hour of the day there was not even the whine of insects. Only when Jack himself roused a gaudy bird from a primitive nest of sticks was the silence shattered and echoes set ringing by a harsh cry that seemed to come out of the abyss of ages. Jack himself shrank at this cry with a hiss of indrawn breath; and for a minute became less a hunter than a furtive thing, ape-like among the tangle of trees.

In the very first paragraph of the book a bird had 'flashed upwards with a witch-like cry'. For Jack, as for human imaginations in all ages, the forest becomes not only a place to hunt in but also a place where one sometimes feels hunted; a place where the human being momentarily locates his intuitions of evil. Jack is in some ways 'reverting to savagery', so that the idea of rescue is hardly real to him any more and pigs matter more than a ship which might take him back to civilization; and so that his eyes sometimes have an 'opaque, mad look' from his compulsion to track and kill. But we are not simply to write this off as evil; he is also acquiring a kind of knowledge that Ralph singularly lacks and would be better for having. Jack understands the littluns and their nightmares, knows that it is not sufficient to proclaim that 'this is a good island'.

But as the difference between the experience of the two boys widens, so understanding becomes more difficult and antagonism mounts. They become 'two continents of experience and feeling, unable to communicate'; and in a later formulation, 'the brilliant world of hunting, tactics, fierce exhilaration, skill ... the world of longing and baffled common sense'.

Both of them are worlds apart from Simon, whom they consider faintly crazy. One can see easily enough what Golding meant by calling Simon a 'saint',* even a 'Christ-figure'. He acts as peacemaker between Jack and Piggy; he is to be seen suffering the little children to come to him, and getting them fruit where flower and fruit grow on the same tree. Afterwards, by himself in the heart of the forest, he has communion with nature or nature's God, in keeping with the poetic and mystical vein that contrasted so markedly, over the candlebuds, with the visions of the utilitarian and the hunter. What the communion is we do not know, but the place is like a church, as the darkness submerges 'the ways between the trees till they were dim and strange, as the bottom of the sea.'

The candle-buds opened their wide white flowers glimmering under the light that pricked down from the first stars. Their scent spilled out into the air and took possession of the island.

There is something saintly in Simon; but such labelling accomplishes far less than one might imagine. What brings Simon alive is

* In an interview with Frank Kermode, *Books and Bookmen*, 5 Oct. 1959.

not good works, or prayer, or faith, or a personal relationship with his creator, and a ten- or eleven-year-old is a slender reed to bear the symbolic weight of saint, let alone of Saviour. This kind of reading will not stand up to examination. What does, demonstrably, bring Simon alive and make the passages where he is by himself among the finest things in the book, is the quality of the imagination that goes into creating his particular sensibility. He is not so much a character, in the sense that the other boys are, as the most inclusive sensibility among the children at this stage.

The presentation of Simon in this chapter is not as symbolic as we think when it starts, and not symbolic at all as it goes on. Those littluns, if we look at them, are 'unintelligible' and 'inscrutable', not paradisal. The flowers and fruit raise the question of Eden, certainly, but they also come direct from *Coral Island*, and represent simple physical fact in the South Seas where many fruit trees bear all the year round. Moreover the enormous fecundity, 'the scent of ripeness and the booming of a million bees at pasture', will strike most readers as excessive for Eden.

This assertive fecundity sets the tone of the scene as it develops. What strikes us with considerable force, as Simon moves through the jungle, is that it is alien to man, and its fecundity is rooted in dissolution. The pale flowers parasitic on the tall trunks are 'unexpected' by the civilized eye; the birds not only 'bright' but 'fantastic'. In the treetops life goes on 'clamorously'; the clearing below is an 'aromatic ... bowl of heat and light'; the 'rapid' climber 'flaunted' red and yellow blossoms; the butterflies are 'gaudy', the colours 'riotous'. Underfoot the soil is markedly soft, and 'the creepers shivered throughout their lengths when he bumped them'. They are dropped 'like the rigging of foundered ships', and the climber is parasitic on a great tree that has fallen and died. This, clearly enough if we look, is no Eden and never was; there was no death in Eden, no riot or urgency, no creepiness.

Simon is the first child to know, to register fully, what the island and its jungle are like in themselves. The qualities that were present in Ralph's daydreaming at the finding of the conch, but have subsequently been overlaid by his need to think and lead, are fully realized in Simon. On the other hand, in solitary communion with nature, he taps Jack's sensitivity to the creepy as well as the beautiful. But he is outside the hunter mentality, the leader mentality, outside even himself. He exists in terms of his sensitivity to what is outside him. This allows him to know comprehensively. He not only registers the heat, the urgency, the riot, the dampness and decay; he also registers the cool and mysterious submergence of the forest in darkness, the pure beauty and fragrance of starlight and nightflower, the peace. Finally he not only registers both, but accepts them equally, as two parts of the same reality. It is these qualities of acceptance and inclusion that give us the 'Simon-ness' of Simon.

In his fourth chapter Golding turns from the 'biguns' to find out whether in the 'passionately emotional and corporate life' of the littluns, when they are too small to have 'characters' or different 'points of view', there may be visible a basic showing-forth of the human that will cast light on *all* the children. When Roger and Maurice romp through the 'castles' and 'interesting stones' and the 'complex of marks, tracks, walls, railway lines' of the littluns' domain, filling Percival's eye with sand, we are still in a recognizable moral landscape:

... Percival began to whimper ... and Maurice hurried away. In his other life Maurice had received chastisement for filling a younger eye with sand. Now, though there was no parent to let fall a heavy hand, Maurice still felt the unease of wrong-doing. At the back of his mind formed the uncertain outlines of an excuse.

It is not very reassuring, however, because the suggestion is that 'morality' is a matter of conditioning and memory, not something innate; and if it depends on memory it may well fade as memory does. What about a child too young to have been conditioned, or to remember?

Percival finished his whimper and went on playing, for the tears had washed the sand away. Johnny watched him with china-blue eyes; then began to fling up sand in a shower, and presently Percival was crying again.

Johnny, almost the tiniest boy on the island, and the first to arrive to the summons of the conch, was the only one whom the author then described as 'innocent'; but although his babyishness makes him morally innocent still, he is clearly not harmless; 'Johnny was well built, with fair hair and a natural belligerence.' The last words may be suggestive.

Meanwhile, rather older and bigger, Henry busies himself at the water's edge:

The great Pacific tide was coming in and every few seconds the relatively still water of the lagoon heaved forwards an inch. There were creatures that lived in this last fling of the sea, tiny transparencies that came questing in with the water over the hot, dry sand. With impalpable organs of sense they examined this new field. Perhaps food had appeared where at the last incursion there had been none; bird droppings, insects perhaps, any of the strewn detritus of landward life. Like a myriad of tiny teeth in a saw, the transparencies came scavenging over the beach.

This was fascinating to Henry. He poked about with a bit of stick, that itself was wave-worn and whitened and a vagrant, and tried to control the motions of the scavengers. He made little runnels that the tide filled and tried to crowd them with creatures. He became absorbed beyond mere happiness as he felt himself exercising control over living things. He talked to them, urging them, ordering them . . .

There is a comment here both on the 'nature' of the 'myriad of tiny teeth'; and on the 'nature' of the human child whose activity goes beyond food and 'beyond happiness'. The chapter is revealed as a commentary on 'nature' and the 'natural man', Johnny's 'natural belligerence' and Henry's absorption in exercising control are basic elements of human nature.

With Roger these elements develop into something more serious. In him, what we noticed in Johnny and Henry becomes deliberately relished. As he throws stones at Henry he is both enjoying exercising power over him, and flirting pleasurably with the idea of hurting him. Roger is becoming a sadist, that is why he is so forbidding. But his 'sadism' is only an excessive development of what we have seen in Henry and Johnny, revealing itself openly because of the absence of grown-up sanctions. For the moment, he throws to miss:

Here, invisible yet strong, was the taboo of the old life. Round the squatting child was the protection of parents and school and policemen and the law. Roger's arm was conditioned by a civilization that knew nothing of him and was in ruins.

But that last sentence shows that the restraint is only a taboo, a social conditioning or superstition, not anything innate. The stone he throws, itself 'a token of preposterous time' which has 'lain on the sands of another shore', speaks of ages which dwarf the waxings and wanings of human civilizations. Moreover, Roger's civilization is in ruins itself because its morality was not sufficient to stop men throwing atom bombs at one another. While he remains conditioned, Roger's incipient sadism is shameful to him: 'a darker shadow crept beneath the swarthiness of his skin'. But we have been made vividly aware, in this chapter on 'The Natural Man', of Roger's connection with Johnny and Henry – who in turn link him with us – and also of the frailty of the conditioning which suppresses that element of basic human nature.

Soon we find out that it is not difficult to invent devices whereby the 'natural' man can be released from shame, and the boys can remember other facets of 'civilization' besides its morality. Jack remembers the dazzle-paint with which ships hunting or hunted conceal themselves from their prey; his face-painting starts off as a reversion to civilization, not to savagery. But when it is done,

He looked in astonishment, no longer at himself but at an awesome stranger ... his sinewy body held up a mask which drew their eyes and appalled them. He began to dance and his laughter became a bloodthirsty snarling ... the mask was a thing on its own, behind which Jack hid, liberated from shame and self-consciousness.

Then the last crucial scene in this fourth chapter throws into relief the distance we have travelled. As a ship slowly passes on the horizon, Jack and his hunters let the fire go out while they kill their first pig. But once again there is no 'evil'. Jack is still 'conditioned'. The arm that failed to descend on the piglet before has descended now, but even the painted hunter still twitches at the memory of the blood; and he is still 'charitable in his happiness', wanting to include everyone.

Nevertheless his new knowledge, 'that they had outwitted a living thing, imposed their will upon it, taken away its life like a long satisfying drink', provides a last link in the chain. We understand now why the compulsion to kill in Jack has meant so much more than the idea of rescue, and has only disguised itself in the need for meat. Moreover the leader, fresh from this total imposition of his will, cannot brook moral condemnation and humiliation at the hands of Ralph and Piggy. His violence and frustration finally erupt as he attacks Piggy and smashes a lens of his spectacles. Here, if we like, is the birth of evil, since irresponsibility has become viciousness; and a will imposed on an animal has now turned in destructive violence on a fellow human being. Yet we would be mistaken to read in these simple moralistic terms. For, as Ralph asserts his chieftainship, as a newly lit fire builds up like a barrier between him and Jack, as the link which bound him to Jack is broken and refastened to Piggy, we ought to remain aware of both sides. There is no defence of Jack's brutality, or his blindness to what it is that he and his hunters have done. Yet the whole chapter has, surely, given us a human understanding of Jack that Ralph and Piggy lack. If it is an emblematic detail that Piggy now only has one eye, it is also humanly fair. Golding's vision is scrupulous. As Jack throws to Piggy the meat that the fat boy is glad enough to eat, he cannot in his rage express his feelings about the dependence on his courage, his cunning and his self-dedication of those who presume to judge him. It is his fate to look round for understanding and find only respect.

III

We hear the Sound of the Shell again, as Ralph summons a second meeting to try to clarify and set right what has gone wrong. Half way through the novel we get a measure of how far we have come; Ralph, discovering his dirt and realizing how much of his time he spends watching his feet to escape falling, smiles 'jeeringly' as he remembers 'that first enthusiastic exploration as though it were part of a brighter childhood'. He and we have grown up since the *Coral Island* stage. This assembly has to be not fun, but business. Ralph is having to realize what it means to be a leader, to take decisions in a hurry, to think things out step by step. This brings out a new scale of values, whereby he sees how little fatness, asthma, myopia and laziness weigh against Piggy's one great quality – his ability to think. But thinking is complicated by the fact that things look different in different lights, and from different points of view. 'If faces were different when lit from above or below – what was a face? What was anything?'

Ralph produces a workmanlike programme to put things straight: a plan for better sanitation, for keeping the fire going, for never cooking except on the mountain-top. But at a level deeper than any programme can reach, things are breaking up because the children are frightened. So the meeting becomes a testing-ground for Ralph's faith that what is wrong can be cured by talking things over reasonably, and coming to a democratic decision on fear itself, on whether or not there is a 'Beast'.

Jack's experience as hunter tells him that there is no fearsome animal on the island, but it also tells him why the littluns are frightened and have nightmares. They are frightened 'because you're like that'; because it is human nature to be frightened of the world and of life when it is dark and man is by himself. But for Jack, 'fear can't hurt you any more than a dream'. Fear can be lived with, and any Beast can be hunted and killed.

Piggy disagrees about fear. For him, everything can be explained and anything wrong, even in the mind, can be cured. Life is scientific. There is no Beast to fear, and there is no need to fear anything 'unless we get frightened of people'. This rationality, however, is greeted with scorn by those whose experience seems to tell them otherwise. Maurice wonders whether science has, in fact, explored the whole of existence and rendered everything explicable and known. The littlun who claims that the Beast comes from the water, and Maurice's memory of being told about great squids only fleetingly glimpsed by man, are both pointers to a sea that may contain a great unknown.

The worst contempt of the meeting, however, is reserved for Simon, who thinks that there may be a Beast that is not any kind of animal: 'What I mean is . . . maybe it's only us.' He is trying to say that man may fear darkness and solitude because they rob him of the world he builds with his daylight mind, and force him to live with his own interior darkness. Perhaps there is something bestial, something absolutely dirty, not external to man but present deep in himself. But Simon is howled down even more than Piggy; and when the vote comes to be taken Ralph is forced to realize that fear cannot be dispelled by voting.

Worse, with the voicing of these internal fears and darknesses, the world of the conch has been brought into question. Piggy is not only scorned, but attacked again by Jack; and this time Jack's rebellion against Ralph also comes out into the open, as well as his growing disrespect for Ralph's concept of order.

'The rules!' shouted Ralph, 'you're breaking the rules!'
'Who cares?'

Ralph summoned his wits.

'Because the rules are the only thing we've got!'

But Jack was shouting against him.

'Bollocks to the rules! We're strong – we hunt! If there's a beast we'll hunt it down. We'll close in and beat and beat and beat –'

He gave a wild whoop and leapt down to the pale sand. At once the platform was full of noise and excitement, scramblings, screams and laughter. The assembly shredded away....

Perhaps they only exchange one kind of 'play' for another. But we have a clear hint of what the other game is: what is happening is a re-enactment of the chant and mime of pig-killing that had fleetingly brought them together again on the mountain. But now, with Jack's 'beat and beat and beat', and littluns staggering away howling, it is taking on significance as an expression of their fear and an incantation against it, while the littluns' cries already foreshadow something worse.

Everywhere there is fear, even among the saner, more responsible ones. Ralph no longer dares to blow the conch in case it should be disobeyed, and all pretence of order be lost in defiance. Piggy, in a telling gloss on what he had said at the meeting, admits to his inner, intuitive fear of Jack. Piggy has a rational mind, but we get a new insight into him; the asthma always appears when he is confronted by something beyond his control and understanding: 'I been in bed so much I done some thinking. I know about people.... If you're scared of someone you hate him but you can't stop thinking about him. You kid yourself he's all right really, an' then when you see him again; it's like asthma an' you can't breathe'. Piggy's asthma is partly an expression of fear, and hate, and how hate may grow from fear and alienation. His sickness tells Piggy truths of human motivation that his rational intelligence, and Ralph's health, are blind to. Jack hates Ralph and Piggy and would hurt both if he could, but Ralph is Piggy's one protection. Simon knows that this is true.

There is fear. In their misery they call to mind the majesty and order of the grown-up world and long for 'a sign or something' from that world; some sort of message that would tell them how to sort things out. But instead:

A thin wail out of the darkness chilled them and set them grabbing for each other. Then the wail rose, remote and unearthly, and turned to an inarticulate gibbering. Percival Wemys Madison, of the Vicarage, Harcourt St Anthony, lying in the long grass, was living through circumstances in which the incantation of his address was powerless to help him.

It may be that other grown-up addresses are as powerless as the vicarage, but the main thing is what has happened to the Sound of the Shell. Man-sound has become a cry of absolute fear – a child lost, alone, in an alien world of nightmare.

IV

The second half of the novel repeats the structure of the first; not however telling us new things, so much as showing the real depths of what we already know.

There is another battle in the night sky three miles above the island, another 'sudden bright explosion and a corkscrew trail'; but instead of the burning plane with the passenger tube, the body of a single parachutist, riddled with bullets, drifts down to lodge on the mountainside. This, with its immediate ironic response to the children's prayer for a sign from the grown-up world, is obviously the most contrived feature of the novel so far. Given the initial situation, the first five chapters have developed with a fatal inevitability, but this, *coup de théâtre* though it be, betrays the novelist's sleight of hand. Yet is it perhaps no more than a fine flourish of rhetoric, to emphasize what we should already have realized.

This is not a novel about children, demonstrating Golding's belief that, without the discipline of grown-ups, children will degenerate into savages. We could think this only if we had forgotten what had brought the children to the island in the first place; and if we had forgotten, the first function of the parachutist is to remind us. The 'majesty of adult life' is a childish delusion. There is no essential difference between the island-world and the grown-up one. There too, order can be and has been overthrown; morality can be and has been inadequate to prevent wholesale destruction and savagery. The parachutist shows man's inhumanity to man, the record of what human beings have done to one another throughout human history. The children are revealing the same nature as the grown-ups, only perhaps more startlingly because of their age and their special situation. The child world is only a microcosm of the adult world.

But the children are already disposed to objectify their inner darkness and expect a Beast who will be other than themselves; so the parachutist becomes identified as the Beast, sitting on the mountain-top, preventing them from keeping the fire and the rescue-signals going. Only Simon cannot believe in 'a beast with claws that scratched, that sat on a mountain-top, that left no tracks and yet was not fast enough to catch Samneric. However Simon thought of the beast, there rose before his inward sight the picture of a human at once heroic and sick.' But Simon, the dreamer who bashes into a tree because he isn't looking where he's going, and who suffers from fits, cannot be accepted uncritically.

The exploration to find the Beast's lair provides a continually ironic commentary on that first golden day and its *Coral Island* explorers. Instead of the peacock-blue of the calm lagoon, Ralph becomes aware for the first time of the other shore, where no reef offers protection against the endless rise and fall of the sea, those eroding tides that 'soon, in a matter of centuries ... would make an island of the castle', and manifest a time as preposterous to man as Roger's stone:

Now he saw the landsman's view of the swell and it seemed like the breathing of some stupendous creature. Slowly the waters sank among the rocks, revealing pink tables of granite, strange growths of coral, polyp, and weed. Down, down, the waters went, whispering like the wind among the heads of the forest. There was one flat rock there, spread like a table, and the waters sucking down on the four weedy sides made them seem like cliffs. Then the sleeping leviathan breathed out – the waters rose, the weed streamed, and the water boiled over the table rock with a roar. There was no sense of the passage of waves; only this minute-long fall and rise and fall.

This, while it has the factuality of the conch and the weed, has no allure; its sinister quality is all the more powerful because it is so muted. It will not carry human meaning, the waters obliterate the table rock, it is utterly 'strange' to man. And if Ralph's mind gives it to him as the breathing of a gigantic beast, it is so inconceivable and alien that it is beyond terror.

Moments of resurgent glamour merely underline the irony.

When Jack cries out excitedly 'What a place for a fort', or discovers a rock that could be rolled onto the causeway, there is a new sense of the need for protection against enemies that gives the excitement a more sinister undertone. It is with a sickening sense of their childishness that we watch through Ralph's eyes as the children roll a rock into the sea. Only, in the midst of his anger, we can detect the beginning of a diminished sense of civilization in Ralph himself:

'Stop it! Stop it!'
  His voice struck a silence among them.
  'Smoke.'
  A strange thing happened in his head. Something flittered there in front of his mind like a bat's wing, obscuring his idea.
  'Smoke.'
  At once the ideas were back, and the anger.
  'We want smoke. And you go wasting your time. You roll rocks.'

He can no longer convince them of the imperative need for rescue, and has to exert sheer authority against their mutinous grumblings.

  If this is the ironic comment on the glamour of Chapter 1, Chapter 7 is even darker than Chapter 2. Ralph becomes vividly aware not only of how dirty and unkempt they have become, but how their standards have fallen so that they accept this situation as normal. Moreover what his eye had already taken in of this 'other side' of the island, now imprints a despair on the understanding:

Here . . . the view was utterly different. The filmy enchantments of mirage could not endure the cold ocean water and the horizon was hard clipped blue. Ralph wandered down to the rocks. Down here, almost on a level with the sea, you could follow with your eye the ceaseless, bulging passage of the deep sea waves. They were miles wide, apparently not breakers or the banked ridges of shallow water. They travelled the length of the island with an air of disregarding it and being set on other business; they were less a progress than a momentous rise and fall of the whole ocean. Now the sea would suck down, making cascades and waterfalls of retreating water, would sink past the rocks and plaster down the seaweed like shining hair: then, pausing, gather and rise with a roar, irresistibly swelling over point and outcrop, climbing the little cliff, sending at last an arm of surf up a gully to end a yard or so from him in fingers of spray.
  Wave after wave, Ralph followed the rise and fall until something of the remoteness of the sea numbed his brain. Then gradually the almost

infinite size of this water forced itself on his attention. This was the divider, the barrier. On the other side of the island, swathed at midday with mirage, defended by the shield of the quiet lagoon, one might dream of rescue; but here, faced by the brute obtuseness of the ocean, the miles of division, one was clamped down, one was helpless, one was condemned, one was –

Simon's quality of sheer faith – 'I just think you'll get back all right' – brings a momentary lightening of despair. But the remembered cottage on the moors (where 'wildness' was ponies, or the snowy moor seen through a window past a copper kettle; and 'spectre', like the awful picture of the spider in the Magician book, was either not looked at at all, or else safely replaced between the *Boys' Book of Trains* and the *Boys' Book of Ships*) is utterly out of reach and unreal; a flimsy dream.

'Reality' is really wild nature; a charging tusker in the forest. But Ralph's first experience of the hunt is also a revelation of his own darker side; he discovers in himself the excitements, the 'fright and apprehension and pride' the others have known. Moreover, as the boys mime to one another again, their underlying tensions suddenly carry them away, including Ralph. They begin really to hurt Robert, who is acting the boar, and his cries of pain excite them still further. Ralph also feels the 'sudden thick excitement'; and as the chant rises ritually, as Robert screams and struggles, 'Ralph too was fighting to get near, to get a handful of that brown, vulnerable flesh. The desire to squeeze and hurt was over-mastering.' The 'game' is becoming dangerous; changing from an imitaion of an action, to a ritual of release for fear, hatred, violence. It begins to need a victim to be wholly satisfactory.

Lastly, in this chapter of darker sides, Jack's hatred of Ralph emerges fully. As soon as he ceases to lead and control, Jack turns vicious; and he has clearly begun to hate the boy who bars his leadership. Any possibility of responsible and sane decision on this expedition is sabotaged as Jack insists on turning it into a personal challenge and duel. The next morning, seizing on Ralph's 'insult' to his hunters as excuse, Jack blows the conch and openly challenges Ralph's courage and leadership. When he fails to displace him, Jack splits away to form his own tribe.

What is most immediately remarkable however is the way that the language shows a reversion, not so much to savage, as to schoolboy: 'He isn't a prefect and we don't know anything about him. He just gives orders and expects people to obey for nothing. . . . All right then . . . I'm not going to play any longer. Not with you . . . I'm not going to be part of Ralph's lot –' Jack has never been able to make real to himself the 'democracy' of the conch, or the leadership of anyone else, or the need for responsible thought, or provision for rescue. All that makes sense to him is his own need to control others and impose himself, and hunting because that is a kind of power assertion. The sudden humiliating tears, and the schoolboy language, affect us in very different ways. There is pathos in the realization that this bogey-figure is only a child. There is the equally sudden realization that power obsession is essentially childish when it is stripped of the disguises of the adult world.

What the coming of the 'Beast' has meant is an acceleration of the divisions among the children. Chapter 8 corresponds with Chapter 3 as an examination of the implications of the division. The hut-builders and home-seekers are now penned to the lagoon and the shoreline. They fear the forest and they no longer have either the view from the mountain or the view from the other side of the island; a limitation of consciousness as well as a limitation of area. Piggy's intellect conceives the daring idea of lighting the fire on the rocks instead of the mountain top; but they cannot disguise the fact that they want it now as much for reassurance against the darkness as for rescue, the idea of which is getting steadily more remote. The fruit diet, the conch, and the platform are an insipid contrast to the life of the tribe. With the departure of Jack, Piggy can be fully recognized and given his rightful voice in affairs, but there remains a question mark over the range of his vision. Is it enough to regard Jack as the reason why everything is breaking up?

Jack, for his part is 'brilliantly happy' now that his leadership is assured. Having renounced communal decision, and having no interest in rescue, the idea of a tribe becomes a satisfying way of life. There is the Beast, but they can keep out of its way and forget it; and if it is a hunter like themselves they can propitiate it with part of the kill. Since a tribe is a power-grouping in a world where strength counts, they believe 'passionately out of the depths of their tormented private lives' that they will dream less as they get nearer to the end of the island where the Fort is sited, and where they can barricade themselves. Hunting is no longer merely a question of getting meat, or even of exercising control or imposing oneself. As the hunters chase a sow through the oppressively hot afternoon, they become 'wedded to her in lust'. As they hurl themselves at her the violence has unmistakably sexual undertones; and finally the sow 'collapsed under them, and they were heavy and fulfilled upon her'. Roger's spear up the pig's privates only shows again a peculiar heightening of an impulse common to all. Having renounced the world of Piggy and Ralph, they begin to reveal what their world of hunting really is. It is only incredible if we think that 'bloodlust' is an empty word; for Golding, in opening out the 'thick excitement' we have already accepted, is vivifying what for him is not a cliché. There is an impulse both in lust and in killing, which seeks the obliteration of the 'other' as the most complete expression of the 'self'. The first killing satisfied Jack's bloodthirstiness 'like a long drink'; now his bloodlust is fulfilled in a killing-wedding.

Meanwhile Simon, as in Chapter 3, is in his place of contemplation, but this time not only watching the butterflies dance in the almost unbearable heat; he is watching also the place erupt with the squeals and the death-struggles, and watching the disembowelling, the decapitation, the offering of the head to the Beast. Into the quiet place have entered the buzzing flies, the spilled guts, the pool of dried blood, the vile thing on the sharpened stick. What Simon 'sees' is the Lord of the Flies, Baal-Zebub, the Devil. The title of the book tells us we have reached its heart.

Simon is tempted to pretend that nothing important has happened, that the offering was a 'joke', that he has made a 'mistake' in taking it seriously. The temptation is to avoid being thought 'batty' by Ralph and the others. He is then tempted to keep quiet for a different reason. To try to make the others see the truth about what has happened will be very dangerous. But these voices come from inside Simon's own head, and from the very first they only tell him what he already knows. In spite of hallucination, one thing he knows quite clearly is that what he sees is not the Beast, but 'Pig's head on a stick'. The worst temptation both for Simon and the reader is to see the encounter as a dialogue with the Devil. The difference is really the difference between Simon's view and Jack's:

'Fancy thinking the Beast was something you could hunt and kill!' said the head. For a moment or two the forest and all the other dimly appreciated places echoed with the parody of laughter. 'You knew, didn't you? I'm part of you? Close, close, close! I'm the reason why it's no go? Why things are what they are?'

To imagine that the evil is in any way in the pig's head; or, more insidiously, that the pig's head symbolizes an evil external to the individual, is in fact to commit the error from which only Simon, in spite of his hallucination, is free. The pig's head is not a symbol of anything abstract or outside the boys, like a Devil; it is, like the parachutist, a solid object with a history that human beings have provided. The hallucination ends with Simon falling into the mouth: he faints into his own emergent consciousness of evil. What is wrong on the island is not Jack, as Ralph and Piggy think, or a Beast or Devil to be propitiated as Jack thinks. What is wrong is that man is inherently evil, as Simon has already maintained; the 'ancient, inescapable recognition' is of something in Ralph and Piggy, and Simon himself, as well as Jack and Roger. This being so, there is reason to fear. Simon has known already an assembly crying out 'savagely' as he tries to tell them of 'mankind's essential illness'. Now the inner voice foretells the cost of trying to tell the truth; warns him not to 'try it on ... or else ... we shall do you. See? Jack and Roger and Maurice and Robert and Bill and Piggy and Ralph. Do you. See?' The macabre echo of Ralph's initial promise that they would have 'fun' on the island gains point when we remember what we have already noticed the 'game' of the dance becoming.

At the same time it is important to realize how Golding's imagination guards him against the simple thesis on original sin he is generally credited with. For if there can be little doubt after reading the whole book that the author is inclined to share this view of Simon's, this is by no means necessarily the impression that the scene would leave on an unprepared reader – or its whole truth. It carries both mystery and ambiguity. Golding has left it open to a humanist to call Simon's vision sick, or even morbid. Simon himself 'hears' the charge that he is an 'ignorant, silly little boy', a 'poor, misguided child' who thinks he can 'know better' than other people. It is true that he 'hears' these voices as cynical, or with the patronizing testiness of a schoolmaster; but with his point of view he would inevitably do so. This doesn't mean that they are necessarily to be discounted. They might be a wider and truer valuation. Moreover his peculiarity has been insisted on ever since we first laid eyes on him as he pitched on his face in the sand. If the heat makes him delirious and causes him to faint – he may be a mild epileptic – then where does the delirium start? Only with the pig's head expanding like a balloon, or is that the climax? Or is it that his vision is so frightening that it brings on 'one of his times' as Piggy's fright brings on his asthma? How can we tell for certain what is true vision and what is sick hallucination? or which is the product of what?

We cannot of course; any more than men have been sure in real life whether the 'prophets' and 'saints' were sick, or possessed, or crazy; or whether they were saner than everybody else, the only sane ones. What does it mean to say 'the fit of prophecy was upon him'? We may suspect what Golding's own view is – but if we read what is on the page the question is certainly posed. This is not because Golding is evading the issue; but because his primary concern is with the creation of an inclusive account. There are three explanations of what has gone wrong, not one; and they amount to three different readings of the universe.

Piggy and Ralph believe in the essential goodness of people and of the island. If things 'break up' – the implication is that they are naturally whole – then it is the fault of individuals, who deviate because there is something wrong with them. In the adult world Jack would be cured by a psychiatrist or restrained by greater power than his, which would also solve the Beast. Horror and wrong happen, but they are deviations which can be overcome by sanity and responsibility.

Jack thinks that evil and destruction are live forces. In a world of power there are powers at work that are stronger than man. But these powers (Beast, Devil, or God), can be propitiated by ritual, ceremony, sacrifice. And if this view strikes us as 'primitive', we ought to be aware at least that Jack has been open to some kinds of human experience that Ralph and Piggy have not; and moreover that it has not always been the least civilized cultures who have held such views.

Simon's view declares that blaming bad men, and the Devil, is both right and wrong: there is evil, but it is not either outside man or confined to certain men, it is in everyone.

Piggy has one eye; Jack is a savage; Simon is a queer little boy who has fits. There are question-marks over all three views. This is not a *roman à thèse*. We are likely to respond most to Ralph emotionally, since we see so much through his eyes, sharing his feelings and his troubles. What is at stake has however not yet been fully disclosed.

Golding's ninth chapter corresponds to the chapter on Natural Man in the first half: it is the test case for establishing a basic conviction. Both the 'View' and the 'Death' of its title are Simon's; the question is whether they endorse his 'explanation'. It is inevitable that Simon should climb the mountain – 'what else is there to do?' He cannot believe in a Beast, but it is established as the Simon-ness of Simon to want to contemplate and understand everything. It is inevitable, too, that we should see behind his slow climb an age-old symbolism that involves Ararat, Sinai, Calvary, and Parnassus:

> On a huge hill
> Cragged and steep, Truth stands, and hee that will
> Reach her, about must, and about must goe,
> And what the hill's suddennes resists, winne so.

But once again, the truth is nothing abstract, and it may not be as simple as we think.

Simon contemplates the rotting corpse, the 'mechanics' of its 'parody' of animation, the 'white nasal bones, the teeth, the colours of corruption' and the foul smell, and he is violently sick. The flies in a dark cloud about the head remind us, accurately, of the pig's head; for both record what human beings have done. One is taken up into the other. But then, after the toil of the ascent, and the sickness that expresses and purges the horror of realization, Simon is able to bend down and release the figure from its tangle of lines. These have made it keep drawing attention to itself, in a parody not only of animation, but of death and resurrection again and again. It won't lie down. Simon, because he has understood, can break the pattern and stop the repetition. He can lay to rest the 'history' of man's inhumanity, can be free and can set free. He goes down to the others to tell them that what they have erected into the Beast is 'harmless and horrible'. On a deeper level he has shown that, by recognizing the truth of man's evil, as it is revealed in what men have done, and by purging oneself from it, one can be free to begin again.

The children, already conditioned to expect a Beast external to themselves, are in a state of hysteria. At the feast which Jack has staged to tempt as many as possible to join him, the sense of his own power has given him a newly sinister quality behind his paint. He has ceased to be Jack, he has become the Chief. Personality is overcome by power and he loses his name. He has begun to adopt ritual and oracular speech, he sits throned 'like an idol', waited on by acolytes, and 'Power lay in the brown swell of his forearms: authority sat on his shoulder and chattered in his ear like an ape'. All day the heat has been building up static electricity in the atmosphere and the tension of the approaching thunderstorm is palpable. Now the human tension of an approaching showdown between Ralph and Jack stretches the nerves still more. As the lightning begins, and the first raindrops fall, so that 'home' and 'shelter' become meaningful again, it seems for a moment that the balance might swing in Ralph's favour. But Jack begins the dance, and we have seen very clearly how that has been turning into a protective ritual, whereby the children first externalize what they fear and hate, and then 'kill' it. As the lightning scars sky and eyes the hysteria mounts with it, in Ralph and Piggy too, until at its peak of intensity Simon staggers out of the forest into the circle, and is taken for the Beast, whose killing becomes no longer mime but reality. In frantic savagery, a 'desire, thick, urgent, blind' that grows out of the fear but is distinct from it, they 'do him in'. As Piggy and Ralph feared when things began to go wrong, they have become animals who 'leapt on to the beast, screamed, struck, bit, tore. There were no words, and no movements but the tearing of teeth and claws'. The squirrel, the jaguar, the ape, have taken human form.

Meanwhile in the high wind on the mountain-top the figure of the parachutist is lifted, and swept in a great arc across the beach to be carried out to sea, as the screaming boys flee into the darkness of the jungle. Again this is a *coup de théâtre*, a calculated artifice of rhetoric. But again it merely emphasizes what we should already know. As the parachutist extended the meaning of the pig's head into a wider 'history' of man, so the parachutist has now been subsumed in Simon. The children have done what their fathers have done. The 'sign' is released, not because the children are free in Simon's terms, but because they have made a sign for themselves and need no other.

The death of Simon is the fact on which the whole novel turns and the evidence by which any theory of its significance must be judged. But the first condition it has to meet is whether it can convincingly happen. The answer must be sought in the resources of the novelist, and not in theology. How does Golding convince us that these boys could and would do this terrible thing?

V

The method of the novel is revelatory as we have seen: the uncovering of an unsuspected depth to something we have already accepted. A backward glance will reveal a cumulative process.

Far back, on the first golden day, Ralph learned Piggy's nickname (and immediately betrayed it, the first betrayal of the novel):

'Piggy! Piggy!'
Ralph danced out into the hot air of the beach and then returned as a fighter-plane, with wings swept back, and machine-gunned Piggy.
'Scha-aa-ow!'
He dived in the sand at Piggy's feet and lay there laughing.

It is a 'game', in 'fun'. Ralph would no more deliberately kill Piggy than Jack can kill the piglet caught in the creepers, though, when we remember how he comes to be here, we might see in Ralph a dangerous blindness to the realities the game imitates. But, looking back, that 'danced' has a reverberation of unease, as is the 'next time' with which Jack drives his knife into the tree when they have allowed the piglet to escape; for the next time will in fact see both the killing of a pig, and the invention of the chant and the dance which will eventually be the death of Simon. Is this a verbal trick, a 'plant'? Or can we accept that a game may be a game and still reflect attitudes that only want opportunity to fulfil themselves; that there is visible in the nickname itself a conversion of human into beast expressing animus towards a nature disliked and distrusted; and, in the mime of the killing, a putting of that animus into action, permissible and humorous simply because it is recognized as 'only a game'? Ralph has already been trying 'to get rid of Piggy'.

'Next time', the reluctance to kill anything with flesh and blood is overcome, though Jack still twitches. The mimed action of driving the knife, at least, can become real action. But while the kill has been taking place the fire has gone out and the ship has passed, so there is real tension between Ralph and Jack. The knife has just been shifted from Jack's right to his left hand, smudging blood across his forehead, when he 'stuck his fist into Piggy's stomach. Piggy sat down with a grunt – Jack stood over him. His voice was vicious with humiliation.' (We suddenly remember a less vicious voice, but still a fierce one: 'You should stick a pig …') And though Piggy doesn't bleed, he is half blinded. Does the animus of the nickname and the 'Scha-aa-ow!' look so far-fetched now, and is this a game?

Not long after this Maurice reduces the tension, and reunites everyone but Ralph, by miming what had actually happened in the killing of the pig. The others sing the chant they made up to keep step by as they carried it back, and to express their triumph:

The twins, still sharing their identical grin, jumped up and ran round each other. Then the rest joined in, making pig-dying noises and shouting.

'One for his nob!'

'Give him a fourpenny one!'

Then Maurice pretended to be a pig and ran squealing into the centre and the hunters, circling still, pretended to beat him. As they danced, they sang.

'*Kill the pig. Cut her throat. Bash her in.*'

Grin, pretence and dance show that this is still a game. But we have seen how in different, tense circumstances, game can turn into actual violence. The tension has only been reduced, it is still there, and what they are acting is already a reality. The line between game, pretence and reality is becoming much more difficult to draw.

After the assembly's discussion of the Beast, and the break-up in disorder (with Jack's 'If there's a beast, we'll hunt it down! We'll close in and beat and beat and beat …'), there is dangerous tension again:

The sound of mock hunting, hysterical laughter and real terror came from the beach …

'If you don't blow, we'll soon be animals anyway. I can't see what they're doing but I can hear.'

The dispersed figures had come together on the sand and were a dense black mass that revolved. They were chanting something and littluns that had had enough were staggering away howling.

The dance is becoming a way of fencing off terror, or even of taking it out on a projection of its cause, not merely of reducing it. Although there is no necessary suggestion that the littluns have been beaten, there is ringing in one's ear, both the first suggestion of hysterical animality, and the first cries of terror. The black, revolving mass, like a miniature tornado, is a forbidding phenomenon.

Next time, Ralph is also involved in the experience of hunting, and is caught up into the heady excitement of the mime. The children had been frightened by the boar and, stronger than ever, there is the tension between Jack and Ralph. This time, in the ring, somebody really hurts Robert who is acting the pig; and his cries of pain and frenzied struggle to escape produce a 'sudden, thick excitement' which carries away Ralph too:

'Kill him! Kill him!'

All at once, Robert was screaming and struggling with the strength of frenzy. Jack had him by the hair and was brandishing his knife. Behind him was Roger, fighting to get close. The chant rose ritually, as at the last moment of a dance or a hunt.

'Kill the pig! Cut his throat! Kill the pig! Bash him in!'

Ralph too was fighting to get near, to get a handful of that brown, vulnerable flesh. The desire to squeeze and hurt was overmastering.

Jack's arm came down; the heaving circle cheered and made pig-dying noises. Then they lay quiet, panting, listening to Robert's frightened snivels ...

'That was a good game.'

The borderline of game has however clearly been crossed, though in a way which often happens in games ('I got jolly badly hurt at rugger once'). This one has clearly revealed not only the riddance of tension and the acting out of fear and hatred, but the excitement of inflicting pain ('Behind him was Roger, fighting to get close'). And, for the first time, the actor has become the victim. The children feel that they are still not doing it properly, they need a drum, someone dressed up as a pig, no, more.

'You need a real pig,' said Robert, still caressing his rump, 'because you've got to kill him.'

'Use a littlun,' said Jack, and everybody laughed.

It is said in fun, but we have become uncomfortably aware of the impossibility of positing a secure barrier between 'fun and games' and the darker passions. After this the hunters discover their bloodlust, and Roger the torturer is rewarded by a more satisfying scream than Robert's, but we are disturbingly reminded of Ralph as we see him 'prodding with his spear whenever pigflesh appeared'. We are not likely to be convinced when the 'voice' of the Lord of the Flies tells Simon: 'It was a joke really – why should you bother?'

Finally, in the lightning and thunder, this whole process of revelation reaches a climax. The boys are hysterical with fear of the lightning, with the tension of the static electricity, with the conflict between Jack and Ralph at its highest. Clearly and unmistakably, dance and chant have wholly moved over from game or narrative, to a protective ritual: 'Piggy and Ralph, under the threat of the sky, found themselves eager to take a place in this demented but partly secure society. They were glad to touch the brown backs of the fence that hemmed in the terror and made it governable.' The ritual enacts the hemming in, and then the killing, of their own terrors, all of which are projected into the Beast. So, now, the words of the chant have changed: '*Kill the beast! Cut his throat! Spill his blood!*' The individual loses himself in the mob; the chant 'began to beat like a steady pulse'. 'There was the throb and stamp of a single organism.' Then, out of the screams of terror, rises once again that other desire 'thick, urgent, blind', the desire to 'beat and beat and beat'.

We have learned how each of these scenes revealed something which contained the potentiality of the next. Though it is a terrible shock to inspect the end in one leap from the beginning, or vice versa, there is no leap in the whole progress. Each step is just the same measured advance on the last, and connected with the same inevitability to what went before and what is to come after. Can we point to any discontinuity? Can we, accepting all the other links, refuse our assent to the last? For the achievement has nothing to do with dogma, or an assertion of Original Sin. Golding does not tell us, he shows us, and that is what makes the book so terrifying, whatever our private beliefs may be. He shows us, at the end of his progress, how 'Roger ceased to be a pig and became a hunter, so that the centre of the ring *yawned emptily*'.

It is impossible not to feel the suspense and menace here; that last phrase crystallizes our whole experience and our own emotions of fear and waiting. We know we are on the brink of tragedy without being able precisely to locate it; we know that blind mouth must close – on something.

So, as Chapter 3 linked Johnny and Henry and Maurice with Roger, and Roger with Jack's 'bloodthirsty snarling', we have now seen all the children as part of a process of becoming which has ended in a second, more terrible death. Whether Simon's view of man be just or not, the prophecy of what the fun and games would lead to has been fulfilled.

Simon's view, however, is not yet complete, even though he is dead, for it has not depended on him only as a character, but on a way of seeing. Golding appeals to no heaven to right the wrong of man and there is no God in his novel; but as the storm gives way to calm and the Pacific tide comes in, Simon's body is beautified, if not beatified, and his kind of vision operates once more, as we take in the fact of its disappearance.

The scene re-orchestrates the earlier one in which Simon's vision was first given to us. The riot and clamour then gave way to peace and beauty; they do so again. After the storm, after even the dripping and running water dies away, the world of tension and violence becomes 'cool, moist and clear'. The residue of the terror, Simon's body, still lies 'huddled' while 'the stains spread, inch by inch'. But as night falls, there advances in the great onward flow of the tide a line of phosphorescence in the 'clear water (which) mirrored the clear sky and the angular bright constellations'. The essence of Simon's view, *acceptance*, becomes explicitly the mode of the writing.

The line of phosphorescence bulged about the sand grains and little pebbles; it held them each in a dimple of tension, then suddenly accepted them with an inaudible syllable and moved on.

The broken detritus of man's barbarity is made into something beautiful, like a work of art. As a pebble is decorated with pearls, as the pitted sand is smoothed and inlaid with silver, so:

The water rose further and dressed Simon's coarse hair with brightness. The line of his cheek silvered and the turn of his shoulder became sculptured marble.

But the beauty is not prettified, it co-exists with the alien, even the sinister and the ugly. The acceptance has to include the bubble of Simon's last breath escaping with a 'wet plop', an ugly, final sound. The beautifying creatures are 'strange, moonbeam-bodied . . . with their fiery eyes and trailing vapours'. Indeed, a moment's reflection will tell us more: they are the same 'transparencies' that come in the daylight scavenging for food like 'myriads of tiny teeth in a saw'.

It was the nature of Simon's view to see things inclusively in both their heroic and their sick aspects, to accept the daylight and the night-time mood. We have to see both tiny teeth and phosphorescent beautification; both the huddled figure, the stains, the wet plop, and the bright hair and sculptured marble; both the riot and clamour of 'day' and the calm, fragrant beauty of 'night'. In the endless processes of the universe, there is the reverse of the terror of the ocean on the 'other side': there is the 'Pacific':

Somewhere over the darkened curve of the world the sun and moon were pulling; and the film of water on the earth planet was held, bulging slightly on one side while the solid core turned. The great wave of the tide moved further along the island and the water lifted. Softly, surrounded by a fringe of inquisitive bright creatures, itself a silver shape beneath the steadfast constellations, Simon's dead body moved out towards the open sea.

The studiously scientific description intimates a sense of quiet order; a huge and universal perspective, which yet does not dwarf because it includes everything, accepts Simon as he had accepted it. In a sense we are asked to experience the fact that he has 'got back to where he belonged', to a vision big and inclusive enough to be 'steadfast', to accept and order all. To be true to Golding's book, we must remember the heroism as well as the sickness: not only the Lord of the Flies, the corrupting flesh of the parachutist, the teeth and claws and huddled body; but also the vision that is given the beautification of this sea-burial.

To the 'world of longing and baffled common-sense' what has happened is shameful and obscene. Ralph struggles, trapped between shame and honesty. Piggy's shrill outrage marks his unwillingness to admit what cannot be hidden. There is attempted excuse: 'It was dark. There was that – that bloody dance. There was thunder and lightning and rain. We was scared.' But Ralph knows how much more was involved. Piggy's excited 'gesticulating, searching for a formula' is stopped short by a voice in which there was 'loathing, and at the same time a kind of feverish excitement' as well as a note 'low and stricken'. But Piggy will not accept guilt:

Ralph continued to rock to and fro.
    'It was an accident,' said Piggy suddenly, 'that's what it was. An accident.' His voice shrilled again. 'Coming in the dark – he hadn't no business crawling like that out of the dark. He was batty. He asked for it.' He gesticulated widely again. 'It was an accident.'
    'You didn't see what they did –'
    'Look, Ralph. We got to forget this. We can't do no good thinking about it, see?'
    'I'm frightened. Of us. I want to go home. O God I want to go home.'
    'It was an accident,' said Piggy stubbornly, 'and that's that.'
    He touched Ralph's bare shoulder and Ralph shuddered at the human contact. 'And look, Ralph,' Piggy glanced round quickly, then leaned close – 'don't let on we was in that dance.'

It is clear on one level that this amounts to a severe criticism of Piggy – 'We never done nothing, we never seen nothing' – and this attempt to deny their involvement, this last pathetic effort to hang on to the simple view that evil is something done by other people, compares ill with Simon's. But it is pathetic, because no one is fooled: 'Memory of the dance that none of them had attended shook all four boys convulsively.' They have got 'frightened of people' as Piggy had said they should not. All that was complacent about Piggy's point of view in the assembly has been pinpointed. 'We can't do no good thinking about it' is not a statement that inspires.

    This however is not a disposal of 'the humanistic view of man', nor, as was obvious after the first assembly, does Piggy merely represent a complacent Humanism. We would even be misreading if we thought that this episode was a weighted demonstration of the superiority of Simon's belief in Original Sin. For, while it is easy to dispose of what is complacent and narrow in Piggy's view, it is not at all easy to dispose of the view itself; nor is it meant to be. For Piggy has a challenging point. Simon's view, we must remember, was of 'mankind's *essential* illness'. What has happened has proved conclusively that there is evil in all human beings, even in those who try to be rational and civilized. But this does not amount to proof that the illness is of the *essence* of man. May it not be an 'accident', as one might argue medical illnesses are, produced by special circumstances? That is precisely the question that Piggy poses, and it is a good question for Golding to ask so openly.

Had Simon any business crawling out of the dark like that? Wasn't he batty? From his own point of view even, isn't the 'saint' crazy to believe that people he sees as inherently evil can be so easily converted into the belief that the projection of their inner darkness is 'harmless and horrible'? Doesn't he, on any point of view allow too little for fear of the dark that he doesn't share? We remember Ralph having to rebuke Simon for terrifying the littluns, in the corresponding chapter in the first section, by moving about in the dark outside the shelters, and he was surely right to do so. That early episode can now be seen to have cast a long shadow. This is a searching psychological question too. If the martyrdom is partly created by the martyr, can he not be truly said to have 'asked for it'? Lastly, if the tragedy happens because of the coming together, at some uniquely dangerous corner, of the special circumstances of hysteria and the special 'case' of the martyr, is it not only the simple truth to speak of accident rather than essence? One is not suggesting that the vision of Simon may not be the more convincing and conclusive; nor that we are not inclined to take the 'impaired vision' of Ralph and Piggy in deeper senses than the physical. But Simon's vision establishes itself, if it does so, by its own imaginative force and the opposing views are given no inconsiderable weight.

On the other hand, both 'longing' and 'common sense' are clearly shown as more and more vulnerable to the darkness. The longing for rescue is more difficult to keep alive, the flapping curtain in Ralph's brain more pronounced, and the barricades of common sense can operate only in daylight. Ralph's nightly game of 'supposing' fails to comfort, because the 'wildness' even of Dartmoor and the ponies is no longer securely attractive.

His mind skated to a consideration of a tamed town where savagery could not set foot. What could be safer than the bus centre with its lamps and wheels?

All at once, Ralph was dancing round a lamp standard. There was a bus crawling out of the bus station, a strange bus ...

The mind releases its secret knowledge that there is no safe barrier between civilization and wild nature. The conch is becoming emptied of significance, seen as fragile: 'I got the conch' is spoken with hysterical irony by a Ralph who sees no future in what he still pathetically caresses.

For Jack's tribe, on the other hand, the death of Simon is a catalyst. They know the horrors of the island well enough; what they proceed to build up is the full tribal technique for coping with them. They barricade themselves in the Castle with the huge rock poised over the causeway and sentries posted. This is an extension into daily living of the 'ring'; and the 'stamp of a single organism' is preserved by the absolute authority of the Chief. They know well enough what they have done, but they overcome the knowledge, not by hiding it, but by extending their projection of evil into the Beast. They persuade themselves that the Devil can take different shapes, and be 'killed' in those, but 'How could we – kill – it?' So far they have realized Simon's truth ('Fancy thinking the beast was something you could hunt and kill'); but they still see the Beast as outside them, an evil capricious force that must be placated. The world has fully become a power situation of 'us' and 'not us'. The strong Beast must be propitiated; but the tribe makes a surprise attack on 'Ralph's lot' to take what they want. The Chief finally secures his authority when he captures the means of fire in Piggy's glasses, and the 'vicious snarling', hitting, biting, scratching, are now deliberately, not accidentally, directed against their fellows.

In this chapter, called *The Shell and the Glasses*, we see that for the tribe the glasses have lost all connection with sight; it is nothing to them that Piggy will be virtually blind and the conch has no meaning whatsoever, so that the raiders show no interest in it. The release of their inner darkness in the killing of Simon has meant an end of all that the conch stood for. If the world is one of power, there is nothing for power to be responsible to. Jack does not have to give reasons for beating Wilfred; and this is a revelation to

Roger, who receives 'as an illumination ... the possibilities of irresponsible authority'. The death of Simon precipitates the worst element in the tribe: there is nothing now but power, war against 'outsiders', and a darker threat behind.

The stage is set for a final confrontation, recalling the assembly at the end of the first section. The conch sounds again. 'The forest re-echoed; and birds lifted, crying, out of the tree-tops, as on that first morning ages ago'; but now 'both ways the beach was deserted'. If the savages will not come to the conch however, Piggy is determined to take the conch to them.

'What can he do more than he has? I'll tell him what's what. You let me carry the conch, Ralph. I'll show him the one thing he hasn't got.'

Piggy paused for a moment and peered round at the dim figures. The shape of the old assembly, trodden in the grass, listened to him.

'I'm going to him with this conch in my hands. I'm going to hold it out. Look, I'm goin' to say, you're stronger than I am and you haven't got asthma. You can see, I'm goin' to say, and with both eyes. But I don't ask for my glasses back, not as a favour. I don't ask you to be a sport, I'll say, not because you're strong, but because what's right's right. Give me my glasses, I'm going to say – you got to!'

Piggy ended, flushed and trembling. He pushed the conch quickly into Ralph's hands as though in a hurry to be rid of it, and wiped the tears from his eyes. The green light was gentle about them, and the conch lay at Ralph's feet, fragile and white. A single drop of water that had escaped Piggy's fingers now flashed on the delicate curve like a star.

The words are brave, but the mode of their reception is already established in the irony of the different salt water that has become the element of the 'fragile' white shell. And, though Ralph dimly 'remembered something that Simon had said to him once, by the rocks', Simon's fate has hardly made his faith reassuring. Nevertheless Piggy is given real stature at this moment, the stature of tragedy.

On the causeway before the castle, we hear the Sound of the Shell for the last time as there is a final hopeless attempt to summon back into the painted savages the consciousness of the British schoolboy. But the language of reminder has lost its meaning, because the standards it appeals to are gone. The 'silvery, unreal laughter' from the height is an insuperable element, dissolving the appeal to civilized value before it can have any effect: ' "If he hasn't got them he can't see. You aren't playing the game –"' The tribe of painted savages giggled and Ralph's mind faltered.' The idea of rescue has quite vanished, and the protest of the twins against their imprisonment only underlines the helplessness, the lack of language, of their cries 'out of the heart of civilization': 'Oh I say!'; '– honestly!'

There is only denunciation, and the language can only be ironic. When Ralph shouts 'You're a beast, and a swine, and a bloody bloody thief', it is only our ears that take in the literal meaning, and even to us it is clear that it is really only an invitation to battle, for moral values have no validity here.

Piggy stops the battle by holding up the conch ... for the last time we see the emblem at work: 'The booing sagged a little, then came up again to strength. "I got the conch!"' But it is only a momentary memory, and when they do listen to Piggy, it is as a clown. While he speaks, there sounds through the air the faint 'Zup!' of the stones that Roger is dropping from the height, where his hand rests on the lever of the great rock, feeling how 'some source of power began to pulse' in his body. From his height the boys are not even human: 'Ralph was a shock of hair, and Piggy a bag of fat.' Then comes the final challenge:

'I got this to say. You're acting like a crowd of kids.'
The booing rose and died again as Piggy lifted the white, magic shell.
'Which is better – to be a pack of painted niggers like you are, or to be sensible like Ralph is?'
A great clamour rose among the savages. Piggy shouted again.
'Which is better – to have rules and agree, or to hunt and kill?'
Again the clamour and again – 'Zup!'
Ralph shouted against the noise.
'Which is better, law and rescue, or hunting and breaking things up?'
Now Jack was yelling too and Ralph could no longer make himself heard. Jack had backed right against the tribe and they were a solid mass of menace that bristled with spears. The intention of a charge was forming among them; they were working up to it and the neck would be swept clear. Ralph stood facing them, a little to one side, his spear ready. By him stood Piggy still holding out the talisman, the fragile, shining beauty of the shell. The storm of sound beat at them, an incantation of hatred. High overhead, Roger, with a sense of delirious abandonment, leaned all his weight on the lever ...
... The rock struck Piggy a glancing blow from chin to knee: the conch exploded into a thousand white fragments and ceased to exist. Piggy, saying nothing, with no time for even a grunt, travelled through the air

sideways from the rock, turning over as he went. The rock bounded twice and was lost in the forest. Piggy fell forty feet and landed on his back across that square, red rock in the sea. His head opened and stuff came out and turned red. Piggy's arms and legs twitched a bit, like a pig's after it has been killed. Then the sea breathed again in a long, slow sigh, the water boiled white and pink, over the rock; and when it went, sucking back again, the body of Piggy was gone.

The boy has now literally been seen and killed like a pig; the implications of his nickname fully brought out; what they hated about him turned into 'red stuff' welling out of an 'opened' head. The 'table' Ralph saw has become a place of sacrifice. 'Viciously, with full intention', Jack hurls his spear at Ralph to kill, while 'anonymous devils' faces swarmed across the neck', and another human Pig obeying 'an instinct he did not know he possessed' swerves in his flight, and goes crashing through foliage to be hidden in the forest. 'Something', the words echo from far back, 'squealed and ran in the undergrowth'. We hear a familiar sound, but this time it is human, and what the Sound of the Shell has become is a 'great noise as of sea-gulls': the harsh sound not of the conch, but of the hunters screaming hatred and bloodlust.

The hunt is called off, for the moment. But there advances on Samneric, finally liberated from all control, almost brushing Jack aside because of the 'nameless unmentionable authority' that surrounds the Executioner and Torturer, the figure of Roger: 'The yelling ceased, and Sam and Eric lay looking up in quiet terror.' There is silence, but we know, although we do not hear it yet, that we are listening for something. Gulls' scream and hunters' cry, and the high scream of a victim in pain, these are only postponed, suspended – for a moment.

VI

Alone and terrified, Ralph goes on trying to believe that 'they're not as bad as that. It was an accident'; but he knows better. There is no further reliance on their 'common sense, their daylight sanity'; and there is that 'indefinable connection between himself and Jack; who therefore will never let him alone; never'. Jack can never be free from the Ralph-in-him till Ralph is dead. There can be no end to this game. It is the nightmare of 'play' that must go on and on past nightfall, with no rules, no 'Sir' or Mummy or Daddy to call a halt.

Might it not be possible to walk boldly into the fort, say – 'I've got pax,' laugh lightly and sleep among the others? Pretend they were still boys, schoolboys who had said, 'Sir, yes, Sir' – and worn caps? Daylight might have answered yes; but darkness and the horrors of death said no. Lying there in the darkness he knew he was an outcast.

'Cos I had some sense.'

But this echo of Piggy poses once more the question of whether the reason for what has happened does not lie a good deal deeper. Ralph suddenly finds himself in the clearing, where a 'pig's skull grinned at him from the top of a stick':

He walked slowly into the middle of the clearing and looked steadily at the skull that gleamed as white as ever the conch had done and seemed to jeer at him cynically. An inquisitive ant was busy in one of the eye sockets but otherwise the thing was lifeless.

Or was it?

Little prickles of sensation ran up and down his back. He stood, the skull about on a level with his face, and held up his hair with two hands. The teeth grinned, the empty sockets seemed to hold his gaze masterfully and without effort.

What was it?

The skull regarded Ralph like one who knows all the answers and won't tell. A sick fear and rage swept him. Fiercely he hit out at the filthy thing in front of him that bobbed like a toy and came back, still grinning into his face, so that he lashed and cried out in loathing. Then he was licking his bruised knuckles and looking at the bare stick, while the skull lay in two pieces, its grin now six feet across. He wrenched the quivering stick from the crack and held it as a spear between him and the white pieces. Then he backed away, keeping his face to the skull that lay grinning at the sky.

Again, Golding himself is silent. We are asked to measure and judge the contrast for ourselves; the skull doesn't, in fact, hold 'answers'. There is the white conch, and the white skull; Ralph's and Piggy's 'meaning', and Simon's. There is the view that accepts the evil and takes it to himself; there is the 'sick fear and rage', the hitting out that expresses the loathing and rejection of something utterly alien. 'What was it?' It is for us, finally, to say.

The next day the inevitable hunt begins. Great rocks, 'big as a car, a tank' are sent crashing down like bombs in a full-scale war.

This is not game, not defence, not even the work of a single sadist, but military strategy. We notice again the familiar opening-out technique spreading from that first delighted dispatch of the 'enraged monster' into the jungle. The forest is set on fire again, but deliberately this time, the smoke is not for rescue, and the drum-roll heralds an execution quite literally. Worse, it heralds a propitiatory sacrifice to a new Lord, not Beelzebub, but Moloch; for though Ralph does not recognize the meaning of the stick sharpened at both ends, we do. Ralph's head will replace the pig's. And Ralph is becoming an animal, launching himself snarling, knowing the experience of being hunted, desperate, with no time to think, and dreading always the flapping curtain in the mind which might black out the sense of danger and make him mindless. Finally he does become Pig. His last thought of rescue, the hopeless memory of Simon's groundless faith, is replaced by a 'scream of fright and anger and desperation. His legs straightened, the screams became continuous and foaming. He shot forward, burst the thicket, was in the open, screaming, snarling, bloody.' There is the cry of the hunters, the roar of the fire, the 'desperate ululation' advancing 'like a jagged fringe of menace', the narrowing pig-run to the beach past the blazing shelters, then certain and horrible death:

Then he was down, rolling over and over in the warm sand, crouching with arm up to ward off, trying to cry for mercy.

He staggered to his feet, tensed for more terrors, and looked up at a huge peaked cap ... He saw white drill, epaulettes, a revolver, a row of gilt buttons down the front of a uniform.

A naval officer stood on the sand, looking down at Ralph ...

There is probably no remark about his work that Golding regretted more than referring to this ending as a 'gimmick'.* For though there is device, there is no suggestion of trickery. The murder of Ralph takes place in the imagination as surely as if Golding had written FINIS under the word 'mercy'. But what happens is like turning on the lights in the theatre before the curtains close, and then letting the cast suddenly step outside the action that had mesmerized us. We are forced to distance the

* Interview with Frank Kermode, *Books and Bookmen*.

completed experience, and measure how far we have travelled. For that measurement Golding needed Ralph's eyes.

The change of perspectives justifies itself as a challenge to us in the midst of shock. Suddenly we see 'a semicircle of little boys, their bodies streaked with coloured clay, sharp sticks in their hands'; some tiny tots 'brown, with the distended bellies of small savages'; a 'little scarecrow' who 'needed a bath, a haircut, a nose-wipe, and a good deal of ointment'; and another 'little boy who wore the remains of an extraordinary black cap on his red hair and who carried the remains of a pair of spectacles at his waist.' Is that all?

There could have been no more dramatic way of bringing home to us how much more there is, than thus forcing us to measure the gap that separates what the officer sees from what we ourselves know, through seeing with the eyes of Ralph. To our horror, the officer's language reveals the kind of attitudes to children and coral islands that we might very well have started with. Each word is filled with corrosive irony: 'Fun and games ... Having a war or something? ... I should have thought that a pack of British boys – you're all British aren't you – would have been able to put up a better show than that ... Like the Coral Island.' We measure the implications of that 'pack' against the Jack who had voiced just such a confidence in the British at the second meeting. 'We've got to have rules and obey them. After all, we're not savages: We're English; and the English are best at everything. So we've got to do the right things.'

But the novel has gone beyond being a critique of *Coral Island*; and there is much more involved than our better knowledge of what children are like. For the measure of the officer's inadequacy is not only that he doesn't know what children are like, but that he doesn't know what adults are like. For as our eyes take in the uniform, the revolver and sub-machine gun, the 'trim cruiser' on which the eyes that are embarrassed by the children prefer to rest, we know the significance of uniforms and weapons as the officer does not. 'Having a war or something' ... in thinking of himself as not only superior to, but even other than the children, it is the man that is the child.

It is Ralph who is 'grown-up', but he shows his adulthood by weeping. Golding needs him not only to see, but to register the proper response in pain and grief.

Ralph looked at him dumbly. For a moment he had a fleeting picture of the strange glamour that had once invested the beaches. But the island was scorched up like dead wood – Simon was dead – and Jack had ... The tears began to flow and sobs shook him. He gave himself up to them now for the first time on the island, great, shuddering spasms of grief that seemed to wrench his whole body. His voice rose under the black smoke before the burning wreckage of the island; and infected by that emotion, the other little boys began to shake and sob too. And in the middle of them, with filthy body, matted hair, and unwiped nose, Ralph wept for the end of innocence, the darkness of man's heart, and the fall through the air of the true, wise friend called Piggy.

This *grief** is the truest of all the sounds; in the sense that it shows the human response to all the others that Golding wishes to leave in our ears.

It is however a *response*, not an answer. What Ralph weeps for is the failure of Piggy's idea of a rational world, Piggy's friendship, Piggy's intelligence. We might ask whether there has not been a truer 'innocence', a greater 'wisdom', a more loving 'kindness', a better attitude to 'darkness' and the 'fall'. If Ralph weeps for Piggy, may it be because he only knows one degree better than the officer? Ought *we* to be weeping ... for Simon? But, though we may ask such questions, the novel will give us no dogmatic answer. Golding's fiction has been too complex and many-sided to be reducible to a thesis and a conclusion. *Lord of the Flies* is imagined with a flexibility and depth which seem evidence of finer art than the polish and clarity of its surface. Even in his first novel, it is not explanation and conclusion, but imaginative impact which is finally memorable.

---

* Golding once summed up the import of the novel as 'grief, sheer grief, grief, grief, grief!' (*A Moving Target*, p. 163)

2

THE INHERITORS

(1955)

I

To come to *The Inheritors* fresh from *Lord of the Flies* is to be made quickly aware of opacity and puzzle not present in the earlier novel. We feel uncertain about both the direction of the narrative and the status of the characters, and it is often difficult to see, on the simplest level, what exactly is going on. It is only as we continue to read that we begin to place our difficulty. The style is simple enough, with a vivid sensuousness that carries us forward in spite of uncertainties. The difficulty lies in the point of view:

As he watched, one of the farther rocks began to change shape. At one side a small bump elongated then disappeared quickly. The top of the rock swelled, the hump fined off at the base and elongated again then halved its height. Then it was gone.

It is because we are placed behind a pair of eyes that only perceive, and cannot understand, that we may have no more idea than Lok what it is that he is watching. Perception is itself, no more; not what we normally expect it to be, a stepping stone to an idea rapidly transferred from the eye to the mind. We come to realize that Golding's Neanderthalers live through their senses. They can infer to a limited extent from their own experience but they cannot go beyond it because they cannot deduce or reason. What we watch is the moment when Neanderthal Man first confronts Homo Sapiens, but all we can be given is sharply focused visual detail of shape and movement. Lok cannot conceive a human creature with a nature wholly unlike his own; cannot deduce such a creature from the behaviour he sees; and consequently cannot understand that behaviour at all. We share his limitations as we use his eyes.

It is of course open to us to use our own reasoning powers on his experience. At several points before this one we could have deduced not only the existence of New Men but the difference in nature between them and Lok's People. They must have removed the communal bridge-log to make their own huge fire; it was their smoke that caused Lok to make his almost fatal mistake on the cliff; they must have been responsible for the disappearance of Ha. As we watch the instinctive miming of Lok the tracker we can accurately deduce the differing natures of Men and People and hazard a shrewd guess at what must have happened to Ha. And once we have deduced Man's hostility, suspicion and fear, the opacity vanishes and Lok's vision sharpens for us. What he watches so uncomprehendingly is a Man treating him as though he were a predatory enemy, a man not 'another', as simple loving and fearless as himself, but peering stealthily round and above the rock he uses as cover, spying.

Any such process of understanding has however to take place outside the fiction itself. The only incitement to interpret, deduce, explain, comes from our own intellectual frustration at being confronted with the apparently unintelligible. This is not what concerns Golding. The response he seeks is essentially the imaginative one of knowing what it is like to look through eyes empty of thought and as innocent of judgement as of hatred, suspicion and fear. He had devoted all his resources to creating that experience, and Lok's incomprehension is a vital part of it. We cannot be prevented from analysing and judging, nor need we; but we would indeed 'murder to dissect' if we thought that analysis and judgement were supposed to be the object of the exercise. Imaginative exploration, through a vision quite unlike our own, comes first. Understanding will follow, but more slowly and mysteriously from a distillation of experience, and it may result in something far more complex than a black-and-white contrast between Men and People. If ever there was a book meant to be read through in one imaginative act, by which we seek to become, and to judge only when the experience is complete, it is *The Inheritors*.

Any account of the novel that does not centre on its qualities of imaginative exploration ought then to be highly suspect. It is easy to suggest apparently useful ways of looking at it, but it is more important to see just how they miss the mark. The epigraph suggests, for example, that Golding wishes to overturn H. G. Wells' account of the Neanderthaler (in both *The Outline of History* and his tale *The Grisly Folk*) as *Lord of the Flies* had subverted Ballantyne. So one could approach the novel as a fictional essay in prehistory, based on considerable knowledge of anthropology, and seeking to substitute a truer picture of Neanderthal Man for one distorted by faulty assumptions. The funeral of Mal, for instance, comes across vividly in just this archaeological and anthropological way.

Yet the novel is also a fictional *tour de force*, taking us to an otherworld and othertime that we enjoy for their own sake, irrespective of historical considerations. Isn't this science fiction if it is science at all: taking us backwards as space fiction takes us forwards, substituting Neanderthalers for Martians, but giving us the same pleasure in the exotic, or the familiar seen through strange eyes?

Yet again, the fiction seems to point to allegory. Golding's Neanderthalers are the true innocents, the harmless ones, not only without evil themselves but incapable of understanding it when it meets and destroys them. They run to meet their killers in love, and are quite incapable of preserving themselves by destroying their oppressors. The title reveals a bitter irony, for it is not the meek who inherit the earth but the killers of the meek. We can contrast every aspect of the 'fallen' life of the New Men with the 'unfallen' life of the People, and take home to ourselves the message that comes from realizing the nature of our ancestry. We may then reach the point when the novel seems no longer essentially about Neanderthal Man at all, but merely uses him as a way of analysing the nature of the Fall. Emblems now emerge: the dead tree from which Lok and Fa look down on the destruction of their Eden; the waterfall which marks the limit of innocence, but beyond which the sinful have to travel towards a line of darkness.

Each of these ways of looking seems momentarily convincing; each indeed contains an aspect of truth; but as soon as one turns back to the novel itself, all are manifestly unsatisfactory, suggesting something smaller and less valuable than what is actually there. For what they all leave out of account is the primary experience of reading: a reaching out through the imagination into the unknown. The mode of *The Inheritors* is one of discovery, not an exercise in literary archaeology, science fiction or a fable about the Fall. By committing himself so radically to the viewpoint of his People, by doing his utmost to ensure that he is kept out of his normal consciousness, Golding does contrive to see things new, not merely to see new things. His imagination is at full stretch throughout because of the challenge of his basic form; it has to be, for the novel to be written at all. That is the real significance of the point of view.

It also drives his style to produce its finest effects. Simon's kind of perception through the senses dominates and does virtually all the work because the People have to be made to live convincingly through their senses. The style also has to persuade us that they are not merely defective, that their faculties of perception are so much richer than ours that the contrast can never be the simple one of 'better' and 'worse' so intrinsic to Wells.

'I have a picture –'
Then the people laughed too because this was Lok's picture, almost the only one he had, and they knew it as well as he did.
'– a picture of finding the little Oa.'
Fantastically the old root was twisted and bulged and smoothed away by age into the likeness of a great-bellied woman.
'– I am standing among the trees. I feel. With this foot I feel –' He mimed for them. His weight was on his left foot and his right was searching in the ground. '– I feel. What do I feel? A bulb? A stick? A bone?' His right foot seized something and passed it up to his left hand. He looked. 'It is the little Oa!' Triumphantly he sunned himself before them. 'And now where Liku is there is the little Oa.'
The people applauded him, grinning, half at Lok, half at the story. Secure in their applause, Lok settled himself by the fire and the people were silent, gazing into the flames.
The sun dropped into the river and light left the overhang. Now the fire was more than ever central, white ash, a spot of red and one flame wavering upwards. The old woman moved softly, pushing in more wood so that the red spot ate and the flame grew strong. The people watched, their faces seeming to quiver in the unsteady light. Their freckled skins were ruddy and the deep caverns beneath their brows were each inhabited by replicas of the fire and all their fires danced together. As they persuaded themselves of the warmth they relaxed limbs and drew the reek into their nostrils gratefully. They flexed their toes and stretched their arms, even leaning away from the fire. One of the deep silences fell on them, that seemed so much more natural than speech, a timeless silence in which there were at first many minds in the overhang; and then perhaps no mind at all. So fully discounted was the roar of the water that the soft touch of the wind on the rocks became audible. Their ears as if endowed with separate life sorted the tangle of tiny sounds and accepted them, the sound of breathing, the sound of wet clay flaking and ashes falling in.

This is not one of the spectacularly beautiful passages that stud the novel, but what it fairly represents is the overall sensuousness and accuracy of the style. Golding conveys the extraordinary experience of living through the feet as much as the hands, and having ears remarkably more sensitive than ours. The sensuous texture is a direct result of his challenge to himself to imagine what it is like to live through sense and instinct, not the mind, breaking the barrier of 'modern' consciousness. To turn from this to *The Grisly Folk* is to perceive that the significant difference is not the contrasting ideas of the moral nature of Neanderthal Man. It is that Golding has accepted the challenge to imagine himself into an alien mode of life, as Wells has not. Without imagination there is nothing between scientific data, obviously susceptible to opposite interpretations, and unsupported fantasy.

Yet his limited point of view presented Golding with a huge stylistic problem, for it involves not only intensification of the sensuous imagination beyond the normal, but also continuous and severe self-denial. He had to deprive himself of all analysis, by himself or his characters, and of most of the possibilities of dialogue, in order to create from within the consciousness of people who neither think nor communicate as we do. Yet he had also to make them credibly human; and create a style which would reach beyond them to us, communicating beyond the limits of their power. The solution is a brilliant one and the chosen discipline faithfully maintained.

In description, Golding allows himself one compromise. Once granted that the People have a vivid accuracy of sense-perception far exceeding ours, he allows himself 'modern' resources of language where these are exactly descriptive of what the People see, feel, hear, or touch, without themselves having words or images to express their activities. This is perfectly fair, their experience is wholly independent of language, and to pin it down to their linguistic resources would falsify totally; whereas to use the full resources of our language only conveys as accurate an equivalent as possible of something communicable in no other way. To take an obvious example from our passage, to speak of eye-caverns 'inhabited by replicas of the fire' merely states accurately what the people themselves see, though it requires a word totally beyond them. Indeed, they have no power of comparison; yet 'the likeness of a great-bellied woman' is the only exact way of conveying what the root looks like to us.

We probably hardly notice this licence, however, because the experience of living in the People's minds is so strong and so strange. There is a peculiar colouring in the style; they see anthropomorphically, investing their whole environment with humanity. The river sleeps or is awake, trees have ears, the island is a huge thigh, shin and foot, logs go away, everything is alive. So, here, the fire eats and dances, and the near-clichés suddenly reveal a freshness when we realize that we are in touch with a linguistic epoch, not only before metaphor has died, but before it has even begun to live as comparison. 'All their fires danced together' is said simply and literally. Metaphor is still the expression of identity. The light dancing in the eyes is not like fire, it is fire. The people see the root as Oa in little, the maternal fecundity incarnate in the wooden shape. There are ice-women, not simply ice shaped like women. The adventure of style escapes mere limitation and begins to carry us imaginatively into a strangeness of living.

In dialogue of course the losses are heavier and more obvious. Lok's words in the passage are little more than verbal accompaniment of mime and gesture, and though he is the simplest of the People, this is true of most of their speech. Words for them are only one stage beyond expressive noises, and we can see how simple the process of verbalization might be if we imagine the 'original' language that Golding translates into English. It might be rather like those first beginnings in a foreign language that the tourist experiences, where he can make do with nouns and action words, without grammar and inflection. Indeed, when Lok becomes excited, his 'words' become emotional noises with little or no meaning; he 'gibbers' or 'babbled happily in admiration, his head thrown back, words coming out at random'. Clearly the limitation for the novelist is a huge one.

Yet there is also a linguistic interest in the People's speech which is an interest in progress. In Ha, and Mal, and Fa, and in Lok too, when circumstances force him to develop from clown to leader, we can watch the People's language trying to transform itself and reach out to the incomprehensible and the incommunicable. On the opening pages Mal can only cope with the problem of the vanished log by calling on his experience and giving orders based on memory; but we watch the quickness of Ha to catch on. Again, we can see how from Mal's version of the myth of creation told in simple narrative, feelings and attitudes are distilled which require a moral or religious language. We watch the struggle of this more complex language to meet the challenges of necessity and change. Fa battles with language as she tries to invent cultivation and irrigation. Such actions cannot exist until they have been conceived. Lok struggles with words, trying to learn to reason, and to use the linguistic tool of comparison and analogy. We start off vividly aware of limitation, but there is also a linguistic experience of unique strangeness and excitement. In the book's dialogue we reach back through history to experience for ourselves how language must have developed in time. By the end we have been forced to make real to ourselves the dimensions, and the cost, of our linguistic inheritance.

The style also has to convey a kind of mental experience totally unknown to nearly all of us, for words are by far the smallest part of the People's resources of communication. They mainly communicate by telepathic picture. For Golding's purposes as a novelist this is a fine invention, for it allows him, as soon as there is something communicable on a basis of past experience, to use among the People and for their own 'thoughts' something of the resources of language he can use descriptively, and with the same justification.

The pictures are of course visualizations, not conceptualizations. If they are part of the People's abnormally rich life of sense and instinct, they are also part of their incapacity for abstract thought. Here however we get not only the experience of growth towards our own consciousness; we get also the experience of a faculty that modern man has almost entirely lost. We can watch the People trying painfully to learn to put pictures together in a chain of thought. But we can also experience a fellow-feeling so intense that the People literally participate in one another when they share pictures, living not as individuals, but as part of a communal whole. Mime becomes far more than an attempt to compensate for linguistic insufficiency; it becomes a method of imaginative sympathy and a mark of natural, instinctive love. The People not only share Mal's mind with its cloud of pain and premonition, they share also his body, and their actions do not merely parody his, they are also a way of participating in his suffering. When, in that firelight scene, 'One of the deep silences fell on them, that seemed far more natural than speech, a timeless silence in which there were at first many minds in the overhang; and then perhaps no mind at all', that 'perhaps' should make us pause. The main point is not their insufficiency of language and the limitation of their minds when compared to ours. We are not looking at the mindlessness of animals; we are not indeed looking at mindlessness at all. What we glimpse is a kind of consciousness wholly without that individual separateness and loneliness which is the definition of human consciousness as we know it; a togetherness so complete (feeling 'one' without needing to feel one about anything in particular), that in our terms it is 'perhaps no mind at all' – more than our language can cope with. We discover imaginatively what it is like to be not Men, a mere collective tag for a number of separate individuals, but People, a collective phenomenon. The style reaches out into the unknown, to bring it within our imaginative comprehension. It is an adventure, and we are the Inheritors; but the novel does not tell us, it makes us discover what that means.

II

Given the primacy of experience over analysis, we can nevertheless see that the effect of the first four chapters is to build up, through our detailed imaginative response to the behaviour of the People, a sense of their nature and way of life. We learn, without knowing that we are learning, how they think, how they govern themselves, how their traditions direct their attitude to their environment, how they have developed a religion, a morality, and a way of looking at life and death that are human, and yet challengingly different from our own.

This growing perception of what it means to be People rather than Men is indeed very nearly the whole fascination of these early chapters; for, in narrative terms, the life of the People has an intractable sameness. 'Today is like yesterday and tomorrow' is no ideal formula for a novel. The People's existence is essentially static: the cave by the sea in winter, the overhang by the waterfall in summer; the search for food and firewood; the endurance or the satisfaction of hunger and thirst; the experience of birth, sex, and death. In such a life there is little pattern or excitement, unless it be some natural disaster or external challenge. Indeed, if we look back on these chapters, we shall see that the Neanderthalers simply come back to their summer home, find a doe, and suffer the death of Mal, and the interest is not in these particulars so much as in their revelation of what it is to live and die as People.

What narrative interest there is comes from the intrusion of the New Men: their removal of the bridge-log which indirectly hastens Mal's death, their smoke which causes Lok to fall on the cliff edge, the disappearance of Ha. It is Lok's fear of the alienation he experiences when tracking and seeing the Other that forces him to risk the sanctuary of the ice-women. The New Men provide the only opportunity for suspense. In addition to the difficulties of putting himself behind the People's eyes, the very nature of their life complicates the novelist's problems: not only will his chosen method make his early chapters obscure, but his chosen subject removes most of the possibilities of narrative excitement. It is hardly surprising that we should find *The Inheritors* more difficult to get into than the other novels. This is partly offset, however, by Golding's use of suspense in the gradual materialization of the New Men, so that curiosity is kept alive. For the rest, he manages to convey so vivid and detailed a sense of the People's life itself that we remain fascinated by its strangeness and caught up unawares by its challenge to our own consciousness.

Their existence is essentially communal. We have seen how they not only protect and warm Mal with their bodies, but also involve themselves, through mime and picture, in sharing his sickness and awareness of death physically, as well as imaginatively. We have seen, too, how the consciousness most natural to them is of so existing in one another that they become one mind. But there are more startling indications of the fact that it is the relationship among them that is central, and the relationships between them only secondary. Their sexuality is promiscuous in our terminology. They seem at first to live in couples, but when Mal touches a rock 'as Lok or Ha might touch Fa' the description turns out to be more pointed than it looks, for though Fa is in one sense Lok's mate, and Nil Ha's, Liku is Lok's daughter by Nil. Nil will dream, in a seriously reassuring way, of herself and Fa being slept with by both men. The sexuality that is as natural as hunger to them can clearly exist among the group as well as between the couples, and is only a part of their feeling for one another as a whole. It is 'animal', yet as Fa pats her hair when Lok touches her, it is recognizably human too. If we call it 'promiscuous' we simply reveal our different assumptions about relationship. Again, the depth of Lok's feeling for Ha is manifested in a sense of his 'Ha-ness' no less physical than his feelings for Fa; and we can make no useful distinction between the mourning of Fa and Nil for him, and the mourning that breaks from Lok's mouth. So when Lok the tracker feels that 'The other had tugged at the strings that bound him to Fa and Mal and Liku and the rest of the people. The strings were not the ornament of life but their substance. If they broke, a man would die . . .', we have to see that though Fa comes first on the list, it is the 'strings' as a whole that are the vital substance of living, and the particular relationships exist only within that feeling of oneness. The baby is not 'Nil's baby' but the New One for them all.

The group is directed both by the Old Man and by the Old Woman. She is the guardian of the Fire and the Hearth, the protective warmth at the heart of their society and their sense of Home; and she guards and uses fire with a sense of its preciousness and mystery. While she holds it she is set apart. She is also the priestess of their matriarchal religion: 'a woman for Oa', a man 'for smelling things out and having pictures'. This makes her numinous, and the other women share something of this; there can develop about them the same aura that makes Fa sometimes untouchable and awesome. Woman as mother is the vessel of the life force: 'As long as there was a woman, there was life.' The Old Man, on the other hand, is the governor. He commands every step of the way, he takes all decisions, and what he formally orders is obeyed without question. The others immediately realize that Mal in his weakness has made a mistake when he orders the young girl, and the nursing mother and her baby, to join in the hunt for food and firewood. There is tension and worry, but when 'it is spoken' it must be obeyed, and tension disappears in obedience. It never occurs to them to question Mal's decision to bring them into the mountains, though he has clearly brought them too early. The Old

Man is the guardian of tradition too. As they settle into their summer quarters he formally reminds them of their Genesis and the continuity of their history, reckoning backwards through the record of each Old Man's name.

The matriarchal religion and the patriarchal government and tradition direct their whole attitude to life and death. We have noticed their animistic view of nature; how everything (with one exception we shall notice later) is instinct with life, reverenced, precious. The world 'belongs' to them in the sense that they feel completely at home in it and see it filled with the same life that pulses through themselves; but nothing 'belongs' to them as property or as of right. They fit the world and the world fits them. To come home to the overhang is to squat in an accustomed place and shuffle one's back until it 'fits', they do not build any sort of dwelling that belongs to them exclusively. It is to lay the hand on a rock which has a place for the thumb and around which the hand fits, with a useful edge for cutting. But such implements are found, not made, and are not carried around as property. Only the fire goes with them from place to place, and is laid on time-honoured hearths around which implements 'wait' to be used again, and nature waits to bring forth its abundance to sustain them.

Their deepest idea of life, including their own genesis, is as a continuous act of feminine creation: 'There was the great Oa. She brought forth the earth from her belly. She gave suck. The earth brought forth woman and the woman brought forth the first man out of her belly.' There is the memory of a paradisal state 'when it was summer all year round and the flowers and fruit hung on the same branch'; but though this has vanished, it was not through human sin, and there was and is no devil-serpent in the People's Garden. They recognize disaster; Mal remembers in his own lifetime the terrible Fire that decimated the People to their present tiny group, but it was a purely natural disaster and not, like Noah's Flood, a punishment for wickedness. Nature can and does destroy, but it is ultimately creative and beneficent, and they treat all its manifestations with reverence. They revere the earth with its abundance that Oa annually brings forth for them, and the air with its riches of scent and information. They are uneasy with fire, but revere it also as their dearest treasure. They fear water as the element most foreign to them; but it is in the water and ice of the ice-women that Oa is most visibly manifested. Their sanctuary is both terrible, and astonishingly beautiful. It is numbing, deathly cold, with the horror of absolute winter. Yet the ice-women are linked together to the heavens like the People themselves. They are the culmination of ice-patterns that embody not only wintriness but the upward energy of growing trees and plants. From their terrible blue loins there issues water deadly cold, but the visible sign of the thaw and the spring. From the glittering ice, even in moonlight, there is reflected dazzling radiance and pure beauty. The description of the 'cathedral' is probably the most spectacularly beautiful thing in the novel; but its essence is the perception of the holiness of death-in-life and life-in-death, a vision that can see both steadily, and how they make each other significant. The religion of feminine creativity holds the terror of death in meaningful tension with the creative energy the People see pulsing through the living world. There is a place for Lok's sick fright, and a place also for his dances of joy and gratitude.

We can see the two strands again in Mal's death and burial. The death is tragic, even more so because it happens in the immediate aftermath of Ha's, and there is no doubting the depth of the People's love and grief. Yet the dominant note is acceptance, both by Mal and his mourners. As Lok digs the grave beside the dying man, the layers of hearth after hearth bear witness both to Time the destroyer, and to the continuity of life. The old bones are treated just like the earth and the stones, and Liku plays with them matter-of-factly before the dying man's face. There is no sense of the gruesome. The People are obviously accustomed to open the skulls and eat the brains of their honoured dead so that the qualities they honour will enter into them. Mal asks them not to, in his case, only because he fears to transmit his weakness. Yet there is nothing ghoulish. The baby plays in the grave, we see death and life in one focus; and the haunch of meat and the handfuls of water, indeterminate though their indication of life after death may be, speak a different language than the ashes and dust of a familiar ritual. As a last word: 'Oa has taken Mal into her belly'. The grave is the womb of nature. In the same way, when the ice-women fall it is summer, but the winter in which they will form again is the gestation of a new spring.

This natural religion contains no idea of crime or punishment, and, while it requires offering, it knows nothing of blood-sacrifice. The only idea of evil they have, in fact, is the destruction of life by violence. This comes out very strongly in the episode of the doe. For the first time we see both hostility and the consciousness of moral dilemma. The People are essentially non-violent; their thornbushes are walking-sticks and balancing rods, or when they are weapons at all they are purely defensive. But the hyenas are regarded with instinctive hatred, the only living things in these four chapters to call forth hostility, even aggression. The rock that Fa thumps into the bitch's ribs is a 'natural blade of stone', however, and the hatred clearly has a kind of moral basis: to the People's ears the hyenas are 'talking evilly'. The reason is of course that the hyenas belong to another 'nature', the world of the sabre-toothed tiger and the cave bear. The People only eat meat when it has been killed by some other agency and there is 'no blame' for shedding blood; moreover even this is only justifiable on the same terms as their feeding on grubs or bulbs or fungi, the terms of human need.

But as Lok and Fa dismember the doe that a 'cat' has killed: 'The air between the rocks was forbidding with violence and sweat, with the rich smell of meat and wickedness.' To enter the world of cruel nature, even by proxy, is to be involved with an atmosphere and feelings unnatural to them. Their actions are described in a new, violent language. Fa tears fiercely, slashes with a splinter of bone, cries out in anger, splits the belly open; Lok pounds at the body 'breaking out the joints', his great 'hands tore and twisted and snapped the sinews', he 'beat in the skull ... and levered open the mouth to wrench away the tongue'. When they finish, 'the limbs were smashed and bloodily jointed', the doe 'wrecked and scattered', leaving only 'torn hide, bones and hoofs' and a collection of 'torn and quivering fragments' with which they move away 'grunting and fierce'.

It is quite clear that they cannot simply be exonerated in their own eyes because they have not done the killing. The air may be 'forbidding' but it is also 'rich', Lok dribbles as he works, and Fa grunts with excitement as well as anger and effort. Yet their essential harmlessness is perhaps proved more by this episode than by any other, since it is here that their values are most consciously recognized and asserted through conflict. We see Lok acknowledging the 'darkness in the air under the watching birds', knowing that what they are doing is 'very bad' even when 'there is no blame'. His reverence for the female creature that Oa brought out of her belly is such that even the violent dismemberment of its dead body requires a penitent awareness, a definite justification: 'There is little food when the people come back from the sea. There are not yet berries nor fruit nor honey nor almost anything to eat. The people are thin with hunger' – we have seen, indeed, that they are famished – 'and they must eat. They do not like the taste of meat but they must eat.' A little later he adds 'a brilliant thought, "The meat is for Mal who is sick."' The whole rhythm of this is one of rationalization, yet it is the deep need Lok feels to justify what he does that really reveals his innocence. In the 'mixture of darkness and joy in his head' the joy is communal as well as personal or greedy; the darkness is known to be dark, and not to be complied with unless there is real justification. After this passage we know that the People are quite incapable of shedding blood themselves.

Perhaps the most astonishing thing is that Golding can convey so much by such limited means. Most of it, of course, comes welling out of description, where his linguistic resources are greatest; the experience distils its implications without needing either explicitness or analysis; we are largely unconscious of taking them in but find them in our minds when we have responded. Speech comes mainly in the narrative of Genesis, Numbers, and the Fire, and a few formulae of the kind that primitive people hand down orally. But in the deer passage the religion that can be conveyed through description begins to issue in a morality that must not only be enacted, but requires also to be brought into overt consciousness. This in turn demands a moral language: evil, wickedness, blame, bad. Objections might be made to this as inappropriate and imported, a breaking of the novelist's linguistic bargain; and the difficulty is real. Yet if it is credible that Neanderthalers should have a religious sense at all – and this must rest on unprovable assumption – such a sense must issue in moral attitudes and these must be communicable to us in moral language. 'Evil' or 'blame' are simply translations of noises which express distress, the desire to disassociate themselves from what is felt to be repugnant, feelings which any human not only feels but is conscious of feeling, as much as pleasure or pain.

By the end of these four chapters, then, Golding has not told us, nor analysed for us, but made us realize through imaginative experience what it is like to be one of the People over the whole range of their lives. 'Today is like yesterday and tomorrow'; they move through a world which contains death, violence, and natural disaster, but their existence in it is stable, reverent, harmless, natural. Behind the fiction lie anthropology and archaeology, and centuries of speculation about the Natural Man, yet it would not be too much to claim that nowhere in our literature has either the primitive man or the Natural Man been realized more imaginatively.

Yet the richness of the imaginative discovery is such that we are also afforded a dim awareness even at this stage, though only the full sweep of the novel will confirm and elucidate it, that the People's life is poised more precariously than they know between the future and the past, in ways that are not confined to the advent of the New Men.

We can see clearly in retrospect, for example, that Nature is not constant but changing. The fact that they have arrived at the overhang too early is neither an accident nor merely the result of Mal's failing powers. In the Neanderthal world the ice-cap is shifting, and the seasons are changing with it. Today is not quite like yesterday, and tomorrow will be different again.

The People are changing too, even before the revolution that the New Men will bring about. On the opening pages, with the problem of the missing log, we see not only the limitations of their thinking but also the way that the most intelligent of them are beginning to push out their mental frontiers. Mal cannot communicate any 'idea' of what he wants by picture, because his picture comes only from his memory and has no counterpart in theirs. But as soon as his orders result in the finding of a new log and its placing in the water, Ha is very quick to learn the mechanics of getting it across and firmly in position. To do this he needs to be able to think by a logical process, and he proves capable, once given a start by Mal. Fa is even more brilliant in the People's terms. We are present at the moment when a human creature invents the idea of cultivation. (p. 49). She is developing the power to connect one picture with another allowing action to be predicted, which could bring about a totally new situation. Edible plants grow here in earth, there is earth there, at the overhang, therefore we could grow plants there. The last step eludes her powers of communication however, because there is no 'therefore' in a picture, and no word for 'therefore' in a language based wholly on experience and memory. She can only make 'bringing together' gestures with her hands. But her intelligence has begun to bridge the gap between inference from experience and deduction. She has begun to think in the new sense, of which Lok is still incapable when he sees the smoke of the New Men's fire a few pages further on. Later, she has another brilliant idea which could have developed into the invention of irrigation (p. 62). We see her struggling to separate out, from an inclusive snapshot memory of the sea-shore, the significant detail of Lok shaking salt water from a shell; and to extract from that the idea of holding fresh water in a container. We then watch her trying to connect this with the significance of Liku carrying the little Oa through the forest. This time she manages to force the two pictures into some sort of combined picture; a picture *made*, not simply remembered, or seen. To Lok it is 'a meaningless jumble of shells and Liku and water, and the overhang', but the Old Woman understands. Only, her response is startling:

... she swayed back, lifted both hands off the earth and poised on her skinny hams. Slowly, deliberately, her face changed to that face she would make suddenly if Liku strayed too near the flaunting colours of the poison berry. Fa shrank before her and put her hands up to her face. The old woman spoke.

'That is a new thing.'

Past and future meet head-on in the present. There is beginning to stir in the People a new power of mind which could bring about a revolution in their existence, so that tomorrow will be utterly different from today. It confronts a hostile conservatism, for which all change is to the worse. With our modern consciousness we are of course on Fa's side, on the side of progress, but we have become sufficiently aware of the Old Woman's wisdom to pause. Are the People's happiness and security, perhaps even their innocence, dependent on the limitations of their consciousness? We can see how Lok's sunniness depends on his living in the present, incapable of predicting the future for good, but also for ill. Uncertainty, coming across the consciousness 'like a cold wind', is a 'knowledge ... nearly like thinking'; in fact, a condition of thought. Moreover, thought is clearly beginning to give Fa the power to impose her will on the world and alter it to the shape of her mind. The inventions we see her making are 'good', but they are not the only ones such mental powers could make. The Old Woman may have a point, that the ability to choose to impose one's will is the beginning of evil, or at least the gateway; something attractively coloured but possibly poisonous. So, in a changing world, the opportunity to change for evil as well as good in the People themselves begins to raise questions about the stability of their innocence. We are only dimly aware of this, if at all, on a first reading; but it is a mark of the depth of the novelist's imagination that it should be there, waiting to be brought into our full consciousness later.

We should notice that an important change of perspective takes place as early as the second chapter, and in that chapter at its most beautiful: the account of Lok on watch. To have seen the People's homecoming is to have seen the natural man completely at home in the world. But now, as Lok's senses respond to the vastness of the night horizon, the stars pricking open, the expanse of country stretching out in darkness to the sea, we are taken imperceptibly beyond the poetry of sense, to a different aspect of the People's limitation. The bulk of the island, separated from him by terrible sliding water, is seen anthropomorphically as ever, in the shape of a giant's leg; but it is as remote as the moon so that 'it had no connection with life as he knew it'. Only a creature 'more agile and frightened' than Lok could reach it, and there is point to the juxtaposition of fear and agility. We are realizing that his consciousness does not operate on the whole world of human possibility, there is a bigger shape of man, requiring a different kind of consciousness to explore its darkness: a creature moved by fear to a daring inconceivable by innocence. Again, there is more than mere confusion in Lok's inability to grasp the relation between the world of his mind and the world out there. 'This part of the country with its confusion of rocks that seemed to be arrested at the most tempestuous moment of swirling' suddenly reveals itself as a whirlpool of 'becoming', not a safe and customary trail. He is given in the mist a further intimation of the Other, and seems 'for a moment on the brink of revelation', but 'he could not hold a new thought when there seemed no danger in it'. A challenge is coming from the darkness beyond the Neanderthal hearth, with a revelation of other human possibilities, but it comes to a consciousness unprepared and unpreparable. The world is bigger than Lok can realize; the shape of a human being more terrible, and also more extensive, than he can grasp. As he settles down to sleep we can see that he is not really fitted to the world, nor the world to him. He curls up *against* a night that is in some senses inimical. His posture cannot help reminding us of a foetus, but can a new life be born?

Hard to get into though they may be, these are four brilliant chapters. They start as Wells does from the scientific facts, but their superiority is not a matter of preferring the conclusions reached by different assumptions; it lies in the density and depth of the imaginative exploration. To imagine like this is to create a world which cannot be confined to categories. To respond to the experience fully is not only to respond to an 'innocence' more convincing than that of Milton's primal people, but to respond also with deep vibrations of unease.

III

We know that *The Inheritors* will reverse *The Grisly Folk*; but the more clearly we know it, the greater the danger of missing the value and power of Golding's fiction. We have continually to guard against moral certainties. Indeed, the value of some under-standing of the implications of his chosen form, and some grasp of the complexity of his exploration of the People, is that these enable us to see with what care and artistry he sets out to frustrate any simple contrast.

It is significant that Lok rather than Fa should be the medium of our vision. Given the incomprehension of the People as a whole, faced with Otherness, to employ the simplest and most loving of them is to forestall our tendency to judge, and to force us for as long as possible to 'look without seeing', as Lok does. The basic mode of perception is affectionate and trusting long after it should have changed; and long after it has changed in Fa because of her greater intelligence. Being made to see familiar things as though we had never seen them before ensures that we respond with fascination, curiosity, even amusement, and certainly delight, before we become aware in darker ways. The uncomprehending eyes that see all things stripped of their implications guarantee at least an initial objectivity. Of course we come to the experience filled also with nascent horror and premonition, and the implications cannot be prevented from welling up in our minds; nor indeed should they. Yet the method can so restrain us that we become open to richer and more complex impressions than we are aware of or expect; and the richness and complexity become available to us because his method has made them available to the author, restraining his initial urge simply to tear Wells to shreds. He becomes Lok, 'there was too much to see and he became eyes again that registered and perhaps would later remember what now he was not aware of'.

It is remarkable, too, how long Golding manages to keep Lok away from a full confrontation with the New Men, so delaying his comprehension even further. In Chapters 5 and 6 the tragic action happens largely offstage, and what we proceed to after the first four chapters is not, as we might have expected, an immediate marking of the opposite, but rather a continued exploration of new kinds of consciousness in the People. Chapter 5 starts us in their inner recesses; it begins in dream, and ends with nightmare coming to the surface in daylight. Then Chapter 6 takes us through Chapter 1 again, exploring revolutionary dimensions in the People before we are allowed really to see the New Men. This means that when we do confront them in Chapters 7–9 we no longer have a stability to judge them by. The points of view have suddenly multiplied. We see through Lok, but we are also aware of Fa, and of the chasm that has opened between their differing visions. Our own consciousness also begins to reach beyond them both, as they see things they cannot possibly understand, and which must remain radically obscure unless we use our own intelligence and powers of deduction. We begin also to be able to see from the point of view of the New Men, to see the People as they see them, and to understand why they behave as they do. No simple contrast emerges from all this. Finally, Golding puts Lok to sleep at the tragic climax of these chapters. We know from Fa's behaviour that something terrible has happened, and we can make certain guesses about it, but we do not and cannot know what it is, and we shall not until the end of the penultimate chapter. This is not wilful mystification, or cheating, but has a serious function. It is the firmest indication of Golding's determination to prevent us from judging until the full experience of both kinds of men is complete, until we know all that is needed for a fully compassionate judgement.

We start then in Chapter 5 with an exploration, not of the New Men, but of new 'deep waters' in the People's consciousness. The shocks they have already suffered, by the disappearance of Ha and the first experience of the Other by Lok and Nil, disturb not only their innocent foetal sleep, but also the stability of their daylight society. They dream, 'beset by a throng of phantoms from the other place', from a realm, which they still think of as Other to themselves, where violence, killing and alienation exist and must be encountered in the subconscious. Lok dreams of being hunted by the Other, but from the depths of his psyche in sleep, the shock he has experienced draws forth an answering strength of reassurance from his oneness with the People. 'Pulled by his desperate need' they come to him physically, 'they drove in until they were being joined to him, body to body. They shared a body as they shared a picture. Lok was safe.' But the strain is shown by the fact that only the fullest physical union can now bring the feeling of safety; and there is a sense of loss too: for in the dream the People are no longer at home in the universe. What was implicit in the foetal sleep is becoming explicit in the unconscious: 'They came in, closer and closer, not as they would come into the overhang, recognizing home and being free of the whole space.' Nil in her dream experiences the same psychological reassurance in a specifically sexual form, but this is no longer sex as natural as hunger, and she whimpers when she wakes. The People's communion with one another copes with the shock, the strings hold, but they have been badly strained.

With the daylight we realize the damage to government and leadership of the two empty spaces, for 'now there is Lok'. It is obvious how much his happy foolishness, his inability to join 'a picture to a picture so that the last of many came out of the first', fall short of the qualities of Mal and Ha; so that the Old Woman has to rescue him from his mistakes and put the right orders in his mouth. It is true that he begins to find words without pictures, to use a new tool of comparison, to conceive necessary actions, control his clowning, and develop responsibility; yet he will never make as good an Old Man as Ha would have done. The traditions remain, of course, and the best must be made of them. Stability must be reasserted. The Old Woman thinks she has the measure of the crisis: 'Now, is like when the fire flew away and ate up all the trees'; when their life could continue in spite of decimation. Yet we wonder.

Indeed the significance of the chapter is that it dismantles the hope of continuity. Among the drifts of green buds, ironically proclaiming the Spring of new life, Lok dances in acrobatic friendliness as he greets the New: 'Hoé man!', 'Hoé new people!', excitedly expecting relationship. But the scene reorchestrates in darker tones the first sight of the Other. There is not only the same failure to respond; there is the sight of the huge logs the New Men use for their fires, at which Lok, though he cannot be said to understand, knows an unreasoning fear as deep as Mal's nightmare of a totally alien and destructive world. Twice the New Men have removed the log-bridges, with their social function of joining a trail for any traveller, to burn them up for themselves. When Lok hears their voices they make 'a picture in his head of interlacing shapes, thin, and complex, voluble and silly, not like the long curve of a hawk's cry, but tangled like line-weed on the beach after a storm, muddled as water'. They contain neither the simple assertion of raptor nature, nor the practical, communal order of the People. Yet we look less at what these things tell us about the New Men, than at what Lok's incomprehension implies. There is the laughter of a child – or an idiot – at what he does not understand, and the reading of himself into what he hears so that the voices become 'laugh sound'. Though we continue to recognize the goodness of this innocence, we become more and more disturbed by its helpless inadequacy. The voices themselves herald deep waters of the mind; again cliché is becoming meaningful. There cuts across them the mindless screaming of Liku, caught in a world of panic and violence, moving 'away across the river'. The river, deep waters; People cannot cross them, but they must.

When Lok sees the New Man's face it is totally unlike his own, with 'white bone things above his eyes and under the mouth so that his face was longer than a face should be'. But now delighted curiosity turns into horror for us, as a poisoned arrow thuds into the trunk at Lok's head while he remains wholly uncomprehending. 'A stick rose upright and there was a lump of bone in the middle ... Suddenly Lok understood that the man was holding the stick out to him but neither he nor Lok could reach across the river.' Innocence cannot hope for continuity; it must change, or be destroyed.

Finally, 'upside down over deep water', Lok experiences not merely the overturning of his world, but also, in daylight, the release of nightmare consciousness in the depth of his own mind. The vision of the Old Woman's body among the weeds of the river is one of those moments in Golding where he seems to write out of some deep psychological cavern,* with a disturbing power that reverberates well beyond what can be made rationally explicit. Not that it is difficult to produce explanations. The wisest of the People, who believed that the crisis confronting them was of the same kind as the Fire, has walked to meet Evil; she has been destroyed by the Fall. Her dead eyes ignore the mutilation of the human shape involved in this, as her living eyes had failed to conceive its possibility. Not death only, but murder has entered the garden. The priestess of Oa has encountered a phenomenon which calls the religion of beneficent creativity in question. The eyes and mouth which saw and voiced the unity of man and nature have no such message now; and in the otherworld of water, skinned over from the sky, death speaks only of deadness: 'the eyes shone as dully as the stones ... her mouth was open, the tongue showing and the specks of dirt were circling slowly in and out as though it had been nothing but a hole in a stone.' The world that knew dread but no fear has gone for ever, betrayed by its inadequate faith.

These are ways of putting it, and they express the upside-downness in a useful analytic way. But the real strength and significance of the passage lies elsewhere; not, again, in points that can be made about it, but in the activity of imaginative experience itself. What we have to respond to is primarily an eerie *rhythm*:

---

* See also our discussion, Ch. 6, p. 213 and footnote.

The weed-tail was shortening. The green tip was withdrawing up river. There was a darkness that was consuming the other end. The darkness became a thing of complex shape, of sluggish and dreamlike movement. Like the specks of dirt, it turned over but not aimlessly. It was touching near the root of the weed-tail, bending the tail, turning over, rolling up the tail towards him. The arms moved a little and the eyes shone as dully as the stones. They revolved with the body, gazing at the surface, at the width of deep water and the hidden bottom with no trace of life or speculation. A skein of weed drew across the face and the eyes did not blink. The body turned with the same smooth and heavy motion as the river itself until its back was towards him rising along the weed-tail. The head turned towards him with dreamlike slowness, rose in the water, came towards his face.

The two references to dream are important, for the rhythm is that of nightmare. A formless thing disengages itself from the depths of the mind, becomes a dark spectre, rises with dreadful slowness, but 'not aimlessly', ... and we are frozen, it is impossible to escape. It reveals sudden intimations of terror; hides them. Then, slowly, relentlessly, it turns towards us the full horror of its face. And as we respond to this we become aware of the sense in which it is happening in Lok, not merely to him. While he watches, the horrible world of water is the only world, whose dimensions the rolling body makes one take in as one follows its eyes: the surface, the bottom, the 'width of deep water'. Its rhythm is that of the river itself, and Lok is made to know it as a rhythm in his own mind. The chapter began with phantoms from another place, capable of being exorcised by inner psychic resources. At this moment there is no place but here, and no resources to meet the spectres. Innocence becomes aware of deep water, inside itself, inescapable.

Narrative now begins to confirm and explore what imagination has revealed. The sixth chapter is full of deliberate echoes of the first, but they mark ironically the nature of the new dimension. As Lok's feet unclench themselves from the bushes to slide down into water, we remember as part of a lost world the delighted onward rush of the clever feet leaping the puddles. As he shivers 'like Mal' the difference is plain to us: this is no natural disease of age. The game with the beech-branch becomes a hysterical release of unbearable grief and rage. In the clearing, there is another poisoned arrow to be plucked from the tree instead of the edible fungus for Liku. As Lok runs up the path to the overhang he sees not only the smoke he had smelt on the platform but one of the men who made it; and we have a sharp sense of what the people's inability to reason and predict has cost. He comes home to an empty overhang, a desecrated hearth, the traces of blood and milk which speak of the murder of the Old Woman and Nil. Fa remains, but the 'strings' have been cut, the links with the past and the future broken (we suddenly remember that Fa has been unable to bear children), the fire that was the centre of a whole warmth of community extinguished. The blood is terrible, but the milk, the abducted children, the dead embers are worse. The raiding party has set out not just to kill persons, but the People, and they have all but succeeded.

We have a fuller notation now of what the Old Woman's body prefigured, and Golding proceeds to explore the implications of both 'upside-downness' and 'deep water'.

The new situation is deeply tragic, and the more we took in of the nature of the People in the opening chapters, the greater will be our sense of loss. Yet the surest sign of a new dimension is that the sense of loss implies no longing to conserve. We know in our bones that any way out of the tragedy depends on Fa, and we become increasingly impatient with Lok as, even now, he cannot understand and continues to behave and feel as the People have always done. As he gallops to the overhang, or scratches himself uncomprehendingly under the chin, we suddenly become aware of his closeness to the ape as we have not been before. We may have mixed feelings as Fa fiercely compels him to accept her leadership, reversing their tradition, but we are in sympathy with her, knowing that revolutionary change is vital if they are to survive at all. As they watch the boat nosing along the bank it is her fear that offers the only way forward, and Lok's innocent incomprehension – 'They have twigs' – can only be disastrous. It is not that Fa will learn to fight the New Men with their own weapons, indeed the outcome of her realization that the arrow is a weapon is the insistence that Lok 'give the twig back'. (It plunges into the water like a stooping hawk, but it is unnatural, and the People reject it.) Yet this does also involve the assertion of alienation from their side; if the action is 'good' because it rejects evil, it is 'difficult' because it involves a break with their nature and their natural vision.

We become still more sharply aware of how upside-downness is related to the deep water of the river and the fall. Far back in the novel, when Mal in his nightmare momentarily saw the world as essentially destructive, we had our first neutral and undramatic glimpse of a log going over the waterfall. There was no reason then to suspect any connection, but there is now. As Fa cries out 'Give the twig back', another trunk slides noiselessly over the lip. When the twig is thrown:

The sun was right down in the gap and the river flamed so that the edge of the fall was burning bright as the ends of sticks in the fire. There were dark logs coming down river, black against the flaming water. There were whole trees, their roots behaving like strange creatures of the sea. One was turning towards the fall beneath them; roots and branches lifting, dragging, going down. It hung for a moment on the lip; the burning water made a great heap of light over the end and then the tree was going down the air to vanish as smoothly as the twig.

Lok spoke over Fa's shoulder.

'The old woman was in the water.'

To assert alienation, to realize the destructiveness abroad in the world in a vision which unites blazing fire and terrible water, is to begin to know the Fall; and even Lok recognizes the connection of this moment with his nightmare vision of deep water. The twig and the mutilated old woman fuse with the logs in a new connection of man and nature, destructive man adding his work to destructive nature. And the People cannot now be free, cannot simply dissociate themselves. The deep waters begin to exist permanently within them. Feeling rushes into Lok 'like a wave of the sea', it 'went through him and over him. It came from nowhere like the river, and like the river it would not be denied. Lok was a log in the river, a drowned animal that the waters treat as they will.' He knows not only the fall without but the tide within, and it never leaves him for long again. The essentially innocent Lok is going.

Then Chapter 6 gives us a last sardonic echo of Chapter 1 as Fa forces Lok to cross the deep water and thread the darkness of the giant's leg. They have become the creatures 'more agile and frightened' who alone would dare to do so; yet the agility is not only the product of fear, there is attraction too. 'The other people with their many pictures were like water that at once horrifies and at the same time dares and invites a man to go near it', and there is an obscure feeling that they are seeking not just the comfort of seeing Liku and taking her food, but also some 'remedy' that the New Men might afford for the misery they have caused. Now Lok and Fa *use* the logs and the river's pull towards the fall; they are made agile not only by fear but by the 'attraction without definition' of the darkness where the witchdoctor dances before the shelters and the huge fire. So, what the echoes of the first chapter measure is the gap between the new consciousness and the old. This new fierce Fa, with her daring ingenuity, her desperate terror, her clutching herself into the earth of the island after the terrible water, contrasts markedly with her former self. The new Lok has no impulse to clown, and the mighty jumper screams with wordless terror like Nil as he crosses the log. Reminders of their old selves occur when the clown's foolish luck achieves what Fa's intelligence is seeking, and when a loving Fa applauds his boasts of his cleverness, but even here there is difference. The boast is anxious, the applause indelibly ironic; and the foolishness of the old Lok of the People nearly destroys them both in the New Men's clearing.

The happiness, the security, the communal unity in the world of Oa, have gone for ever. When they get back to the overhang the hyenas have desecrated Mal's grave. Without the fire the past is as vulnerable as the present. They have only each other, but their sexuality in the new dimension is a 'new thing' too. 'The two pressed themselves against each other, they clung, searching for a centre, they fell, still clinging face to face. The fire of their bodies lit, and they strained towards it.' This is not the old natural hunger. Nor is it Nil's search for a centre in a sexuality essentially communal. The note is of strain, of a different kind of fire lit in the body to cure the sickness and fear of the soul, by two individuals isolated in a world unsuffused by the glow of a hearth. They don't lie, they fall together.

Only now, when the old stability of the People has modulated into the instability of Lok and Fa caught between two worlds, is Golding ready to give us a full look at the New Men. This can no longer involve any simple measurement of contrast; the points of view have multiplied and the experience must be complex. We have to measure Lok's fascination and objectivity against our sense of implication; measure his incomprehension against the hints in

Fa's behaviour; measure both, against the point of view of the New Men and against our own fuller awareness; and finally recognize the limits of even our knowledge. Chapters 7–9 are amongst the most obscure and difficult in Golding's work, but the difficulty is functional and the rewards are great.

The fascination of seeing our savage ancestors through eyes which find them 'incomprehensibly strange' is fused with the upside-down discovery by Lok that they are utterly different from himself. The 'masks' of white bone are skin and there is no Neanderthal face hidden beneath them. The grey hairy skins are suddenly revealed as clothes out of which a naked body can step without pain. The hair-styles show that they are primarily individuals, developing and proclaiming their difference even from one another. The clothes show that they are creatures alien to their physical environment and needing to protect themselves from it. To eyes accustomed to the faces of the People, the New Men's eyes look little, dark and busy. Their nostrils are narrow slits between which the bone is drawn out to a point. Their ears are not pointed and movable, but tiny and screwed tightly into the sides of their heads. These sense organs testify to the New Men's alienation from the People's life of the senses. Such eyes will not see in the dark and will need fire for illumination as well as protection. Such noses will not perform 'miracles of perception'; the New Men cannot track Lok to the tree, let alone inhibit their scents as he can. Such ears have neither the power nor the fine discrimination of Lok's. On a darker level of implication, the teeth 'remember wolf'. (Even Wells notes that Neanderthal teeth have no canines, but are big, even, grinders; though he doesn't draw the conclusion that such teeth are primarily vegetarian.) The eyebrows are thin, menacing, wasp-like; the scent is a 'sea-smell, meat-smell, fearsome and exciting'; there are necklaces of teeth and shells, the fangs of sabre-toothed tigers as earrings. These are meat-eaters, hunters, killers. On the other hand, the thin lips which 'putter' and 'flap' can speak with a quickness and delicacy, a complexity of utterance beyond the People's power; and they have no need of mime, whether 'communal' or to make up for linguistic deficiency. Once again Golding's physical imagination authenticates the differences, while the multiple viewpoints ensure that the contrast is not simple. Repulsion, attraction, fascination hold us in eddying feelings as they hold Lok.

This is even clearer in the perception of the New Men's movement:

They were balanced on top of their legs, their waists were so wasp-thin that when they moved their bodies swayed backwards and forwards. They did not look at the earth but straight ahead. And they were not merely hungry. Lok knew famine when he saw it. The new people were dying . . . Their movements, though they had in their bodies the bending grace of a young bough, were dream-slow. They walked upright and they should be dead. It was as though something that Lok could not see were supporting them, holding up their heads, thrusting them slowly and irresistibly forward. Lok knew that if he were as thin as they, he would be dead already.

The perceptiveness and the limitations of Lok's viewpoint stand side by side. The New Men are half-starved, but nowhere near death; their slowness is largely a consequence of their carriage and a completely different physical structure. The evocation of a creature that has evolved to walk upright through the eyes of one that has not is beautifully exact and uncomprehending. Here the objectivity begins to bear fruit, so that we also take in the eyes that can look straight ahead because the figure is upright, the bending grace of a young bough, the sense of an evolutionary life-force driving them upwards and onwards at a higher level than Lok's.

The New Men build shelters against the world, fashion a defensive stockade behind which to feel safe, post armed guards, not merely look-outs. They manufacture implements, as against the natural blades of stone or bone that the People pick up and use. Both weapons and tools make implements of offence: we see Tuami making a bone knife that could stab a man through his rib-cage and watch him strike off a man's finger with a stone axe. Nil combs her curls with her fingers, Vivani has a bone comb; but Vivani is self-absorbed as well as better equipped. Greater techno-logical efficiency is balanced against a different consciousness: these Men are individualists, killers, frightened, greedy, proud, as well as clever and inventive. The People play with gold and throw it away, the New Men use it in adornment. Tanakil's doll is a triumph of sculpture, wonderfully life-like to the People's eyes; but it hasn't the religious significance that makes the little Oa more than a doll. The New Men carry loads of property about. Their dugouts, with eyes also pointing forwards across the sea and up the river, are marvels of ingenuity, daring and skill, giving them the power to push out the human frontiers in exploration. But, as we watch the huge effort of humping them ashore, we become aware also of the new fear of theft, damage and loss that property brings, and of the cumbrous machinery of transport that it demands.

The differences grow deeper as we watch the New Men's relationships. There are moments when they share the People's togetherness. Watching Vivani suckle the New One, Tanakil and Liku playing and laughing together, Tuft and Chestnut-head sharing a burden and working in unison, brings the sunshine into Lok's head again. But, in the children, Tanakil's urge to dominate becomes cruelty when her will is thwarted, playing sharply against Liku's 'adoration' of her superior intellect. In Tanakil's mother we see again the Old Woman's poison-face, but there is not only misunderstanding and ignorance of natural good, but also violence, and readiness to see Liku as a hostile and treacherous creature. Yet there is penitence too, and the desire to atone, which Liku understands as little as the anger. There is no sense of community so basic that it controls all other relationships. Tuami the artist and highbrow considers himself apart from and above the others, 'and carries on a dangerous affair with Marlan's woman. Various kinds of dissension crackle beneath the surface. The society is wholly man-directed and the women are inferior, without the division of function that makes each sex equally precious. Their sexuality contains violence and exploitation. Tuami consumes Vivani and is consumed by her, sex contains fighting and eating so that there is blood on face and shoulder. They hunt pleasure like a wolf running down his prey or a fox playing with his victim, but 'there was no animal on the mountain and the plain, no lithe and able creature of the bushes or the forest that had the subtlety and imagination to invent games like these, nor the leisure and incessant wakefulness to play them.' When they walk back to the shelters, they do not walk together. Yet here we must be careful too. Tuami and Vivani are drunk, and they are drunk because they are frightened. Moreover, though Lok is bored by the play, he is absorbed and excited by the copulation itself. We ought to recognize the difference that instability has made to the apparently simple contrast. It is not just the natural hunger we have to compare this with, but the new sexuality born of fear that has brought Lok to the point where he can understand what he sees. (Later, we shall watch Lok and Fa when they are drunk.)

The New Men go beyond human need to indulgence, and beyond indulgence to excess. The People's hunger, thirst, and sexual desire are similar, and forgotten as soon as assuaged. Meat is shared and eaten to capacity, but there is nothing like Marlan's furtive wolfing while his people starve. The New Men have discovered wine and spirits; and drink has become a source of stimulus, and reassurance, and finally oblivion. There is drunkenness and the noise of vomiting in the darkness. Their fire becomes an inferno, going beyond their need for protection, warmth and light into an expression of frenzied revelry against the darkness and in it blazes the log which 'killed' Mal. Firewood, meat, and water are too precious for the People to squander. Yet with the inventiveness Fa has groped for, the stone bottles and the wineskin, the transport of logs by water, there has arrived the possibility of excess. If we admired Fa, we can now see where her ideas could lead, and with what loss of the reverence born of scarcity and of natural religion.

The New Men's religion and government are one, and are based on fear and the politics of power. Marlan's authority as ruler-priest prevails only as long as the tribe fear him more than they resent him, and as long as his magic satisfies their needs. Behind failure lie mutiny and death. It is here that Lok's incomprehension is absolute, so that on a first reading it is very difficult to know what is happening, let alone take in its implications. Yet once again the description is so exact and vivid that our imagination and intelligence can reach beyond the powers of the People's understanding and see through the New Men's eyes as well.

Marlan is the witchdoctor of the totem cult of the Stag, and Tuami is the tribal artist. The tribe is half-starved, and terrified of the ogres who seem to block their path up-river. They leave the island because even there they prove not to be safe from Lok and Fa. In the clearing they build a stockade to keep the ogres out from landward while the river guards their backs. Tuami promises them that they will be able to make a sortie from this fortress to exterminate the last of the ogres, but to ensure success they need the help of their ritual magic. He begins to paint the image of the Stag. (To create an image of something brings it within one's power to influence.) The others begin a rhythmic incantation, chanting and clapping. As the witchdoctor in his stag-pelt dances in, they bow their heads to the ground in homage. He presides over the creation of the image while lots are drawn to determine who shall hunt and who provide the necessary sacrifice. This lot falls on Pine-tree, who allows a finger to be cut off in offering to the Stag, proving the seriousness of the crisis. The witchdoctor censes the chosen hunters and touches them with his fern-wand. They then ritually 'kill' the Stag in enactment of the power they believe the magic has given them. (The ritual imitation of an action helps to bring it about and gives one the strength to do it.) The tribe chants and abases itself again as the hunters leave the stockade. Tuami and Tuft close their eyes to avoid seeing the 'fey' ones who now contain the power of the god. Chestnut-head and Bush are setting out for food, and to exterminate the last of the People, to liberate the tribe from their terrible hunger and their terrible fear.

The religion is a death-religion, which gives man the power to impose his will on nature, at the cost of blood-sacrifice. It contains reverence, but born of fear not dread; and because its whole business is with results, it must succeed or bring rebellion from devotees who have sacrificed in vain.

Here the deepest significance of what Lok watches so uncomprehendingly ought to begin to dawn on us. For after the hunters have left, the tribe still cluster round Marlan clamouring for food, and are told by Tuami that they must trust to the Stag. Marlan allows them a ration of wine to keep them quiet, but after drinking on empty stomachs they bitterly resent being forced to get the boats on dry land, and finally refuse to move the second one any further despite Marlan's rage. They are drowsy and irritable. Suddenly Pine-trees catches Marlan furtively wolfing the meat Lok had thrown at his feet on the island, which he has hidden and kept for himself. Irritation turns into dangerous anger, and pointing at the stag has lost its power to control them. They move on Marlan shouting 'Meat, meat, meat!' Vivani rescues him by bringing the wineskin out again, but this time they refuse to be rationed, a fight breaks out, and the wineskin is burst. Marlan reasserts his authority, taking advantage of their sheepishness in towering rage, and they are temporarily cowed. But quickly their hunger becomes greater than their fear, and a furious woman displays the evidence of her empty belly and flattened breasts, while she screams and spits at Marlan. Again he refers to the Stag ... but at just this moment of crisis the hunters return empty-handed. They have failed to find the ogres, they have failed to get meat, and Chestnut-head has been wounded (by a stag, a bear, or a 'cat'). Marlan's magic has failed, and when the wounded man hears about the hiding of the meat, there are the makings of a murderous situation. He advances on Marlan with bow and arrow ready.

Now obscurity begins to thicken. Marlan tries to get hold of the New One but Vivani bites his hand. The bow is bent, and the crisis arrives. In utter silence Marlan faces Chestnut-head and moves his arm round until his index finger points to one of the shelters. Vivani laughs once, hysterically. 'The old man glanced round the clearing, peered out to where the darkness was crowded under the trees and then back at the people. None of them said anything.'

At this terrifying moment Lok falls asleep, bored with watching what he cannot understand, and tired out by the two terrible nights and the succession of shocks. Our source of information has gone. We know that something tragic must happen when hatred, fear and hunger have been raised to such a pitch. Having got this far we could even hazard some guess at the form it is taking. Marlan is trying to shift the blame onto the People, saving himself by converting them from 'ogres' into 'devils' who have thwarted the Stag-magic. Having failed to get hold of the New One, he points, it must be, to the shelter where Liku is. But that is the most we can even guess. Only the terrible face of Fa, who throughout has understood something of what she sees, reflects the horror of what is taking place, while like a mother she keeps Lok from seeing, and cradles him into a child's exhausted sleep. Her mouth opens, her breathing quickens, her face 'was like the face of a sleeper who wrestles with a terrible dream', 'her eyes, open, open for ever, watching'. When he wakes, she is streaming with sweat, but the crisis and its tragedy are over. The tribe are like a wolf-pack in cry, the fire has become a demented inferno, destructive 'like the fall, like a cat', the wild light makes everything leap up and down, the New Men are all roaring drunk on spirits. When they fall asleep Fa searches for the New One while Lok tries to track Liku down against her orders, but the sleepers awake in nightmare, and the two People are forced to leap the stockade, alone. Fa is wounded, and as Lok follows her trail it leads into the marsh, and ends.

Yet, however terrible the intimations of tragedy have become, it is clear that Golding has done everything in his power to prevent us from making a simple contrast, and to force us to defer judgement until the experience and our understanding of it are complete.

We respond still to Lok's lovingness, to the strength of the bond with Liku that will not let him submit to Fa's desire to run away and make a fresh start, in the hope that she will bear children after all. We can see that Fa's development has taken her further and further away from the consciousness of the People towards that of the New Men. But over and over again we are also aware that it is Lok's retention of the People's consciousness that makes him blind, and doomed, without Fa's intelligence and understanding. There is no simple choice, no obvious way to say that one path is 'better' than the other.

Moreover, more surely than ever before, we can see that Lok is changing too. There is not only the way that his experience has made him capable of understanding beings like Tuami and Vivani which the old Lok would have found wholly alien. There is the steady development of that new consciousness born of fear, whose beginnings we watched at an earlier stage. When he faced the crossing of deep water he became aware that 'there was outside of Lok and inside'. As he watches the stockade being built, Fa's fear begins to call forth in him too an 'agonized attention, a motionless and tensed awareness . . . Now, more clearly than ever before there were two Loks, outside and inside. The inner Lok could look for ever. But the outer that breathed and heard and smelt and was awake always, was insistent and tightening on him like another skin. It forced the knowledge of its fear, its sense of peril on him long before his brain could understand the picture.' The 'inside' of the man of the People plays against the 'outside' that knows in fear as the New Men do. But is this an 'advance', or a 'fall'? Is it an invitation to bitter contrast, as when 'Mal's voice of the summer land' blends in his sleepy confusion with the voice of Marlan below him? Is it some secure indication to us that, when the lottery takes place, 'Lok's head began to fill with the fall', and when the finger falls on the stag-image 'the fall sounded nearer'? Outside-Lok demonstrably makes him less spontaneous and affectionate. Yet it demonstrably also makes him more intelligent, more prudent, more responsible. Finally, after whatever tragedy takes place is over, Lok gets from Fa a dim premonition that links the new outside sense with the inner nightmare and the deep waters, and heralds a further inner growth:

A kind of half-knowledge, terrible in its very formlessness, filtered into Lok as though he were sharing a picture with her but had no eyes inside his head and could not see it. The knowledge was something like that sense of extreme peril that outside-Lok had shared with her earlier; but this was for inside-Lok and he had no room for it. It pushed into him ... He was possessed by it and did not know what it was.

Fa turned her head sideways slowly. The eyes with her twin fires came round like the eyes of the old woman moving up through the water. A movement round her mouth – not a grimace or preparation for speech – set her lips fluttering like the lips of the new people; and then they were open again and still.

'Oa did not bring them out of her belly.'

In the dead-tree, within earshot of the waterfall, Fa has experienced 'the knowledge of good and evil'. In that knowledge she becomes for Lok like the Old Woman, within the nightmare rising in the mind, summoning him to an awareness fully double, inside and out. It is still half-knowledge now, or premonition. He can only sense, not know it, yet it must come. Can we be sure, however, before it is completed in him and in us, of the calculus of gain and loss? If Fa has known the fallen consciousness, should we wish that Lok might be spared the disaster, as she does? Or is it, however terrible, also necessary to realize that the world is not ruled by Oa; and that a consciousness which cannot fall (or climb?) beyond People-feeling and Oa-religion may be an evolutionary and human failure? Is the speech of the New Men, which Fa has come within an ace of uttering, the terrible but necessary goal?

For, we remember, Lok has himself seen, beyond any easy contrast or calculus, the life-force pushing them forward, and eyes that can see ahead. At the first experience of the stag-ritual in the darkness of the island, his sensitivity has captured something we must not overlook. The belling of the Stag-Man is 'harsh and furious, full of pain and desire. It was the voice of the greatest of all stags and the world was not wide enough for him.' The eyes of the stag-pelt were 'looking up, past the new people, past Fa and Lok'. We should not lose the sense of desire and aspiration in our response of horror to the harshness, the fury and the pain. We should at least keep open the possibility that the world we look at is not yet wide enough, so that we too need to look past both kinds of men.

We must certainly begin to understand the New Men, and why they behave as they do. Their terror of the ogres who block their path upwards and onwards is bitterly ironic. But it ought not to be impossible to sense what was in the mind of that first Other when he saw the strange red hairy figures, and found Ha bounding up the cliff after him; what he felt when he heard Lok's bellowings at him across the river, and heard them again from the bushes on the island where he had felt so safe. We can see for ourselves how the People, appearing as if by magic from the dead tree and leaping the big stockade, must seem to the eyes of men just awakened from nightmare:

The guard who had run after Fa was dancing in front of the new people. He crawled like a snake, he went to the wreck of the caves; he stood; he came back to the fire snapping like a wolf so that the people shrank from him. He pointed; he created a running, crouching thing, his arms flapped like the wings of a bird. He stopped by the thorn bushes, sketched a line in the air over them, a line up and up towards the trees till it ended in a gesture of ignorance.

Of ignorance; it is not enough to see the error and the irony, or reflect that they come from the New Men's preconception about a world red in tooth and claw. For, in re-orchestrating the scene in which Lok had mimed the Other, this scene also has the effect of suggesting that *we* may have a vision of the New Men no less ignorant, because equally incomplete. We still need to know both the worst and the best about them. We need to know the full extent of the horrible thing they acted out in the clearing. We also need to know more about what thrusts them on up the river, the desire, both painful and heroic, to widen the world, the force that got them onto their hind-legs and made them invent the boats that can explore and cross deep water, the eyes that see the way ahead.

The tragedy cannot be understood in the simple categories of better and worse, praise and blame.

IV

A new day begins with Lok hiding in the marshes alone. What we watch is, however, more than pain, it is the way that Lok achieves through it, one by one, the steps by which the lost Fa had grown mentally beyond him. He clutches himself into the earth as she had done on the island:

He writhed himself against the dead leaves and twigs, his head came up, turned, and his eyes swept round, astonished eyes over a mouth that was strained open. The sound of mourning burst out of his mouth, prolonged, harsh, pain-sound, man-sound ... Far off, the stag blared again.

This is different from the keening over Ha or Mal; and there is no reassurance in the earth after the terrible water. The leaves and twigs are, simply, dead. The sound is man-sound not people-sound; it has the mixture of harshness and pain of the stag's blare. Far back, we had begun to associate thinking with the chill wind of uncertainty, but Lok's new knowledge is coming from a level of suffering beyond the People's world. In our response, progress is fused with 'the pity of it'. Suddenly Lok finds that he can think, can deduce, from his memory of the dugouts being moved, what the noises the New Men are making must mean: 'This was an upheaval in the brain, and he felt proud and sad and like Mal ... All at once it seemed to him that his head was new, as though a sheaf of pictures lay there to be sorted.' He can not only feel the solitary life-string binding him to Liku and the New One; but understand for the first time the 'terrified love' of outside and inside Lok for the New Men, and know now that they 'would kill him if they could'. It is with new clarity that he feels again the terrible inner tide of grief and loss swirling through him. Now, as he watches the dugouts being heaved through the forest, he becomes absorbed again, but is prudent in time to save himself. Unreasoning fear contains within it the perception of bloody illness: 'He was frightened of the new people, and sorry for them as for a woman who has the sickness.' But the illness is in him too; he instinctively reacts as animals or the People would, eating things that will make him vomit and purge the badness, but in vain:

The new head knew that certain things were gone and done with like a wave of the sea. It knew that the misery must be embraced painfully as a man might hug thorns to him and it sought to comprehend the new people from whom all changes came.

Finally, for that comprehension, 'in a convulsion of the under-standing Lok found himself using likeness as a tool'. He has become capable of using analogy for deliberate analysis; and the comprehension it gives him is not only full but complex. The hunters are 'like a famished wolf'; but, remembering their moments of togetherness they are also 'like honey'. Tanakil's cleverness, her laughter, and her stick, are 'like honey in the round stones, the new honey that smells of dead things and fire', sweet, but rotten and burning. The Men are terrible, essentially destruc-tive: 'They are like the river and the fall ... nothing stands against them.' But lastly, most significant of all, they are creative too, 'they are like Oa', part of a life-force.

Shaped by grief and suffering, a new Lok stands before us; no longer a clown, but a rapidly maturing thinker who has begun at last to understand. He is 'like Mal', but also greater than Mal, knowing far more than Mal ever did because of what has happened to him. He has caught up with Fa; and we cannot but respond with admiration as well as pity.

All this time he has been unconsciously retracing his steps to the water where Fa's scent had ended ... and suddenly, beyond hope, he catches it again and finds her coming towards him, wounded, but alive. They meet with an intensity of love unique in Golding's work and beautifully, tactfully rendered because we do not need to be told what the reunion means: the possibility of 'Peopleness' again, the intensity of shared feelings and pictures, seen at their most precious and exciting because they had seemed lost for ever.

Yet, as they commune, we become aware that Lok has not only caught up with Fa in consciousness, he has surpassed her. In the next few pages the 'point of view' of the novel becomes its hero in full stature. They are both unconsciously aware that the new people 'could not be left alone. Terrible they might be as the fire or the river, but they drew like honey or meat'; but only Lok has been able to bring the attractiveness of the New Men into conscious focus. All Fa's images are unremittingly hostile, full of the sad sense of destruction. While he is with her, he loses the sense of their 'Oa-ness'. Following the train of her thoughts leads only to the limited perception of Mal and the Old Woman, the terrible image, from memory now, that the situation is 'like when the fire flew away and ate up the trees'. But there has been more, and will be more again. Of course it is easy enough to explain why Fa sees as she does: every time Lok mentions Liku there is a reaction from Fa which reminds us that she has experienced something that Lok has not, and makes it steadily more certain that it was the murder of Liku. Yet the sense of Lok's new maturity remains, and finds physical expression too. As they move through the forest they walk abreast, but when they come to the clearing and see 'the pictures and the gifts', Lok takes the lead again while a frightened Fa slips in behind him.

The scene that follows is one of the most crucial in the novel because, while it brings them to (and, momentarily, over) the brink of fallen consciousness, it also begins to define that brink, and prove that they will never finally cross it because they remain People. Terror and pain have enabled them more and more to use their minds in ways that the New Men do. A new sense of the deep waters through which the New Men move has welled up tidally within them, they have known something of the consciousness of the river and the fall. But they have never acted like the New Men, and they have never entered the kind of being that is expressed in the stag-cult.

On the ground, Tuami has finished the new painting we saw him beginning as the guard mimed the ogres' escape. There is another stag-image, but superimposed on it and pinned to it by a driven stake is an image of the People as Tuami sees them, as though 'in the act of some frantic cruelty'. Swinging from the stake is a stag's haunch, and by the figure's head is an open stone bottle of honey-drink. Propitiatory offering and death-magic go together. Convinced by Marlan that the People are not just ogres but devils who have thwarted the stag-magic, the New Men have tried to tap the powers of, and exert control over, both God and Devil. The gifts are the propitiation born of fear, but the stake speaks of ritual killing.

The People see 'gifts'. But by eating the New Men's only 'comparatively bloodless' meat, and drinking their rotten honey, they do experience for the only time what it is to act like New Men. In a tragic novel this is a finely comic scene; unique in

Golding, so far. Yet knowing Lok and Fa as we do, we may find it also more and less than funny. In their drunkenness they discover excess, a reeling world, oblivion, ended by vomiting and a sick head and eyes. They become greedy, selfish, aggressive, sulky, furious, violent. Lok's voice comes out 'high and loud and savage'; Fa crawls round the ashes of the fire as the savage man had done 'like a moth with a burnt wing ... talking to herself of hyenas'. When Fa laughs drunkenly, 'kicking her legs in the air' we laugh too, but, as 'Lok and the honey fire responded to this invitation clumsily', they have taken another step towards Tuami and Vivani. Soon Lok belts her over the rump as Tanakil had beaten Liku, for not obeying his will, and Fa hits back devastatingly. Loving turns to fighting. Finally Lok 'discovered the power of the new people in him. He was one of them. There was nothing he could not do.' He feels himself imposing his will on the universe, he walks 'with what he thought was the slow swaying carriage of the new people', he lumbers round to tell Fa she must cut his finger off. 'The fall was roaring in the clearing, inside Lok's head.'

Yet the comedy remains secure. The fallen behaviour is purely the result of drunkenness, and when the People's stomachs vomit the rotten honey out they become themselves again. Our laughter has been a response to the extraordinary. When Fa strikes Lok she is immediately filled with tears as well as laughter, and the experience frightens them both. At the moment when he is closest to the New Men, claiming identity, we realize most emphatically that Lok will always be essentially different. He can think and be conscious in many of their ways, and for the duration of his drunkenness he can even act like them, but he can never *be* as they are. This is because, for Golding, it is the basic 'religious' attitude to the world that determines 'being', and only being can determine the kind of action that can define one's nature.* Lok can only think of the severed finger as some vague kind of initiation, he is quite incapable of the religious attitudes that lie behind blood-sacrifice and ritual killing. The alien behaviour he is trapped into, by what he sees as gifts, is founded on no basic self within and consequently disappears without trace. For a moment, in 'action', he crosses the boundary of the Fall, but there is no counterpart in his true 'being',

* See this developed in *Free Fall*.

and the effect of the experience is only to clarify our sense of how essentially unfallen that being is. Actions unfounded in being have only temporary significance.

Fa, in her recovered self, teeters nearer the brink than Lok, as she has always done. In his hangover he allows her to take the lead again, and she proceeds to act in a way that for the first time looks like confronting the New Men on their own terms. She hurls stones at them as they shoot arrows at her. She conceives the idea of abducting Tanakil as they abducted Liku. Her teeth show, like Chestnut-head's as he comes at Lok. As a by-product of her strategy, one of the dugouts splits and smashes on the rocks, while for the first time a New Man takes the death-dive over the waterfall. Yet Fa's nearness to the borderline only emphasizes how impassable it is for her too. The rocks are only a distraction while Lok tries to rescue the New One, the abduction of Tanakil is conceived only for exchange, the death of Chestnut-head and the destruction of the dugout pure accident. Again the necessary basis in being is absent.

We realize this with finality when the differing 'religious' attitudes are juxtaposed in the overhang. Both Fa and Lok have become consciously aware of the terror of the New Men that lies behind their every movement, and their consent to the whip, as they frantically toil up the slope which leads above the waterfall to open waters, away from the devil-haunted forests. The awareness, now so explicit, comes from the new dimension of conscious knowledge; having experienced terror, not just dread, they can recognize it fully. But they think the New Men are baselessly terrified of the empty air, since there is nothing in the forest to fear; and this is because they can never, even for a moment, conceive of themselves as capable of harm. Without the willingness to impose the will at any cost; without the world-view that recognizes no more essential value than the preservation of the self and its imposition on the universe, if need be by destroying whatever is in the way, there can be no Fall. In their desperate extremity, the witch-doctor and the religious artist reveal the extent of the cost they are prepared to bear. Blood-offering, if necessary of part of oneself, turns into human sacrifice, as Beelzebub turned into Moloch in Lord of the Flies. There is no stag-image now, for the Devil has proved stronger than the God. The devil is 'savagely' drawn and far more terrible than before, with its pebble eyes supplemented by the tigers' teeth; and the stake has been driven through its heart with hysterical strength. They offer their young girl in propitiation for the death of Liku (no doubt warned by the 'anger' of Lok's cries of 'Liku'); but they give her also as a human offering for the devils to consume as they would consume the stag's haunch and the honey-drink, and the purpose is to acquire the power to kill.

Faced by the tethered Tanakil in her fit, 'Fa began to make noises. They were not words and they were not screams.' We are not told what they were, but Lok hears Tanakil's screaming as like Liku's crossing the water, and that was utter horror and revulsion. They work frantically to free her, and when they run to the terrace in a last despairing hope of the New One, they run without weapons and without any idea of using Tanakil as an exchange, since they immediately release her to her mother. On the terrace, by the waterfall, the Fallen finally confront the eternally Innocent; but with a last terrible irony, the death-magic works. A concussed Fa is carried over the Fall in a sunset river of blood. There can be no doubt which of the two natures is stronger, and must survive.

So, against the fiery water and the fall, there is the first of the final perspectives; a double one. On the one hand we have to set against Fa (the red squirrel running on all fours up the slope), the brilliant inventiveness, the scientific technology which has begun to understand the principles of the conveyor belt and the fulcrum and lever. On the other hand we have to set her essential innocence against the destructive fire and river, the terror, the whips, the blood-sacrifice and ritual killing, the murderous fallen nature. The harmless one, holding the blinding pain inflicted on a head which could conceive no evil, is trapped by a dead tree she can neither escape nor surmount, and swept by the bloody river over a fall she cannot survive. She is never a person of the fall, the river, the fire or the blood. Golding has taken her to the brink of the fall but she herself could never pass that brink. She is killed, carried back below, because she is the kind of being who cannot even begin to conceive of preserving herself by trying to destroy her enemy.

Before we can settle into any final horror of the Inheritors, however, we are made to look again. If the novel had ended here, where its action ends, our response would have been relatively clear-cut; the title a severe, but relatively simple irony. But it is always just where we expect Golding to end that the deepest insights begin.

The surprise ending of *Lord of the Flies* forced us, by a sudden change of perspective which 'distanced' the novel, to look at it again as a whole. This Golding contrives to do now, at the end of the penultimate chapter. Having made us live for ten and a half chapters within Lok's mind, Golding suddenly becomes a distant, impersonal, and coldly objective narrator. This involves a different style, with a fully modern vocabulary, but there is a chilly scientific accuracy recording what it sees with no understanding or emotion. There is a 'red creature', and 'a dark hollow in the side of the cliff where there was evidence of occupation'. If we want a way of measuring the gap between the anthropologist and the imaginative novelist, we have it here.

These eyes can record only what Lok looks like, and the effect is as though we have never seen him before.

It was a strange creature, smallish, and bowed. The legs and thighs were bent, and there was a whole thatch of curls on the outside of the legs and the arms. The back was high, and covered over the shoulders with curly hair. Its feet and hands were broad, and flat, the great toe projecting inwards to grip. The square hands swung down to the knees. The head was set slightly forward on the strong neck that seemed to lead straight on to the row of curls under the lip. The mouth was wide and soft and above the curls of the upper lip the great nostrils were flared like wings. There was no bridge to the nose and the moon-shadow of the jutting brow lay just above the tip. The shadows lay most darkly in the caverns above its cheeks, and the eyes were invisible in them. Above this again, the brow was a straight line fledged with hair; and above that there was nothing.

The gap between this and our knowledge is like the gap between the Officer and Ralph; what is seen is accurate, and yet meaningless without the understanding that so manifestly does not accompany the vision. What we measure is the extent of what the novel has achieved for us by making us live behind Lok's eyes instead of looking at him with our own. We can, for the first time, appreciate the tactic of Golding's choice of point of view, because if this kind of vision had appeared in its logical place on the opening page, we could never have responded to such a figure as we have responded to Lok. We could never have been made to realize his true humanity, let alone his greater humanity, in some directions, than our own. Every detail here seems to speak of the innate superiority of *homo sapiens*, though no conclusions are drawn. The temptation must have been to regard such a creature complacently, with a readiness to draw inferences not only of difference, but of inferiority ... as Wells did. Indeed that is exactly the point. These are the eyes of Wells, and to take in the difference is to take in the full measure of what Golding has done to *The Outline of History* and *The Grisly Folk*.

To watch Lok so coldly, while his eyes follow the tree that has killed Fa until he loses sight of it in the distance, is to make us uneasily aware of how blind we would have been even if some accident of time had placed us on the terrace at that moment. We watch while he retraces the whole circuit of the tragic action, so small-looking now; while he revisits one by one the stations of his agony, and the effect is like looking through the wrong end of a telescope so that everything is diminished. Yet the final effect is just the opposite, and the tactic reveals an unexpected stroke of genius. For there rises in us a passionate reaction against this vision, a sense of poignant pity and loss far more powerful through this excess of understatement than could have been achieved by any direct appeal to emotion. As the creature 'seized a great swinging beech bough and lugged it back and forwards until its breathing was fierce and uneven' the full emotional impact hits us of what has happened to that first happy onrush, and the delighted game between the sunny father and the laughing red-haired child.

Only now is the full horror revealed, moreover, as the creature digs from the churned earth and ashes of the fire 'a small, white bone':

The creature stood and the splashes of moonlight stirred over it. The eye-hollows gazed not at the bone but at an invisible point towards the river. Now the right leg began to move. The creature's attention seemed to gather and focus in the leg and the foot began to pick and search in the earth like a hand. The big toe bored and gripped and the toes folded round an object that had been almost completely buried in the churned soil. The foot rose, the leg bent and presented an object to the lowered hand. The head came down a little, the gaze swept inward from that invisible point and regarded what was in the hand. It was a root, old and rotted, worn away at both ends but preserving the exaggerated contours of a female body.

The old Lok's 'only picture' is transformed into a 'still' from a horror-film. Liku has not only been killed, she has been *eaten*. What Marlan did was not only to save himself by shifting the blame onto the devils, whose representative could be ritually slaughtered in vengeance; but also to offer her as meat to the famished tribe for a cannibalistic orgy. (This is Golding's bitterest rejoinder to Wells, whose Grisly Folk 'thought the little children of men fair game and pleasant eating'.) We are frozen with the same horror as Lok. The wrong end of the telescope seems unable to give us any reaction. Or does it?

The creature looked again towards the water. Both hands were full, the bar of its brow glistened in the moonlight, over the great caverns where the eyes were hidden. There was light poured down over the cheek-bones and the wide lips and there was a twist of light caught like a white hair in every curl. But the caverns were dark as though already the whole head was nothing but a skull ...

There was light now in each cavern, lights faint as the starlight reflected in the crystals of a granite cliff. The lights increased, acquired definition, brightened, lay each sparkling at the lower edge of a cavern. Suddenly, noiselessly, the lights became thin crescents, went out, and streaks glistened on each cheek. The lights appeared again, caught among the silvered curls of the beard. They hung, elongated, dropped from curl to curl and gathered at the lowest tip. The streaks on the cheeks pulsed as the drops swam down them, a great drop swelled at the end of a hair of the beard, shivering and bright. It detached itself and fell in a silver flash, striking a withered leaf with a sharp pat.

We realize that Lok is weeping without making the slightest sound. The objective accuracy of the description not only protects the moment from any trace of sentimentality or exploitation, it also puts the experience into our minds before we know it is there, and the delayed-action response is all the more powerful. We watch what must be said, quite simply, to be one of the most tragic moments in contemporary fiction.

Nevertheless, though our knowledge and our response seem now so complete that we can hardly believe there can be more to come, Golding is not finished with us yet. For the sudden distancing proves to be more than a device to produce, without sentimentality, a welling up of horror, and grief, and love for innocence destroyed. It may be *necessary* to get to a distance, or we may still see and respond too simply.

'If the strings broke, a man would die', and Lok does. The cliché of 'a broken heart' receives its full meaning because there is not only nothing to live for, but no way of living. Lok tries to get into Mal's grave, but he is already too weak to move the stone. He curls up into a foetal position again, but now he seems 'to be growing into the earth, drawing the soft flesh of [his] body into a contact so close that the movements of pulse and breathing were inhibited'. This foetus is inhibiting life, it is 'growing' only backwards into the womb; and with the little Oa before his face Lok cannot but make us think of a dead child, which has failed to develop into the full shape of a man.

Throughout these chapters we ought to have been aware, as an ironic undertone announcing itself more and more strongly, of the advance of spring into summer: the sun getting hotter, the leaves burgeoning, the wood-pigeons nesting. The fullness of the river speaks of the thaw in the mountains, and water cascades from the ice-woman sanctuary onto the rocks beyond the terrace. As the hyenas approach the body they know to be dead, 'a sudden tremendous noise' sends them 'shivering back'. It is the avalanche proclaiming the beginning of summer, and probably also the end of the ice-age. There is the irony that the abundance so eagerly awaited has come too late; but there ought also to be the sense that it is not enough to feel that Innocence has been wantonly destroyed. The People have failed to grow beyond the Spring of mankind, have failed to move beyond the waterfall, the full evolutionary march of man has necessarily left them behind. If we are filled with grief and pity at the extinction of Innocence, we should not fail also to take in its inability to surmount the Fall, and move forward into a life beyond.

So it becomes necessary to take in a final perspective; to enter for the first time the mind of a New Man, and discover what moving beyond the Fall entails. The language is immediately the nautical one of the seafarer. The tree-trunk that slips past the solitary boat with one root lifted 'like a mammoth's tusk' reminds us that the time is prehistoric, but the boat itself, the navigational calculations, the mind of the helmsman, point straight into the future, however slowly and hesitantly.

We find out their past, and the explanation of much we could not know before. We know their names, with the sense of personality that proper names give. In some directions the darkness of their history merely confirms impressions we already have. Marlan has stolen Vivani from her husband, and his followers are consequently not merely exploring, but flying from the vengeance of their tribe. Tuami wants Vivani too, and the ivory knife he is making is destined for Marlan's heart as, we remember from the scene in the clearing, Marlan himself has sensed. Vivani's statuesque self-absorption and magnificent selfishness are reinforced; and so are our impressions of their malice, their lust, their deadliness. Yet, as we see them from inside, we see that they are not quite what we thought. We take in also a confirmation of Lok's other impressions. Though the People could never have called anyone 'Master', or have snapped at each other with faces so twisted by grief and hate, these men and women can remind us of Peopleness. As the New One sucks at Vivani's breast 'the people were grinning at her too as if they felt the strange, tugging mouth'. Moreover their voyage has not simply begun in lust and rapaciousness and fear. There has been something else, 'whatever it was', that impelled them to voyage on. There is also a level of motivation unknowable to Lok. Vivani, like Fa, has lost her baby, and the New One was taken to ease the pain of her swollen breasts and console her for her loss; while Tuami spared Liku arbitrarily, 'as a joke'. It is not, perhaps, very much of a qualification, but it does mean that they are less deliberately and strategically destructive than we thought.

More important, however, is that hitherto we have unconsciously tended always to regard them statically, as determined. Now we begin to see that for them, as much as for the People they destroyed, the encounter has involved new dimensions of growth, and the waterfall has been a Rubicon. To Tuami 'It seemed as though the portage ... from that forest to the top of the fall had taken them on to a new level not only of land, but of experience and emotion'.

At first this new level is wholly appalling. Tuami feels 'haunted, bedevilled, full of strange irrational grief ... the world with the boat moving so slowly at the centre was dark amid the light, was untidy, hopeless, dirty.' The world is defiled, in a way that cannot be remedied by squaring off the boat. In Tanakil's mad eyes he sees 'the night going on'; and the encounter with the People has made her 'a changeling'. It has made 'a new Tuami too'. We watch again, as we watched with Lok, the release of a new sense of the mind's deepest waters: 'I am like a pool, he thought, some tide has filled me, the sand is swirling, the waters are obscured and strange things are creeping out of the cracks and crannies in my mind.' There is nightmare again, as the red leg of the New One suddenly seems part of a monstrous hairy spider creeping from a crevice, but the horror is in the mind behind the eyes, not in the harmless baby. If the world has become dirty and dark, and the brain filled with visions of nightmare, it is because of guilt. 'What else could we have done?' he cries. 'If we had not, we should have died.' The diagnosis, we know, is tragically wrong; but the feeling is not, and it is a wholly new human dimension beyond the capacity of the Innocent.

It is also beyond the Old Man in the boat. Marlan has not changed; he is still confined within his old self-justifying categories. The People were 'devils', the evil was within them, not himself, and he escapes any sense of its continuity by the assurance that the 'devils' will not cross water. Yet this can only be the birth of superstition; while the other is the birth of a new 'religious' sense of the world. Tanakil's terrible cry of 'Liku' is born of the horror of what they have done; it is not a devil's name which only she can speak because she is 'possessed' by an external evil. Tuami sees with utter clarity how much smaller and weaker Marlan has become in his sameness. He looks at the witchdoctor to find something to hold onto, but the new dawn reveals his inadequacy in a light as horrifying, in its way, as Lok's vision of the Old Woman below the fall: 'The sun was blazing on the red sail and Marlan was red. His arms and legs were contracted, his hair stood out and his beard, his teeth were wolf's teeth and his eyes like blind stones. The mouth was opening and shutting.' He is the relic of the old dead way, himself the embodiment of the blind, vicious, insensible evil he had read into the People, his hope of escaping the darkness by keeping to the waters and the plain a manifest stupidity. There is no way out, by flight, or by fight. Tuami's ivory blade is useless: 'What was the use of sharpening it against a man? Who would sharpen a point against the darkness of the world?' In the consciousness of guilt is the fear of the price to be paid: 'What sacrifice would they be forced to perform to a world of confusion? They were as different from the group of bold hunters and magicians who had sailed up the river towards the fall as a soaked feather is from a dry one.' They, as much as the People, have been immersed in deep water, from which there can be no escape.

Yet there is a thoroughfare. The people in the boat already respond to the New One with a 'well of feeling' which includes not only fear, but love. Suddenly the tremendous booming of the avalanche reverberates across the water with its intimation of a new season, and a new age. The baby scuttles into Vivani's furs as we have often seen him do with his mother, and in a sudden release of tension 'the people, released as if a lifted weapon had been lowered, turned their relief and laughter on the devil'. This is simple psychology; but for Tuami there is a revelation, and a cure, not a mere diversion: 'The sun shone on the head and the rump and quite suddenly everything was all right again and the sands had sunk back to the bottom of the pool.' Why?

The 'rump' of the old and the 'face' of the new have suddenly become a single shape, unified and harmonious; contrasted, but seen to fit:

The rump and the head fitted each other and made a shape you could feel with your hands. They were waiting in the rough ivory of the knife-haft that was so much more important than the blade. They were an answer, the frightened angry love of the woman and the ridiculous, intimidating rump that was wagging at her head, they were a password. His hands felt for the ivory in the bilges and he could feel in his fingers how Vivani and her devil fitted it.

The sculptor will change the death-weapon to a form of loving, even religious vision, an answer to guilt, a password to a new expedition of the spirit. This starts from the ability to love both the fallen and the unfallen nature, and to see the downward path of the innocent and the surmounting movement of the guilty as essentially related. The People's plunge to extinction by the fall is necessary to the progress of the New Men beyond it. The new vision and love are the product of sin and shame unknowable to innocence. Neither the People, nor Marlan with his mutterings about darkness and his Wellsian ogre-consciousness, can grow; the dead 'evil' and the dead 'good' are left behind. But the sculptor creates something one can see all round. He finds a way to voyage beyond the fall to a creative knowledge of good *through* evil, perceptible only to a consciousness newly aware of guilt, but offering a password to go forward. This is the vision 'past the new people, past Fa and Lok' which Lok glimpsed on the island but could never himself achieve. The ability to focus good and evil in essential relationship, and see lovable human shape in both, is a better vision than that of either the children of darkness or the children of light. This makes Golding's novel explicitly what it has always been implicitly, not a mere lament for lost innocence, but also a subdued testimony to the ability to know the worst and remain loving. Tuami cannot see to the end of the deep water, or 'if the line of darkness had an ending', but this may be because he is blinded by the light the water reflects. Whatever the end, the new beginning is good. The artist has captured a new vision. It is for his people to inherit.

V

More accurately, the vision can neither be 'given' nor simply 'inherited'. It had to be discovered by its author, and has to be discovered by his readers, by imagination at full stretch, laying hold of a complex truth graspable in no other way. By comparison, although we have been anxious to point to ways in which it arrives at a vision richer than its apparent thesis, *Lord of the Flies* remains a smaller and simpler work. *The Inheritors* also began from a thesis – and a quarrel – but it transforms and expands itself to a far greater extent. The manuscript version had no waterfall, no last chapter; it was wholly the tragedy of the People, with neither as complex an exploration of their consciousness, nor as full a perspective on its implications. The most symbolic elements came last of all. Golding's way of writing turns out to be more like Lawrence than Milton, in ways that can hardly be accounted for by treating him as fabulist and pattern-maker. After finishing a first version that is already a considerable achievement, he clearly felt he had only begun to see what his novel was about, and started again. The discovery implies an even bigger and more difficult adventure of the imagination. It is equally discovery, not pattern-making, that *The Inheritors* forces on its readers by the nature of Golding's art.

The triumph of technique hardly needs further emphasis, the novel appears in retrospect as a dazzling *tour de force*. Yet it is never pyrotechnic, but always functional, and the function is always to keep the imagination alert and flexible, so that there can be no stasis until the whole act of discovery is complete. The revelation technique of *Lord of the Flies* reappears as situations are reorchestrated to bring out ever richer levels of implication. This means that Golding can pack an extraordinary weight of meaning into a single sentence: 'Terrible they might be as the fire and the river, but they drew like honey or meat'; and can bring the entire novel behind the tragic plunge of Fa over the waterfall. But the purpose of writing like this is to force the imagination to hold all its knowledge in tension, so that in the final chapters the entire experience can be gathered together and re-viewed. The shifts of perspective ensure that we should be able to see all round what has been discovered. The basic choice of point of view ensures that we have experienced imaginatively before being allowed to analyse or judge; and ensures also that we will have experienced a growth of thought and a history of language.

In some ways the book gives a sense of perfection; of being one of those rare novels which seems to encompass the whole of its subject. In this respect it is perhaps the most perfect of Golding's works, but it is a perfection within limits.

Partly these are inherent in archetypal myth with its constant drive towards the essential and its relative impatience with the contingent. In character, for example, the search is for the being of Man rather than the complexities of the individual. There is less concern with relationship as a complicated and mysterious flux between individuals, than with defining the essential nature of relationships. Oddly, the one between Lok and Fa is probably the most fully developed in Golding's first five novels, yet he uses it always to explore through, to Peopleness, Deep Waters, the Brink of the Fall. Relationship itself is never the statue. It is the marble in which the statue has to be revealed by cutting away what is non-essential.

The subject of *The Inheritors* cannot but increase this selectivity, and hence the sense of limitation. It is obviously a great advantage to work on a subject which offers the least resistance to treating Man, rather than individuals in complex social relationships. Prehistory suits Golding's art better than an island and a group of boys. There is even less marble to cut away. But it then becomes inevitable that our powerful sense of the archetypal should be accompanied by a rather startled realization of just how much in human existence as we usually encounter it is rendered contingent by such vision. How deeply and richly significant from one point of view, how startlingly *naked* from another, Golding's statue turns out to be.

If, however, it is a valid idea of art to see the artist whittling away to find the shape of the basic human condition, then Tuami with his ivory images his author's achievements. Yet the stress in *The Inheritors* should be on the more inclusive image of the artist as voyager through deep waters. The art has grown deeper and more complex in the second novel, and the vision which concludes the book looks forward to an exploration of individual man in society. The next two novels will seek to extend Golding's range in different ways, until Tuami's vision of unified opposites can become the single vision of *The Spire*. *The Inheritors* reveals Golding as an explorer, and his art 'not still, but still moving'.

3

PINCHER MARTIN

(1956)

I

This, it seems, is a book about a man alone on a rock in mid-Atlantic – a bleak prospect; but the novel at its simplest is already a *tour de force*, the challenge met by a vivid realization of the castaway's predicament. We feel in their grandeur and terror the realities of rock, sky, and sea; the pressure on a man of a Nature crushingly alien to him; the struggle to stay alive and sane; the physical and mental deterioration; the madness that is convincing on a naturalistic level before it is anything else. Golding's first achievement, to borrow words from Philip Larkin, is that he can 'overwhelmingly persuade' that this is a real man on a real rock, 'in every sense empirically true'.

Yet 'realism' is a notoriously treacherous concept for the critic of the novel, and we need to remind ourselves that there are as many 'realities' as there are kinds of imaginative vision that can persuade. If we feel tempted to pinpoint Golding's achievement by contrast with, say, Defoe's, this cannot be a matter of praising him for greater fidelity to some supposed criterion of 'reality'. The usefulness of the comparison will be that it may help us to define the kind of imaginative vision we are dealing with, by contrast with another kind:

... the Sea having hurried me along as before, landed me, or rather dash'd me against a Piece of Rock, and that with such Force, as it left me senseless, and indeed helpless, as to my own Deliverance; for the Blow taking my Side and Breast, beat the Breathe as it were quite out of my Body; and had it returned again immediately, I must have been strangled in the Water; but I recover'd a little before the return of the Waves, and seeing I should be cover'd again with the Water, I resolv'd to hold fast by a Piece of the Rock, and so to hold my Breath, if possible, till the Wave went back; now as the Waves were not so high as at first, being nearer Land, I held my Hold till the Wave abated, and then fetch'd another Run, which brought me so near the Shore, that the next Wave, tho' it went over me, yet did not swallow me up as to carry me away, and the next Run I took, I got to the main Land, where, to my great Comfort, I clamber'd up the Clifts of the Shore, and sat me down upon the Grass free from Danger, and quite out of the Reach of the Water ...

... I walk'd about on the Shore, lifting up my Hands, and my whole Being, as I may say, wrapt up in the Contemplation of my Deliverance, making a Thousand Gestures and Motions which I cannot describe, reflecting upon all my Comrades that were drown'd, and that there should not be one Soul sav'd but my self; for, as for them, I never saw them afterwards, or any sign of them, except three of their Hats, one Cap, and two Shoes that were not Fellows.

Defoe keeps our attention fixed on the man, so that although the sea threatens to overwhelm him, we never doubt that he is in control. The verbs accumulate to establish our response; for a short while they belong to the sea, but the loose syntax turns, the object becomes the subject and the passive the active. 'I must have been strangl'd in the Water; but I recover'd ...', 'I resolv'd ...', 'I held ...', 'I clamber'd up ... sat me down ... quite out of the Reach of the Water'. The things denoted by capitals are objects, with no resonance, that the 'I' and the actions deal with. The imaginative vision sees the world as one of objects for humans to act on, objects dangerous, or useful, or not useful like the shoes that are largely denuded of their pathos by the automatic recording of their uselessness. It is clear that the 'reality' Defoe seeks to convey has little to do with the experience of what it must feel like nearly to drown and then be saved. His is the 'realism' of pure record – this happened and then this. The very absence of personal feeling testifies to the 'truth' of what is said, the 'facts' are presented as they have to be in a law-court, stripped of imaginative connotation with nothing between them and us. We are aware not so much of an individual character, or even an individual situation, as of a detached narrative voice neutrally recording a crisis overcome.

Pincher Martin shows another man drowning and seeming to strike shore:

Then he was there, suddenly, enduring pain but in deep communion with the solidity that held up his body. He remembered how eyes should be used and brought the two lines of sight together so that the patterns fused and made a distance.

The pebbles were close to his face, pressing against his cheek and jaw. They were white quartz, dulled and rounded, a miscellany of potato-shapes. Their whiteness was qualified by yellow stains and flecks of darker material. There was a whiter thing beyond them. He examined it without curiosity, noting the bleached wrinkles, the blue roots of nails, the corrugations at the fingertips. He did not move his head, but followed the line of the hand back to an oilskin sleeve, the beginnings of a shoulder. His eyes returned to the pebbles and watched them idly as if they were about to perform some operation for which he was waiting without much interest. The hand did not move.

Water welled up among the pebbles. It stirred them slightly, paused, then sank away while the pebbles clicked and chirruped. It swilled down past his body and pulled gently at his stockinged feet. He watched the pebbles while the water came back and this time the last touch of the sea lopped into his open mouth. Without change of expression he began to shake, a deep shake that included the whole of his body. Inside his head it seemed that the pebbles were shaking because the movement of his white hand forward and back was matched by the movement of his body. Under the side of his face the pebbles nagged.

Where Defoe's passage is dominated by the personal pronoun, in Golding it is not the beholder but what is beheld that takes all our attention. He works to make us experience as directly as possible what is being described; these are the sensations that might have been ours if we were skilful enough to catch and record them. Defoe's scene is framed within the will of his character, in Golding the scene itself is hypnotic, drawing the eye to note with increasing intensity whatever is placed before it. The pebbles are first felt, then seen: 'solidity ... dulled and rounded ... potato-shapes ... whiteness ... qualified by yellow stains and flecks of darker material'. Attention is gradually focused, we are made to see with the same kind of riveted attention as Pincher. Then, almost imperceptibly, out of sensation wells emotion. The passage seems to start even more disinterestedly than Defoe's, but the dulled objectivity is charged because we sense the suffering that has produced it. We are dimly aware that the obsessively detailed vision is somehow abnormal; as the body begins to shake there is released in us a veiled kind of horror, diffuse, undirected. We are never, as in Defoe, an audience for a narrator. We are inside a head, we are a pair of eyes, a consciousness aware of fear and pain.

The two kinds of 'realism' these passages aim at is an

inseparable part of the imaginative vision, and hence the structure of the novels from which they come; we can detect in the organization of each a hint of an overall rhythm. Defoe's narrative stance and cataloguing tone have the immediate effect of distancing his story so that we feel it capable of swift onward movement. The novel will be a loose, widely ranging, rapid account of actions which gradually impose a man's organization on the world. Golding, on the contrary, will do everything to cut down distance, to maximize detail, to build up the narrative in the detail itself. The novel will be hypnotic, densely textured, a growth not of action but of consciousness. It will seem at first that the awareness is mainly, even obsessively, physical; an experience through the senses of a man's subjection to his environment. But in fact where the 'realism' is taking us is inside his head. We might not be able to predict the full outcome, but it will eventually reveal a fearful imaginative logic. The rock, whose 'realism' is itself so considerable an achievement, will disappear; the inside of the head will remain the only 'reality' that exists.

Realism in *Pincher Martin*, then, turns out to be increasingly ironic. Yet we must begin with the convincing rendering of rock and sea and sky, for these are the primary imaginative experience, it is their hypnotism that rivets us, and it is only in and through them that Golding can hope to capture the full resonance of his myth:

He worked across the rock and back from trench to trench. He came on the mouldering bones of fish and a dead gull, its upturned breast-bone like the keel of a derelict boat. He found patches of grey and yellow lichen, traces even of earth, a button of moss. There were the empty shells of crabs, pieces of dead weed, and the claws of a lobster...

He lowered himself carefully and inspected the cliff. Under water the harvest of food was even thicker for the mussels were bigger down there and water-snails were crawling over them. And among the limpets, the mussels, the snails and barnacles, dotted like sucked sweets, were the red blobs of jelly, the anemones. Under water they opened their mouths in a circle of petals, but up by his face, waiting for the increase of the tide they were pursed up and slumped like breasts when the milk has been drawn from them...

There was something peculiar about the sound that came out of his mouth... He held his nose with his right hand and tried to blow through

it until the pressure rounded his cheeks. Nothing cracked in his ears ...
He stood up, facing a whole amphitheatre of water and sang a scale ...
The sound ended at his mouth ... He closed his lips, lowered his hand
slowly. The blue, igloo-roof over the rock went away to a vast distance,
the visible world expanded with a leap. The water lopped round a tiny
rock in the middle of the Atlantic. The strain tautened his face.

The man's physical predicament is vividly there. Food is nauseous,
water perilous, the body blotched with bruises and urticaria, the
mind and senses swept by waves of fever through exposure. We are
made to experience the bruising rock, the crushing weight of air,
the idiot depth of water, the suffering body, and the agonized mind
trying to keep an ever more precarious hold on identity and sanity.

Moreover, it is against this experience that the stature of the
man's struggle to survive becomes measurable. The terrible food
underlines the indomitable will that forces him to eat; the tasteless
water held in so precariously by furry red silt heightens our
appreciation of the intelligence which creates the 'Claudian
aqueduct'. The way we get to know the rock ourselves in all its
bleak inhospitability, allows us the measure of the 'naming of
parts', the attempt of frightened and solitary man to tame his
environment by netting it down with names. The creation of 'man-
shape' – the 'dwarf' with the silver-paper face, the line of seaweed
as a man-mark visible from the air – has a heroic as well as a
pathetic side. On the one hand the rock cuts man-shape down to
size. The dwarf enacts the diminishing, and how in the absence of
other faces the 'face' merely reflects an alien, inhuman environment. The seaweed measures the puniness of unaccommodated
man whose intelligence sees so much, but whose frame can
accomplish so very little. Man is seen unromantically, clinically,
for what he is in himself: Pharaoh without the ant-hordes who
built the pyramids, the officer without the great machinery of his
century. Yet for all this, man is not simply diminished: his qualities
of endurance, courage, resourcefulness are also thrown into sharp
relief.

So we spend an entire novel on a tiny rock, fascinated, convinced, and imaginatively extended by a deeper understanding of
the pressures of sea, sky, and rock on unaccommodated man, and
involved with what is in some sense an epic of human endurance,
whatever else it may turn into. The man is an Atlas holding up an

alien world that threatens to crush him; but the scene is not facile because we can feel the strain on the physical muscles. He is a Prometheus tortured on a rock; but when pain, delirium, and madness arrive, they are very far from notional or 'poetic'. There is about his predicament, and his response to it, the stature of Man against the Elements. Is Man no more than this, this bare fork'd animal? Perhaps, but he is certainly no less.

On the level we have been discussing so far, *Pincher Martin* has in common with *Robinson Crusoe* a lack of concern with individual character; we find it easy in both cases to talk about 'the man', or even Man. Nothing we have said so far depends upon what the particular man was like in society, what he had done, the nature of his personality and relationships. But a substantial part of *Pincher Martin* is very much concerned – in a special way – with the character indicated by its title, and his past. Here, necessarily, a very different imaginative vision is at work.

We are left in no doubt about the nature of that character. He was an actor, and the part he played most successfully in life, summarized in his nickname, is sufficiently indicated when the producer of a morality play introduces him to the masks of the seven deadly sins:

'What's it supposed to be, old man?'
  'Darling, it's simply *you!* Don't you think, George?'
  'Definitely, old man, definitely.'
  'Chris – Greed. Greed – Chris. Know each other.'
  'Anything to please you, Pete.'
  'Let me make you two better acquainted. This painted bastard here takes anything he can lay his hands on. Not food, Chris, that's far too simple. He takes the best part, the best seat, the most money, the best notice, the best woman. He was born with his mouth and his flies open and both hands out to grab. He's a cosmic case of the bugger who gets his penny and someone else's bun. Isn't that right, George?'

'Chris – Greed. Greed – Chris' – the identification is documented in the manner of a dossier throughout the novel. The record is almost altogether black, the element stark and unqualified. There is remorseless self-assertion: the young Pincher on a new bike manoeuvring a rival into a crash rather than be beaten; the resisting girl given the choice of walking home from a parked car or being maimed in a speeding one. There is sex for power and sex for advancement, sex with men and sex with a boy. There is theft plain and simple, a rifled cash-box and a conscience at ease: 'What are you going to do about it? There was nothing written down.' At strategic moments there are elaborate images which serve as choric commentary on these episodes. One of the most dominant is a carefully set scene between Martin and the producer he has betrayed, in which, with overtones borrowed from *Hamlet*, we get both moral anatomy and prophecy:

'I love you, Chris. Father and mother is one flesh. And so my uncle. My prophetic uncle. Shall I elect you to my club?'

'How about toddling home, now, Pete?'

'Call it the Dirty Maggot Club ... We maggots are there all the week. Y'see when the Chinese want to prepare a very rare dish they bury a fish in a tin box. Presently all the lil' maggots peep out and start to eat. Presently no fish. Only maggots. It's no bloody joke being a maggot ... It's a lousy job crawling round the inside of a tin box and Denmark's one of the worst. Well, when they've finished the fish, Chris, they start on each other.'

'Cheerful thought, old man.'

'The little ones eat the tiny ones. The middle-sized ones eat the little ones. The big ones eat the middle-sized ones. Then the big ones eat each other. Then there are two, and then one, and where there was a fish there is now one huge, successful maggot. Rare dish ... 'N when there's only one maggot left the Chinese dig it up – ... Have you ever heard a spade knocking on the side of a tin box, Chris? Boom! Boom! Just like thunder. You a member?'

As the flashbacks to the past accumulate the world they reveal was 'eat or be eaten', and in that world the man on the rock, Pincher Martin, was, for the moment, king.

In the course of the flashback record, however, two characters stand out in total contrast: Martin's great friend Nathaniel Walterson and the girl Nat marries, Mary Lovell. Mary is a first version of the girl who was to become Beatrice in *Free Fall*. For Martin she is a maddening contradiction: an anthology of petit-bourgeois convention, 'gloved and hatted for church, the Mary who ate with such maddening refinement ... the pursed up mouth, the too high forehead, the mousey hair'; but also 'a treasure of demoniac and musky attractiveness that was all the more terrible because she was almost unconscious of it'. She calls his whole view of life in question: 'set there in the road to power and success, unbreakable yet tormenting with the need to conquer and break'. His feeling for her is not lust so much as a kind of hate, his 'nights of imagined copulation' go not with sensation or satisfaction but with the rhythm of 'take that and that'. Sexually obsessed, he understands nothing of the values which give her life its quality (the unity of Mary and Lovewell); yet she eats into his kind of existence like acid. He can only seek to break her will; but fails to do so in the desperate car journey in which he threatens that she will be 'burst and bitched', and earns only her contempt and loathing.

Nathaniel is a more elaborated figure. He is the 'saint' of the novel – wholly unworldly and innocent, genuine, humble, unselfish, loving. He is, it is true, presented as peculiar and even ludicrous – the extraordinary spidery lankiness, the language of 'meditation', the theories of soul-migration and astrology, the spiritual lecturing, the total lack of humour. But this is no more than a familiar technique whereby one tries to win acceptance and credit for 'goodness' by making it slightly comic. There is little doubt that 'sheer niceness' is meant to be our predominant and final impression. He marries Mary, asking Chris to be best man. In the darkest hour Chris knows before he hits the water: in Oxford, when, hearing the communal summoning of the bells, he recognizes in himself a complete blackness of solitude and exclusion – 'Because of what I did I am an outsider and alone' – it is Nathaniel who arrives as Comforter, with a warning, but also with the warmth of companionship and love, and a promise about dying into heaven. He is entrusted on this occasion with the novel's central 'ideas'. And he produces in Chris the only unselfish moment that the whole kaleidoscope of memory reveals: a moment when he is driven to give warning against himself, before calculation and jealous hatred take over again. He cannot help loving Nat 'unwillingly ... for the face that was always rearranged from within, for the serious attention, for love given without thought'; but he also hates him 'quiveringly ... as though he were the only enemy'. This of course is what he is. The face whose expressions come from genuine movements of feeling and relationship within, is a continual reproach to the actor's manipulation of a mask that conceals the true features of Greed; the serious attention and love a standing index to the loveless

egotism. The affection for Nat is the only feeling he has apart from
that of self; but the goodness is hateful and must be destroyed
because it threatens the autonomy of the selfish ego. It is far more
than jealousy over Mary; Nat stands in the way of his whole
existence. So, as with Mary, he plots to destroy him. At the
moment when the torpedo strikes the destroyer, Chris had shouted
the order 'Hard a-starboard, for Christ's sake', which would have
been the right order for avoiding the torpedo if it had been given a
few seconds earlier. But in fact the order was attempted murder;
for Nat, swaying unsteadily against the rail with eyes closed and
hands before his face in prayer, is vulnerable to a sudden change in
direction and a sea taken over the starboard bow. The final motive
however is not rage, or jealousy, or hatred. Martin is searching for
'a kind of peace' – and only the destruction of Nat (or the
destruction of himself) could give it to him.

From the drift of the flashbacks and the treatment of Nathaniel
and Mary it can easily be seen that Golding is aiming at a very
different kind of reality from that on the rock. There everything
was excessively concentrated, densely particularized; here everything is distanced and type-cast, the web of circumstance calculatedly removed. We do not in fact find 'character' in the sense we
tend to expect from fiction; we are confronted with moral figures in
the past where we had been confronted with archetypal Man in the
present. So there exist in constant and even violent juxtaposition a
world of dense, non-individualistic sensation, and a world of
morality-play or illustrated catalogue for the confessional.

One's first reaction is probably to see these contrasted realities in
succinct terms of imaginative success and failure: to insist that the
morality play is a rhetoric of statement rather than imaginative
creation; that its attitudes are damagingly oversimplified to the
point, often, of crudity; that it is frequently artificial and uncon-
vincing as a portrait of credible people in credible situations; that
its language tends both to the unimaginatively coarse and the
imaginatively over-elaborated; that, in a word, the worst and the
best of Golding lie side by side. Moreover, is there not a curious gap
in causality between the two worlds? We hardly needed Golding to
tell us* that he set out to make his protagonist as unpleasant as he

* Interview with Frank Kermode, *Books and Bookmen*.

possibly could, but why? Rock, sea, and sky, are great levellers; it hardly seems to matter, when we are cast away with Martin, what kind of a man he is. He could not, it is true, be gutless or stupid, but do we really need to assume so monstrous a character to explain his will, courage, endurance or resourcefulness? Are the novelist's left and right hands not only doing different, but essentially unrelated things?

Yet we had better pause again. For the effect of the flashbacks is obviously calculated; and if there is a failure it must lie in the conception rather than the realization. Indeed the cliché term flashback is itself more accurate than usual, for Pincher makes continual photographic and cinematic reference to his memories as 'pictures', 'glossy and illuminated scenes', 'snapshots', 'film trailers'. Golding clearly wants the memories to have only the same relation to real life as photography has: they must seem framed all round, artificially lit and polished, stills rather than motion pictures aiming at the illusion of reality, and, if they do move, giving the sense of being deliberately selected from a bigger film in order to provide an artificially heightened sense of the nature of the whole. He has deliberately chosen to emphasize the artificiality by making Pincher's past an actor's world and its language a theatrical argot. Above all, the technique is designed to enforce the sense of the past as utterly over, completed, with that quality of a vanished world that old films and photographs possess.

There will be reasons for this – but for the moment it may be useful to notice a new sense of the peculiarity of the novel's conception: for behind the superficially violent contrast of the 'real' world of the rock and the glossy pictures with their moral configuration, there can now be seen to lie a more significant resemblance. Both are essentially static, outside time. Both are already determined, incapable of change. This is immediately obvious in the flashbacks; but it will not take us long to perceive that the 'life' on the rock, too, can only be further revealed for what it already is. The man may become more aware of his situation, or fulfil it, but he cannot change it. He may die, but he is already dying.

In fact, of course, the last page of the novel notoriously reveals that its hero is dead, and has been dead since the second page:

But the man lay suspended behind the whole commotion, detached from his jerking body. The luminous pictures that were shuffled before him were drenched in light but he paid no attention to them. Could he have controlled the nerves of his face, or could a face have been fashioned to fit the attitude of his consciousness where it lay suspended between life and death that face would have worn a snarl. But the real jaw was contorted down and distant, the mouth was slopped full. The green tracer that flew from the centre began to spin into a disc. The throat at such a distance from the snarling man vomited water and drew it in again. The hard lumps of water no longer hurt. There was a kind of truce, observation of the body. There was no face but there was a snarl.

A second later, 'his distant body stilled itself and relaxed'. This is the moment of Pincher's death: 'the real jaw was contorted ... the mouth slopped full'; yet 'there was no face but there was a snarl'. The disparity between reality and moral figure, and the resemblance, are exposed in two sentences. The novel is static: it exists out of time, where a lifetime can be expressed in a moment, the moment of death. Both kinds of rhetoric are ways of expressing a stasis. On the one hand Golding sets up his obsessional rhythms of sensation so that we are caught and held in an overwhelming now (this is what it is like to drown). On the other, the now reveals just as starkly and statically the eternal figure of the man (a mask of Greed, snarling). There remains only the question of the connection between the present and the past, the face and the snarl: but that is what the novel is going to be about. What is absolutely and necessarily missing is the future.

Where then does the dynamism of the novel come from, our immediate sense that there is a future as we read, that the situation can change? It comes from what can now be seen to be the novel's most cardinal fact: it can only exist if its protagonist is the kind of man who is totally incapable of accepting his own extinction and who must refuse to die, to the point where the greatest conceivable leap of the novelist's imagination will fail to follow him into the unknown. That is why the protagonist had to be, not Everyman, but a particular kind of man pursued to the limit of his figure: the Christ-bearer become Pincher.

What will a Pincher do at the moment of death? – the moment when there is either no time or eternity? He *invents* a world in which the ego he will not relinquish can continue to exist. And it is his invention of a future that gives the novel its dynamism and its meaning. This is where we shall find the energy of the fiction and its conflict; yet increasingly we are also made aware that it is all illusory, that we exist in a moment blown up like a bubble to the point at which it will and must burst ... A 'present' that overwhelms the senses, a 'past' so remote that it is like 'a show of trailers of old films', both of them determined – the novel is the record of the unique moment when these two are precariously brought together through a wholly invented 'reality'. It is this invention which gives the novel both its subject and its form. Neither 'a real man on a real rock' nor 'a morality play' are the 'real world' of the novel ... it has no real world outside the moment of death on which it begins and ends. But we have to learn to see that moment for what it is. The novel is like one of those tapestries that show different pictures when one stands on one side of the room or the other; but we only look from the right angle when we can see a third perspective coming magically into focus, containing and explaining the others.

II

In the split second of death, Pincher Martin conceives an image which gives him a world of consciousness into which he can try desperately to escape.

The jam jar was standing on a table, brightly lit from O.P. It might have been a huge jar in the centre of a stage or a small one almost touching the face, but it was interesting because one could see into a little world there which was quite separate but which one could control. The jar was nearly full of clear water and a tiny glass figure floated upright in it. The top of the jar was covered with a thin membrane – white rubber. He watched the jar without moving or thinking while his distant body stilled itself and relaxed. The pleasure of the jar lay in the fact that the little glass figure was so delicately balanced between opposing forces. Lay a finger on the membrane and you would compress the air below it which in turn would press more strongly on the water. Then the water would force itself farther up the little tube in the figure, and it would begin to sink. By varying the pressure on the membrane you could do anything you liked with the glass figure which was wholly in your power. You could mutter, – sink now! And down it would go, down, down; you could steady it and relent. You could let it struggle towards the surface, give it almost a bit of air then send it steadily, slowly, remorselessly down and down.

The delicate balance of the glass figure related itself to his body. In a moment of wordless realization he saw himself touching the surface of the sea with just such a dangerous stability, poised between floating and going down. The snarl thought words to itself. They were not articulate, but they were there in a luminous way as a realization.

Of course. My lifebelt . . . Suddenly he knew who he was and where he was. He was lying suspended in the water like the glass figure; he was not struggling but limp. A swell was washing regularly over his head.

And so the body of the sailor lifts its head, pulls off its seaboots, inflates its life-belt, and 'lives'. Refusing to accept extinction he plays God to himself, raising the pressure on his own rubber membrane so that the figure of Pincher Martin rises to the surface of a world he himself creates. But if the novel wryly illustrates Nat's lecture-topic, 'the sort of heaven we invent for ourselves after death, if we aren't ready for the real one'; the essence of the experience is the knowledge that existence is only possible by a kind of temporary permission, a rope paid out, an inscrutable game going on below the surface. The jar and the glass figure, the little world 'quite separate, but which one could control', in fact only give the appearance of control. The operator thinks in his Pincherish way that he is the power-wielder exercising his will. But 'the pleasure of the jar lay in the fact that the little glass figure was so delicately balanced between opposing forces'; and these are not under the finger's control, though they may allow it to operate while they remain constant. There are physical forces like water and the body, but there is a controlling factor above all: the pressure of the real heavens outside the little world of the jar, of God if He exists, or of the blank immensity of empty space if He does not.

Consequently when one re-reads the book with its last sentence still in one's ear – 'He didn't even have time to kick off his seaboots' – the experience of the first reading is radically altered. The world which one had hailed for its dense and detailed 'reality', now reveals for page after page the terrifying strain of maintaining it, indeed, of making it up. What the experience *is* is that of surface tension, of inflating the bubble with infinite care and precision because it has to keep out absolute nothingness; or of teetering along a tightrope over an infinite chasm, never knowing, not only when one's own foot might slip, but when some cosmic hand might decide to give the rope a sudden twitch. And the mind must never allow itself consciously to know what it is doing; or the whole of existence will be annihilated. Pincher must invent his whole world by a kind of deliberate dreaming which must always obey every law of being awake so that he never finds out it is a dream. And there is a wry game going on all the time which can never be admitted either; there is a secret Antagonist.

> Now his wars on God begin,
> At stroke of midnight God shall win.

God, or utter nothingness.

There plays across the narrative chapters, in fact, another structure altogether: a kind of parody of the Divine Week of Creation, but ending at the beginning of the Seventh Day when the work of human hands must be set aside.

On the first Day the Will creates sea and sky around itself, creates day and night, creates the rock. A convulsion of will moves the body into buoyancy, but the move leaves him 'no better off than I was' because the Antagonist counters with the necessity, if the dream is not to be revealed as dream, of experiencing numbing cold, terrible depth of water, absolute blackness, of facing (though alive) an 'Eternity, inseparable from pain'. He creates dawn, but pictures in his mind like the one of a jam jar try to tell him the truth and get between him and the urgency of his movement towards the dim light – yet the will sees them in a way that robs them of significance. All the same the cold seeps in, and the hopelessness. But the will summons him to another effort. 'Think. My last chance. Think what can be done' – and the imagination summons up a shape. A ship? No, too complicated; a not-ship, a rock, that in its own way is no less terrible than the water, but promises a kind of safety.

As he lies slumped in exhaustion on the pebbles, there is still danger. The pictures in the mind and the pebbles under the face are perilously interchangeable, as though one were as real, or as unreal, as the other. The mind still treacherously threatens to give the game away by remembering sailor and jam jar. As the will recovers its sense of identity the abyss can always open without notice, at any moment. To think of the rock as 'one tooth set in the ancient jaw of a sunken world, projecting through the inconceivable vastness of the whole ocean' can, for a reason still obscure, produce a 'deep and generalized terror (which) set him clawing at the rock with his blunt fingers ... "Think, you bloody fool, think."' Hastily he 'remembers' a captain pointing to a rock on a chart whose real name cannot, had better not, be remembered. (Rockall is too near a miss to an obscenity whose meaning would be disastrous.)

He is still 'no better off than I was', though 'the consciousness was moving and poking about among the pictures and revelations ... like an animal ceaselessly examining its cage', and finding some reassurance in the knowledge of its own intelligence. But, suddenly, the Adversary moves again. If this is a real sea and rock there must be tides – the cleft cannot be safety – it must be a sea-trap. He must climb. But though he imagines an initial foothold, an opening shaped like an ashtray, suspiciously facile, there is something in the mind which knows the real nature of the imagined surface and knows that it would be too smooth, like ivory. So the panicking consciousness traps itself, stuck, 'Like a dead man'. The snarl returns. But the mind makes another desperate convulsion: *not* like a dead man, 'Like a limpet' – and in a panic-shot blind leap of imagination the body fantastically climbs through the funnel, on top of the rock, by using two limpets like mountaineering wedges. The Adversary has won the first round on points. The Will has survived, the thing was not absolutely impossible, but the bounds of credibility have had to be stretched to breaking-point.

Immediately, in near collapse, the Will makes what will turn out to be a serious error. There is a painful consciousness trying to get in through the 'eye', a needle continually probing the brain through the visual imagination. The Will tries to explain it, and so get rid of it. Remembering real rocks, and knowing at the back of the mind that the nature of this 'rock' requires the presence of whitish matter, the Will brilliantly invents guano, and then goes on triumphantly to explain the eye-pain as the effect of a solution of guano and water smeared across the eye when the body fell across the trench. But success is only partial: salt water will not wash the pain out. 'The idea that he must ignore pain came and sat in the centre of his darkness where he could not avoid it.' Hopelessness returns:

The chill and the exhaustion spoke to him clearly. Give up, they said, lie still. Give up the thought of return, the thought of living. Break up, leave go ... An hour on this rock is a lifetime. What have you to lose? There is nothing here but torture ...
  His body began to crawl again ... There was at the centre of all the pictures and pains and voices a fact like a bar of steel, a thing – that which was so nakedly the centre of everything that it could not even examine itself. In the darkness of the skull, it existed, a darker dark, self-existent and indestructible.
  'Shelter. Must have shelter.'

So the first 'Day' ends with the body crawling into a crevice like a lobster. In the 'Night' the consciousness that wishes to rest, but cannot, edges around the realization of his predicament. There is a kind of being in which he floats, in the dark side of a kind of globe, 'like a waterlogged body':

He knew as an axiom of existence that he must be content with the smallest of all small mercies as he floated there ... If he could hit some particular mode of inactive being, some subtlety of interior balance, he might be allowed ... to float, still and painless in the centre of the globe.

But always the needle jabs the eye, forcing him to go on making the physical situation real and justifying its reality. So a new Day of creation must begin.
  He imagines a gull clucking to wake him; but the second Day (pp. 56–72) starts with what will turn out to be another serious mistake. He 'sees' the gulls wrong, not as smooth-outlined birds but as 'flying reptiles' – but mistakes don't matter unless they are realized. The work of the Second Day is the food and water he needs to 'live'; but with horrible irony the 'rules' set limits within which he has to operate, and the cry of 'Bloody Hell' voices his horror at the 'oval brown foot' of the limpet and the 'blobs of red jelly'. What he is inventing, *pace* Nathaniel, is no Heaven. His invention of a water-supply is also an image of the perilous nature of his situation: the tasteless necessity only just held in by the furry silt mirrors his own predicament, 'held back so delicately that the merest touch would set his life irrevocably flowing – He backed away with staring eyes and breath that came quick. "Forget it!" '

But he cannot. The imagination also shows a submerged but perceptible hint of what the true reality of tiny cavity and red slimy rim might be; as does the language which describes the sea, the 'constant gurgling and sucking that ranged from a stony smack to a ruminative swallow. There were sounds that seemed every moment to be on the point of articulation but lapsed into a liquid slapping like appetite.' This also applies to a strangeness about the other great creation of the Second Day, the man-shape of the dwarf. On one of the jagged rocks that he has lugged from its place and manhandled across the trenches there is an unexplained trace of blood. The mind stirs treacherously again beneath the carefully maintained surface, always hinting at what it dare not express: exactly what the 'rock' is, and how he came to imagine *that* in his moment of need.

In the Night of the Second Day the Will, while ever more nearly admitting its predicament, nevertheless asserts itself more strongly than ever, in spite of everything. He remembers, dangerously, Nathaniel's words. 'You could say that I know it is important for you personally to understand about heaven – about dying – because in only a few years –' On the rock, as in the room at Oxford, stinging pain whips into the 'globe' as the consciousness anticipates the words that must not be spoken – 'you will be dead'. The Will immediately 'wakes' itself from this dangerous corner, which nevertheless can safely be thought of as a 'dream' of the past. The response however is intense: 'I'm damned if I'll die!' We can see clearly enough that it isn't a case of inventing one's own 'heaven' because one isn't ready for the real one. Pincher asserts himself *in spite of* 'everything'. There is the shout, a burst of jeering laughter, a 'hosing gesture' of urination at the horizon.

The morning of the Third Day (pp. 72–96) has begun. This is the zenith of Pincher's creative achievement: he makes his body real to himself, battered, but all the more convincing; he imagines in reassuring detail what there is in his pockets; above all, he remembers his identity disc and summons its objective statements before his eyes:

'Christopher Hadley Martin. Martin. Chris. I am what I always was!'
    All at once it seemed to him that he came out of his curious isolation inside the globe of his head and was extended normally through his limbs. He lived again on the surface of his eyes, he was out in the air ... The

solid rock was coherent as an object, with layered guano, with fresh water and shell-fish. It was a position in a finite sea at the intersection of two lines, there were real ships passing under the horizon.

He assures the quiet sea that with health and education and intelligence he will win; but he knows that he is 'really' talking to himself. For him now, as for Robinson Crusoe, the island has become an 'estate', which can be 'inspected not only with eyes but with understanding'. It has a rational geological history which can incorporate without strain the image of how 'the tooth bursts out of the fleshy jaw'. Even when this becomes a mental picture of the line of rocks as like teeth gradually being worn away, there is irritation rather than fright, for the suggestiveness is buried in millennia of geological time. 'The process is so slow, it has no relevance to –'

But the sentence never gets finished, for the Antagonist moves again; the words spoken aloud seem to fall dead at the lips. For the situation which the wearing process is too slow to be relevant to is dependent on the pressure of an atmosphere; and if the rock is to be a real one, its isolation in enormous space without resonance must act thus on the human voice. Involuntarily he cries out 'My God!', clutches the Dwarf in his horror – and its head falls off. The moment that there is no faith in the ability of the human head to control reality, manshape is broken; but in a fury of willed activity he builds the Dwarf up again, bigger than before. 'Out of this nettle danger –' he has managed to pluck this flower safety, for the moment.

He preaches a sermon to himself, a practical one like Ralph's, about a rescue, about survival, about what must be done to keep the body going and the thread of life unbroken in spite of sickness and suffering – but there is more obviously now a Spectre to be feared for him as well as Ralph. He starts to admit that he has already had 'hallucinations'; and though he cannot carry the admission through, he warns himself against insanity stealing up and taking him by surprise. For he has been shaken, in broad 'daylight', and his consciousness cannot settle its grip. He has stopped living on the surface of his eyes, and finds himself seeing through a window with three lights – eye, nose, eye – and a window-box of moustache; but the vision sometimes suddenly reverses itself so that 'reality' is outside him looking in: 'The window was surrounded by

inscrutable darkness which extended throughout his body.' He tries
to persuade himself that this 'is the ordinary experience of living'.
He insists in imposing himself on the rock, refusing to adapt himself
to its ways, netting it down and taming it with names. But the peak
of achievement is past, and as the Third Day ends in Night the
tiring brain drops its guard once more.

This rock.
   'I shall call those three rocks out there the Teeth.'
   All at once he was gripping the lifebelt with both hands and tensing his
muscles to defeat the deep shudders that were sweeping through him.
   'No! Not the Teeth!'
   The teeth were here, inside his mouth. He felt them with his tongue, the
double barrier of bone, each known and individual except the gaps – and
there they persisted as a memory if one troubled to think. But to lie on a
row of teeth in the middle of the sea –
   He began to think desperately about sleep.

But he is afraid to sleep, afraid to let 'the carefully hoarded and
enjoyed personality, our only treasure and at the same time our
only defence ... die into the ultimate truth of things, the black
lightning that splits and destroys all, the positive, unquestionable
nothingness'.
   In extremity the material and the immaterial become confused
again. A series of sharply distinct snapshot memories, whose
meaning remains obscure because the mind will not explore them,
is succeeded by one terribly focused because it speaks of the
present as well as the past and is horribly meaningful:

This was a bright patch, sometimes like a figure eight lying on its side and
sometimes a circle. The circle was filled with blue sea where gulls were
wheeling and settling and loving to eat and fight. He felt the swing of the
ship under him, sensed the bleak stillness and silence that settled on the
bridge as the destroyer slid by the thing floating in the water – a thing,
humble and abused and still, among the fighting beaks, an instrument of
pleasure.
   He struggled out into the sun, stood up and cried flatly in the great air.
'I am awake!'

With a convulsion of his whole being, he creates a new Day.
   The Fourth Day (pp. 96–122), the 'thinking day' he had
promised himself, turns out to be one in which his imagination
overtaxes itself. Existence becomes purposeful with the brilliant

idea of supplementing the Dwarf's assertion to the sea with the line of seaweed asserting himself to the air. He is able to commit himself to the water again to gather weed, and he works hard – so hard that his concentrating mind makes another mistake about a lobster, which goes completely unnoticed, but will turn out to be disastrous. And what he has conceived is too huge to be done in reality; half of his mind is assailing him with hopelessness. The other half tries to distract him – there's a plop in the sea, is it a fish? – but not for long. He oscillates between assertion and despair:

I may never get away from this rock at all.
   Speech is identity.
   'You are all a machine. I know you, wetness, hardness, movement. You have no mercy but you have no intelligence. I can outwit you. All I have to do is to endure. I breathe this air into my own furnace. I kill and eat. There is nothing to –'
   He paused for a moment and watched the gull drifting nearer; but not so near that the reptile under the white was visible.
   'There is nothing to fear.'

This has a dying fall. And after a day of empty waiting and endurance there is a night when the thoughts and pictures always contain an obscure threat, and the 'fires' in his aching body become 'a luminous landscape ... a universe, and he oscillated between moments of hanging in space observing them, and of being extended to every excruciating corner'. What he has constructed is hell.

   This time he does not 'wake', which is itself significant. He is forced to admit that he has never been asleep at all. On the Fifth Day (pp. 122–67) day and night lose their maintained distinction, time begins to have its stop, and the laboriously constructed world begins to lose conviction. The High Street looks like 'a picture. He shut his eyes and then opened them again but the rock and the sea seemed no more real.' Looking into a crack in the rock no wider than an eighth of an inch he looks into 'a terrible darkness'. His mind begins 'envisaging the whole rock as a thing in the water ... familiar ... remembered ... imagined as a shape one's fingers can feel in the air –'. Only another loud plop from the warning side of his mind manages to turn the dangerously freewheeling consciousness aside. He is becoming aware 'outside' of more and more weight, a 'ponderous squeezing. Agoraphobia or anyway the opposite of claustrophobia. A pressure' – the vast pressure of the heavens on the glass sailor. 'Inside', the mind is becoming more and more difficult to control. ' "I must have a beard pretty well. Bristles anyway. Strange that bristles go on growing even when the rest of you is –" He went quickly to Prospect Cliff and got a load of weed.' He plans the Claudian aqueduct and begins to work on it, 'imposing purpose on the senseless rock', but: 'There is something venomous about the hardness of this rock. It is harder than rock should be. And – familiar.' In the very act of self-congratulation there lurks the abyss, ever nearer: 'Anyway I'll hand it to you Chris. I don't think many people would –' Would what? Would have been able to keep it up this long? The confident talk is replaced by agonized cries ... 'Christopher' ... 'Oh, my God'. Two arms reach out to grab an identity vanishing before his eyes in a gesture that pre-figures the last that Pincher will ever make.

The Will goes on asserting but it is clearly losing its grip. He mistakes his hand for a lobster, and this tells us something about the colour of the one he saw before, as well as pointing to the state of his consciousness now. He cries out against his lessening sense of identity now that there are no other people to define him for himself in their love or hate. The pools on the rock will not reflect a definite image of his face because he cannot remember it accurately enough. And fantasy begins to proclaim itself as such: a seal suddenly becomes capable of being ridden to the Hebrides before the imagination can stop itself. It is like the waking nightmares of childhood, when the mind is uncontrollable:

'... those nights when I was a kid, lying awake thinking the darkness would go on for ever. And I couldn't go back to sleep because of the dream of the whatever it was in the cellar coming out of the corner. I'd lie in the hot, rumpled bed, hot burning hot, trying to shut myself away and know that there were three eternities before the dawn ... And I'd think of anything because if I didn't go on thinking I'd remember whatever it was in the cellar down there, and my mind would go walking away from my body and go down three stories defenceless, down the dark stairs past the tall, haunted clock, through the whining door, down the terrible steps to where the coffin ends were crushed in the walls of the cellar* – and I'd be held helpless on the stone floor, trying to run back, run away, climb up –'

* This has a source in Golding's childhood. See 'The Ladder and the Tree', *The Hot Gates*, pp. 166–7, for the cellar and the graveyard, and the whole essay for a gloss on

The child's horror is the man's; it exactly expresses (while veiling itself, if only just, as 'memory') the way he is being forced to confront what is there in the inmost darkness of his mind. He may try to assert that he and the child have nothing in common, but there is something crushing him, something terrible just ahead, a part of the play he doesn't know about.

Cleverly, he seeks a new sanctuary in delirium; for in fever one can let go for a while and still come out again. So he lapses into a state which can 'realize' without committing itself to acceptance. In delirium all the faces from his past are stone, hung in rows in a corridor leading away from the 'theatre' of daily life. At the far end is the

other room, to be avoided, because there the gods sat behind their terrible knees and feet of black stone, but here the stone faces wept and had wept. Their stone cheeks were furrowed, they were blurred and only recognizable by some indefinite mode of identity. Their tears made a pool on the stone floor so that his feet were burned to the ankles. He scrabbled to climb up the wall and the scalding stuff welled up his ankles to his calves, his knees. He was struggling, half-swimming, half-climbing. The wall was turning over, curving like the wall of a tunnel in the underground. The tears were no longer running down the stone to join the burning sea. They were falling freely, dropping on him. One came, a dot, a pearl, a ball, a globe, that moved on him, spread. He began to scream. He was inside the ball of water that was burning him to the bone and past. It consumed him utterly. He was dissolved and spread throughout the tear an extension of sheer, disembodied pain.

He burst the surface and grabbed at a stone wall. There was hardly any light but he knew better than to waste time because of what was coming. There were projections in the wall of the tunnel so that though it was more nearly a well than a tunnel he could still climb. He laid hold, pulled himself up, projection after projection. The light was bright enough to show him the projections. They were faces, like the ones in the endless corridor. They were not weeping but they were trodden. They appeared to be made of some chalky material for when he put his weight on them they would break away so that only by constant movement upward was he able to keep up at all. He could hear his voice shouting in the well.

'I am! I am! I am!'

---

the 'two worlds without a bridge' of *Free Fall*. The mysterious experience in *Free Fall*, p. 154, is also apparently a childhood memory.

The talking voice, drooling away with its 'explanation' that this is all Freudian stuff, tunnels and wells and water, just sexual and familiar, known, cannot fool him, let alone us. This, and the insight of the cellar, are the 'truest' things to have happened since the opening pages, more essential than the manufactured present, or the snapshotted past which now merely glosses the insights which bring it into focus.

Now the 'pressure of the sky and air was right inside his head. A thought was forming like a piece of sculpture behind the eyes but in front of the unexamined centre ... But he knew the thought was an enemy and so although he saw it he did not consent or allow it to become attached to him in realization.' What he sees through his 'window' has become only a pattern of colour, not exterior, but 'like a lighted picture on the wall', 'the only visible thing in a dark room'. Inexorably, the 'thought' rises like a Kraken from the depths:

'There is a pattern emerging. I do not know what the pattern is but even my dim guess at it makes my reason falter.'

The lower half of his face moved round the mouth till the teeth were bare.

'Weapons. I have things that I can use.'

Intelligence. Will like a last ditch. Will like a monolith. Survival ...

Almost for the last time the snarl rallies: 'Why drag in good and evil when the serpent lies coiled in my own body?' The Will makes a last effort to localize the poison that threatens its existence in a place where it can be purged. The administration of the enema curiously, but necessarily, mingles the heroic, the pathetic and the comic-grotesque. For a moment it seems to work. He has the sense that life has begun anew. Until, inevitably, real disaster strikes through apparent triumph.

On a real island, rocks seem to move when the tide is running strongly. The Antagonist feints, but Pincher is not fooled. He knows it is an optical illusion. But he is shaken – and as he looks sharply down at his feet to see that the rock is steady, the gesture brings back what he had seen the last time he made it, gathering weed. Now the appalled mind takes in what it 'saw' then: ' "Whoever saw a lobster like that swimming in the sea? A red lobster?" ' As we ought to have deduced from the mistake about his hands, he had forgotten that lobsters are only red when they are cooked. When he 'saw' the lobster, 'as if his eye had created it ... among the weed, different in dragon shape, different in colour', he over-reached himself. Now the irony of the language comes home. In one shattering second, truth appears: 'Something was taken away. For an instant he felt himself falling; and then there came a gap of darkness in which there was no one.' The five-day-creation vanishes. Time stops. The abyss opens:

Something was coming up to the surface. It was uncertain of its identity because it had forgotten its name. It was disorganized in pieces. It struggled to get these pieces together because then it would know what it was. There was a rhythmical noise and disconnection. The pieces came shakily together ... There was a separation between now, whenever now was, and the instant of terror. The separation enabled him to forget what had caused that terror. The darkness of separation was deeper than that of sleep. It was deeper than any living darkness because time had stopped or come to an end. It was a gap of not-being, a well opening out of the world and now the effort of mere being was so exhausting that he could only lie sideways and live.

Presently he thought.

'Then I was dead. That was death. I have been frightened to death. Now the pieces of me have come together and I am just alive.'

It is only possible for Pincher to exist at all because the eye does play tricks in real life, and the Will can seize on one optical illusion it has just experienced, as a subconscious theory to explain another, provided it can forget what happened. But existence is utterly precarious now, depending on total lapse of memory and bound to fail. The 'reality' of the rock cannot be recaptured: 'This side of the gap is different from the other. It's like when you have finished a lights rehearsal and they cut. Then where there was bright, solid scenery is now only painted stuff, grey under the pilot light. It's like chess. You've got an exultant attack moving but overlooked a check and now the game is a fight. And you're tied down.'

Though there is a Sixth Day, it is no longer under Pincher's control. Lightning flickers, and 'some deep seat of rationality' in him sees, indeed creates for the last time, the promised rain from the lambent threat. Yet, as it pours torrentially, flooding him out of his crevice, we may remember another rain that fell and destroyed a false world, and we can certainly see that Pincher neither controls it, nor does it bring him the expected satisfaction. He tries to rebuild his precarious sanity, but while his mouth lectures uneasily about the uncertain borders between sanity and mania or neurosis, the 'centre [. . .] was moving and flinching from isolated outcrops of knowledge. It averted attention from one only to discover another.' It cannot last. Only too soon, on this Rock which is also the Cellar to which all the paths of his life have led, and where the Spectre he most feared must be faced, knowledge cannot be avoided any longer. Not only has he seen a red lobster which might be an optical illusion; he has also forgotten that guano is insoluble. To be sane is to be forced to admit what he has done; what cannot be explained away once it has been explained:

His tongue felt along the barrier of his teeth – round to the side where the big ones were and the gap . . . His tongue was remembering. It pried into the gap between the teeth and re-created the old, aching shape. It touched the rough edge of the cliff, traced the slope down, trench after aching trench, down towards the smooth surface where the Red Lion was, just above the gum – understood what was so hauntingly familiar and painful about an isolated and decaying rock in the middle of the sea.

One could draw Pincher's 'rock' only too easily now – that decaying and creviced molar set between the canine of Safety Rock before the Gap he came through, and the three other eroding grinders of Oxford Circus, Piccadilly, and Leicester Square. This is the foundation on which he has built his unreal heaven, his temporary hell, his escape from death.

'Now there was nothing to do but protect normality.' Knowing what he does, he will still not accept its implications. He goes on performing meaningless actions like eating, while his voice quacks away: 'I was always two things, mind and body. Nothing has altered. Only I did not realize it before so clearly.' Meanwhile 'the centre thought of the next move . . . The will could resist.' But the Spectres from the Cellar cannot be locked away now. In one moment of terror he sees in the Dwarf the Old Woman who lived in the darkest corner of childhood's cellar. He flinches away: 'That is not the next move.' But the moves are no longer in his hands. A piece of rock in the shape of a book has fallen from one of the trenches, engraved, not like that other Tablet of stone, with words 'which would have killed him immediately', but with a pattern that the eye can follow, a signature repeated, in the recess from which the stone has split, by the Engraver:

It was like a tree upside down and growing down from the old edge where the leaves were weathered by wind and rain. The trunk was a deep, perpendicular groove with flaky edges. Lower down, the trunk divided into three branches and these again into a complication of twigs like the ramifications of bookworm. The trunk and the branches and the twigs were terrible black. Round the twigs was an apple blossom of grey and silver stain. As he watched, drops of water dulled the stain and lay in the branches like tasteless fruit.

　His mouth quacked.
　'Lightning!'
But the dark centre was shrunk and dreadful and knowing. The knowing was so dreadful that the centre made the mouth work deliberately.
　'Black lightning.'

The formulation is Nat's, in that conversation which has kept making its way into Pincher's mind: 'Take us as we are now and heaven would be sheer negation. Without form and void. You see? a sort of black lightning destroying everything that we call life.' On this view, because we are wholly egotistic, the Heaven that we could reach if we were only prepared to die to ourselves must seem totally destructive of all we hold most precious. What the saint knows as perfect love, compassion, peace, is a black destroyer to the sinner. The Creator who formed him with the choice of enduring death for heaven, and the Love which watched over him, must appear as the spectres of the Executioner and the Executioner's Wife whom the child pictured in the cellar under the graveyard. So, having seen and flinched from the Old Woman, Pincher recognizes the signature of her Husband. The 'tree' is the appletree of Eden as seen upside down through evil eyes: a tree terribly black, its blossom bleached of colour to grey and silver, the fruit of the knowledge and love of God dull, watery, tasteless, the whole a signpost to destruction.

　One last escape remains to be tried: 'There was still a part that could be played – there was the Bedlamite, Poor Tom, protected from knowledge of the sign of the black lightning.' Where sanity is hopeless, madness may be a hiding-place. So the brain begins to spiral as he beseeches the Old Woman-Helen, the Producer's Wife, for comfort and reassurance. Confusing past and present he relives the child's waking nightmare as he is compelled to the cellar: that ordinary coal-cellar transfigured into the 'death door' through which one meets 'the master'. But he keeps insisting that he must be mad, must have been mad to see the red lobster, the soluble guano, the flying lizards; or the 'kindling from coffins' and the axe and block 'not worn for firewood but by executions'.

'Seals aren't inimical and a madman wouldn't sleep properly. He would feel the rock was too hard, too real; he would superimpose a reality especially if he had too much imagination. He would be capable of seeing the engraving as a split into the whole nature of things – wouldn't he?'
And then fettered in the darkness by the feet, trying to lift one and finding a glue, finding a weakness where there should be strength now needed because by nature there was nothing to do but scream and try to escape. Darkness in the corner doubly dark, thing looming, feet tied, near, an unknown looming, an opening darkness, the heart and being of all imaginable terror. Pattern repeated from the beginning of time, approach of the unknown thing, a dark centre that turned its back on the thing that created it and struggled to escape.
'Wouldn't he? Say he would!'

Perhaps one could know that one's nightmare is an insanity, as the child knows, and such an 'explanation' behind the horror might reassure even Poor Tom? But no:

There is no centre of sanity in madness. Nothing like this 'I' sitting in here, staving off the time that must come. The last repeat of the pattern. Then the black lightning.
The centre cried out.
'I'm so alone! Christ! I'm so alone!'

The mind cannot but recognize what it is and why it is as it is. Finally the whole flashback world resolves itself into two pictured scenes hung side by side. There is, once more, that scene with Nat which now reveals how much he loved him, and how much the goodness meant, that came to comfort him in the moment of blackness and exclusion that prefigured this one. Beside it is the scene which tells how he tried to murder that love and goodness. The 'centre' experiences again all the grief: 'Because of what I did I am an outsider and alone ... Now there is no hope. There is nothing ... If I could only be part of something ...' But it also experiences the rage at the explosion which was an opportunity to become part of God by the death of Pincher – the rage of the eater eaten. Nothing is changed. He *will* not die.

So the madness increases in the mouth while the centre goes on trying to pretend in the physical rock. The mouth shouts high in self-pity, rage or defiance, trying to drown the 'other noise' behind the storm; playing part after part – Prometheus defying the Thunderer, the drummer-boy whose Emperor is taken, the adulterer moving into the love-nest and threatening to leave it. Explanation follows explanation – running together fact and fantasy – trying to escape the noise of the spade against the box:

'Mad,' said the mouth, 'raving mad. I can account for everything, lobsters, maggots, hardness, brilliant reality, the laws of nature, film-trailers, snapshots of sight and sound, flying lizards, enmity – how should a man not be mad?'

'Mouth' and 'centre' become one, shouting against the storm and the lightning: 'You bloody great bully!'

The body acts its part of naked madman. It hunts the Old Woman/Nat/Mary/Actress across the rock and slashes her to pieces with its knife for being the spectre which has been at his back, calling his identity in question, all his life. But he is not mad: 'he and his voice were one. They knew that the blood was sea-water and the cold, crumpling flesh that was ripped and torn nothing but oilskin.'

Finally there appears, as the terrified voice had predicted, what is either the Truth itself, or Madness indeed; either the last figment of Pincher's crazy imagination, or that great Mind of which Pincher is only a projection, the producer of the whole drama. It is a figure exactly like Pincher Martin in every particular but one. 'On the sixth day he created God. Therefore I permit you to use nothing but my own vocabulary. In his own image created he Him.' But the figure is wearing seaboots. If it is 'Martin', it is a Martin who died and was united with God. If it is not madness, it speaks with the voice of God insofar as Pincher can hear; and the 'seaboots, good and shiny and wet and solid ... made the rock behind them seem like cardboard, like a painted flat'. It is an opportunity for Pincher to face what he could be, the 'self' he has rejected, to choose again:

'Have you had enough, Christopher?' ...
'Enough of what?'
'Surviving. Hanging on.' ...
'I hadn't considered.'
'Consider now.' ...
'I won't. I can't.'
'What do you believe in?'
Down to the black boot, coal black, darkness of the cellar, but now down to a forced answer.
'The thread of my life.'
'At all costs.'
Repeat after me:
'At all costs.'
'So you survived.' ...
He snarled. 'I have a right to live if I can!'
'Where is that written?'
'Then nothing is written.'
'Consider.'
He raged on the cardboard rock before the immovable, black feet.
'I will not consider! I have created you and I can create my own heaven.'
'You have created it.'
He glanced sideways along the twitching water, down at his skeleton legs and knees, felt the rain and spray and the savage cold on his flesh.
He began to mutter.
'I prefer it. You gave me the power to choose and all my life you led me carefully to this suffering because my choice was my own. Oh yes! I understand the pattern. All my life, whatever I had done I should have found myself in the end on that same bridge, at that same time, giving that same order – the right order, the wrong order. Yet, suppose I climbed away from the cellar over the bodies of used and defeated people, broke them to make steps on the road away from you, why should you torture me? If I ate them, who gave me a mouth?'
'There is no answer in your vocabulary.'
He squatted back and glared up at the face. He shouted.
'I have considered. I prefer it, pain and all.'
'To what?'
He began to rage weakly and strike out at the boots.
'To the black lightning! Go back! Go back!'

He prefers madness on his rock to sanity, heaven, with loss of himself. He chooses to reject what he will not even bring himself to admit may be the Love of God. He insists on black lightning, so black lightning it is. He finally does go mad, riding the rock like a horse into the storm, holding out his identity disc, and shouting what is at last a recognition: 'I spit on your compassion!' As the spade thunder is heard, and the first tendrils of black lightning lie across the western sky, the 'centre' tries to prove its madness by destroying the water-supply it needs to 'live'. But, as the voice above the seaboots has said so quietly, even madness is only another crevice that will crumble.

In two brilliant pages, the whole physical universe whose 'reality' seemed so persuasive, is dismantled with equal conviction, chillingly:

There were branches of the black lightning over the sky, there were noises. One branch ran down into the sea, through the great waves, petered out. It remained there. The sea stopped moving, froze, became paper, painted paper that was torn by a black line. The rock was painted on the same paper. The whole of the painted sea was tilted but nothing ran downhill into the black crack which had opened in it. The crack was utter, was absolute, was three times real.

The 'lightning' is only the fissure of dark nothingness that opens up as the paper world is torn apart. There is no noise. Then there is no mouth.

Still the centre resisted. It made the lightning do its work according to the laws of this heaven. It perceived in some mode of sight without eyes that pieces of the sky between the branches of black lightning were replaced by pits of nothing. This made the fear of the centre, the rage of the centre vomit in a mode that required no mouth. It screamed into the pit of nothing voicelessly, wordlessly.
'I shit on your heaven!'

At any moment, if Nat is right, the black lightning can be converted into the everlasting arms of the real heaven, and the pit of nothing into the face of the Living God. But as sea and sky and Safety Rock vanish, the 'centre' that is still Pincher clutches the rock like the claws of a lobster:

The lines of absolute blackness felt forward into the rock and it was proved to be as insubstantial as the painted water. Pieces went and there was no more than an island of papery stuff round the claws and everywhere else there was the mode that the centre knew as nothing.
The rock between the claws was solid. It was square and there was an engraving on the surface. The black lines sank in, went through and joined.

The rock between the claws was gone.

There was nothing but the centre and the claws. They were huge and strong and inflamed to red. They closed on each other. They contracted. They were outlined like a night sign against the absolute nothingness and they gripped their whole strength into each other. The serrations of the claws broke. They were lambent and real and locked.

The lightning crept in. The centre was unaware of anything but the claws and the threat. It focused its awareness on the crumbled serrations and the blazing red. The lightning came forward. Some of the lines pointed to the centre, waiting for the moment when they could pierce it. Others lay against the claws, playing over them, prying for a weakness, wearing them away in a compassion that was timeless and without mercy.

In a sense the situation on page three of the novel has simply been revealed for what it then really was, as the six-days-long pretence that masked it is ripped away. As the seventh (God's day?) opens, the Divine Love that can only appear as merciless waits to take Martin to itself by destroying Pincher. Or, from the other point of view, black nothingness waits to engulf him utterly, finally.

III

There *are* different ways of looking.

The final chapter, as in Golding's first two novels, is itself a device to get the author and his readers outside the consciousness in which we have lived, and to make us take stock of it. So when the corpse-disposal officer arrives at the Hebridean island to remove what is left of Christopher Martin, the episode has on a first reading the shock-value of the ending of *Lord of the Flies*. Indeed, where that invited us to judge our experience by taking in how much our consciousness had been changed, this challenges us with the disclosure that a whole relatively new experience and consciousness still lie ahead if we will read the book again. But when we understand what the full experience is, the significant resemblance is to the end of *The Inheritors*: the unsettling of any moral and emotional certainties the tale may have seemed to encourage.

The tone of the scene is delicately set. In the wintry sunset there is a strange, sad beauty – black drifter, leaden water, 'valley of red and rose and black', as the last of the sun lies across the sea in the drifter's path. Silence and soft voices contrast strongly with the overheated, frenzied consciousness we have been living in. But, if the sadness of death comes across for the first time in the novel, it does so quite without sentimentality; for the horror is present too, in the alliance of the body with lineweed and flotsam, the drinking that alone makes Davidson able to face his job, the paraffin poured for an obvious reason over the corrupting flesh, the effect of the body on Campbell's dreams. There has been an inevitable tendency in the novel to make death dramatic. Now the sadness, the gruesome pathos of dereliction are gently but firmly established.

Within this setting the questions, the large questions, seem right and even inevitable. Campbell has been looking at the lean-to while the naval man inspects the body inside. The broken-down building gives him a language to ask in:

Broken, defiled. Returning to the earth, the rafters rotted, the roof fallen in – a wreck. Would you believe that anything ever lived there? ...

The harvest. The sad harvest. You know nothing of my – shall I say – official beliefs, Mr Davidson; but living for all these days next to that poor derelict – Mr Davidson. Would you say that there was any – surviving? Or is that all? Like the lean-to?

The new 'distance' is new also for Golding, pushing aside the manuscript in which he has been living all this time; and whatever we think his official views may be, there can be no doubt that his imaginative voyage in the novel has not made him assertive. The tentative, gently posed question has a proper tact.

Davidson cannot understand, and converts it into a simpler question of whether the dead man had time to suffer. But even this can be filled with significance by Campbell's quiet voice. For the greatest 'suffering' might not be physical at all; it might lie precisely in there being no Time. It might be just to go down like the sun 'seemingly for ever', leaving 'nothing for a reminder but clouds like smoke' – or an identity disc in a stranger's pocket that no longer refers to anybody. It might be ...

The emphasis is on suffering, wonder, mystery. One official view of Golding's we do know about is the belief that novels should try to tell the truth. But how to tell the truth about death? No matter what any of us believes officially about surviving, in our minds there obstinately lurks the opposite spectre. Only saints (religious or pagan) and simpletons escape the sense that the 'other side' might just be right after all. The pressure that allows the finger to work on the jar's membrane could be nothing but empty space. The seabooted figure, the force against which Pincher shouts defiance, could be figments of his mad imagination. The terrible final experience may be terrible precisely because it is a hopeless battle against Nothing and Nobody.

Again, there is real imaginative ambivalence about our attitude to the 'poor derelict'. The treatment of his past makes us see the struggle on the rock as emblematic of a life of ferocious self-concern, the ravening ego refusing the selfless act of dying. But his 'present' cannot escape, as an imaginative experience, a sense of the heroic. The 'selfless act of dying' is felt to be only a submission to an overwhelmingly greater power, and this, whether God or Void, is felt to be destructive. If, in Nat's terms, the black lightning destroys 'everything we call life', everything may well seem too high a price, and to shout 'You bloody great bully' or 'I shit on your heaven' can seem either heroic or a damnable folly. Where 'heaven', 'love', 'mercy' are in fact absent (necessarily of course, for the character), the effect of the experience may be to push a deliberately violent contradiction like 'a compassion that was ... without mercy' beyond the frontiers of imaginative realization. And this is all deliberately done. There are a large number of allusions that are both ironic and heroic. One imaginative eye sees Paradise Lost, the other sees a human hero fighting destruction and terror. It may be that the 'religious' view prevails, but the other has real imaginative resonance. An atheist setting out to rewrite the book would only have to change the lighting, the myth itself would still hold true. And at the end, deliberately pointing up the uncertainty, Golding is content to give a phrase like 'the harvest' a summarizing prominence, the novelist's metaphors fading into the ambivalence and euphemism of ordinary speech. Answers give way to questions.

Yet again, there are different ways of looking at the nature of the fiction. On one view it is the most myth-like of all Golding's fictions. If myth selects from multitudinous complexity an archetypal situation, there could be nothing more rigidly exclusive than the man on the rock, and nothing more archetypal than the vision which insists that even that might be stripped away to leave man facing God or Void, nakedly. It would be impossible to imagine anything more universal, timeless, basic ... the ultimate situation, the final recognition. Seen in this way it is tremendous – and a complete dead end. What development could there possibly be beyond this point? On the other hand, though we have seen that *Pincher Martin* denies assumptions about 'character' and 'relationships' which we may tend to think of as central and axiomatic for the novel, we have only to compare it with Golding's previous novels to make an opposite point. For there is here, demonstrably, the beginning of *some* new kind of concern with character. This is the first Golding novel to bear for its title the name of an individual, the first to be told from a point of view within an individual consciousness, the first to have an adult, contemporary protagonist, drawn at length, and concerned (at whatever level) with sexual and social relationships in a modern world. The choice of point of view, moreover, has significant implications for style. Here for the first time the protagonist creates the fictional world. In the previous myths, which were purely archetypal, Golding used the full range of the concrete poetic style which is so uniquely his. (There were limitations in *The Inheritors*, but they tended if anything to maximize the effect of what Golding does best.) But in *Pincher Martin* the style must express an imperfect human being with an imperfect vision – for the first time in Golding we meet vulgarity, insensitivity, ugliness, banality, fitted to the consciousness we have to live in. There is a voice with a snarl, a voice different from Golding's own.

So, for the critic too, answers must give way to questions. Is this peculiar book dualistic, an unresolved conflict of warring opposites; or is it a unified whole, whose apparent dualism only comes from our failing to look at it from the right angle?

Any attempt at an answer must surely begin by trying to define the peculiarity of Golding's basic conception of character. We have argued that *all* the novel's 'worlds' (the past, the apparent present, and the real present) are essentially determined and static. Pincher is revealed as he has always been; his situation is revealed as it always essentially was. What are the implications of this for character?

The first essential implication is that the choice of protagonist absolutely and necessarily excludes complexity of character. The novel could not have been written if its protagonist were not a Pincher incapable of dying; and if he is Pincher he cannot be complex. Macbeth is a complex man who becomes a monster, Pincher is always a monster. Indeed we can now go on to see that despite the many references to Shakespeare, the basic concept is Sophoclean.

This is because Golding is essentially concerned with *Being*, not *Becoming*; and consequently his concept of character is static, not dynamic. Oedipus too might have cried that whatever he had done in life, whatever his relationships might have been like, he would still have found himself in the same position, giving 'the same order, the right order, the wrong order'. Oedipus also carries within himself a central darkness, determined and unchangeable; he too journeys through a world which looks like the ethical world in which a man acts, directing his own course and that of others; but the journey is an illusory progress through unrealities, and the false 'time' of his humanly constructed world has to give way to the eternal moment of the revelation of his Being, in which he is acted upon.

The Greek drama also helps us to see how the emphasis in a novel like this is on recognition. What there is to be seen has always been there, but men have tried to escape seeing it. The function of the art is to get the protagonist stripped of false seemings and get the audience looking from the right angle, so that knowledge of reality can no longer be escaped. And, only now is there choice. Neither Oedipus's nor Pincher Martin's is a moral tragedy, for neither can be said strictly to have chosen his Being. At the very end they choose, but what they choose is whether or not to accept the Being that they are, and always have been.

We can see this more clearly in *Pincher Martin* if we ask a question which Golding clearly, and very significantly, never thought it necessary or relevant to ask: How did Christopher Martin become Pincher? For as soon as we ask it, we see that it is a 'becoming' question that lies right outside the scope of Golding's conception, as it lies outside Sophocles'. The centrepiece of all Pincher's memories is the child and the cellar; 'psychologically' this seems to lie at the heart of the book. The man in the tunnel trying to escape the gods and the annihilating tears by trampling the faces, the drowning sailor constructing his world to escape into, the madman slashing the oilskin, all simply reorchestrate the child's horrified rejection of the cellar and the darkness. The cellar connects with the tunnel of Pincher's life, the tunnel with the rock, and the rock leads back to the cellar. But there is no chain of *causality* here at all, as we can see immediately by the absurdity of positing one. Golding is not saying that the moral character of Pincher is caused by the child's trauma. He is not concerned with cause and effect at all. He is interested in the Being of Pincher and its implications; and the child, the man, the madman are all simply and equally revelations of that Being. Indeed all the flashbacks, all the illusory Six Days' Creation, and the final terror, are pictures of the same thing, whose essence is a pair of claws locked against black lightning. It looks like a novel in which one thing leads to another: it is in fact a maze in which all paths lead back to the centre, and the centre is a single, simple image of a Being reacting to Non-Being.

We can see now why Golding wanted his flashbacks to be what they are; not what we expect in the cinema – glimpses of a past which explains how the present came to be – but a series of stills which focus more clearly the single image building up behind the apparent dynamism of the rock. On a naturalistic level we could say that the past must seem artificial and static at the moment of death; another country; a distant stage on which actors strut and fret. Or again, at one's last moment, the 'whole life' that is supposed to flash before the eyes might very well seem less like a travel-film, dense with complex detail, than a map starkly outlining the essential pattern. But the most basic reason is that the novelist of Being *sees* the past like that, as essentially static anyway; and sees artifice as the way of extracting from the cluttering complexities of ordinary life the essential signature of Being, by making use of the one perspective which is outside all possibility of time and change: the moment at which all the stills are on file together and the clearest ones, most definitely exposed in black and white, can be most tellingly mounted, juxtaposed.

Yet we may find ourselves still stubbornly objecting, finding it hard to accept that human beings, their relationships, their actions, can be validly treated in such simply reductive terms. Aren't the flashbacks too like posters in excessively flat primary colours, too diagrammatic? Taking this a step further: is it not too easy for the author to blacken a tooth or block in some disfigurement, since the mode is one of statement incapable of the kind of imaginative verification we demand from a Casaubon or an Osmond? Does not working in such swift and shallow sketches mean that Golding is never involved and imaginatively stretched beyond his existing vision? One step further: where the basic insights are already dangerously simple, does not the deliberately imperfect style tend to vulgarize and crudify even further until we find difficulty in adjusting the man who saw and spoke like *that*, with the man using the full range of his author's imagination and language on the rock?

We are however in difficulties if we want to voice such criticisms, for we are bound to become uneasily aware of how dependent they are on a basic objection to the mode of vision itself, a philosophic rather than a literary objection. A novel of pure Being may offend both against expectations based on more than two and a half centuries of novels, and against unspoken assumptions about 'real life and real people'. What we might see as fiction lacking necessary complexity, Golding sees as going to the heart of the matter undistracted by what, for all their fascinating unevennesses of surface, are irrelevances – like the rock which must be cut away to get at the pure form of the statue. He might have been more tactful, but he is a man much given to facing consequences without disguise. We can state our criticisms in such a way that they will seem to be literary ones; but as soon as we begin to ask why and how they come about, they lead us back to the concept behind the novel and reveal themselves as extensions of a basic objection to that concept. Questions of style are dependent on stance and treatment; questions of stance and treatment dependent on the basic nature of the informing vision. Moreover we cannot even distinguish, basically, the flashback world and the world of the rock, for the underlying vision is common to both. If we do not feel the same objections to the latter, it is surely only because the situation is so radically peculiar and other-worldly that it never challenges expectations based on 'ordinary life', and never reveals its awkward implications until we come to reflect afterwards.

Perhaps we might say that the whole myth is both too specific and too general – too specific to be really archetypal, for Pincher is a highly special case; too general because we find ourselves asking questions about this particular man that the fiction cannot or will not answer. But still we reveal ourselves as wedded to concepts of becoming, with a right to ask how a man becomes his being. How does the child in the cellar become the man on the rock? How, if a man carries within him so determined a signature of Being, can he be said to choose? Childhood is too early. Is not manhood – when for example, he recognizes his love for Nathaniel – too late? Still what we are criticizing is the basic concept itself. Once we look from his angle, we see as the author saw with great power. Yet have we explained our criticisms away?

The fiction however is certainly wholly consistent and not dualistic at all. It may be ambiguous in the sense that we are made aware that there are two ways of reacting to it (according to whether God exists or not), but not in the sense that both views are right. We cannot expect Golding to know the answer to that problem; and it is a positive strength that he has created an image of man that will respond to either view. The image in all its aspects reflects a single vision of human life: an essential confrontation of Being with non-Being.

Yet it is not irrelevant to question the validity of that kind of vision, for this is precisely what Golding himself proceeded to do. The writing of *Pincher Martin* brought him up against questions strictly outside the scope of the fiction, but obviously vital for a novelist committed to seeking the truth. The questions we formulate are exactly those he poses to himself in *Free Fall*, and the need to answer them is the turning-point in his development so far. This marks an end and a beginning: the end of a set of novels in which the state of man is explored as a finite concept; the beginning of a set in which complex, searching, philosophically difficult questions begin to be asked about how one should look at man. These are necessarily more difficult, obscure and tortured for both author and reader, for they are significantly about authorship and ways of reading. The protagonist becomes himself an artist, asking not just 'what am I?', but also 'how did I become what I am?', and 'how do I find a way of looking at my being and becoming that will reconcile the contradictions I see?' The first three novels are visions, the next two seek a path through irreconcilable kinds of vision. They try to discover not what, but how, to see.

4

FREE FALL

(1959)

I

If *Free Fall* seems the most elusive and difficult of Golding's novels so far, it is because Golding is now questioning the nature of understanding itself. Our first impression is likely to recall E. M. Forster's reaction to Conrad: 'Is there not a central obscurity – something noble, heroic, beautiful . . . but obscure, obscure? While reading one doesn't or shouldn't ask such a question, but it occurs not improperly, when the author professes to be personal and take us into his confidence.' Yet we can do a great deal to understand the nature of the obscurity if we come to the novel with *Pincher Martin* in mind, for *Free Fall* is profoundly illuminated by its predecessor.

We are immediately aware of both similarities and differences. We recognize familiar portraits: Mary has become Beatrice; Sammy is a subtilized Pincher; the love-affair that was only one set of stills among many is now the central tragedy which challenges the understanding. The flashback world has, as it were, increased in scope and complexity so as to become the main picture.

There is, however, a major difference immediately evident: the tragedy now has a before and after, we are led to examine what led up to it and what necessarily followed. In *Pincher Martin* the past merely focused the present to give sharper definition to the same picture: the static, determined self of the protagonist. The activity of the book was one of recognition. Now we hear Sammy Mountjoy asking the kind of questions the earlier novel neither asked nor could answer: seeking to discover how he became what he is, seeking to explain how his childhood innocence came to be destroyed by the consciously choosing will, deliberately and self-consciously exploring his past in search of a pattern of development governed by choice. Revelation and recognition of Being, then, gives way to exploration, explanation, discovery of Becoming. Consequently the new novel is concerned with moral analysis, and is inevitably about character, in exactly the way that *Pincher Martin* was not. So for the first time Golding seems wholly to abandon his isolated and isolating settings and give us the social scene. The novel takes place in the Britain of the nineteen thirties, forties and fifties, and is in some ways a representative experience. It is also the portrait of the artist as a young man: the slum childhood, the tough schooldays, the growing ability to paint, the college of art, first and overwhelming love. It looks like a novel of character and environment, shadows of Dickens, Wells, Joyce Cary fall across the pages. Such a novel would seem to have its centre of gravity in notions of responsibility; and so we find Sammy Mountjoy asking an explicit question: 'What am I looking for? I am looking for the beginning of responsibility ...' The question takes us inevitably into the world of Becoming, motive, choice, behaviour; it seeks a moral explanation of the story.

Yet this will not explain the form of the novel, or satisfy us as even a shorthand account of the nature of the experience. For Golding has not decided that the mode of vision of *Pincher Martin* was wrong and so changed to a better one, and the new novel is by no means as different from its predecessor as it looks. Both novels reveal life 'islanded in pictures', there is still a careful composition, a deliberate framing. There is, once more, a series of crucial moments which are 'a split into the whole nature of things'. And Sammy asks not only about the beginning of responsibility, but about its end. 'How did I lose my freedom? I must go back and tell the story ...' Indeed, his story might seem to have little to do with moral analysis of free choice. For the more that Sammy searches his past for moments of choice and responsibility, the more determinism he reveals. What looks like a detective movie, following clue after clue to a solution, resolves into a series of stills, all showing the same pattern of freedom already lost. We are back in the world of Pincher.

as I remembered ... I could find no moment when I was free to do as I would. In all that lamentable story of seduction I could not remember one moment when being what I was I could do other than I did.

Here 'moral' questions – What ought I to have done? – or 'becoming' questions – How did I get to be like this? – seem irrelevant and meaningless; the world of responsibility and the possibility of change gives way to another in which wisdom resides in the humble recognition of what we unalterably are.

Neither of these patterns will cover the novel because both are inescapably there. Indeed, the form of the novel can now be seen to be the deliberate posing of one against the other, and its subject, the contradictions that result. Obscurity is inevitable when the experience is of looking at a human life through a pair of eyes, each of which sees in a different way and consequently sees different things. The novel is the result of Golding's need to explore the tensions between Being and Becoming which *Pincher Martin* had raised for him, but which he could not deal with in that form. How does a man become what he is? How can he be said to choose? If he is first free, then determined, where is freedom lost? In childhood? Is that not too early? In manhood? Is that not too late? Golding had written three novels using one mode of vision, and felt it to be true; but he had come to realize how peculiar it was, and how different from another, more 'ordinary' mode of vision which could also command his imaginative consent, how many problems it raised. As a myth-maker he is committed to trying to tell the truth about human beings, but how if the truth is Janus-faced and one finds oneself imaginatively committed to both faces? So the pattern-finder is obliged to question the validity of patterns. The tentativeness which had grown over the three novels now occupies the centre. In *Free Fall* Myth becomes no longer a form designed to enforce the recognition of truths deeper than the surface of ordinary life; but a form designed to explore the nature of looking for truth. In one novel two different kinds of novel are allowed to fight it out, and this accounts for the elusiveness of the book. Of necessity, clarity gives way to opacity, revelation to agonized search, assured poetry to a violent opposition of styles and voices. Everywhere contradictions mount: a voyage of discovery into what is already known; paintings that reveal truths opposed to those of experience; vivid characters in commonplace situations and brilliant apocalyptic situations peopled by archetypes; the need to explain countered by the knowledge that explanation is futile.

The opening of the novel plunges us immediately into these contradictions; yet it also presents us with an opportunity to tune the opposed voices so that the distinction between them is clarified and they do not simply jam each other. We begin with the apocalyptic and fixed, but the next paragraph sets this firmly against the world of becoming.

I have walked by stalls in the market-place where books, dog-eared and faded from their purple, have burst with a white hosanna. I have seen people crowned with a double crown, holding in either hand the crook and flail, the power and the glory. I have understood how the scar becomes a star, I have felt the flake of fire fall, miraculous and pentecostal ... I live on Paradise Hill, ten minutes from the station, thirty seconds from the shops and the local.

Sammy in this mode needs no exploration; what there is to know has already been revealed to him and can be expressed in an old symbolism of revelation. This paragraph metaphorically summarizes all the facts of Being that the novel but for its final page will expand and annotate. The ordinary world of market-place, shops and local and the better-class suburb is seen to contain the eternal verities of the Spirit. Sammy has seen Lent and Easter revealed in ordinary biographies, has seen souls, having decayed from the Imperial, burst into pure resurrection through repentance. He has seen how ordinary people can reveal a royalty greater than Egypt's, a glorious martyrdom, where the punishments of justice are counter-balanced by the love which lifts the fallen from the pit. He has himself experienced suffering that turns into glorification; has known in his own being the transfiguration through pentecostal fire. So the old symbolism is a true reflection of what can happen to a man when he is touched by the world of the spirit. Yet Sammy is no born-again Christian. 'My yesterdays walk with me. They keep step, they are grey faces that peer over my shoulder.' Sammy has known no forgiveness. To have been touched by the power and the glory is only to be the more violently 'self-condemned', to experience a sharper sense of the spectres of his guilty past. The being that is revealed to him is irreconcilably split: the ordinary transfigured, but the evil simultaneously underlined. Yet in this mode of awareness a whole human life can be summarized in a paragraph. Before we can understand its symbols fully, they may need to be translated into the facts whose patterns they reveal, but when we do understand we shall more fully recognize what we already know. By the top of the last page we can truly comprehend the first one; its pattern fulfilled rather than changed. In this mode, *Free Fall* might seem as essentially static as *Pincher Martin*.

Here however the first paragraph's coherent pattern and expert knowledge do not satisfy. For Sammy remains 'a burning amateur, torn by the irrational and incoherent, violently searching and self-condemned. When did I lose my freedom? For once, I was free. I had power to choose.' Sammy cannot accept any determinism in which causes lead to effects by unalterable laws. He is sure of his Being, but equally sure that it lies within the human will to choose and change one's whole direction. So, against the static, eternal images of being we find a language of Becoming asserted: 'Free-will cannot be debated but only experienced, like a colour or the taste of potatoes'. A human life in this mode is like a child in a garden where the central fountain is surrounded by many different paths radiating outwards, and he can choose to go down one or another.

But how can these two modes be related? If there was freedom, how is it lost? So Sammy begins to search for an explanation of what he already knows, to review his past in order to discover how he became his being, but he cannot escape the contradictions. He has 'hung all systems on the wall like a row of useless hats', yet he desperately desires some all-embracing pattern and looks to the writing of the book, the act of communication itself, as a way of finding one. But his two modes of vision cannot but affect the writing. First, we find them reflected in different ways of experiencing time:

For time is not to be laid out endlessly like a row of bricks . . . Time is two modes. The one is an effortless perception native to us as water to the mackerel. The other is a memory, a sense of shuffle fold and coil, of that day nearer than that because more important, of that event mirroring this, or those three set apart, exceptional and out of the straight line altogether.

One is a mode of being, the other of becoming; and this in turn means that the historian of his own past finds himself playing different roles. Mere chronology is a 'dead thing'; to keep the life and truth, the tale must unfold as it appears to the imaginative eye, but Sammy inevitably finds himself pulled in different directions because he has a double vision. He will see himself as a faithful transcriber of events ('I have no responsibility for some of the pictures'), when to record is simply to bear witness. But he is also a self-conscious artist, ordering his narrative with Jamesian expertise, for 'understanding requires a sweep that takes in the whole of remembered time and then can pause. Perhaps if I write my story as it appears to me, I shall be able to go back and select.' Yet again, he knows that to select is to falsify and that any pattern is reductive. He knows that communication is impossible, that each of us exists in the loneliness of a 'dark thing that sees as at the atom furnace by reflection, feels by remote control and hears only words phoned to it in a foreign tongue'. He knows, finally, the truth of Gerontion's cry: 'After such knowledge what forgiveness?'

So the contradictions ebb and flow as the voice speaks, or, rather, as one kind of voice changes into another and back again. The novel may seem a hopeless proposition: each pattern contradicts the other, yet patternlessness would be simply incoherence. But to have tuned the voices, to have got the differences and their implications clear to ourselves, is already to have begun to move beyond Sammy. His search will eventually achieve a full tuning for him, whereby the dichotomy will be revealed in utter starkness; but we can begin to anticipate, to see as Sammy does not as we watch him voyage into his past, to detect which mode is operating where and why. And there may be more than this, for we must not forget that behind Sammy's confusions there lurks a greater writer allowing him to explore different roles, juxtaposing them, playing a waiting game. The more clearly we can see what Sammy is doing, the nearer we are likely to come to Golding. Will he be able to take us beyond Sammy, to find a path beyond the dichotomy so deliberately created by the form and advertised by the title? 'Free fall' is at once the momentous choice in Eden, and the effortless being in space. Are either, or both enough? Are they reconcilable? Golding's fourth novel represents a determination to find out.

II

Rotten Row, the world of Sammy's earliest memories, is seen in the mode of Being. In common with the apocalyptic opening it shows the ordinary lit from within so that the lighting is more important than what it plays on. The surface of Rotten Row is a rural slum: poverty, hardship, dirt and moral delinquency. Sammy is a bastard, his mother and Evie are 'sodding liars', Ma Donovan's pretty daughter may have the pox, and so on. Yet this is not 'the truth'. When Ma provides Sammy with a father from her fantasies: a soldier, an airman, a clergyman, the Prince of Wales, 'the glittering myth lay in the middle of the dirty floor, accepted with gratitude', because it points to something anterior to the cold world of 'reality' and 'fiction', 'truth' and 'lies'. The small boy's world is lit with romance, beauty, drama, mystery, that are quite as 'real' as, or more real than, the 'realities' they illuminate. Evie's uncle in the suit of armour, the long spoons, the girl who becomes a boy who can pee higher than the others, the lodger's Snow-Maiden swan's feathers, all point in the same direction. The slop-pool from a drain is iridescent with life and colour in the two-foot world, the bogs on wash-day become a vividly dramatic setting for epic action which wholly transcends its basis in defecation, half-held-up bloomers and superstitions about syphilis. In Rotten Row there is a rich vitality, a sense of community, a security, a boozy comfort. It *is* an Eden, untroubled by dirt, presided over by Ma and Evie, and life continues, not uniformly happy, but 'permanent and inevitable in this shape'.

Ma is not so much a person, or a relationship, as an archetypal creature of myth permanently fixed in the eye of childhood: 'These last few months I have been trying to catch her in two handfuls of clay – not, I mean, her appearance; but more accurately, my sense of her hugeness and reality, her matter-of-fact blocking of the view.' Later he will see her 'as a stranger might see her, a massive, sagging creature, mottled and dirty. Her hair was in wisps over her brown forehead, her face was a square-ish, drawn-down mass with a minute fag sticking in one corner of her mouth'. But when we get there we know that this is only an 'appearance', for we have known what it is to see her and her world through the eyes of the 'infant Samuel'.

These eyes transmute evil, suffering, dirt. When Rotten Row's devious scrap-dealers are arrested they appear handcuffed 'between two dark blue pillars surmounted by silver spikes'. When death comes to the lodger the stopping of the heart is no more than the stopping of the clock with which it is confused; a black car with panes of chased and frosted glass; a missed opportunity of seeing the magical cap of white feathers. The teachers at the infant school are tall trees. Occasionally a shadow falls; a Downs child disgraces herself, 'she was taken home by one of the trees, for we watched them pass through the gate, hand in hand'. But the shadow lifts, and Sammy doesn't go through any gate, even when he passes from childhood into boyhood.

In the primary school we become much more aware of the darker side of the boy's world. Now there is violence and gang warfare. Under Philip Arnold's influence the young Sammy learns robbery with violence as he bullies smaller boys for their precious fag-cards of the Kings of Egypt. Yet Philip, belonging to a different order of being – 'clever, complex, never a child' – can only make Sammy do evil things. He does not make him evil even when, cunningly playing upon his weaknesses, he persuades him to spit upon the altar of the church. There is a collapse, but it is purely physical, not 'moral' or 'religious'. The verger's blow on the ear 'lays him open' only in the sense that it bursts a mastoid infection and puts him in hospital, no more. For the boy's essential innocence cannot change or be changed; he can do bad things but he cannot *be* bad.*

The central episode of this section sums up the nature of the child's being and pinpoints its implications. On the airfield, 'trespassing', Johnny and Sammy see tragedy – a plane crashing in flames. But there is no sense of transgression or suffering: only a man, tall, hatless, smeared with black, shouting: 'You kids shove off! If I catch you here again I'll put the police on you . . .'; and a sensible getaway. Then they trespass again, into the General's garden, avoiding a policeman by hiding behind a bush and disappearing noiselessly across the lawn. Having seen tragedy, they see transfiguration:

We were in the upper part of the garden, looking back and down. The moon was flowering. She had a kind of sanctuary of light round her, sapphire. All the garden was black and white. There was one tree between me and the lawns, the stillest tree that ever grew, a tree that grew when no one was looking. The trunk was huge and each branch splayed up to a given level; and there, the black leaves floated out like a level of oil on

* See Ch. 2, pp. 85–7.

water. Level after horizontal level these leaves cut across the splaying branches and there was a crumpled, silver-paper depth, an ivory quiet beyond them. Later, I should have called the tree a cedar and passed on, but then, it was an apocalypse.

But they only *see* what is revealed; as 'two points of perception, wandering in paradise' ('we were eyes'), they see, but they do not understand.

This is an Eden because it is illuminated from within by the light of Innocence; it is as true of the whole world of childhood as it is true of the hospital ward that 'remembered, they shine'. Innocence is the nature of the existence described – it is useless to look here for the beginning of responsibility. The grey faces have no source here and the only scar is from Sammy's operation; trespass, violence, stealing, blasphemy, do not spell out 'guilt'. It is easy to see why. The purity of vision is possible because of the total absence of self-consciousness; perception has not yet given way to reflection.* The General's garden, like all the other scenes, is a setting for Blake's *Songs of Innocence*. There is no calculation, choice, responsibility, and without these there is lacking a dimension essential to evil or guilt. Philip has it, but that is why he is never a child. Sammy makes the diagnosis explicit: 'I was innocent of guilt, unconscious of innocence.'

The infant Samuel, then, opposes to the kind of Being described in the opening paragraph one qualitatively different, yet seen in the same mode. This one is innocent, the other guilty. One is unconscious, the other conscious. One cannot find forgiveness, the other does not need and cannot give it, because it cannot understand. One has lost the power of moral choice, the other has not yet acquired it. Yet both are *states*, 'islanded in pictures', with a sheer gulf between.

Golding can be seen to have gone behind *Lord of the Flies* and *Pincher Martin* to show that there is an innocence in childhood and that the child does not automatically father the man. He has re-phrased *The Inheritors* so that, in child and man, Lok again faces Tuami across the Gap between innocence and experience. Yet the net effect is to pose all the more awkwardly the problem of Becoming, how one changes into the other.

* See Ch. 2, pp. 48–9.

III

The orthodox 'moral' way of accounting for such a change would be to look for an action, a freely chosen crossing of some moral Rubicon, which led to further decisions and actions, amounting together to a change in one's inner nature. So Sammy turns next to just such a moment: the initial action in his seduction of Beatrice.

Yet we have already noticed that innocent being can do bad actions without becoming bad; whereas Sammy, looking back, sees from the start that his Rubicon found him already determined, so that he cannot be said to have chosen to do what he did. The laconic opening sentence of the new section: 'Even by the time I was on the bike by the traffic light I was no longer free', undermines at the outset the validity of a moral account.

This is Sammy's *Vita Nuova*, acridly rewriting Dante's experience of the revolution of Love. Sammy's Beatrice, first manifested to him at school in front of a picture of a Palladian bridge in the art-room, is as much a showing-forth of another world as Dante's, a miraculous Being, equally unattainable. But Sammy sets out to attain her (his Beatrice is rather too explicitly surnamed I-for). A greeting is for Dante a grace beyond deserving but Sammy intrigues for one as a prelude to possession. So we find him on another bridge at a traffic light, initiating the first move in what certainly looks like a moral metaphor. The bridge is crossed, the red light of warning first breaks down and is then ignored. Yet we are told from the beginning that this cannot be so. Where there is no freedom there can be no morality; the moral metaphors and language are ironic; signs and warnings are as irrelevant to Sammy as the huge baked-bean advertisement to which he cries 'I didn't ask to fall in love'.

Yet it does look like a story in the mode of Becoming. It is, convincingly, an adolescent tragedy with both the poignancy and the rather tawdry absurdity of millions of such affairs in real life. The presentation catches the absurd/pathetic tang of the elaborately casual cyclist separating his girl from her knowing companions; the mechanisms of Lyons, busrides, country walks, the bed-sitter with the Van Gogh flowerpiece, the fierce high-talk to uncomprehending ears, the self-dramatization, the narrow bed, the sexual failure. It is psychologically convincing too: the obsessed, salt boy and the unawakened, socially and sexually inhibited girl;

the passionate proposals, meeting a reluctance which alternates between the prim and the inhibitedly neurotic. Unable either to reject or accept, it seems, Beatrice is driven first into engagement and then into an increasingly lubricious and unsatisfactory sexual relationship. Happiness is caught with the right touch of immaturity: 'I rode home, my heart molten with delight, goodness and gratitude. For it was good. She was nineteen and I was nineteen; we were male and female, we would marry though she did not know that yet . . .', but such moments are rare and the story is even more convincing in its record of how frustration turns into exploitation as Sammy tries desperately to break through to an impossible togetherness. Inevitably, disillusion becomes desertion, another woman and a more satisfying love, marriage and children.

Looked at from this angle the story does seem to have the scope and complexity of a well-observed and credible human relationship, the kind of treatment Golding never gave in *Pincher Martin*, as we can easily see by comparing it with its source in the Mary episodes. Even its vulgarities and lapses from 'good taste' have a realistic basis. Golding was clearly determined to get the peculiar tang of adolescence across at whatever cost in grace and power; so the language veers from the flat to the melodramatic, the humour can be excruciating, the experience is absurd, irritating, embarrassing, as well as pathetic, in the ways that adolescence itself can be.

This means that we are led to reflect in largely social and psychological terms. When Sammy talks of losing his freedom, we think of this as a result of his obsession with a girl whose behaviour is irritatingly provocative, and we think of that behaviour as both psychological and socially conditioned by the *mores* of the time. We might consider the whole thing as a flatter, slangier, less 'poetic' version of the story of Paul and Miriam in *Sons and Lovers*. If Sammy speaks of loss of freedom he seems merely to echo the age-old lament of the anxious lover:

For now there were rough ropes on my wrists and ankles and round my neck. They led through the streets, they lay at her feet and she could pick them up or not as she chose.

And yet it is no less clear that Sammy, looking back, is once again aware of the tension between the two modes of explanation. We have noticed how, if he is already determined at the moment by the traffic light, he can only be said to become more strongly what he already is, and we can only read the episode in terms of Becoming in that special sense. Constantly, also, we become aware of a bedrock of altered Being jutting through the surface, so that the loss of freedom acquires different and darker overtones from those we have been considering:

Once a human being has lost freedom there is no end to the coils of cruelty. I must I must I must. They said the damned in hell were forced to torture the innocent live people with disease. But I know now that life is perhaps more terrible than that innocent medieval misconception. We are forced here and now to torture each other ... Those who lose freedom can watch themselves forced helplessly to do this ...

We cannot see this as simply an intensification of the drama: it creates a sense that somehow, beyond or below, there is a determinism far deeper than the psychological. The terrible seduction scenes, credible as they are, reveal some sort of metaphysical dimension; the narrative carries within itself some point which only a later gloss can reveal. Or we could say that the tale has suddenly outpaced the teller's ability to explain what he nevertheless knows to be true. When he reflects: 'the descent we were now to embark upon and at my hands was one I was powerless to control or stop', we can share an impression that this is true of the story as he represents it, and yet in terms of 'character' or 'plot' there is no adequate explanation for so terrible a determinism. Another kind of picture, as yet obscure in its significance, is being drawn behind the one we are watching; and across every incident, however casual, falls the shadow of an ominously larger meaning. So, for example, we begin to feel that Beatrice's repeated 'maybe' is more than the irritating and provocative revelation of her inability to say yes or no:

I would try to explain.

'I'm trying to find out about you. After all, if we're going to spend our lives together – where are you? What are you? What is it like to be you?'

Her arms would shake – those arms that bent in at the elbows, were so delicate that they seemed for receiving only – her breasts and her face would push against me, be hidden.

Impatient and angry. Continue the catechism.

'Aren't you human, then? Aren't you a person at all?'

And with shudders of her wrists and shaking of the long, fair hair she would whisper against me:

'Maybe.'

If 'maybe' was a 'sign of all our times', it becomes a chord sounding uneasily again and again throughout the episode, and hinting at a growing uncertainty. Sammy, continually brought up short by the word, is shown at the limit of his 'explanations'; the word blocks and undermines the psychological, the social, the behavioural certainties.

Indeed, we can see in this instance how the love affair itself is based on perceptions of Being, in a way that makes the reference to the *Vita Nuova* more than morally disparaging irony. For all Sammy's questions are Being questions: where are you, what are you, what is it like to be you? Just as much for him as for Dante Beatrice is a revelation, of a nature wholly other and superior to his own – 'the most mysterious and beautiful thing in the universe' – and it is *that* he longs for. The basis of his tragedy is that he confuses, as Dante never did, sharing in that Being with possession of the body that manifests it. We shall not understand the obsession which drives him to torture and exploit her unless we understand what kind of an obsession it is, and how little, basically, it has to do with the sexual act it is so readily confused with:

'I said I loved you. Oh God, don't you know what that means? I want you, I want all of you, not just cold kisses and walks – I want to be with you and in you and on you and round you – I want fusion and identity – I want to understand and be understood – oh God, Beatrice, Beatrice, I love you – I want to be you!'

The same uneasy sense that there is some metaphysical dimension operating below the physical, is shown in the difference between Sammy the painter and Sammy the lover. Through the paintings the story is again pushed away from questions of psychology and sex, motive and behaviour; yet Sammy the lover cannot understand this because he identifies his paintings with his lust:

'I shan't paint your face at all. I just want your body. No. Don't rearrange it. Just lie still.'
Beatrice lay still and I began to draw.
When the drawing was finished I made love to her again. Or rather, I repeated what my pencil had done, finished what my pencil had begun.

In fact, however, the painting records what he has *not* done and in it, as in all his good paintings, he 'stands the world of appearances on its head'. The climactic picture to which, after a particularly degrading exploitation, he adds 'the electric light-shades of Guernica to catch the terror', reveals when he looks at it later in a public gallery no sign of the rape, the brutality, the suffering and devastation of Picasso's masterpiece:

The electric light that ought to sear like a public prostitution seems an irrelevance. There is gold, rather, scattered from the window. There was dog faith and big eyes and submission. I look at the picture and I remember what the hidden face looked like; how after my act and my self-contempt she lay, looking out of the window as though she had been blessed.

Does the painting reveal a reality which contradicts the lover's dossier, though implied by the name itself and the reference to Dante? Maybe ...

Finally, the tension can also be detected in the oddly double tone which governs the whole episode and gives it its peculiar flavour. Here again contradictions meet, for the tone is a mixture of sympathy and searing contempt; and the fluctuations are traceable to Being and Becoming too. The eyes that see and record the lovers are the eyes that have recognized the kind of being described in the opening paragraph. The knowledge that the younger self is no less determined and helpless than the older carries with it a sympathy, no matter how horrible or ridiculous the situation may be. When the young Sammy is repulsed, and weeps, the older narrator records clearly enough an impression of 'that ridiculous, unmanly, trembling creature' – and yet the effect of the scene as a whole is so different that our predominant response is a compassion strong enough to override both ridicule and laconic amusement:

I was trembling regularly from head to foot as if my button had been pressed. There in the winter sunlight, among the raindrops and rusted foliage I stood and trembled regularly as if I should never stop and a sadness reached out of me that did not know what it wanted; for it is a part of my nature that I should need to worship, and this was not in the textbooks, not in the behaviour of those I had chosen and so without knowing I had thrown it away.

After the first dismissive sentence the tone suddenly warms; and though we can go on to see that the *behaviour* is ridiculous, the young man revealing the nature of his inner being, helplessly, is not. Indeed he only becomes ridiculous when he 'turned away and made a dramatic effort to master my emotion. That was a cliché of behaviour and therefore not frightening.' But it is absurd. The distinction seems clear enough. Whenever the Being of the lovers is recognized, however diminishing the context, the tone is one of understanding. Sammy looks back over the years with a sad grasp of what then was ungraspable. But the moment the narrative eye sees only Becoming, the motives and behaviour of the lovers acting out a drama produced, directed, played out as though this were all, the tone sharpens, and can flay. Indeed, the moments which we may feel are raw, embarrassing, in dubious taste, are directly traceable to the contempt Sammy feels for the blindness of the lovers, as they strut and fret in what they think are actions of their own devising and decision:

Unconsciously we were both setting ourselves to music. The gesture with which she opened her knees was, so to speak, operatic, heroic, dramatic and daunting. I could not accompany her. My instrument was flat.

This is more than the sour comedy of impotence, and isn't finally reducible to the slangishness, awkwardness, embarrassment and indignity appropriate to adolescence. The ultimate sourness is, as in *Pincher Martin*, directed to the posturing and self-dramatization of the 'hero' who cannot realize his inability to master himself or his situation, and whose heroics are radically false. When Sammy reveals Being he cannot but sympathize; but he cannot explain motive, decision, behaviour without conveying a sense of contempt so raw that it cares nothing for niceties of taste. If we have learnt to tune the voices in the prelude, we can detect the nature of the discord everywhere.

Yet we must not simplify: there is another side to the world of behaviour, action, and decision. The contemptuous flick lashes the Communist Party too, and the young man who thinks that Comrades Alsopp and Wimbury are a movement which knows where it is going and can explain the actions of men both past and future. Yet there is also 'a certain generosity' in the Party, 'a sense of martyrdom and a sense of purpose'; and it is through his membership that he meets Taffy, who in a few weeks becomes his wife. Taffy is hardly present in the book, yet she has a definite importance; for we can see that the relationship has real value. It neither threatens nor exploits, and it exists happily within a behavioural world. When Sammy records that. 'We achieved that extraordinary level of security when we did not expect entire truth from each other, knowing it to be impossible and extending a *carte blanche* of forgiveness beforehand', truth and forgiveness have to do with what they have done, with their 'histories', not with what they are. This relationship does not pierce through to Being, it exists solely in terms of behaviour and in that region they can offer and receive explanations, however edited. Explanation cannot be total, but it is possible and satisfying. The lovers demand far less, but they achieve far more. When the nonsense of Party belief is swept away, there is in the clasp of these sublunary lovers something that is generous, and something that suffers to some purpose. It would seem to be, then, the dimension of Being and the determination to touch it that causes the torture. The world of Taffy and Sammy is smaller, but it does not destroy, and what it gives is real.

Yet we do not forget the deeper perspective either. There is the picture of Johnny: a 'still' of perfect, joyous Being flying into the air on the brow of a hill at 100 m.p.h., and kissing his girl in a mode where there is no before and after, no cause and effect; simply a revelation of love so perfectly unified that consequences cease to matter and the eyes are turned quite away from the road of Becoming that can lead to one thing or another. This 'remains a measure' in Sammy's mind 'of the difference between us'.

Moreover it is Taffy's Sammy who 'explains' his relationship with Beatrice as

the mind's self-deception. Certainly there was no light in her face ... Her only power now was that of the accuser, the skeleton in the cupboard; and in this bounded universe we can easily put paid to that.

But this cannot satisfy his own deeper self, let alone us. His vision of the cat mangled by the motorcar, and the nightmare in which Beatrice runs crying for him, through a rising water that he has escaped, are visions in the mode of Being which will not be explained, and point to a universe that is boundless, without possibility of forgiveness or atonement.

Finally, we return to determinism. The child's world revealed innocence, the lover's world guilt, but in neither is there free choice or responsibility:

What else could I have done but run away from Beatrice? I do not mean what ought I to have done or what someone else could have done. I simply mean that as I have described myself, as I see myself in my backward eye, I could do nothing but run away. I could not kill the cat to stop it suffering. I had lost my power to choose. I had given away my freedom. I cannot be blamed for the mechanical and helpless reaction of my nature. What I was, I had become. The young man who put her on the rack is different in every particular from the child who was towed along the street past the duke in the antique shop. Where was the division? What choice had he?

'What I was I had become' ... but we are no nearer to knowing how. We only know that looking at the guilty *action* will not tell us.

IV

It would seem, then, that guilt must be located in some choice of what to *be*; and if Sammy cannot put his finger on its beginning, he can at least pinpoint exactly the first realization of its nature. 'Becoming' questions are put aside for the while and the focus of the novel narrows again to isolation, as we find Sammy interrogated in the P.O.W. camp by a Gestapo psychologist and forced to recognize the nature of what he now is, in the horror of the cell. We move firmly back into the world of *Pincher Martin*; it is the 'unnameable, unfathomable and invisible darkness that sits at the centre' of Sammy that takes the attention. Halde's remark that 'there is a mystery in you which is opaque to both of us' defines the nature and function of a journey into the darkest interior.

He is being questioned to extract information that will allow Dr Halde to prevent a mass escape. He is being asked to betray his fellow-prisoners; or, in another sense, he is invited to prevent a massacre in which fifty lives might be lost instead of the two who have just been shot. The situation is a cliché but the treatment is complex: the Gestapo *éminence grise* is a man of great civilization and humanity, and the moral problem a tangle of relativities in which there can be no simple right or wrong. Yet the real problem, as always, is wholly anterior to any question of moral decision.

In what sense can Sammy be said to 'know' anything? Halde wants 'to raid the camp swiftly and suddenly and with absolute certainty of what I am going to find and where'; he wants the location of the tools, tunnel, radio, and civilian clothes. Sammy does not know any of this. His fellow prisoners do not trust him enough. What he does 'know' is the result simply of his painter's eye and its perceptions of Being: the eyes which instinctively study his fellows day after day could tell at any time that out of hundreds, perhaps twenty-five are the kind of beings who would try to escape. But such 'knowledge' might be everything or nothing; it cannot be defined, verified or explained, and only an explanation would satisfy. In the interrogation Sammy is trapped again between the worlds of fact and action, and of being; asked questions in one language that he could only answer in another, and so cannot answer at all. He refuses to talk, not because he is either a hero or a 'chuckle-headed' conformist to some 'little code' of loyalty or patriotism, but because he is as helpless as the infant Sammy interrogated by the verger and facing the impossibility of communication.

So the whole interrogation becomes a parody of the temptation of Christ, where the irony lies only partly in the different 'world' the tempter offers; but far more in the hero's different capacity to answer. Sammy, as Halde points out, 'has no health in him':

'You do not believe in anything enough to suffer for it or be glad. There is no point at which something has knocked on your door and taken possession of you ... You wait in a dusty waiting room on no particular line for no particular train.'

Christ, like the dead men, 'could say no because (He) could say yes;· He had 'some simple knowledge, some certainty to die for', some purposive Being. Sammy can say nothing. He is indeed, as a tiny but significant moment makes clear ('Do you feel nothing?' 'Maybe.') in the position of Beatrice responding to the catechisms he put her through, before he too is given over to torture.

The torture starts with the cell's darkness, for Sammy, like Pincher, is terrified of the dark. In *Pincher Martin* we could not ask why, or how he became so, but now Sammy proceeds to do just that. There is a break in the narrative as he resolutely attempts to localize and explain his fear. He thinks back to the lonely child in the cold, loveless rectory, after Father Watts-Watt had adopted him; remembering the rattle of the handle on the bolted door, the draughts and tapping pictures, the timid homosexual advances, the persecution-mania with its talk of signals and unusual happenings in the middle of the night. But when all has been remembered, the fear remains stubbornly inexplicable. Father Watts-Watt added nothing to the terror of the dark. 'Now I have been back in these pages to find out why I am frightened of the dark and I cannot tell. Once upon a time I was not frightened of the dark and later on I was.' The drift, and the significance of the narrative break just here, is apparent. Whatever fear there is in Sammy, and however it has influenced his actions, it is part of his being and cannot be 'explained' in terms of environment or behaviour. Once again Becoming questions are blocked, this time with full deliberation and purpose; but the blocking is no longer because the questions are excluded, but because they cannot be answered before what Sammy *is* has been investigated. As the darkness of the cell begins to press on Sammy's eyeballs, we know that his 'history' can tell us nothing more. Only the revelation afforded by myth will serve.

So in Chapter 9 we find ourselves back in the characteristic Golding world of isolated man. Dr Halde, 'Doctor Slope', precipitates him into the pit of his own being so that its nature is fully and horribly revealed to him. He is not tortured, but allowed to torture himself, and his terror of the dark elucidates for him and for us the kind of mind that fears this thing rather than that thing. The fictions of his horrified imagination define the shape of what he is, stands for, believes in at the centre of himself. The nature of his fear becomes explicit, 'It cared only to protect my privates'; and the worst thing he can imagine to torture himself is the severed penis he thinks he discovers lying in its blood in the middle of the floor. This is both a pointer to a self for whom his sexuality is the central reality and value and, in the horror of the organ divorced from the complex humanity it ought to be only part of, an exact symbol of that Being.

The crux of the entire novel is, however, as with all the previous ones, not the revelation itself but the response to it. Sammy's life 'centred round the fact of the next few minutes I spent alone and panic-stricken in the dark'. He shrieks for help, the cry of the rat when the terrier shakes it, a hopeless sound, the raw signature of one savage act. My cry meant no more, was instinctive, said here is flesh of which the nature is to suffer and do thus. I cried out not with hope of an ear but as accepting a shut door, darkness and a shut sky.

But the very act of crying out changed the thing that cried ...

There is no help in the present, nor in the past, and the future holds only imaginations of increasing terror to the point of extinction. Yet ...

The thing that cried fled forward over those steps because there was no other way to go, was shot forward screaming as into a furnace, as over unimaginable steps that were all that might be borne, were more, were too searing for the refuge of madness, were destructive of the centre. The thing that screamed left all living behind and came to the entry where death is as close as darkness against eyeballs.

And burst that door.

But Sammy does not die; instead the door of the cell bursts open too, and he walks out into the prison camp with his innocent vision miraculously restored.

Now at last we begin to 'cash' the apocalyptic language of the novel's opening; and Chapter 10 (a chapter of resurrection following temptation and torture) is perhaps its finest imaginative achievement. The prison camp becomes the General's Garden seen again, but now with the qualities of conscious awareness leading to reflection that were missing from the child's vision. The drab huts 'shone with the innocent light of their own created nature'; the dust 'was a universe of brilliant and fantastic crystals, that miracles supported instantly in their being'.

Those crowded shapes extending up into the air and down into the rich earth, those deeds of far space and deep earth were aflame at the surface and daunting by right of their own natures though a day before I should have disguised them as trees. Beyond them the mountains were not only clear all through like purple glass, but living. They sang and were conjubilant.

And now the landscape reveals also the power and the glory of man. The Kings of Egypt of the child's cigarette-cards take flesh, and proclaim a wonder and beauty in the midst of suffering and dirt. As he looks at them he cries out again, and 'This cry travelled away and along a fourth dimension' where love flows, so naturally,

powerfully, and incandescently that 'Standing between the understood huts, among jewels and music, I was visited by a flake of fire,
miraculous and pentecostal; and fire transmuted me, once and for
ever'. At last the painter's eye, always devoted to Being, comes into
its own in love of nature and man, and the 'secret, smuggled
sketches of the haggard, unshaven kings of Egypt in their glory are
the glory of my right hand and likely to remain so'.

Yet we must recognize the cost of such a vision. The Kings are of
Egypt, not of Israel, and they are seen through tears, by one who
has just staggered out of a sea of death. The eyes are dead because
the old Sammy Mons Veneris who could live content with himself
and his world is gone for ever. Yet the being they look out from
remains, and the vision so full of love for fallen man and a fallen
universe is filled with loathing when it turns inward on himself.

Now at last, the eyes of Sammy turned and looked where Halde had
directed them ... what they saw was not beautiful but fearsome ... here
was a point, a single point which was my own interior identity, without
shape or size but only position. Yet this position was miraculous as
everything else since it continually defied the law of conservation of
energy, rule one as it were, and created shapes that ... could be likened to
nothing but the most loathsome substances that man knows of, or
perhaps the most loathsome and abject creatures, continuously created ...
and this was the human nature I found inhabiting the centre of my own
awareness ... But now to live with such a thing was unendurable.

In the last phrase we find the driving force of Sammy's novel, and
are very nearly at the position he occupied when he began it.
Looking back at Beatrice now, the ordinary eye can understand the
painter's eye and bring her into focus:

The beauty of her simplicity struck me a blow in the face. That negative
personality, that clear absence of being, that vacuum which I had finally
deduced from her silences, I now saw to have been full ... She was simple
and loving and generous and humble ...

Yet the cell which has given him insight into the value of himself
and his past has done nothing to suggest that the way was anything
but inevitable. We can understand with a new accuracy the
violence of his self-condemnation, but also appreciate the force
that makes him go on searching for a *cause*.

V

Now, however, we can also detect a shape that the strategy of search has fallen into. The evidence for understanding the kind of Being revealed in the opening paragraph is almost complete, but the problem of Becoming is apparently no nearer solution. Yet this is far from the case. For to have realized that guilt cannot be localized in action but must be sought in Being, and to have discovered the exact nature of the guilty self, is to be able to define the question of Becoming with an accuracy impossible before. The choice, if it existed, must have been *a choice of being*, anterior to action, and the question then becomes: How did I choose to *be* like *that*? Moreover if childhood is too early, and the start of the guilty action too late, then such a choice if it happened at all, must have occurred in the missing space – the time of adolescence. There, and only there, if anywhere. The peculiar chronology of *Free Fall* is not wilfully obscure, but logical. Insight into the beginning can only *follow* insight into the nature of what is begun, and that is far more difficult than it sounds; achieved only by the process of exclusion that we have gone through. After three necessary sighting shots, the target area is pinpointed.

There is however a difference from the earlier school episodes that goes beyond the difference in the age and vulnerability of the boy, and depends on a new position of the narrator. Coming after the cell, the account cannot be on the level of mere reminiscence; it is bound to have a new quality of explicit analysis. So Sammy recalls through his younger self, but arranges the episodes with an emphasis and definition that always demonstrate an adult under-standing. We move sharply back for the second time into the mode of Becoming. Once again the voices, the actions, the psychology, are sharply observed and realistically convincing; but this time the vision is carefully ordered to bring out a pattern of choice. So the young Sammy confronts his spiritual parentage, two views of reality, artistically juxtaposed. There is the ordered universe of scientifically predictable cause and effect, taught by Nick Shales with a deep sense of its logic and beauty. And there is the miraculous world of the spirit, of Moses and the burning bush, taught with vivid power by Rowena Pringle. For a while Sammy moves easily between them without realizing their incompatibility, until the cruelty of the scripture-mistress forces him to choose. Inevitably, however, he chooses between the philosophies, not as they were, but as they were presented. He chooses Nick's instinctive goodness which is logically no part of his philosophy; he rejects the tortured and torturing spinster though what she taught had compelled his belief. Yet he remains innocent, so this cannot be the determining choice. It is the goodness of Nick that is chosen; the cruel nastiness of Rowena that is rejected: 'People are the walls of our room, not philosophies.'

There comes a time however when Sammy uses Nick's philosophy to deny the goodness for which he chose it. The wine of sex has been spilt in the children's blood and Sammy, having dashed down without thinking a portrait of a hardly-noticed girl in the art-room, finds he has been captured not only by the light in her face and her beauty, but by the body that holds them. He can never draw her again; she becomes an obsession. The idea of possessing her sexually receives dramatic formulation when the attractive French mistress and the games master are caught together in the boiler-room – their dismissal sends a shudder of pleasure round the school. This is what sex is, the dangerous, forbidden, but utterly fascinating fruit, and Sammy is enthralled. He turns to Nick, but for him, 'if the Devil had invented man he couldn't have played him a dirtier, wickeder, a more shameful trick than when he gave him sex!'. In Nick's rational and scientific universe there is no place for the mysterious irrationality of sex; it is branded shameful, reduced to a trick, and in the wake of such diminution comes evil. Sammy is willing enough not only to see sex as the Devil's trick but to espouse it, because of his compulsion to possess Beatrice; and he converts Nick's rationalism into an egotistic ethic where good and evil become relative, the only absolute being one's own desires and the eleventh commandment. In words recalling Milton's Satan he begins to deify his own urges: 'musk, shameful and heady, be thou my good'; and with this he begins to move into 'the world of the lads' – Mercutio, Valentine, Claudio – who made the law the servant of passion and desire. Now at last Sammy really focuses on the gap between behaviour and being that his novel has been opening up more and more: 'For this guilt' he 'found occasion to *invent* a crime that fitted the punishment. Guilty am I, therefore wicked I will be ...*Guilt comes before the crime and can cause it*' (our italics). He seems to be accepting himself as irretrievably fallen, if that word can be used of someone whose 'good' is what he himself decides. All that is needed now is the conscious and deliberate decision that fixes the guilt. As he bids farewell to school Nick tells him to commit himself totally to whatever he chooses to do. The headmaster goes a little further:

> If you want something enough, you can always get it provided you are willing to make the appropriate sacrifice. Something, anything. But what you get is never quite what you thought; and sooner or later the sacrifice is always regretted.

Sammy's future being is already coming into existence, already being robed as a destiny; yet he is not finally committed to it, nor has he clarified and accepted the cost. He is still free ... just.

He walks out into the hot summer day, and as he enters his 'bower of blisse' the answer to the headmaster's question 'What is important to you?' becomes clear, namely 'the white, unseen body of Beatrice Ifor, her obedience, and for all time my protection of her; and for the pain she has caused me, her utter abjection this side death'. It is the crucial moment, and as he emerges from the wood, so that 'there should be no doubt I now see', it is as though the angel of the gate of paradise holds a sword between him and the spices. Below the weir lies the water, the angel breathes on it, 'it seemed to me that the water was waiting for me'. It is a final chance of purification, an opportunity to see whole, but he takes from the water only the experience of his own sexuality, and when he emerges fresh, composed, self-sufficient, he faces and chooses between the alternatives. He moves away from 'the providential waters' and, on the hillside between earth and sky, cloister and street, the free decision we have been searching for takes place:

> What is important to you?
>   'Beatrice Ifor.'
>   She thinks you depraved already. She dislikes you.
>   'If I want something enough I can always get it provided I am willing to make the appropriate sacrifice.'
>   What will you sacrifice?
>   'Everything.'

It is the formal catechism of self-damnation, the deliberate choosing of a part for the whole. Sammy ratifies his guilt, determines the course of his life, and loses his freedom. Here Being and Becoming meet as Sammy chooses his determinism. It is only in a special sense an action ... Sammy 'does' nothing ... but it determines all future action and all future being. It is his free fall.

Then, having discovered the beginning, we see what it led to in the end. We go back to the General's Garden, now the grounds of a mental asylum; and just as years before the eyes of the boy had witnessed an apocalypse and manifested innocence, so now the no less contemplative eyes of the man see his guilt made flesh. 'Beatrice sat, looking at the wall, looking at nothing. Her face was in the shadow of her body ...' Desperately, Sammy tries to communicate with her, but she has become what he chose, Miss Ifor, a body without mind or spirit. Like Minnie in the infant class, she is only minimally human; she disgraces herself and is led away. There can be no atonement, no forgiveness. Sammy is left to live with himself in all the violence of his self-condemnation. We return to the condition of the opening paragraph, recognizing the full enormity of what it means to live in two worlds that cannot be unified:

All day long the trains run on rails. Eclipses are predictable. Penicillin cures pneumonia and the atom splits to order. All day long, year in, year out, the daylight explanation drives back the mystery and reveals a reality usable, understandable, and detached. The scalpel and the microscope fail, the oscilloscope moves closer to behaviour. The gorgeous dance is self-contained, then; does not need the music which in my mad moments I have heard. Nick's universe is real.

All day long action is weighed in the balance and found not opportune nor fortunate or ill-advised, but good or evil. For this mode which we must call the spirit breathes through the universe and does not touch it; touches only the dark things, held prisoner, incommunicado, touches, judges, sentences and passes on.

Her world was real, both worlds are real. There is no bridge.

VI

This conducts us to the limits of Sammy's understanding. We come round full circle to a definition of the dichotomy implied by the first paragraph, and gradually explored and focused until it can be explicitly stated in its full starkness. He has apparently solved the problem he set out to solve. He has contrived to show how he became his being. Yet if we should find it extremely peculiar and difficult to accept, it is not simply because the conceptual frame-work is so different from any we are likely to have met. There is brought to a head in the final section a critical problem that affects the novel as a whole.

Are we convinced by the moment of free fall to which the whole quest leads? Because it cannot be an action within a human relationship, it is curiously removed from the world of behaviour in which moral decision is usually shown in novels; but so enormous a determinism depends on it that we must be imaginat-ively convinced, or the whole novel surely collapses in ruin. Golding has to create a moment in which Sammy does nothing; yet it must be demonstrably crucial enough to determine all the actions and behaviour of the book. Can we truly feel that the boy wandering through the musky wood, bathing in the water, climbing the hillside, and there formally damning himself, is capable of such terrible self-determination, and that the moment convincingly represents so irretrievable a decision? There is certainly a claim to Miltonic consequence:

> ingrate, he had of mee
> All he could have; I made him just and right,
> Sufficient to have stood, though free to fall.

But at that moment – 'What will you sacrifice?' 'Everything' – if we do not feel that, in the fiction, Sammy has had all he could have from Golding, and been made just and right, the novel will collapse as a novel, and reduce itself to a theological treatise which we accept or reject on conceptual grounds alone. If we felt that the episode was a construct, a text-book illustration for moral theologians indicating the exact conditions necessary for grave sin, rather than the solidly convincing achievement of a novelist, realizing dramatic truth through protagonist and scene, and capable of satisfying the full testing conditions of novels of becom-ing, we could only fully respond to it by a kind of faith in the theology which determines it. Or again, if we doubt the convin-cingness of the scene, would this not suggest that there is some-thing wrong with the theology?

The problem however is far from simple; for it is partly a question of the way that art itself demands a localization and articulation that are not like life, and uniquely so in the situation to which Golding's explorations, and their form, have led him. In 'life' terms, whatever our philosophy, there seems to be no particular difficulty about conceiving that a boy of nineteen, before he actually does anything, might be so self-conditioned that he cannot help himself when the moment of apparent choice of action appears. In life this would be a process, only gradually becoming conscious. But just as a parabola must contain a single point which belongs neither to the up curve nor the down, but is the point where one turns into the other, so such a process would have to contain a single moment of determination. Yet to represent such a moment fully, any artist would have to give it a prominence and explicitness out of keeping with its true place in the curve; though he could try to minimize this to a greater or lesser extent by gradual preparation and consequence.

The real difficulty then is not the 'theology'; rather that Golding chooses to maximize his highlighting, and to give his scene a clarity of analysis and an explicitness of language that stretch realistic credibility to breaking point. Why is this?

Most obviously, it is because this is Sammy's book, and the whole driving force of it is his search precisely for a *moment* of choice. This must inevitably 'island' it 'in a picture', since he is not interested in the re-creation of the process, the accumulation of tiny nudges towards it, or confirming it afterwards. The process is of course implicitly there, but we do not experience it in lifelike graduation because of the analytic mode that Sammy imposes on the whole section. This in turn, as we have seen, is because his search has reached after the cell a point where he knows exactly what he is looking for and where to find it. He is a man hastening to a destination, superimposing upon the features of experience a grid-map of itinerary. When he reaches the scene, we experience it as his clarification to himself of what the boy was doing. The boy must have been conscious and deliberate, morally speaking, in the movements of consciousness within the mind, but not in that way or that language; yet what is important for Sammy is not at all to experience the boy realistically, but to get the implications precisely clear. Finally we might quote Sammy on his own painting. He knows that 'the rectangle of a canvas' is 'a limited area however ingeniously you paint ... Living ... is too subtle and copious for unassisted thought. Painting is like a single attribute, a selected thing.' But he sees also the peculiar nature of his success in catching Beatrice in a picture:

I had put the girl on paper in a way that my laborious portraitures could never come at. The line leapt, it was joyous, free, authoritative. It achieved little miracles of implication so that the viewer's eye created her small hands though my pencil had not touched them. That free line had raced past and created her face, had thinned and broken where no pencil could go, but only the imagination.

This is obviously Golding on his own art too, or what he would like it to be. (We have seen how this new novel is bound to be about writing a novel and reading a novel because of the new problems Golding was posing himself.) Ought we not, then, to look at the scene of Sammy's fall in the same way, to see that it implies what it does not need to show in detail? If it 'breaks', it merely honestly indicates the boundary-line where – if we want what 'really' must have occurred – art must no longer seek to encapsulate, but rather to liberate the imagination?

Yet this will not altogether dismiss the difficulty either; because there remains a sense in which it is part of the whole clash of Being and Becoming in the novel. Sammy's painting, as we have seen many times, is an Art of Being; what the portrait of Beatrice does is 'catch this particular signature of being which made her unique'. Yet the moment of Sammy's fall is a moment of Becoming. And we may ask how far an *Art* of Becoming exists in the novel as a whole?

Its 'Being' sections – Rotten Row and boyhood, the cell and the transfigured camp – are both assured and homogeneous. There *is* an Art of Becoming: its sections – the affair with Beatrice and the closing section – do exhibit a strength new in Golding's work. In their richness of observed detail, speech, motivation, psychology, behaviour, they are also imaginatively resourceful and confident. Yet, significantly, they are not homogeneous. The first, as we saw, is continually shot through with intimations of Being; the second is patterned analytically as we have just been arguing. Page by page the scenes convince, but they are always felt to be in the service of some governing purpose which frames them, islands them (in that significant phrase we may now complete) '*out* of the complexities of living'. Surely, however reasonable the technical explanation, it is true that in pitting one kind of novel against another, Golding's art remains finally weighted towards an art of Being? It is much less so than in any of the previous novels; it is capable of dealing with new complexities in a new way; but it never wholly commits itself to that way without revealing a clear tendency to veer back. So, at the key moment of choice, we may still feel that the 'islanding' is excessive, and that some more marked move towards the Art of Becoming would have been more appropriate. The novelist's eyes which saw no need to take longer, to do far more filling in of what is only implied, to place one more firmly in the boy's consciousness, are eyes still primarily concerned with Being. Yet, on the evidence of the novel, it is by no means a question of incapacity. Golding clearly possessed the means, if he had been convinced of the need, for more 'laborious portraitures'.

VII

Yet such criticism pales beside Golding's self-criticism, once we see the significance of the novel's final page. We may object that in pitting one mode of explanation against the other, he is still caught in a too reductive pattern of Being; and that he ought to have swung over to more development of character, where signpostings like 'Beatrice Ifor', let alone Beatrice turning into Ifor, would have to be paid for in a different currency. But Golding himself is altogether more thoroughgoing.

In *Free Fall*, finally, he comes to see both Becoming and Being as patterns, and sees *all* pattern as reductive. What we have been discussing is Sammy's book; but it ends at the top of page 253, and for the rest of the page Golding himself takes over as we have been expecting him to do, and the effect is revolutionary. In the end neither Being nor Becoming, nor yet Sammy's attempt to adjust them to each other, will do.

Let us recapitulate Sammy's two worlds without a bridge, conceptually. There is one kind of pattern where cause and effect operate, man chooses, and becomes what he chooses by acting. In Nick's language: 'If you do that sort of thing you become that sort of animal. The universe is wonderfully exact, Sammy. You can't have your penny and your bun. Conservation of energy holds good mentally as well as physically.' The exactness of cause and effect may have to be studied with greater and greater subtlety, beyond, say, the uncertainty of Kenneth on the cause of Beatrice's insanity, but behaviour is ultimately explicable. Humans are free to change, but only from one state into another, they cannot combine both states. There is responsibility, but there is also the possibility of forgiveness through understanding. There is nothing that cannot be explained.

Conversely, in the other kind of pattern, man chooses to *be* one thing or another, and this determines all his actions. Nick's phrases are reversed. If you are that sort of being you do that sort of thing – and have no freedom to do otherwise. But here there is no conservation of energy: the bush burns unconsumed; the good shine, even if they behave badly or foolishly, continually generating light from within; the evil generate vile shapes unceasingly. The self cannot be changed. There can be a change of vision, but this only clarifies the nature of the being it inhabits. There is responsibility, but no forgiveness. There is no 'explanation'; there is revelation, apocalypse, recognition.

Both patterns are true; hence neither can be true in itself. Sammy uses both, but he also manages to adjust them to each other at two points. Being and Becoming cross at the moment of free fall, where Sammy becomes what he chooses. They cross again at the moment of resurrection, when the lips utter the cry in the cell. This is in one sense a death and a new beginning. But the beginning is only one of *judgement*; the fourth dimension crosses the other three only to condemn.

We have also to adjust the characters to these worlds. Most live in only one pattern. Taffy, Kenneth, Sammy himself in his marriage, live purely in a world of Becoming, where forgiveness is possible and there are no grey faces. The Good, like Johnny and Nick, and the infant Samuel, live purely in the realm of Being and neither need nor can give forgiveness. The Wicked, like Rowena and Philip, also live in that single world, and do not recognize any need for forgiveness. But there is a new distinction between the Wicked and the Guilty: 'The innocent and the wicked live in one world ... But we are neither the innocent nor the wicked. We are the guilty ... We weep and tear each other.' The Guilty live in both worlds, so that they recognize what they are, understand how they became as they are, but can find no forgiveness. These are Sammy and perhaps his guardian, who knows what's what, and outgrows his Christian biretta. For them, most terrible of all, 'both worlds are true. There is no bridge.'

Sammy has explained how he became what he is; but if the deeper object of the search was the reconciliation of the two worlds, it is self-defeating. Both patterns are true, but their truths remain contradictory; they touch, only to condemn. Sammy fails to find what he was looking for most.

On the last page, however, Golding moves beyond him. The ending differs from those of the previous novels in that it contains no surprise or shock; indeed, it could hardly be more ordinary, less dramatic. Yet it is like them in that the author looks again at what has been achieved as a whole, and asks us to do the same; and its effect is more unsettling than ever before.

One tiny piece is missing from the jigsaw of Sammy's experience; and while the gap is emphasized by the rest, it must also in some sense give a new and final orientation to everything else. Narratively it is utterly simple: just the moment when the cell door opens and Sammy emerges to find the commandant sitting where Halde had been. Behind Sammy is an ordinary cupboard with a wet floorcloth on the concrete, and four utterly simple sentences are spoken. Yet they leave Sammy puzzling, as though they were the Sphinx's riddle 'what is man?'.

This, indeed, is just what they are, and their cryptic density and opacity is Golding's hard-won answer to the reductiveness of *all* pattern. The puzzled Sammy of the final sentence is a wiser man than the one who penned the confident statement at the top of the page. For it is not merely that Being and Becoming are both reductive patterns. Sammy's dichotomy is a pattern too, albeit a more complex one than the twin components it tries to adjust. At the very end we are given an opportunity to see without pattern; a hint of how cryptic and intensely difficult such seeing must be, a challenge to achieve it.

For the difficulty is not that the simple sentences are meaningless; it is the opposite. They mean too much, too contradictorily, and they must mean their contradictions simultaneously. The moment that we 'explain' them as meaning one thing, or even one thing *or* another, we fail the challenge of seeing that they mean both at once. We fall again into pattern, into reduction.

'Heraus' is a curt, brutal-sounding order from the world of

punishment and imprisonment; a command only to change one prison for another. It is also – Go out – an offer of an open door, and Compassion sitting where the Judge had been expected. It is neither; because it is and must be both together. We must also complete 'You have heard?' in two opposite ways at once. Have you heard the good news? that there is no judgement, that you are free, forgiven, have died into new life? And – we remember the same words on the lips of the lieutenant – Have you heard the bad news? The two indefatigable cricketers have been shot, the weeping Sammy tortured. 'This should not be happening. I am sorry.' 'Sorry, Sammy. They're a lot of bloody murderers.' 'Bloody swine!' But have you heard that you are a swine and murderer too, that we all are, sorry, and self-condemned? Yet again it cannot mean either because it must mean both, simultaneously. So, 'the Herr Doctor does not know about peoples'. He does of course: has he not tapped Sammy's loathsomeness, revealed him to himself? But he also does not, because he is an 'explainer', an 'either/or man' ('are you a hero or not, Sammy?'), a reducer. The moment we fail Golding's challenge and 'reduce' the cryptograms, we too are on the slippery slope. It is only in riddle, in dense opacity, total ambiguity, that things can be seen as they really are.

And what then of Sammy's book?

For Golding, it can only be a failure. Sammy's paintings of the Kings of Egypt in simultaneous misery and glory are not only his greatest work, but 'likely to remain so', for they point to where his book cannot go. At its end we see clearly why only the man who has experienced both worlds should have even the opportunity to see truly. Certainly none of the reductive characters could do so. Miss Ifor, Nick and Rowena, Johnny and Philip, Taffy and Kenneth, Dr Halde, all escape the agony, but necessarily forfeit the vision. Yet we do not see Sammy the writer achieving it, nor know whether he could, ever. From the old standpoint of Becoming we might have objected that while we can accept what Sammy sees after the cell as true for him, we never have a chance to verify for ourselves something like the 'real' radiance of Beatrice. But the criticism now is a far deeper one. We are *not* meant to substitute the painter's Beatrice for the lover's. She is both a girl with a light in her face and a shining being; a girl sexually inhibited, frustrated and frustrating; both Beatrice and Ifor at once. So Nick is saint and devil, radiant and evilly reductive, simultaneously. But the objection is not that we do not see as Sammy sees. For Sammy does not see like this. The objection is that because Sammy cannot see truly, neither can we. His split vision may be only an eyelash away from meeting the conditions of true sight that Golding has come to realize by struggling in and through him. But the eyelash splits the focus. Sammy's pattern of mutually exclusive modes would only have to be altered by bringing them, superimposed, into the same focus; but this is the whole difference between single and double vision. And there is no achievement of single vision: only a cryptic challenge to try it for ourselves in its astonishing difficulty, and an obscure indication of the conditions it must meet. Self-mockingly, Golding adopts a comic German-English to tell us that Herr Doctor/Sammy/Golding 'does not know about peoples'. No criticism of *Free Fall* has been nearly as trenchant as its author's.

Yet it is surely not perverse to claim the book as a considerable achievement, not in spite of but because of all this. It is only through a huge effort of exploration, analysis, and discovery that we have been able first to recognize the problem, and then to see at least the way to overcome it.* The author of the first three Golding novels was already a novelist of real stature. To read *Free Fall* properly is to watch that novelist in the act of transforming himself, not without pain. And as *Pincher Martin* produced the problem which led to *Free Fall*, so the writing of his fourth novel clarified for Golding what he had to attempt in *The Spire*. *Free Fall* diagnoses true, single vision. *The Spire* seeks to attain it.

---

* The goal is strikingly similar to Iris Murdoch's in her interesting essay *Against Dryness* (*Encounter*, January 1961, pp. 16–20). See our different, but related discussion of 'fable', 'history' and 'myth' in Ch. 6.

5

THE SPIRE

(1964)

I

In some ways *The Spire* reverses the psalmist's cry; the straight is made crooked and the plain places rough. Ambiguity, paradox, reversal, these are the words that come most readily to mind when we try to give an account of the book, and they seem no less just when we agree that in its purely narrative trajectory *The Spire* is the most straightforward of Golding's novels since *Lord of the Flies*. The story has none of the obscurity of *The Inheritors*, springing from the imaginative demand that we enter the consciousness of primitive people; nor the double structure behind *Pincher Martin*'s remorseless concentration on a single moment; nor the sudden shifts in time, direction and mode of *Free Fall*. The narrative is generally as clear as the spire itself; any obstruction in reading comes from the density and intensity with which its implications are investigated. For the moment we pause to make sure that we have understood the detail, the atmosphere changes. What looked like firm ground turns into a mirage, cross-lights begin to play on the scene, so that fair seems foul and foul fair.

It is useful to begin by recording this dual impression of the novel – extreme clarity accompanied by extreme opacity – because if it is part of our experience of reading, it is also part of the meaning. This curious impression is not a sequential one, we do not find light giving way to darkness. Rather, the light changes constantly as we read. We can often see, caught in a single paragraph, different reflections of the book as a whole. One such moment occurs at the beginning of the novel, when Jocelin stands at the great west door of his cathedral looking up the aisle:

The most solid thing was the light. It smashed through the rows of windows in the south aisle, so that they exploded with colour, it slanted before him from right to left in an exact formation, to hit the bottom yard of the pillars on the north side of the nave. Everywhere, fine dust gave these rods and trunks of light the importance of a dimension. He blinked at them again, seeing, near at hand, how the individual grains of dust turned over each other, or bounced all together, like mayfly in a breath of wind. He saw how further away they drifted cloudily, coiled, or hung in a moment of pause, becoming, in the most distant rods and trunks, nothing but colour, honey-colour slashed across the body of the cathedral. Where the south transept lighted the crossways from a hundred and fifty foot of grisaille, the honey thickened in a pillar that lifted straight as Abel's from the men working with crows at the pavement.

He shook his head in rueful wonder at the solid sunlight. If it were not for that Abel's pillar, he thought, I would take the important level of light to be a true dimension, and so believe that my stone ship lay aground on her side; and he smiled a little, to think how the mind touches all things with law, yet deceives itself as easily as a child.

An immediate response to such a passage is likely to be to its visual brilliance, the perceptive rendering of intense sunlight in the dark and dusty nave. When we come like Jocelin to see 'near at hand', we see that the light is trapped and seen in terms of the very different element of dust. In the foreground, the individual grains dance in relation to one another; further off, the dance becomes collective; in the distance, there is a blending into 'sundust', honey-coloured against the darkness, so solid that it seems no less of a pillar than those of stone. The confidence of the eye is shaken, and the paragraph concludes by questioning the vision itself, knowing that the eye can get the angles, the certainties of horizontal and vertical, wrong.

We see that this is not simply a description of the vagaries of light in darkness. The scene has dramatic content, a subject. Cathedrals are not usually in a state of dust and chaos, and in the relation between the sunlight and the dust kicked up by Jocelin's decision to build the spire, there exists one of the main tensions in the plot itself. The novel will turn out to be about seeing in a very literal sense, seeing neither sun nor dust but 'sundust'. It will not be surprising when the comparison of individual speck and mayfly makes its reappearance as a bleak comment on human beings. Abel's pillar reminds us of something also suggested by the stained glass window of Abraham and Isaac with which the novel opens. The work of God, the building of the church, may include bloodshed, sacrifice, murder. The pillar looks straight, the window looks beautiful – but the story they tell is of crookedness and suffering. When Jocelin smiles 'to think how the mind touches all things with law, yet deceives itself as easily as a child', we seem to have an authorial comment; but later we shall come to see that this reflection has a dangerous facility, that it exhibits Jocelin's complacent handling of a truth to which, personally, he is blind. His smile is actually the measure of his self-indulgence, created for us also by the exalted, 'whipped-up' style with which the book opens. This use of style has been characteristic since *Pincher Martin*.

And so we come back to the paragraph, not simply as an expression of something finely seen and rendered, but as a dramatization of what it is to see only what one wants to see, and to see without understanding or insight. Jocelin's vision operates at a level of dangerous intensity: the light 'smashed through the rows of windows in the south aisle, so that they exploded with colour', the honey colour is 'slashed across the body of the cathedral'. Though Jocelin may smile at 'the important level of light', *he* is in no doubt of the 'true dimension'. The progress of the novel will consist in the taming of metaphors of violence, the overturning of certainties, the transformation of primary colours to depth and shade. The book which opens with such explosive confidence will end in puzzle, with a truth not seen so much as glimpsed from the very corner of the eye, expressed not with the bold assumptions of emblematic metaphor, but with the tentativeness of simile: *'It's like the appletree!'*

II

From emblem to simile – we could see *The Spire* as developing in that way, and in saying this we would be establishing a wavelength for reading. Golding's boldness is to make his central character an 'alter-novelist', a patternmaker, an emblematist, a refiner of the raw material of experience. His church is a man lying on his back, the nave his legs placed together, the transepts his arms outstretched. ' "We are labour" said the walls. The ogival windows clasped their hands and sang; "We are prayer" ... I had seen the whole building as an image of living praying man ... inside it was a written book to instruct that man.' But the 'written book' that Golding creates, for Jocelin's instruction and ours, tells the price of having a meaning but missing the experience. The whole of Golding's art is concerned to create a spire in the place occupied, in Jocelin's mind, by a diagram of prayer; glass, stone and steel, not only the 'fabric of constant praise'. The two voices are clearly caught in dialogue between Jocelin and his master mason:

'We're surrounded by new things. We guess; and go on building. . . . we've come to something different because we were chosen, both of us. We're mayfly. We can't tell what it'll be like up there from foot to foot; but we must live from the morning to the evening every minute with a new thing.'

To which Roger replies:

'I don't know what you mean. But I know how much the spire will weigh, and I don't know how strong it'll be. Look down, Father – right over the parapet, all the way down, past the lights, the buttresses, all the way down to the cedar top in the cloister.'
'I see it.'

These eyes have to be forced to look 'down' or 'at'; their natural tendency is to look 'above' or 'through'.

This strategy of Golding's, the building into his novel of a counter-novel, is one that we examined in relation to *Free Fall*, but here it is used with a much greater consciousness of purpose. In the earlier novel it sprang initially from a degree of uncertainty on the part of the author, and issued in an exploration that belonged to life as well as to art. Here the two 'novels' continuously follow the progress of the spire itself from the beginning. They interplay rather than intersect, one is never supplanted or defeated by the other, there is genuine equipoise until they finally come together. What Jocelin makes abstract, Golding must make concrete; Jocelin's explanations must be Golding's explorations; where Jocelin sees God the Father in a glory of sunlight, Golding must see 'God as lying between people and to be found there'. In this way Golding, like the master mason, 'barters strength for weight, weight for strength'; the novel, no less than the spire, being 'a great dare'. If it reaches its pinnacle in simile, it is because that figure maintains a tension between the things that divide, no less than the things which bring together. The two poles create a field of force only when neither takes over the other.

What exactly *The Spire* is 'like', however, takes us into an analysis of the novel as it unfolds.

III

From the outset of the novel Dean Jocelin dominates the scene and our imaginations. Our response to him is however continuously ambivalent – is he a saint or a destructive monomaniac, self-deceived? The first four chapters suggest that any answer will be paradoxical.

The first chapter is ablaze with sunlight and exaltation; but we are presented with a visionary who sees nothing. We encounter him laughing, crying with happiness as God the Father seems to explode in radiance through the stained glass; but his eyes are half-closed and the upthrust chin does not make for clear sight. The meaning of the stained glass, that story of Abraham and Isaac and the cost of faith, passes him by; and it does so because his glance is so fixedly upwards. He cannot focus on Pangall and the tear he sheds:

There was a sharp tap on the instep of Jocelin's shoe; and as he looked he saw a wet star there with arms to it and tiny globes of water that slid off the dubbin into the mud of the yard. Impatiently, he let out his breath and looked round for something to say. But the sunlight on stone drew his eye upward, to the empty air above the crossways. . . .

'Joy', 'love', 'patience', 'forgiveness' – such words are constantly on Jocelin's lips; but of the realities which give the words meaning he remains tragically unaware. Pangall is an irritation. Father Adam has 'no face at all. He is the same all round like the top of a clothespeg'. Jocelin is deaf to the depths of God's 'simplicities' as the choir sings the creed. He is just as deaf to the voice of Caesar when, reading the letter from his patroness in the bright light of the crossways, he refuses her any answer.

The second chapter reverses the strategy of the first. Dust obscures the sunshine. In a thick yellow fog workmen with de-formed, cloth-covered faces caked with dirt and sweat, chant obscene songs in the transepts. The pit dug at the crossways reveals that the church rests on rubble, brushwood, mud. The human instruments of the work are no more reliable. The master mason sees his assignment in the light of his own ends, and turns a blind eye to the fighting among his men and their sadistic treatment of Pangall. His wife Rachel is vulgar, 'emancipated', a ceaseless torrent of words. The Sacrist, Father Anselm, with his beautiful head, silver-haired and saintly, has a cold unloving heart, and a mind bound by rule and prescription. On the other hand, if the first chapter was concerned to point to the pride beneath Jocelin's sunny faith, here in the dust of the cathedral we are reminded of his warmth. We are not in doubt of his superiority as a human being to the others we meet. The power of his faith is thrown into high relief by the scepticism of the master builder. His heart may be on his sleeve, but it exists as the Sacrist's does not: ' "Father Anselm. Friendship is a precious thing. . . . What have we done to it?" "Is that a real question, my Lord, or a rhetorical one?" ' But, even with Anselm, Golding is fair. Amusement, a curious kindness, flicker across that pseudo-noble face and we are made, in Jocelin's words, to balance one scale against another.

Sunshine, Dust, these elements belong to the surface. The third chapter introduces another element, Water, which takes us below ground, to places which are hidden, either in the church or in the human mind. Water seeps into the pit, into the graves in the choir and arcades, and the cathedral fills with the smell of corruption. There is irrational fear among the workmen, hysteria, and one of them falls from the roof leaving 'a scream scored all the way down the air'. The old Chancellor lapses into imbecility. Plague threatens; 'and the voices rose, in fear of age and death, in fear of weight and dimension, in fear of darkness and a universe without hope'. Jocelin is taken into the human cellarage. He learns of Pangall's impotence, Rachel's coital giggle that makes her incapable of giving or receiving fulfilment. Above all, he begins to be made aware of the growing relation between Pangall's wife and Roger Mason. To these intimations of mortality Jocelin's attitude is one of uncomprehending revulsion:

[Rachel] stripped the business of living down to where horror and farce took over ... He spoke viciously ... 'The impervious insolence of the woman!' ... He cried out loud. 'Filth! Filth!'

His feelings toward Roger and Goody bring together the subterranean worlds of the mind and the earth:

Then an anger rose out of some pit inside Jocelin ... He lifted his chin, and the word burst out over it from an obscure place of indignation and hurt. 'No!' All at once it seemed to him that the renewing life of the world was a filthy thing, a rising tide of muck so that he gasped for air ...

The very vehemence of Jocelin's disgust is however an indication of his own 'cellarage'. When he looks at a stained glass window now it is not to see 'God the Father exploding in a glory of sunlight' but a 'dully rich story ... and the light of the altar was a divided thing, a light in each eye'. His mind is inhabited now by the devil as well as the angel; he can no longer suppress his own sexuality; the revelation of others' begins to reveal him to himself. In the sexual dream which closes the chapter the world within and the world without are seen within one perspective. The devil masturbates the phallus/spire of his body. And the dream poses the question: is the building of the Spire a similar self-erection and self-fulfilment, a distortion and degradation of God-given creativity?

The fourth chapter literally clears the air, and lifts us into the sky. The wind blows the rain away and dries the earth. On the roof of the crossways the lead is rolled back to reveal blue sky; and at once the explosive ecstatic language is back, the old perspective resumed. Delightedly, Jocelin climbs into the tower, where

the pit was no more than a black dot, a hundred and twenty feet below ... It seemed suddenly to Jocelin that now he loved everybody with ease and delight ... So Jocelin clasped his hands, lifted up his head and included the boys and the dumb man and Roger Mason and Goody in one tremendous ejaculation: 'Rejoice, O daughters of Jerusalem!'

But though the language may be back, the tone has lost its assurance since the opening chapter. The brilliant sunshine causes confusion, shadows, after-images. The church at Easter is divided: flowers in the Lady Chapel, but on the other side of the screen 'the body of the church was as secular as a stable or an empty tythe barn'.

Throughout Lent Jocelin preaches, but does not confess or repent. He cannot stay 'above' in the tower, cannot forget or ignore what he has learnt of Rachel, Roger, Goody and Pangall. The internal turmoil of visitation by angel and devil grows worse, robs him of sleep, makes his head ache and flashes of pain dart across his eyes. And suddenly those eyes are forced to concentrate on the pit at the crossways where a sheet of metal has been set up to throw light to the bottom. There he sees what it is for a building to aspire beyond the nature of its foundations:

Then, as Jocelin looked, he saw a pebble drop with two clods of earth; and immediately a patch perhaps a yard square fell out of the side below him and struck the bottom with a soft thud. The pebbles that fell with it lay shining dully in the reflected light, and settled themselves in their new bed. But as he watched them and waited for them to settle, the hair rose on the nape of his neck; for they never settled completely. He saw one stir, as with a sudden restlessness; and then he saw that they were all moving more or less, with a slow stirring, like the stirring of grubs. The earth was moving under the grubs, urging them this way and that, like porridge coming to the boil in a pot ...

As the pavement splits and the pillars sing with unbearable strain, the whole army of workers become hysterical with fear. Frantically, they try to fill the pit with, amongst other rubble, the blindly ecstatic stone heads of Jocelin the dumb sculptor had been carving. The Dean himself kneels directly under the central keystone of the crossing. Defiantly he 'knelt, stiff, painful and enduring; and all the time, the singing of the stones operated on the inside of his head. At last, when he understood nothing else at all, he knew that the whole weight of the building was resting on his back.' This is a parody of prayer in that it is dominantly self-assertion, self-will. There is no hint of penance or humility, no abandonment to the will of another. Nevertheless there are intensities of courage, faith, and vision here, and beside these the attitude of the master mason to the building seems puny and cynical. But Jocelin is willing to sacrifice not only himself but Roger too, in his absolute determination to see the spire built: 'I'm only learning now, how terrible it is. It's a refiner's fire. The man knows a little perhaps of the purpose, but nothing of the cost ...' The story of Abraham and Isaac is more than a picture now.

But the sacrifice which in fact follows is a terrible parody of the story of the man of faith. This is one of the few points in the novel where the narrative becomes obscure. The presentation is extremely elliptical because Golding wishes his reader, like Jocelin himself, to be made to realize only very slowly the full implications of Roger's frantic warning: 'You just don't know what'll come out of our going on!' Jocelin's view of the scene is obscured, and so is ours. The full realization of what actually happens will come only much later. But for clarity's sake we may anticipate.

As so often in Golding – the murder of Simon, the sacrifice of Liku – it is panic which precipitates tragedy. The army of workmen, shattered by seeing the foundations move, are waiting for the obvious decision that they are to abandon the spire. Roger returns to tell them that Jocelin has left them no choice but to go on, in the face of what seems inevitable disaster. Their response is a 'fierce yell'. They have become used to using Pangall as their 'fool', who brings them luck because they objectify in him their sense of the misshapen and ridiculous, and neutralize it in mime and mockery. At this moment of panic and rage they turn on him *en masse*. With a victim so helpless (as with Simon in *Lord of the Flies*), tormenting turns to sadism and vilification to bloodlust. But, once again, there is more – there is primitive magic. In Pangall, Misshapenness and Impotence are ritually murdered. The sacrificial victim is built into the pit to strengthen the inadequate foundations. Across the terrible scene Roger and Goody face each other 'in anguish and appeal, in acknowledgement of consent and defeat'. Jocelin, protected against the mob by the dumb man's body, has no real idea of what he has done; but after these four chapters he, and we, will have to learn to 'count the cost' in a more terrible currency.

IV

The first four chapters are intensive, the next four are extensive, as the tower rises and permits wider and higher views. 'Up here' there is growth, certainty, happiness; 'below' is darkness, incomprehension, distraction. Or – so it seems.

... he passed through the close from the deanery to the west door, hardly able to see his feet for fog; and though the nave was clear of it, like a sort of bubble, it was near enough pitch dark. He climbed, and came out of the corkscrew stair on to the beams, and in a blinding dazzle. For up here, the sun was shining ... there was downland visible all round but nothing else. The fog lay in a dazzling, burning patch over the valley and the city, with nothing but the spire or the tower at least, piercing it. Then he was strangely comforted, and for a time, almost at peace.

A sense of claustrophobia gives way to relief as the novel opens out, as Jocelin climbs away from the nave. But this is only 'for a time'. The cellarage cannot be ignored by climbing into the tower. 'Up here', 'out yonder', 'down there', turn out to be part one of the other, as chapters five to eight make clear.

The terrible scene by the pillar marks a watershed for Jocelin, even though he does not understand it consciously. He emerges noticeably changed, not in his will, which is even more a 'blazing certainty', but in the disturbance of his mind, his sudden high-pitched giggles, his kaleidoscope of emotions. Prayer, confession, human relationship, are all locked out of his mind. He absorbs himself in the work. But the cellarage lies in constant wait:

Among the rubbish at the bottom of the pillar he saw there was a twig lying across his shoe, with a rotting berry that clung obscenely to the leather. He scuffed his foot irritably; and as now so often seemed to happen, the berry and the twig could not be forgotten, but set off a whole train of memories and worries and associations which were altogether random. He found himself thinking of the ship that was built of timber so unseasoned, a twig in her hold put out one green leaf. He had an instant vision of the spire warping and branching and sprouting; and the terror of that had him on his feet. I must learn about wood, he thought ...

This passage catches admirably the disturbance of a mind uncon-sciously aware of things it does not wish to know consciously, things which insist on intruding. The odd pressure behind the word 'obscenely', the onrush of not-so-random associations, betray his subterranean awareness that his spire has become a branching and sprouting evil, sidestepped by a 'practical' thought which is nevertheless loaded with irony. In fact he is trying not to learn, not to see, what he does not wish to know. He looks straight through Rachel, 'so he never saw the astonishment under the red paint'. What had been myopia before is now a deliberate act of exclusion. When he tries to speak to Goody there is significant misunderstanding and distress, met with a characteristic evasion: 'I must climb away from all this confusion.' And so he does, but to do so he has to twist away the cassock which marks him out as a man of God and a minister. As he climbs above it all, he feels 'the same appalled delight as a small boy feels when first he climbs too high in a forbidden tree'.

From the tower the landscape can be seen in a new way as a unified whole to the eye, an order which the growing, dominating spire arranges with new rationality around itself. Here there seems no confusion, though the new perspective has to include the old man seen stumbling into his privy, the cheating milkmaid, the drunk lying in the ditch, as well as the enclosed nuns behind the walls of their garth. But the view, the landscape, is not in fact just

something 'out there below'. The inner eye also shapes it into
pattern:

He examined the strips and patches of cultivation, the rounded down-
lands that rose to a wooded and notched edge. They were soft and warm
and smooth as a young body.

He got down on his knees, hard, eyes shut, crossing himself and
praying. I bring my essential wickedness even here into thy air. For the
world is not like that. The earth is a huddle of noseless men grinning
upward, there are gallows everywhere, the blood of childbirth never
ceases to flow, nor sweat in the furrow, the brothels are down there and
drunk men lie in the gutter. There is no good thing in all this circle but the
great house, the ark, the refuge, a ship to contain all these people and now
fitted with a mast. Forgive me.

'The world is not like that' – Jocelin's confidence has been
transposed into a different key, but it is still there, only this time
in a radical rejection which amounts again to revulsion. And,
prompting that revulsion, we see the pressure of the sexuality
which is revealed as soon as Jocelin's consciously willed exclusions
are momentarily relaxed.

He cannot live with the eagle and raven; and though he increasingly fears the descent to face life below, face it he must. In Rachel's
babble he learns that Goody is pregnant, and since he knows that
Pangall was impotent this can only be the result of an adultery he
has condoned, and indeed exploited, in forcing Roger to stay.
Jocelin's tears are of rage and disgust at sexuality, not (as he tells
himself) at the drunkenness he has seen; the thick parody of the
Magnificat a transparent self-deception. The learning, the 'wood' of
the evil tree, the lesson of 'the height, the weight, the cost', goes on.

In the sixth chapter the metaphorical overtones these words
have acquired are subjected to a new scrutiny.

We, like Jocelin, are reminded that whatever inner meanings
may be released by the spire, it is first and foremost a technical
fact, an exercise in building. Jocelin turns it into an emblem, an
occasion for a sermon. Our lives are like the mayfly, we can never
tell about the future, 'we must live from the morning to the evening
every minute with a new thing'. The spire is a diagram of prayer,
'each new foot reveals a new effect, a new purpose'. Against this
there is now pitched the full weight of the spire as a physical
reality, the spire which Roger Mason sees:

'Let your eye crawl down like an insect, foot by foot. You think these walls are strong because they're stone; but I know better. We've nothing but a skin of glass and stone stretched between four stone rods, one at each corner. D'you understand that? The stone is no stronger than the glass between the verticals because every inch of the way I have to save weight, bartering strength for weight or weight for strength, guessing how much, how far, how little, how near, until my very heart stops when I think of it. Look down, Father. Don't look at me – look down! See ...'

It is physical sight that Roger tries to restore for Jocelin, and we are made to feel its unquestionable rightness. And yet, just at the point where Jocelin's belief looks too simply an evasion, we are reminded of its quality, its courage, its willingness to trust: 'Roger – He isn't needlessly cruel, you know ... A good workman never uses a tool for something it can't do; never ignores it; takes care of it ... But build quickly ...' It is a mark of Golding's control of this book that he never allows us to adopt a position or settle for a conclusion. A sudden delicate change of tone, the direction of criticism changes, and a new exploration begins.

Jocelin is not the only one who encourages Roger Mason to overcome his fear of heights. Goody in the 'swallow's nest', high in the tower, grips her hand on Roger's as white shows at his knuckles. She too has climbed up the tree from the terror and the shame, as her voice is heard 'pleading, ingenuous, and sweet. "But I didn't laugh – did I?" ' Roger's cry 'as if from the very pit bottom' is, however, one more recognition of the guilt 'up there'. A tower built in faith, built in heavy stone, built in sin: all three perspectives are true. Hence none can be exclusively true.

The incident of the swallow's nest tugs Jocelin out of security into chaos. As far as the building itself is concerned, Roger's 'curious, valuable mind' finds a way around an apparently impossible problem, as Jocelin had foreseen. The disintegration of the spire is prevented by the invention and installation of a steel band riveted around the stonework, taking the strain. Jocelin has to take the full responsibility for the extra cost of the work upon himself alone. But though the band does its work, and imparts a 'new quality' to the stone, there is inevitably a new lesson to be learnt in the light of the new achievement. Jocelin looks down on the cloisters:

The boys of the songschool had left their game on the sill of the arcade again. He could not see the squares of the board scratched in stone, but he could see the white, bone counters of the game that lay on it. He could see some of them; but only some, for the stone between the battlements cut off a corner of the board from his eye. There was a kind of childish security in looking at the game, the white counters, one, two, three, four, five –

His cheek was hard against the pinnacle and he knew he had not moved. But a sixth counter had appeared, had slid into view with another square of board under it. He knew he had not moved; but he knew that the tower had moved, gently, soundlessly up here, though down there the pillars might have cried – eeee – at the movement. Time after time, he watched the white counter slide into view, then disappear again; and he knew that the tower was swaying under him like a tall tree.

There is no secure basis for observation or escape 'up here' at all. The truest knowledge that can be gained here is of the fearful strain on the pillars below that makes them sing; and to listen to such singing is 'a penance'.

The attempt to contain the 'chaos' below is less successful still. Jocelin tries not steel, but money; but the gold with which he hopes to have Goody sent away to the garth at Stilbury comes too late. He is forced to watch one brutal exposure after another. The blood on the money (blood which comes from the abortive birth of Roger's and Goody's child) seems at first sight too crude an emblem, too insistent. Yet there is far more involved here than the blood-money of betrayal. Jocelin had insisted to Roger that God would solve the physical problem of the disintegrating spire if he would trust the promptings of his mind; and the mason duly produced the band of steel. The cost was great, the Chapter would not accept it, and Jocelin took full responsibility himself. Red sparks fly, there is a cry of pain from an injured worker, the white stone is scarred and broken, but Roger has dared to obey his inner prompting, and the steel band holds the tower.

That the 'chaos' below cannot be held is not just attributable to the greater complexity of the human situation. Jocelin, too, has had inner promptings about Goody, but he has done nothing. He seeks now not to include but to exclude her. So he has to watch red blood from Roger's head, red hair twisted round Rachel's fingers, red blood from the 'knife-pains' in the white flesh, all that pain issuing in a birth wholly abortive. The blood on the money summarizes all this and precipitates the agonized recognition, 'this have I done for my true love' – and it raises to a new level Jocelin's appalled understanding of his inadequate sense of human cost. 'I was a protected man', he cries. 'I never came up against beldame.' ('Sex' in that sense being a modern word, this is one of the very few times when Golding's medieval setting appears to have given him any difficulty.) Jocelin has been seriously ignorant of human nature, priding himself in his attempt to exclude sexuality in excessive and morbid revulsion. 'This have I done for my true love': the words of the Easter carol refer directly to the betrayal of Christ, who sacrificed himself for love of fallen man, while Jocelin has both sacrificed others and exploited their fall in 'the dreadful glow of his dedicated will'. Deeper still, and still hidden from Jocelin, the words carry a hint of the secret of his true feelings for this girl – a hinted betrayal not only of her, and of God, but of himself.

In the eighth chapter any remaining distinction between 'up here', 'out yonder' and 'down there' is finally demolished. The death of Goody loosens in Jocelin the dykes that kept the dark inner water from flowing into consciousness. Now 'he would be aware of a feeling rising in him, coming up towards the chest like a level of dark water'. With a new clarity of eye ('pain did it, pain did it, pain did it'), and a new humility ('I'm not very intelligent'), he begins to examine internal feelings and external relationships: 'What's this called? And this?' With a shock, we realize that these are the first genuine questions in the book. Anselm had a point after all; the others were merely rhetorical.

As the cone of the spire rises, the light fades within while the octagons narrow and enclose. The snaking rope that hangs from the louvre seems 'haunted', possessed of an evilly destructive spirit. The pillars can no longer take the strain of remaining upright, they bend and become crooked – though the singing stops, for good. At this discovery Roger, already sodden with drink, not only bends but breaks. The human singing to God stops too, since services can no longer be held in the cathedral. Even the godless curse Jocelin. The 'little ones', the children of God who must be suffered to come unto him, are driven out by 'the great ones, the builders'; the capstone hanging round the spire's neck reminding us of the biblical penalty. Faith at such a price becomes indistinguishable from blasphemy.

'In', 'yonder', 'below': in a swift summarizing series the perspectives are put before us, merge, and fade into one another. 'In' – Jocelin sees himself reflected in the metal sheet that had thrown light into the pit:

For a moment he thought of exorcism, but when he lifted his hand, the figure raised one too. So he crawled across the boards on hands and knees and the figure crawled towards him. He knelt and peered in at the wild halo of hair, the skinny arms and legs that stuck out of a girt and dirty robe. He peered in closer and closer until his breath dimmed his own image and he had to smear it off with his sleeve. After that he knelt and peered for a long time. He examined his eyes, deep in sockets over which the skin was dragged – dragged too over the cheekbones, then sucked in. He examined the nose like a beak and now nearly as sharp, the deep grooves in the face, the gleam of teeth.

The kneeling image cleared his head. Well Jocelin, he said soundlessly to the kneeling image; Well Jocelin, this is where we have come.

It is a moment in which we are made sharply aware of the cost to Jocelin himself, his suffering, borne without self-pity; and yet at the same time the image inclines towards parody. The kneeling, the halo, the girt robe dramatize the man away into an ironic gargoyle.

Having looked 'in', his gaze turns outward towards the 'cup' of the horizon:

The evening turned green over the rim of the cup. Then the rim went black and shadows filled it silently so that before he was well aware of it, night had fallen and the faint stars come out. He saw a fire on the rim and guessed it was a haystack burning; but as he moved round the rim of the cone, he saw more and more fires round the rim of the world. Then a terrible dread fell on him for he knew these were the fires of Midsummer Night, lighted by the devil worshippers out on the hills. Over there, in the valley of the Hanging Stones, a vast fire shuddered brightly. All at once he cried out, not in terror but in grief. For he remembered his crew of good men, and he knew why they had knocked off work and where they were gone. So he shouted aloud in anger at someone.

'They are good men! I say so!'

But this was only one feeling. Inside them, his mind knew what it knew.

It is a bitter irony on the growing love between Jocelin and the men he thinks he knows better than anyone he has ever known. Moreover, the 'lesson for this height' is not just the cross 'up here' fighting the devil 'out yonder'. 'Up here' is a temple built by a

David with blood on his hands; a gargoyle-priest wondering whether the loss of God has been 'included' in the cost. Now, faced with the fiery horizon, 'a host of memories flew together. He watched, powerless to stop as they added to each other. They were like sentences from a story, which though they left great gaps, still told enough.' Knowing now that his beloved men are Druidic devil-worshippers, he realizes at long last what must have happened to Pangall – the significance of the rotting mistletoe berry. But if his men are sacrificers, so is he. Evil is not just 'out yonder' in the bale fires 'on the rim of the world'. It is 'up here' where 'the story, with the disjunct sentences, burned before his mind'; it is 'down there' at the crossways where 'the replaced paving stones were hot to his feet with all the fires of hell'.

V

The third and final part of the book opens with what looks like an ending. In Roger's absence his foreman Jehan loosens too quickly the cable around the wedges. The octagons come thundering down; with a breaking of stone and a splintering of woodwork the spire impacts itself into the parapet, while terrified workmen fight down the ladders. The great work still stands. Yet it openly manifests its crookedness. The novel about building a spire is over.

Following the pattern of the earlier novels, Golding alters the viewpoint when the action is completed. But the change marked by the arrival of the Visitor and his Commission is not obtrusive; and much more a starting-point for a farther journey than a milestone showing how far we have travelled. It is illuminating to compare the arrival of the Visitor with the arrival of the naval officer in *Lord of the Flies*.

At first it does look as if the pattern in the earlier novel is to be repeated. Anselm's muttered 'Why shouldn't he see him as he is' seems to prepare for an ironical scene in which appearances will be played off against realities – though it is Jocelin's 'adult' vision that sees the Chapter as a crowd of little children, growing smaller. The real change from the earlier novel lies however in the Visitor himself, and his treatment. There is no incomprehension here, no complacency. He is full-size, powerful, intuitive, sympathetic. We can have nothing but respect for his handling of Anselm and for his acceptance of Jocelin's definitions of faith and service. If we can understand why Jocelin feels the interrogation 'unfair and unanswerable', we can also see how lethal the exposure of the tainted money and the tainted workmen is, and how myopic and desperate Jocelin's answers sound when the questions are put. The Visitor retains a real sense of Jocelin's faith, and though there is a gap between his experience and ours, the interrogation is still rightly directed.

As the questioning proceeds, the direction becomes clear. Jocelin is forced into answers which sharpen his self-knowledge:

She's woven into it everywhere. She died and then she came alive in my mind. She's there now. She haunts me. She wasn't alive before, not in that way. And I must have known about him before, you see, down in the vaults, the cellarage of my mind.

It is these vaults that the interrogation opens for Jocelin. For the first time he becomes consciously aware of 'levels':

... on the purely human level of course, it's a story of shame and folly – Jocelin's Folly, they call it. I had a vision you see, a clear and explicit vision. It was so simple! It was to be my work. I was chosen for it. But then the complications began. A single green shoot at first, then clinging tendrils, then branches, then at last a riotous confusion ...

Even now, however, this is still too crisply analytic. Metaphors block the work of understanding. Every item has now to be examined by bringing it into focused experience. The image of the Tree of Evil, burgeoning in the work, in the mind, in the heart, contains whatever 'explanation' there seems to be, but that explanation can only be earned when the image has been destroyed and replaced by physical and psychological reality. As the inquisition ends, we see Jocelin girding himself for a terrible and difficult climb, not like Simon's up an external Mountain of Truth, but within his own being.

The farewell to the old Jocelin and the embarkation on the new can be seen in the bitter ambiguity with which the chapter ends. He still has absolute faith in the power of the God he has lost. He believes in the ability of the crucified Christ to transfigure his Church and make it prevail. The driving of the Holy Nail into the capstone enacts his faith in the way the second Tree redeems the first. With the nail, the spire cannot fall.

But, for himself, he feels the Kingdom to be irretrievably lost 'for want of a nail'. The old rhyme finally opens the last cellar and reveals what he has locked away there; the essential sexuality of his feeling for Goody Pangall. Knowing 'in the cellarage' of Pangall's impotence, he had used it for unadmitted reasons, to keep her from belonging sexually to anyone else. Memory restores her girlhood to him and exposes his unconsciously prurient reaching out to her. Another sexual dream reveals to him the meaning hidden in the earlier ones, the identify of the 'devil' of his lust:

She came towards him naked in her red hair. She was smiling and humming from an empty mouth. He knew the sound explained every-thing, removed all hurt and all concealment, for this was the nature of the uncountry. He could not see the devil's face for this was the nature of the uncountry too; but he knew she was there, and moving towards him totally as he was moving towards her. Then there was a wave of ineffable good sweetness, wave after wave, and an atonement.

And then there was nothing.

He never cared for the girl's personality, hence the facelessness. What he wanted was the dog-like devotion of the dumb man coupled with her body. Refusing to recognize this, let alone crucify it, he created the bogus marriage, which led to the adultery, which led to her death. He exploited Pangall, and, in exploiting the adultery as a hold over Roger, he caused Pangall's death. The 'atonement' contains the final irony. By Christ's Nail there is an atonement for the corrupt material and workmen of the spire. But for Jocelin there is no Nail; the only 'at-one-ment' he has ever desired is the relief of pent-up sexuality in the uncountry of dream with a dehumanized phantom. After that there is nothing. This is the 'darkness of man's heart', found within himself, rather than by the race with the Beast across the churchyard. But where *Lord of the Flies* ends with a weeping recognition, the last three chapters of *The Spire* travel on within the darkness to discover whether all is yet 'included'.

The tenth chapter knocks away the remaining props that might have supported and sustained Jocelin. Was he not 'chosen'? The Lady Alison comes to tell him that, if he was, it was not by God but by the whim of a cynical young king and his courtesan: '"I have a sister and she has a son." ... "We shall drop a plum in his mouth."' Jocelin's deanship is as corrupt as

Ivo's canonry. Is the Nail not holy? Lady Alison has a new perspective for this too.

'Our bishop Walter in Rome –' ... 'I asked him for money, blind fool that I was. He did better.' ...

'You asked him for money – and he sent you a nail!'

'I said so.'

'*Walter!*'

She began to laugh, round after round of laughter that built up high, until it took away her breath, and in the silence he heard the singing of pillars in his ears. It was not that he understood anything or worked out anything by logical steps in his head; but that there was a sickness driving in and a shuddering of the body to his very fingertips.

And then the man of faith, the man who had given Jocelin such unquestioning loyalty (to the point of saving his life), arrives as the final 'messenger'* to tell him that the stone pillars, on which his whole spire depends, are as corrupt as he had made his four human ones. The polished stone skin, gleaming and dust-repellent, covers only rubble. The 'giants' of the past, who built 'a miracle of faith', were liars and cheats without even 'Builder's Honour'. The vocation, the relic, the very material of his work – everything turns to ashes.

Then all things came together. His spirit threw itself down an interior gulf, down, throw away, offer, destroy utterly, build me in with the rest of them; and as he did this he threw his physical body down too, knees, face, chest, smashing on the stone.

Then his angel put away the two wings from the cloven hoof and struck him from arse to the head with a whitehot flail. It filled his spine with sick fire and he shrieked because he could not bear it yet knew he would have to. At some point there were clumsy hands that tried to pick him up; but he could not tell them of the flail because of the way his body threw itself round the crossways like a broken snake. So the body shrieked and the hands fought with him and under the heap was Jocelin who knew that at last one good prayer had been answered.

When the pain ebbed he found they were carrying him back from the place of the sacrifice with careful hands. He lay on an absence of back, and waited.

---

* The strange word becomes accurate if it is a reminiscence, conscious or unconscious, of the role of the messenger in the *peripeteia* and *anagnorisis* of Greek tragedy.

This is the turning-point of the novel, and it establishes itself as such when we recall not merely the continual shift and counter-shift between 'inner' and 'outer', but, more precisely, the identity of Jocelin's spine with Jocelin's spire. We recall the moment when he first realizes the absence of foundations: 'The singing of the stones pierced him ... His will began to burn fiercely and he thrust it into the four pillars, tamped it in with the pain of his neck and his head and his back ... he knew that the whole weight of the building was resting on his back.' But now the very pillars are rubble, and the burning will no longer hides the secret motives which fuelled it: 'His spirit threw itself down ... as he did this he threw his physical body down too, knees, face, chest, smashing on the stone.' Although the significance of the scene must be grasped in terms of the resolution of a radically dualistic vision into a unity, the physical 'foreground' is no less important. Jocelin is the Snake struck by the flail beneath the Evil Tree, but the tubercular spine and the body contorted in pain are not merely emblematic. The metaphor is authenticated by experience, but the physical seizure exists in its own order of reality too. The tuberculosis is itself an adequate 'explanation' of Jocelin's euphoria, the 'angel' at his back warming him, his increased sexuality. Both physical and spiritual violence are caught in the language, calculatedly shocking as the pain travels from the bottom to the top of his being. As 'head' is united with 'arse' the physiological, the psychological, the philosophical are convulsed within a single spasm.

And if the old Jocelin lies like a snake destroyed by the flail of Judgement, the snake seeks its own destruction, and it is out of this destruction that contrition and humility are to come. He is carried not from the place of judgement but 'the place of the sacrifice', and he speaks, at last, of a real atonement: 'I have given it my back. Him. Her. Thou.' There is no longer any blazing certainty, only a series of possibilities, an acceptance of truth infinitely refracted. It is true that even destruction as fierce as this can provoke a flicker of spiritual pride, playing against Jocelin's helpless turning to others: 'What can you know, Father Anonymous? You see the outside of things. You don't know the tenth of it.' But these flickers are part of pain and felt to be punished. As Father Adam kneels in prayer, Jocelin sees 'how mistaken they were who thought of him as faceless. It was just that what had been written there, had been written small in a delicate calligraphy ...' The eyes of the visionary are focusing into sight: 'He cried out to the face before he knew he was going to. "Help me!" It was as if these words were a key.'

The first thing the key turns is the lock in the chest where Jocelin's old notebook lies. Here he recorded his original 'revelation'. We can measure how far we have travelled when we hear again the old language, brash, ecstatic, ironically prophetic:

My body lay on the soft stones, changed in a moment, the twinkling of an eye, resurrected from daily life. The vision left me at last; and the memory of it, which I savoured as manna, shaped itself to the spire ...

Now Jocelin can only groan: 'It's an ungainly, crumbling thing. Nothing like. Nothing at all.'

But what is most interesting about the extracts which Father Adam reads from Jocelin's notebook is that they are not destroyed by the ironic counterpoint. In the end they carry their own conviction. We *do* feel that the young Jocelin – in a phrase of Lawrence's – was momentarily 'tapping wild life at the source'. The passage asks us to respond to the genuineness of Jocelin's past as well as to his present, and to see that there was a moment when he seemed to have access to the springs of creativity. This is the moment known, however fleetingly, by every genuine artist when the wholeness and radiance of his conception flashes before him; though remembering that moment in the face of the completed object, spire or novel, he can only say: 'It's an ungainly, crumbling thing. Nothing like. Nothing at all.' (On one level, like *Free Fall* before it, *The Spire* is a novel about writing a novel.) And so, quietly and unobtrusively, the movement of the novel begins once again to turn in upon itself. For so long we have been concerned with the blindness of vision, the crookedness of the spire. Now, initiated by these extracts from the notebooks, we are made to contemplate with new insight, a degree of wonder in the spire, and the serenity of acceptance. We contended earlier that this was a novel in which we were never allowed to settle into a view. It has seemed that we were doing so, acquiring a single vision of corruption and evil. But the scene at the crossways marks a turning-point here too, because, while for Jocelin it marks a dark climax, for us it begins to undermine the darkness with reminders of excluded light. Looking back now, perhaps we should begin to wonder whether there has not been something too stark in the outlining of the gargoyle-priest, the Evil Tree, and the Hell at the Crossways.

Having learnt to see Father Adam as more than anonymous, Jocelin tries to see Anselm anew. This indeed is no case of mining a new rift of virtue. The interview follows a familiar pattern: Anselm's spiteful jealousy, his stonyheartedness, Jocelin's old emotional claims pressed home unavailingly. There can be no resolution; but again there is acceptance, even of Anselm's deliberately wounding charge that Jocelin has blight on his hands that kills or ruins everything he touches. He asks Anselm's forgiveness, not for what he has done, but for what he *is*.

Having failed to find forgiveness in a brother-priest, he turns to seek it 'from those who were not Christian folk'. Bent almost double like an old man, a 'stinking corpse', Jocelin confronts the drunken degenerate that Roger Mason has become. This is a much more complex meeting, for Jocelin has a real respect for Roger; they do to some extent understand each other; and Roger does at first respond to Jocelin's appeal.

'I'm a building with a vast cellarage where the rats live; and there's some kind of blight on my hands. I injure everyone I touch, particularly those I love. Now I've come in pain and shame, to ask you to forgive me.'

In a burst of emotion, Roger does. Then, however, Jocelin probes deeper, and suddenly he seems to Roger a missioner of vengeance come to remind him of the terrors he has tried to escape in drink, and the punishment that awaits him. Questions about Goody, questions about the folly of the building, these can be contained. But not this:

'What holds it up Roger? I? The Nail? Does she or do you? Or is it poor Pangall, crouched beneath the crossways, with a sliver of mistletoe between his ribs?'

Evil and terror banish forgiveness, and the two men destroy each other. After Jocelin is thrown down the stairs his death agony begins, as he crawls in the gutter, mocked and reviled. On the other hand his words, 'there's still something you can do, Roger, my son', misunderstood as a demand for atonement, lead directly to Roger's abortive suicide and the helpless imbecility which follows. Jocelin seems to have failed utterly, first with Anselm, now with Roger. He can find no hope through others.

There has been, however, something embedded in his own experience which is both true to Vision and true to the blindness of Vision, true to the love of human beings and true also to their murderous cruelty.

To find it, we need to return first to the moment when, shuffling through his own back-yard on his way to Roger, Jocelin saw an appletree and a kingfisher, glimpsed suddenly from the corner of the eye:

He twisted his neck and looked up sideways. There was a cloud of angels flashing in the sunlight, they were pink and gold and white; and they were uttering this sweet scent for joy of the light and the air. They brought with them a scatter of clear leaves, and among the leaves a long, black springing thing. His head swam with the angels, and suddenly he understood there was more to the appletree than one branch. It was there beyond the wall, bursting up with cloud and scatter, laying hold of the earth and the air, a fountain, a marvel, an appletree; and this made him weep in a childish way so that he could not tell whether he was glad or sorry. Then, where the yard of the deanery came to the river and trees lay over the sliding water, he saw all the blue of the sky condensed to a winged sapphire, that flashed once.

He cried out.

'Come back!'

But the bird was gone, an arrow shot once. It will never come back, he thought, not if I sat here all day. He began to play with the thought that the bird might return, to sit on a post only a few yards away in all its splendour, but his heart knew better.

'No kingfisher will return for me.'

All the same, he said to himself, I was lucky to see it.

This flash of sudden unalloyed beauty in the midst of so much that is crooked, dark and sordid, has a striking dramatic effect. It is right to talk of 'effect' rather than 'meaning', because the passage comes to us, as the experience does to Jocelin, directly and without conscious reflection. It simply happens. Appletree and kingfisher establish themselves as part of his universe. It is only *after* the experiences he is about to undergo that his sight will become insight.

These experiences begin with the scene with Roger. There, as we have noticed, Jocelin achieves an act of contrition that is wholly convincing and has it accepted in real love, if only for a moment. He lays aside the last remnants of his priesthood because he knows he is unworthy of them. He cannot remove his tonsure, but he sees it as a mark of heresy and blasphemy, and considers himself as a dead-dog gargoyle through which no clean water could run. Now, however, as he experiences the reality of human love, 'he found himself babbling foolish things about an appletree, saying foolish, nursery things and patting a broad, shaking back. He is such a good man, he thought, so good – whatever that is! Something is being born here under the painted, swinging sign.' The beauty he had glimpsed in the world is unconsciously fused with the goodness he finds in the man. The sign is the sign of Letoyle, the Star, that moment when the robes of the priest and visionary are laid aside for a 'birth' in the dying sinner. True love is born into Jocelin's world beneath that starry sign. If it does not last; if, indeed, so little later, the arms that have embraced expel to death ... that, too, carries a reminiscence.

Jocelin also meets the fate of Simon and all those who remind men of their guilt; but the gap between the two novels is nowhere clearer than in the dimension of his realization, by comparison with the enigmatic little boy's. Jocelin's encounter with the mob is much more obliquely presented than Simon's. Motivation is never made clear, and even their identity is obscure. If the mob is the townspeople, do they continue to hate and curse Jocelin for what he has done to the Cathedral? If the mob is the 'army' of workers, do they hate him for what he has done to Roger, without whom they are nothing? It could be either or both. But the significance of the mob-scene is to be sought in another direction altogether. What Jocelin hears, above everything else, is laughter. He has become a re-embodiment of Pangall, re-enacting his death. We are in at the beginning of another hunt to the death as the clown becomes the scapegoat: 'The noises began to bray and yelp. They created their own mouths, fanged and slavering.'

The naked perception of physical beauty, the acknowledgement of love, and now the manifestation of the Beast: in these rhythms we have the coda which is to lead into the final pages of the novel. It is important to notice that it is the experience that comes over to Jocelin, and the meaning to us. He has now become a perceiving eye, a generous heart in a broken body. And if the mob break away from him, stopping short of Simon's fate, it is because the work of torture and death is already done. The spire stands crookedly. Jocelin's back is one vast suppurating tubercular lesion.

He does not merely know about Pangall now, he has become him; and he becomes also, in a way that is carefully hinted at, another follower of the Via Dolorosa. In his agony he manages the Christ-like response to his murderers: 'My children, my children.' There is only acceptance; not a trace of anger, bitterness, self-pity. 'Here I show what I am', he thinks, as he falls into the filth of the gutter. He does indeed show himself, but not as he thinks. It is through indifference to self that his new sanctity is revealed. But this sanctity comes about not, as in the case of Simon, by statement, but through the deliberate balance and counterbalance of the action, as Golding has taken it beyond the Inquisition and the crooked spire.

VI

It is to the spire itself, moreover, that we finally return. We could say of the last chapter that Golding replaces Vision by vision, the physical eye's ability to see things as they are. It can only do so when the Visionary himself ceases to come between us and what he sees.

The 'eye' of the last chapter is capable of examining with the same objectivity and exactitude a face, or a fly cleaning its legs on the vault of the ceiling. It sees the 'self' it inhabits with clinical clarity, beyond all feeling. Jocelin orders Gilbert to sculpt him for his tomb as he is, far removed from the ecstatic bird-heads of the visionary, 'stripped in death of clothing and flesh, a prone skeleton lapped in skin, head fallen back, mouth open'. The dumb man draws 'with a face of fascinated disgust', but to Jocelin this is merely the objective memorial of what he has become.

While Father Adam is summoning him to the last rites, the moment of death arrives. With it come three complete 'explanations', but the last is the decisive one, and on it his eyes close.

The endings of Golding's novels are always extremely important, and contain vital shifts of meaning. Analysis must become more detailed here, where 'all things' really do 'come together'. Formally, the action of the closing pages can be swiftly described.

Father Adam summons Jocelin by name, to help him into heaven. He must however assent to his faith. With growing urgency, as the moment of death approaches, the priest tries to get him to say the words 'I believe', or, if he cannot, to make a gesture of assent. But there is nothing. Only, at the very end, 'he saw a tremor of the lips that might be interpreted as a cry of: *God! God! God!* So of the charity to which he had access, he laid the Host on the dead man's tongue.' Since we know that it was *not* 'God! God! God!', the stark irony seems to be that the Man of Faith, the Visionary, has died seeing nothing but despair. The gift of the Redeeming Body is useless, a mark only of the Christian charity of the giver.

To see whether this is true, however, we have to enter and understand the incoherences of Jocelin's mind at the moment of its extinction.

On the first call of his name, knowing how near he is to death, Jocelin's freewheeling mind gives him the first of the three 'explanations':

He looked up experimentally to see if at this late hour the witchcraft had left him; and there was the tangle of hair, blazing among the stars; and the great club of his spire lifted towards it. That's all, he thought, that's the explanation if I had time: and he made a word for Father Adam.
  'Berenice.'
  The smile became puzzled and anxious. Then it cleared.
  'Saint?'

This is the 'psychological' explanation. Berenice dedicated her hair, her 'crowning glory', to sexual love, and erected it to the stars. So Jocelin's spire can be seen as an erect phallus lifted towards the girl he lusted after. The whole thing was a substitute gratification for a need he would never consciously acknowledge, a self-erection for self-fulfilment. 'That's all, he thought.' If it is all, it turns Father Adam's response into a macabre joke. He doesn't understand, but he desperately wants Jocelin to be 'saved', and there *was* an obscure early Christian martyr called Berenice. Jocelin, 'when he was properly balanced' after the racking desire to laugh, falls in with the deception because 'he had a sudden liking for Father Adam and desired to give him something'. But there could hardly be a less saintly 'explanation' than the first one.

Unless it be the second. As the little man taps his forehead,

Jocelin sees him as dying too, and his own *memento mori* vision of himself intensifies into a vision of the universal Adam:

he saw what an extraordinary creature Father Adam was, covered in parchment from head to foot, parchment stretched or tucked in, with curious hairs on top and a mad structure of bones to keep it apart. Immediately, as in a dream that came between him and the face, he saw all people naked, creatures of light brown parchment, which bound in their pipes or struts. He saw them pace or prance in sheets of woven stuff, with the skins of dead animals under their feet and he began to struggle and gasp to leave this vision behind him in words that never reached the air.

How proud their hope of hell is. There is no innocent work. God knows where God may be.

The world of man is wholly absurd, irrational, and evil. For in his absurdity and irrationality man is proud. There is no hope of good or beauty; only hell awaiting pride. His own aspiration towards heaven destroyed the man and the woman who alone could make heaven meaningful, since God is to be found 'between people'. His Faith 'traded a stone hammer for four people'; built a crooked work on the breaking strain of four human pillars. The propositions: 'There is no innocent work' and 'God knows where God may be' sum up despair with bleak finality.

But only now, when the italics on the penultimate page seem to proclaim the 'message' of the novel in despair, does the *literal*, *physical*, *seeing* occur. Looking back now, we can perhaps realize in a new way what Golding's real purpose has been. Behind all the endless complications of the book we could measure its progress and establish its basic structure in terms of stages of physical seeing: First, the explosive light through Abraham's window. Then, the vertically divided light above the altar, one light for each eye, and the horizontal division between the light above and the darkness below. After that came a single Vision of uniform evil, when 'all things came together': the work 'a plant with strange flowers and fruit, complex, twining, engulfing, destroying, strangling ... the anguished faces that cried out from among it'; and the universal Adam in his pride of hell. But this is Vision not vision; the mind and imagination reading itself into the world, not the objective eye. The Vision of universal Adam is 'a dream that came between him and the face' of Adam himself. The whole strategy of the novel, its basic form, has been to manoeuvre us through the obsessive world of Jocelin's mind, emblem-haunted, until we reach the point at which we now stand.

In the final split second the physical eye opens anew. The physical double vision and the mental single one are focused anew, at the point where Jocelin's selfhood is extinguished. Having come through confusion we are brought to the right opening for the light to impinge, in a moment of sheer perception. The 'whole truth' at last impacts upon the retina:

There were two eyes looking at him through the panic. They were the only steady things, and before them, he was like a building about to fall. They looked in, an eye for an eye, one eye for each eye. He bit more air and clung to the eyes with his own as the only steady things in living.

The two eyes slid together.

It was the window, bright and open. Something divided it. Round the division was the blue of the sky. The division was still and silent, but rushing upward to some point at the sky's end, and with a silent cry. It was slim as a girl, translucent. It had grown from some seed of rosecoloured substance that glittered like a waterfall, an upward waterfall. The substance was one thing, that broke all the way to infinity in cascades of exultation that nothing could trammel.

We return to the physical beauty of the 'sundust' vision, so long ago. Since then we have seen the sun, known the dust only too well. We have seen how the individual grains 'bounced together', and have inspected the mayfly lives in their blind ignorance. In a more distant perspective we have seen how the four human relationships made a collective, mysterious shape, the Tree of the Knowledge of Good and Evil, with anguished faces crying out from among the dark overripe fruit. But we have lost sight of what Jocelin's eye then told him, when he was 'absentminded' enough to follow it. There remains the ultimate perspective; that dust gives solidity to sunlight and softens it to sweeter colour, that light gives life to dust, that 'sundust' to the human eye is a beautiful and solid phenomenon, though it is ephemeral, and though it may involve the upsetting of apparent certitudes and angles of vision if we are to see it.

So now, after the confusion, the flowering of emblematic meanings, the complexities, we still have to see for the very first time the completed spire as a thing in itself, whole and one. We have plumbed heights and depths which show conclusively enough that the spire must go down as far as it goes up, and vice versa, and we have developed deeper and deeper understanding of man and his work. But the whole has to be rehabilitated, seen objectively and inclusively, with an eye cleaned of Jocelin. It is *one* thing, a unity that moves the eyes into focus. We do not have to be reminded that it is crooked, leaning to fall. But it is also 'slim as a girl', with an upward 'fall' rushing like a fountain, cascading, exulting, as it connects 'above' and 'below', the earth and infinity. We have got to a sufficient distance to see 'crooked beauty' as Jocelin saw 'sundust'. It too has a colour, the colour both of human flesh and of the mystic rose.

In that moment of perception the certainty of Jocelin's despair is demolished: 'Now – I know nothing at all!' But through all his amazement and terror, the 'wild flashes of thought' that 'split the darkness' seize on a truth which directs the irony away from Jocelin to the language of Father Adam. 'Our very stones cry out.' The spire itself and Jocelin's inevitable response to it proclaim a Belief and an Assent on a different and altogether deeper level than an abstract credal statement like 'I believe in one God'. Stones and flesh and blood cry out, proclaim, because they *must*.

But no 'message' is announced. We get a glimpse of something out of the very corner of our eyes because we have been put in the right position to catch the flash if we can. It cannot be decoded, conceptualized, explained. It can only be conveyed at all, not in the form of a statement, but first a question, then an outcry without a verb, and finally 'words of magic and incomprehension' – something suggested only by analogy.

What is terror and joy, how should they be mixed, why are they the same, the flashing, the flying through the panicshot darkness like a bluebird over water? ...
  In the tide, flying like a bluebird, struggling, shouting, screaming to leave behind the words of magic and incomprehension –
  It's like the appletree!

The whole weight has to rest on what our eyes took in unwittingly of that casual moment in Jocelin's back-yard. It is a weight of being, not of 'meaning'. Yet it is more than what is seen with the eye. If Vision has had to give way to sight, this in turn has to be assumed into insight. We cannot do this by translating imaginative analogies into conceptual terms. The physical remains primary, and the similes insist that analogy remain on the level of suggestion rather than 'explanation'. Nevertheless there is the 'magic' of revelation as well as 'incomprehension'; we have to keep the balance right. We need to explore the imagination which not only sees, but 'sees into the life of things'.

The first analogy works in the dimension of time. The kingfisher flashes just once, like an arrow shot over sliding water, concentrating into utmost intensity all the blue of the sky, but so transiently that one cannot take it in until it is gone – and it never comes again. There is a 'panicshot darkness' before and after man's time on earth that is 'like' the sliding water, the tide, over which the bird flies (and into that darkness Jocelin's life is on the point of vanishing). There is a transient moment of purposeful being that is 'like' the bird, concentrated infinity, intensest bluefire, flashing light. Jocelin sees the life of the spire as a fusion of utmost intensity with utmost transience; one thing, revealed in one glimpse, like kingfishershotoverslidingwater. The 'elements' are meaningless apart.

The second analogy works in space. The appletree goes on being there, dancing. It unites the flashing pink, white, and gold 'angels' of the blossom, filling the air with vivid colour and scent, with the 'long black springing thing' of the branch, like a snake; unites them into a single organism. There is more of it than the one branch, it spans walls and barriers, bursts up and out, lays hold of earth and air like a fountain, miraculously. It remains the Tree which was the source of all our woe; it remains also a scatter of clear leaf and blossom, a marvel – both.

So, framed by the window, caught in one glimpse of the perceiving eye, are the intensest blue transience seen for one instant and the rosecoloured beautyskew cascading to infinity: the spire as one thing, 'like' the kingfisher and the appletree. *All* the 'meanings' are enfolded within the concrete being. That is the 'magic'. They can never be fully or satisfactorily expounded, defined, or conceptualized. That is the 'incomprehension'.

But they do amount to a statement of Faith. Although it is not

'God! God! God!' in the way Father Adam means, it is, one suspects, God! God! God! in the way Golding means, and in its love and exultation, despite evil, it has its own inclusive charity.

Free Fall diagnosed the reductiveness of pattern; *The Spire* takes up the challenge to see without it. Golding sets a whole series of patterns at war in order to convince us that none will do. The Spire is built in heavy stone, in faith, in sin; all three things are true, and contradictory. For Jocelin there are explanations physiological, psychological, moral, religious, social; all are convincing in themselves, and none is satisfactory. But we have to be made to know and understand them all, in wrestling with twelve complex and difficult chapters, before we can be brought to the right position, with sufficient breadth and depth of knowledge, to receive from the corner of the eye in the deliberate tentativeness of simile a single glimpse of what it is to be human. The 'idea' of the novel might seem trite and obvious, but the 'world of difference' is the novelist's world of experience and insight.

6

PERSPECTIVES

He holds him with his glittering eye –
The wedding guest stood still,
And listens like a three years' child:
The Mariner hath his will.

Ultimately, the appeal of every literary artist must be that of
Coleridge's Mariner. He is there for us to talk about only because
he has caught and held our imaginations. So far in this study of
Golding we have been trying to describe the effect of the 'glittering
eye' as it has revealed itself in the particularities of individual
works; in this chapter we hope to shift the perspective and see the
particular kind of 'will' that Golding has exerted over us. How, in
other words, do we judge the imaginative form, the mode of
structuring, in Golding's fiction up to *The Spire*?

To put the question like that is to feel a special sympathy for
Blake's dictum that to generalize is to be an idiot, and reasons for
this feeling are not far to seek. The trouble lies initially in the
concept of 'the novel' itself. Over the two and a half centuries of its
existence, the novel has come to cater for so many different needs
and pressures of the imagination that it cannot accommodate them
meaningfully under a single label. Nevertheless the range and
disposition of a particular imagination tend to elude us if we
concentrate our attention exclusively on its specific manifestations.
A novelist's *oeuvre* becomes something more than an aggregation
of books; it can reach a point of definition where seeing one book
in the light of another gives us new insight into the nature of the
imagination which is operating. To describe this body of work
takes us immediately into describing the kind of novel which this
imagination instinctively offers. And at once we have to deal in a
vocabulary which has had to do duty for so many purposes that it
can be used only if it is buttressed by closer definition and example.
We hope to distinguish Golding's particular kind of novel by

bringing together the terms 'fable', 'history' and 'myth', and trying to make clear our understanding of them and their relevance to the five books we have discussed.

Literary concepts are precipitated by impressions, so we might turn first to the impressions made by a Golding novel. We might think of it as something heavily patterned, uniformly intense, severely exclusive. The patterning can be observed even in the externalities of length and chapter division, virtually the same in every novel. The general form is so markedly dialectical that we are invariably led into describing each novel in terms of different worlds brought into stark confrontation. The moment of confrontation is of high dramatic intensity, though as the novels progress the 'moment' becomes less precise, and consequently less stark in its effect. The books are uniformly intense in that the mood in which each is written hardly changes; though there may be violent shifts in the point of view. The central characters may interrogate themselves remorselessly, may indeed alter, but always they remain the eye of a storm. Related to this homogeneity of mood is the dominant impression of exclusiveness. The shaping spirit of the imagination seems always at work in the foreground of our attention. There is a determination to follow what is thought to be the main road, so that we can only glimpse the possible extensions of a relationship, a place, a sub-topic. Hence we feel that, however densely imagined a particular character or episode may be, everything has been pared down, stripped of irrelevant detail. Bringing these impressions together, we might say that a Golding novel gives the effect of something dedicatedly made, every strain and stress calculated and overcome, so that the final product leads us to think in terms of a sculpture.

This however is only half the story. Our impressions are formed not only by the shape of the fiction but also, where its movement takes us – and here we seem to be faced with paradox. These books, so emphatic in pattern, so exclusive in structure, have as an increasingly dominant theme the limitations of the pattern-maker and the tragic consequences of his vision. This is already present in *Lord of the Flies*. Piggy and Jack try to press their patterns of human nature into action; but neither can bear to see man as he is. Only Simon achieves a vision more inclusive and accepting, but he is destroyed by the excluders who translate the boy into the Beast. The problem of pattern becomes the overt theme of *Free Fall*, it is Sammy's obsession:

I have hung all systems on the wall like a row of useless hats. They do not fit. They come in from outside, they are suggested patterns, some dull and some of great beauty. But I have lived enough of my life to require a pattern that fits over everything I know; and where shall I find that? Then why do I write this down? Is it a pattern that I am looking for?

It is there most complicatedly in *The Spire*, where Jocelin seeks explanation or comfort in one pattern after another, until, 'knowing nothing', he is left staring at an object, seeing it, as it is, for the first time.

Our general impressions are founded on paradox: books of calculated and obtrusive design work towards the creation of a mysterious centre, visionary eyes have to learn to see, novels of purpose insist on the importance of discovery. Basically a Golding novel grows through the tension between its form and his imagination. To describe this tension we must enlarge the context of discussion and the terms 'fable', 'history' and 'myth' help to establish a useful perspective.

Fable brings Aesop to mind as a point of departure. Broadly speaking, the fabulous world is one that proclaims it is made up. It exists deliberately outside the world which we inhabit, and fidelity to common experience is a very minor or even an irrelevant consideration. Aesop's world is inhabited by animals with human traits; other fabulists may write of giants and monsters, or, if they write of men, it is in the mode of dreams and vision, or of an 'un-country' where the boundaries of probability can be crossed and recrossed at will. Yet if the world of fable is quite unlike the world of everyday, it has direct bearing on it. We enter the other world to analyse our own with greater clarity and freedom. We look continually for point; so that the process of reading involves a continuous need for translation. Our awareness of meaning depends on our awareness of correspondence. Nothing is offered for its own sake. Situations, relationships, protagonists, figures, are selected, controlled for a purpose beyond themselves, serving an analytic design or debate.

Curiosity rather than analysis is the motive behind the imagination we describe as history. This is the imagination which Virginia Woolf sketches in her essay on Arnold Bennett:

Mr Bennett would keep his eyes in the carriage. He indeed would observe every detail with immense care. He would notice the advertisements; the pictures of Swanage and Portsmouth; the way in which the cushion bulged between the buttons; how Mrs Brown wore a brooch which had cost three-and-ten at Whitworth's bazaar; and had mended both gloves – indeed the thumb of the left hand glove had been replaced. And he would observe, at length, how this was the non-stop train from Windsor which calls at Richmond for the convenience of middle-class residents, who can afford to go to the theatre but have not reached the social rank which can afford motor cars, though it is true, there are occasions (he would tell us what) when they hire them from a company (he would tell us which).

Virginia Woolf is polemical; but setting this aside, we can see the kind of imagination involved. History recognizes no other level of 'reality' than the phenomenal or contingent. It is anti-formal; not in the sense that it attempts to escape form, which would be impossible for art, but in the sense that it rejects any idea of imposing form on multifarious experience. It seeks always by complicated interrogation to expand, extend, or even subvert what it feels to be the restrictions of pattern. It wishes to include everything and willingly pays the price. It cheerfully accepts 'bagginess' and 'monstrosity' in the service of faithful representation. Since its horizons tend theoretically to infinity, its ending – a death, a marriage, a birth – will be an arbitrary pause rather than a conclusion. By definition, history can never tell all there is to be told, there is always another story. History as fiction begins with historians themselves filling in the lacunae between facts, writing scene or dialogue by inference to lend plausibility to 'what must have been', while remaining true to the facts as they have found them. Fiction as history tries to persuade us that it is merely a transparency through which we view a complicated phenomenal world, its persons and places empirically 'true'. Such fiction may be weighted towards the portrayal of individuals, or societies, or epochs. In the first case we have fictive biography whose basic shape is the shape of a person's life. In the others, a number of such biographies are made to interact. But whatever the weighting there is the same fundamental drive towards inclusiveness – Mr Bennett 'would observe every detail with immense care'.

Of the structure of anthropological myth we can predicate nothing; each story of gods and their dealings with men has the shape of its own vision. But literary myth so deals with men as to reveal an archetypal 'truth' hidden below the surface of everyday life. This cannot simply be 'made', it must be discovered. If fable suggests Aesop, myth takes us back to Aristotle and his citation of *Oedipus Rex* as the perfect tragic *mythos*. In *Oedipus* we have an imaginative mode quite different from either fable or history. The rhetorical structure is not designed for translation into correspondence; equally, it is not concerned with the self-sufficiency of the phenomenal world. Rather, we begin with the world we know, and examine it in such a way that we no longer seem to know it. The essence of literary myth is process, and, more precisely, reversal and discovery. *Oedipus* opens with the assertion of a stable world (I am Oedipus of Corinth, saviour of Thebes, this is my wife Jocasta, these are my children), but it dissolves in the acid of a different truth. Swellfoot of Thebes, deformed bringer of plague, patricide, incestuous husband and father-brother, puts out the eyes which had persuaded him that the world was the explicable world of man and not the inscrutable world of the gods. Myth is history seen through an X-ray lens which reveals a more basic structure than that of the surface body of life.

Fable, history, myth – it is important to insist that nothing qualitative is implied in these terms. They are three different ways of looking at life, each of which has a different stance towards 'truth'. Myth may seem to make larger claims than the others, but there are as many realities and truths as there are ways of looking; and we are concerned with modes of imagination not philosophical views. Each has a fundamental strength of a different sort, but when looked at from an angle other than its own, each has also fundamental limitations. From the viewpoint of history, myth and fable seem too rigidly patterned, taking too exclusive a grip on the complex processes of life. From the viewpoint of fable, history is a baggy monster, capable of testifying only to its own muddle; while myth is mystification, depriving itself of intellectual freedom through its pretensions to a historical reality. From the viewpoint of myth, history tries to include too much, fable too little. Each mode affords a definably different satisfaction as it proceeds from a different imaginative urge. Fable offers the pleasures of analysis, history those of recognition, myth those of revelation.

To see the varying treatments of character in these different modes is to see from another angle their distinctive emphases. It is history that gives us our normative idea of fictional character, an idea typified, for example, in the opening of *Emma*:

Emma Woodhouse, handsome, clever, and rich, with a comfortable home and happy disposition, seemed to unite some of the best blessings of existence; and had lived nearly twenty-one years in the world with very little to distress or vex her. She was the youngest of the two daughters of a most affectionate, indulgent father, and had in consequence of her sister's marriage, been mistress of his house from a very early period. Her mother had died too long ago for her to have more than an indistinct remembrance of her caresses, and her place had been supplied by an excellent woman as governess, who had fallen little short of a mother in affection. Sixteen years had Miss Taylor been in Mr Woodhouse's family ...

The mode is established: the heroine is put before us, age, disposition, upbringing. Her relations with her family, the indulgence of her father, the early death of her mother, the maternal affection of her governess – it is out of this material that the novel will be woven. The assumptions governing fictional character here are almost too familiar for us to be able to recognize them. There is no theoretical limit to the facts that we ought to know, and our knowledge of characters presented in this way (in terms of family, relationships, education, outlook) is analogous to our knowledge of people in daily life. Or, more strictly, it is analogous to a convention of expressing that knowledge to ourselves or to others. A character-sketch such as Jane Austen gives us of Emma, and the 'reference' we might be asked to give for such a person, assume a similar structure, a similar vocabulary.

We could not say the same for the presentation of Mr Gradgrind.

'Now what I want is, Facts. Teach these boys and girls nothing but Facts. Facts alone are wanted in life. Plant nothing else, and root out everything else. You can only form the minds of reasoning animals upon Facts: nothing else will ever be of any service to them. This is the principle on which I bring up my own children, and this is the principle on which I bring up these children. Stick to Facts, sir!'

The scene was a plain, bare, monotonous vault of a schoolroom, and the speaker's square forefinger emphasized his observation by under-scoring every sentence with a line on the schoolmaster's sleeve. The emphasis was helped by the speaker's square wall of a forehead, which had his eyebrows for a base, while his eyes found commodious cellarage in two dark caves, overshadowed by the wall. The emphasis was helped by the speaker's mouth, which was wide, thin, and hard set. The emphasis was helped by the speaker's voice, which was inflexible, dry, and dictatorial ...

We are immediately presented not with character, but with attitude, a stance deliberately posed for purposes of argument and analysis. We sense that every detail of scene and speaker, no matter how tiny, is not descriptive but pointed; and we begin at once to translate them into their point. The predominant impression is of the artifice of the author. The rhetorical performance rivets our attention to his design. We know that action will be important, but will not be the inevitable outcome of character so much as of careful plotting; and that the total pattern will be created not by the way the characters act upon one another but by the way they fit in with one another as functional components of a single informing analysis. With this we know that we are in the world of fable.

Interestingly, and of necessity, myth eludes such brief illustra-tion. It begins in a way indistinguishable from history; but its underlying structure is only gradually discovered by the special ordering of the narrative. Like history, myth has to persuade us that its characters are real people in real places, but it has links with fable in that it persuades us to question the nature of this reality. Unlike fable however, the revelation of myth will be gradual, unobtrusive, taking shape beneath the surface. As far as the presentation of character is concerned, this means that individual features fade to reveal archetypal forces, like those classified by the great psychologists. But just as these forces, however archetypal, cannot be truly conceived apart from this and that individual, so myth can only be expressed in personal terms, and never in the abstract terms of fable. It is possible to go further and say that the more myth is concerned with isolating the archetype, the more banal it becomes, because it has lost contact with the complexities of the individual, without whom this imaginative process can have no life. Oedipus again will indicate the kind of interest in character we find in myth. He begins in a world of history, so that we can talk of his character in terms of leadership, assurance, hot temper; but then this alters to reveal the 'character' or 'signature' inscribed upon him by the gods, one not peculiar to him but a part of the human condition. The complexity of Oedipus is refocused in the light of the sphinx's riddle 'what is man?', but it is this man in this situation which gives the riddle all the imaginative life it has. If we try to see myth in terms of its 'message', it trembles on the edge of the received, or even the trite. But it is a sense of the powerful imaginative resonance of the archetypal that drives an author to seek to capture it in fiction, as it is the imaginative power and richness of the capture that makes the fiction valuable and not the thesis we could abstract from it.

Perhaps these varying treatments of character are sufficiently distinct to require a different terminology, so that 'character' might be reserved for history, 'type' or 'attitude' for fable, and 'archetype' for myth. But this terminology should be purely descriptive in purpose. If we see the mode of history dominant in *The Prelude*, *War and Peace*, *A la Recherche du Temps Perdu*, the mode of fable in *The Faerie Queen*, *The Pilgrim's Progress*, *Gulliver's Travels*, the mode of myth in *Oedipus Rex*, *The Ancient Mariner*, *Moby Dick*, then it becomes clear that by no earthly standard could we want to rank imaginative works of this order. We have been using history, fable, and myth in an attempt to characterize certain modes of the imagination, hence they are anterior to specific literary genres. They may be found in poetry, drama, and fiction. Further, there is no reason why these modes should not co-exist within a single work of art, and they often do. The imagination, though it may travel one line more than another, is not confined to a single track. (Allegories, for example, often combine fable and myth, novels – like Jane Austen's – history and fable.) Nevertheless, the recognition of these varying predilections of the imagination, whatever labels we pin to them, should prevent us from applying to one predominant mode criteria appropriate to another.

With these terms in mind we can return to our general impressions of a Golding novel. If his first five books are considered collectively, they seem to constitute a phase of work which we might reasonably consider complete. This is not to say that they are a step-by-step achievement in which each step must be 'higher' than the last. Rather, they provide a series of variations on a problem, which within his own terms he now seems to have resolved, and this series of variations can be plotted in terms of fable, history, and myth; the twelve years' work can be seen as an exploration of the problem of disengaging myth from fable, and of giving it a sufficiently historical location.

To think of *Lord of the Flies* is to think of the qualities of immediate accessibility, clarity of design and intention, which mark it off from the novels which followed, and explain its popular success. The island setting, isolated from the complexities of society; the exclusiveness of its characters, not merely children but boys before puberty; the firm direction of its plot; all minister to that creation of a deliberate artefact which is the hallmark of fable. It affords the satisfaction of a ship-in-a-bottle, it is a world of equivalences, of meticulous scaling-down. We seem to be able to review it in its detail and in its total design simultaneously. The author seems in conscious control, doing with virtuoso skill and success what he has obviously set out to do. *Lord of the Flies* is in fact the closest of Golding's novels to fable.

Our criticism however has attempted to show how much the novel differs from any such account. There is an important openness in the presentation, especially of Piggy and Simon, which raises questions about the overt design of the book; in one sense making it considerably less definitive than it seems, in another, giving it a new dimension of interest. Looking back now, we can see that this dimension is the stirring of myth imagination in a world primarily fabulous.* Golding's imagination is more complex and less articulate than his design and structure. His basic art is already one of revelation rather than demonstration, and what is eventually revealed is more mysterious than author or reader expected. Also, although the novel is calculatedly isolating both in setting and in its characters, it depends on our acceptance of a

---

* In 'Fable', *The Hot Gates*, pp. 98–9, Golding records how his imagination seemed to him to 'get out of hand' in the first episode with the pig's head. What he there regards as a fault 'of excess', however, we regard as a point of growth.

psychological reality 'true to life'. The boys have to be entirely credible as boys if we are to respond to the novel's vision, and in the imagining of the island and its inhabitants there is a pronounced drive towards the mode of history which plays against the thesis, the translation and the analysis of fable. *Lord of the Flies* in retrospect reveals the myth-imagination already seeking to liberate itself from a mode which, from its viewpoint, is too confidently analytic, too restrictive.

In that respect *The Inheritors* is a long leap forward. In one sense, at the level of 'subject', Golding takes a world so completely 'other' that it might seem unequivocally to invite the description of fable, taking its place with Utopia, Brobdingnag, Erewhon. Moreover he seems to have begun from a thesis-quarrel, a conscious design to demonstrate the inadequacies of Wells. But Golding establishes the novel's 'otherworld' by employing all his imaginative resources, not as More, Swift and Butler do, to manoeuvre analytically between 'their' world and 'ours', but rather to make us forget our world and become imaginatively immersed in the dense mystery of his. The essential element in the writing is the discovery of a procedure which inhibits analysis and judgement, becoming for the first time essentially exploratory and tentative. In other words, the datum of *The Inheritors* seems to belong to fable, but its whole realization belongs to history in which myth is located by imaginative exploration. This is not to say that Golding's interest is that of the historical novelist trying to recapture the past, though his anthropological knowledge continually tethers his imagination to fact. His mode is not history but myth, in that it seeks to reveal archetypal truth within history; it is not fable, in that the myth is demonstrably discovered by the process of writing the novel, could be discovered in no other way, and turns out to be far more complex and difficult to grasp than the novelist thought when he started.

In *Lord of the Flies* we are continually made to look *at* a scene in order to pinpoint its significance within the whole analysis; in *The Inheritors* we are drawn into the scene, incapable of seeing where we are going, but immersed in a mysterious act of discovery. A comparison of the death of Simon with the death of the Old Woman may illustrate this better than a general statement can do:

The water rose further and dressed Simon's coarse hair with brightness. The line of his cheek silvered and the turn of his shoulder became sculptured marble. The strange, attendant creatures, with their fiery eyes and trailing vapours, busied themselves round his head. The body lifted a fraction of an inch from the sand and a bubble of air escaped from the mouth with a wet plop. Then it turned gently in the water. Somewhere over the darkened curve of the world the sun and moon were pulling; and the film of water on the earth planet was held, bulging slightly on one side while the solid core turned.

Although, as we argued, the total imaginative context of this surrounds it with a much more ambiguous suggestiveness than is apparent, the first response is to its clarity and the certainty of its design, the serene confidence with which Golding relates the fraction of an inch and the wet plop with the ordered and beautiful processes of the cosmos. At this moment he seems exactly sure of the placing of Simon's death against the 'darkened curve of the world' and the phosphorescent tide pulled by sun and moon. In contrast with the two scenes with the pig's head, Golding seems to tell us exactly how to see. What we are most aware of is the conscious artistry of the novelist – and this holds good even when we take in the irony of the phosphorescence.

In *The Inheritors*, Lok is confronted suddenly by the dead body of the Old Woman coming up at him as he hangs 'upside down' over 'deep water':

The weed-tail was shortening. The green tip was withdrawing up-river. There was a darkness that was consuming the other end. The darkness became a thing of complex shape, of sluggish and dreamlike movement. Like the specks of dirt, it turned over but not aimlessly. It was touching near the root of the weed-tail, bending the tail, turning over, rolling up the tail towards him. The arms moved a little and the eyes shone as dully as the stones. They revolved with the body, gazing at the surface, at the width of deep water and the hidden bottom with no trace of life or speculation. A skein of weed drew across the face and the eyes did not blink. The body turned with the same smooth and heavy motion as the river itself until its back was towards him rising along the weed-tail. The head turned towards him with dreamlike slowness, rose in the water, came towards his face ... She was ignoring the injuries to her body, her mouth was open, the tongue showing and the specks of dirt were circling slowly in and out as though it had been nothing but a hole in a stone. Her eyes swept across the bushes, across his face, looked through him without seeing him, rolled away and were gone.

The immediate effect of this is to create an experience of
bewildered incomprehension. We are no longer looking at a
dead body so much as entering a mind for whom violent death
is inconceivable. Hence detail, unrelated, finely particularized, is
everything, pattern nothing; the rhetoric keeps 'significance' at
bay. There is significance, but it comes to us unstated and
unstatable, released in our imaginations with the rhythm of
nightmare. 'Upside down', 'deep water': the disorientation involved here will be stabilized only at the end of the last chapter.
And the writing in this passage strikes an obsessive note* quite
unlike the conscious artistry of *Lord of the Flies*.

Paradoxically, however, it is *The Inheritors* which first focuses
Golding's attention on the nature of his art – so much so that it is
given an almost conceptual description in the closing chapter, as
Tuami prepares to carve his ivory, and in the particularity of that
'shape' senses the destiny of the People and of the Inheritors. But
the explicitness with which this is done shows that Golding is in
danger of slipping back into fable, this time the fable of the artist
as myth-maker. For what *The Inheritors* as a whole has made plain
is that the novel as myth, unlike the novel as fable, can never be
aimed at directly. If it is, it will tend to become fable. The three
novels that follow are increasingly profound recognitions that
Hamlet's plan, by indirections to find directions out, must be
Golding's also. More and more clearly, we shall find conscious
artistry replaced by an art of discovery.

In *The Inheritors* Golding tried to reveal the nature of man by
imagining his origins; in *Pincher Martin* he looks at his end. There
is a significant change, however, which prevents these accounts
from being complementary. In *The Inheritors* he is concerned with
a group; in *Pincher Martin* he comes for the first time to look at
individual man, not mankind. A sense of 'shape' has to be found,
not in the emblematic figure of the artist carving the ivory, but in
the particularities of a personal life. With *Pincher Martin* Golding

---

* P. N. Furbank in a review of *The Spire*, *Encounter*, 22 May 1964, pp. 59–61,
observes that the image of a broken or suffering body in water is found in all the
novels. Here, as in *Pincher Martin* (especially p. 96, pp. 144–5), *Free Fall* (p. 130),
and *The Spire* (pp. 64–5), but not in *Lord of the Flies* (pp. 189–90, 222–3), the image
occurs in a context connected with dream.

confronts for the first time the problems that 'character' presents for the writer of myths.

In *The Inheritors* Golding was concerned with the way things 'fit', and consequently with a moment of discovery – not in the sense of a fleeting moment, but rather that given the right moment, a whole lifetime can be caught within it. Obviously, no moment offers itself more dramatically than the moment of death, and Golding avails himself of this to show 'what we are'. Choosing an individual character, however, inevitably raises the past and the question of its relation to the present. Man may be the sum of his actions, but we need to know how. So Golding writes on two levels, giving us Pincher's struggles on the rock in the mode of history, and giving us also the background to his being in the series of flashbacks from his past. Because he is so concerned with being, however, these flashbacks are in the mode not of history but of fable.

Neither of course represents the true mode of the novel. On a second reading the myth is discovered beneath the encounter of history and fable, with its own hidden structure of days and nights behind the chapter divisions, its own tentativeness of explanation behind the clarities of Chris-Greed, or the self-dramatizing of Prometheus-Faust, its disclaimer of official views.

This myth is a powerful and extraordinary achievement. But the clash of history and fable on the surface raises explicit problems for the reader, and also raises implicit questions about the myth's exclusive concern with being, as we tried to show. In this retrospective summary we need only emphasize again how the difficulties spring from Golding's first encounter with the precise problem of character. Dissatisfaction arises from the insufficiency of the 'stills' in the mode of fable to explain how the man on the rock becomes his being. For Golding, Martin's past has only an emblematic and analytic connection with his present, but this translates itself for the reader into Golding's indifference to the character of the man whose struggle he creates so marvellously. The design is now unhappily at odds with the imagination. Although Golding has moved from the group to the individual, he treats Pincher as an attitude, capable of being rendered in a series of analytic vignettes. Though he has realized, properly enough, that the myth-writer must come to terms with the individual, the individual he presents us with is allowed to breathe only in an oxygen chamber of the author's devising. The glass jar is a world, but the more Golding has tried to get a character into it, the more it becomes clear that the atmosphere is too rarified for human life. It could not be extended. It will have, somehow, to be broken open.

The three years that separated *Pincher Martin* from *Free Fall* obviously constituted an artistic stocktaking. As he moved away from fable towards myth the treatment of character had become of crucial importance. Abstractly, it was a question of reconciling the essential being of a character with that process of 'historical' becoming without which no character can satisfactorily exist. However much the myth-maker may be concerned with a moment of definition, he must include in his process of discovery a past for his character that has the reality of his present, and can satisfactorily account for it. These are the considerations that shape *Free Fall*. The ambiguity of the title itself suggests the abandonment of all claim to the certainty implicit in the title of its predecessor. The new novel is explicitly about the problems of writing a novel. 'How shall I understand my art?' becomes for Golding both his subject and his object.

Golding chooses a central character who can be an *alter ego*: a successful artist in one mode trying to understand himself in another, a pattern-maker resolutely interrogating his own experience. With Sammy Mountjoy, the crucial 'moment' of his life is now something to be searched for, not merely shown. Consequently he is genuinely involved from the outset in his own history. But his search is to explain a pattern of being already definite and known to him. So Sammy's purpose and Golding's seem more or less the same; but both the difficulty and the way forward lie precisely in that 'more or less'. For Sammy the novelist remains always, inescapably, a pattern-maker. Although Golding succeeds in creating a character of a depth and resilience that were lacking in *Pincher Martin*, the world of Sammy's novel never frees itself from the collision of differing patterns. The dominant experience of the novel he writes is of learning to 'tune' the differing frequencies, until in his 'conclusion' the worlds of being and becoming are starkly opposed, irreconcilable. But 'two worlds without a bridge' is itself a pattern; the last of Sammy's 'hats' and the only one that will fit for him. The imagination of myth is there in Sammy's novel in the mysterious experience of revelation in the 'being' sections. The imagination of history is there in the particularized experience of the 'becoming' sections. But, because Sammy always seeks an explanation, both are always stratified by the patternings and analytic formulations of fable. As we argued, Golding can use the painter's eye or the myth experience to take Sammy beyond his conscious knowledge; but in Sammy's novel there is no fusion of an art of becoming with an art of being into one vision. Of that novel, as much as of Sammy's paintings, we must finally say that the art is one of 'islanding in pictures' out of the complexity of living.

Golding's long and difficult exploration of the problem through his *alter ego* does however show him, at last, a way beyond, though he can only indicate its direction, not follow its path. His purpose does eventually separate itself from his protagonist's. The final page of the book tries to challenge us to glimpse the complexity of living, upsetting Sammy's certainties. Not only is all hope of an inclusive pattern abandoned, but all pattern is seen as reductive. In other words, Golding in *Free Fall* comes to realize that myth cannot be satisfactorily located in history until a way is found to circumvent fable altogether. There can be no 'answer' to the Sphinx's riddle; what myth must aspire to is the revelation of the nature of the riddle. It is not enough to create a character who can lead a fictive life free from mere author-manipulation. The myth-writer must also create a historical world fit for him to live in; a world similarly free from reduction.

In *The Spire* Golding finds such a world. Once again he takes as central figure the artist as pattern-maker, though with a much greater assurance than in *Free Fall*. Jocelin is less self-conscious than Sammy and there is no danger of identifying his explanations with Golding's. There is a return to third person narration with a corresponding gain in objectivity. Jocelin doesn't talk about seeking patterns, his whole behaviour enacts them. Golding is now quite clear about the nature and limitations of the world of fable – and it is this world he gives to Jocelin. But the world of fable is circumvented, neutralized, in two different ways. It is tethered to the world of history because they have a point of common reference – the spire itself. Seen from one point of view, the spire is the diagram of prayer (or the tree of evil); but from another it is 'a skin of glass and stone' ... with the builders 'bartering strength for weight or weight for strength, guessing how much, how far, how little, how near'. And as soon as we think about the spire, built in faith, in heavy stone, in sin, the very diversity of the explanations means that none will do. By the end of the novel fable disappears, as Jocelin dies. We look at the spire the novel has built, and glimpse its mythic revelation because we know all we need to know.*

The building of the spire pierces every level of the novel, so that fable is taken up into history. To look at the spire is to see Jocelin, to look at Jocelin is to see the spire:

The singing of the stones pierced him, and he fought it with jaws and fists clenched. His will began to burn fiercely and he thrust it into the four pillars, tamped it in with the pain of his neck and his head and his back, welcomed in some obscurity of feeling the wheels and flashes of light, and let them hurt his open eyes as much as they would.

There is no question now of self-consciously feeling for the shape in the ivory. Jocelin is shaped by the spire as surely as he shapes it. This perfect fusion between the inner and the outer world is what gives the novel its immense solidity. The building of the spire becomes different at every level, and presents new problems both physically and metaphysically. It is not history, for it seeks the revelation of archetypal truth, but it founds itself satisfactorily in historical process, gradually unfolding.

It is in the process of discovery within history that the essence of the myth also lies, using the insights of fable, but allowing its clarities and exclusions to cancel one another out. There is no final analysis or formulated wisdom, the emphasis is on the journey and not on the arrival. Hence again and again in *The Spire* we balance faith against the cost of faith, and explanation against explanation. Is it tubercular euphoria that drives Jocelin on? Is it religion – the

---

* This would not be true if the mode *were* history. For example, we know virtually nothing of Goody, not even her name, and little of Jocelin's early relationship with Anselm. Golding cut out, as irrelevant, an account of the latter. Without seeing this, it is impossible to know whether he was right, but it seems likely. We know all we need to know for myth *in* history. By 'historical' criteria myth will always be seen as exclusive, but our argument is that we must not blur the different criteria. Golding may have set out to subvert Trollope, as he had done Ballantyne and Wells.

saint's vision? Is it psychological – sexual sublimation? Is it moral – the blindness of human pride? Is it social – the privilege of secular advantage? As the questions mount and cut across one another, the answers become a matter of increasing indifference to us. What matters is to realize, in Sammy Mountjoy's words 'the unnameable, unfathomable, and invisible darkness that sits at the centre'. But, as Golding's novels have developed into this stage, the 'darkness' has also lost its definite label, it is opacity rather than blackness. It is no longer simply associated with evil and violence, but also with good. It is shrouded in mystery, alien to definition, the most we can hope for is momentary insight. Yet mystery is not muddle. The spire against the sky is a solid object with a solid history, and it reveals, though we cannot 'explain' what it reveals. It leans askew, in constant danger of falling. The myth-maker has realized that he can present no longer a moment of absolute definition, but only a transitory moment of revelation glimpsed from the corner of the eye. But it also cascades to infinity, 'fixing' the otherwise incomprehensible in a moment of time. In one way it is 'nothing like' the novelist's original conception, a failure; in another it is a successful discovery of a far more difficult and complex truth. Golding has rid himself of fable and achieved, not history, but that satisfactory location in history without which myth is still fabulous.

Looking back over the novels we can see the change not only in form, but in the nature of the insight which has required formal development to express it. The fable-like structure of *Lord of the Flies* insisted on the darkness of man's heart. In *The Inheritors* the darkness is no longer simply evil, though it is still fearful. Yet Tuami's eyes, unlike the officer's resting complacently on the trim cruiser, or Ralph's weeping, 'peer forward ... to see what lay at the other end of the lake [but] there was such a flashing from the water that he could not see if the line of darkness had an ending.' It is the strength of *Pincher Martin* that there is no definite 'official view' about where the line of darkness is to be drawn. From one point of view, Pincher lies awake in the night 'helpless on the stone floor, trying to run back, run away, climb up', a victim of his own nature; from another, his darkness is the darkness of depravity; from yet another, he is not Judas but Prometheus struggling against extinction. Though on the level of its flashbacks it is more simply fabulous than *Lord of the Flies*, on others it is more mysterious than anything Golding had written. The new feeling for character it gave him is built on in *Free Fall*, dramatizing his new problems. The door of the cell where Sammy had entered into himself in darkness, eventually opens onto a genuinely ambiguous world. 'There is a mystery in you which is opaque to us both', Dr Halde had remarked, but the psychology of the cell itself is the too simple design of the Herr Doctor who does not know about peoples. The spirit of the remark however shapes the art of *The Spire*. Where Sammy's novel had been programmatic about 'mystery', *The Spire* reveals it, and we can no longer talk simply of 'darkness'. All of Golding's novels have been concerned in one way or another with the Sphinx's riddle, but, as they have developed, the emphasis has shifted from the necessity of getting the right answers to the necessity of posing right questions, setting the riddle in the right way. As explanations have given way to explorations, fable has gradually been assumed into myth located in history.

Put in these terms, we might incline to regard Golding's achievement from *Lord of the Flies* to *The Spire* as a continual progress, in that in his last novel he seems to have found a satisfying shape for myth. In a way this is true, but we are saying less than we might think about the actual achievement in fiction. The solution of artistic 'problems' is something that can be seen only in retrospect, and consequently it is an abstraction from the individual works of art. To think of 'solutions' as synonymous with 'achievements' would be to misunderstand the nature of the artistic process – to become, in fact, a pattern-maker without the imaginative strength of the art of fable. All we can say, as we look at the various transformations which Golding's imagination has undergone in his first five novels, is that it would seem that *The Spire* marks the end of a phase in his work; the resolution established in that work is of such a kind that it is not easy to see how it can be extended. In saying this, the critic can claim no foresight. He can only try to learn to see what is there already, and what is there in Golding's case seems to be a body of work which has resolved what seem to have been its predominant tensions, leaving the artist free for further exploration. Criticism itself constantly aspires to the condition of fable. It is the lesson derived from working on Golding's novels that it should recognize the limitations of its patterns and welcome opacity, remembering Eliot's words:

> ... knowledge imposes a pattern, and falsifies,
> For the pattern is new in every moment
> And every moment is a new and shocking
> Valuation of all we have been.

Criticism can speak only of 'all we have been'; but in doing so, it seeks to prepare us to understand the 'new and shocking valuation' when it comes, as it surely will for a writer who has shown the imaginative vitality and resourcefulness of Golding.

7

THE PYRAMID

(1967)

I A STEP BACK, BUT TO LEAP FURTHER?

When it appeared, *The Spire* seemed not so much a fifth novel as the destination of the preceding four. We remarked in 1967 that it seemed to mark the end of a phase, a resolution 'of such a kind that it is not easy to see how it can be extended'. For *The Spire* seemed to fulfil all the paradoxical demands of the Golding imagination – that the fiction be clear yet mysterious, narratively compelling yet complex, fully formed yet open-ended and tentative – and it did so with an exact and intricate match of substance with form. The building of the spire kept pace at every step with the building of the novel; every height revealed a new depth; patterns multiplied to defeat any overall patterning; and everything came together at the end to make possible a unifying glimpse – but of irreducible mystery beyond. Moreover *The Spire* seemed the purest instance yet in Golding of the work of art acutely *aware* of itself taking up, bringing together and unifying the paradoxes which had emerged from the previous novels. And Jocelin's intense nature ensured greater intensity of vision than ever before, while opening up in its excesses an ever more searching criticism.

Yet in this very completeness, self-consciousness, intensity, was there not a problem, at least for its author? How was he to go beyond? He certainly seemed in difficulties. Three years later *The Pyramid*, inevitably compared with its predecessor, seemed disappointing. Golding himself described it as a step backwards, hoping to leap forward. But there followed a long silence of more than ten years; except for two new stories in *The Scorpion God*, accomplished and amusing in their own fashion, but doing nothing to point the way ahead: an attractive sort of aside, perhaps, to satisfy an anxious publisher. Then the silence was broken dramatically: by two powerful novels appearing in such rapid succession that they seemed almost to have been written in tandem,* but startlingly different, and producing very different responses.

The Journals and a future biography will shed light on this decade of difficulty but perhaps, taking advantage of hindsight about the eventual breakthrough, something can be said now in critical terms about the way Golding eventually managed to get around and beyond the blockage of *The Spire*.

If the urge to completeness and the growth of self-conscious intensity were what seemed to bar the way, then a form would have to be found that was less monolithic, and a texture somehow lighter. New themes, moreover, might come from attempting to deal more searchingly with contemporary society, and thus more in the mode of 'history' (in our terminology) than Golding had attempted before. The 'step backwards' seems to have come from a sense of unfinished business left over from *Free Fall*, both in content and form.

There he had set out to deal more fully than in *Pincher Martin* with a contemporary world; but as Sammy searched – under the rival influences and metaphysics of Nick and Rowena – for a moment of individual self-determination, what had never really come into focus was the *social* determinism of the English class system. About this Golding actually felt very strongly. 'I think an Englishman who is not aware of the classic disease of society in this country, that is to say, the rigidity of its class structure – he's not really aware of anything, not in social terms.'[†] In English life the public-school motto 'Manners Makyth Man' has a classifying sense, and Golding had never tried the novel of manners, such as Jane Austen's 'three or four families in a Country Village', which she thought 'the very thing to work on'. And perhaps this new content would go well with a more fractured form? To a reader coming to *The Spire* from *Free Fall*, the calling into question of Sammy's split vision by the mysterious ambiguity of the final fragment can seem to anticipate the unity, bringing the eyes together, at the culmination of *The Spire*. Looking back now, however, once a sense of monolithic unity had come to seem the

---

* This guess is borne out by Golding's Journals: see p. 395 below.
† Interview in *Twentieth Century Literature*, Summer 1982.

very thing blocking the way, might there not be much to be gained by a deliberate splitting of the new story, not by metaphysics this time but rather into different genres? So, stepping back to the world of *Free Fall* with a newly ironic focus on the 'disease' of English society, and a new diversity of form – a spire ironically recast into three surfaces, yet allowing a focus on the same subject from differing angles – might allow Golding to move forward again. So it did, with mixed success in *The Pyramid* itself, but eventually in two very different strategies that grew out of it.

Perhaps, then, we should free *The Pyramid* from competition with *The Spire*, and appreciate how radically Golding's aim had come to differ from the intensity and continuous concentration of its predecessor. Three juxtaposed stories, from different stages of their common narrator's life, try for different kinds of comedy, apparently casual in their linkages. The new social focus and the new fractured form serve to hold back, for the time being, the visionary Golding and the intense exploration of good and evil, in favour of something lighter and brighter: laughter, satire, playful ingenuity, and above all the structural irony in which Jane Austen excelled. Indeed an underlying unity lies there: not merely in the shared narrator but in the pervasive irony that operates in differing degrees between the lines of all his narratives. Irony, indeed, begins wryly from the title, with its sardonic difference from the spire: no solid object with multiple mythic meanings now, but three *surfaces* that, through the narrator's myopia, challenge a reader's perception, between the lines, of class-ridden attitudes which hide the truth of people. Most obvious of course, would be the specific and detailed operations of the social 'pyramid', the class distinctions and assumptions of a small town in all their destructive prejudice and blindness. The instinctive awareness and communication of these by the characters, moreover, is a matter of signals expertly sent and received, as if through prisms in crystal sets behind curtained windows, tuning in wavelengths of discrimination and judgement. Most insinuating of all is the ironic role of music, present in all three stories, but exposing more and more the absence of concord, harmony, measure, in the places where it is played – a discarded metronome, finally, cast on a rubbish heap. These 'pyramids' are signposts to fields of ironic perception and response, welling through the lines of a comedy of manners which itself is tonally varied throughout the novel. An ironic comedy of adolescence becomes less and less funny, is then satirically offset against an operatic farce, and darkens finally into tragicomedy: loveless waste, desperation, and relationship stillborn.

II 'ON THE ESCARPMENT'

The opening story, first published separately under that title, maps the diseased social ground in an ironically named small town, but in a comedy of adolescence for which there can be amused sympathy at first. Oliver, at eighteen, bangs out Chopin in hopeless grief over the lovely Imogen, who is out of his social reach and about to marry a newspaper proprietor. Sammy Mountjoy, adopted from a slum, 'boasted with rudimentary feeling for the shape of our social pyramid that I was the rector's son', but Oliver knows the gradients more exactly. He is the son of a pharmacist, and will go with a scholarship to Oxford – but Robert next door is the son of a doctor, has a public school education and a motorbike, and is about to become a flying officer-and-gentleman. And if Imogen is far above Oliver, Evie Babbacombe, the local sexpot, is as far below: the town crier's daughter 'from the tumbledown cottages of Chandler's Close. But of course we had never spoken. Never met. Obviously.' When however a pebble at his window summons him to rescue Evie and his unloved neighbour from the farcical mire that sex has got them into, he becomes obsessed with having her sexually – and we become more and more aware how incapable he is of knowing her as a person.

If the full irony of the story is to reveal itself however, it is important that we should be clear about the point of view. Though the first-person narrative lets us into an adolescent consciousness in all its tumescent frustration, snobbery and bafflement, we should pick up the signals that it is not *that* Oliver who is telling the story, but a much older one, recreating him. The lad could not, for example, have observed on the second page that 'Eighteen is a good time for suffering. One has all the necessary strength, and no defences.' Yet the last words of the story will confirm that the older Oliver never spells out what his younger self fails to see about Evie. It is we who must do that, reading between the lines. And this may be more testing than it seems at first.

The story in its first phase is clear enough, however, and at its funniest. The rescue gives Oliver a psychological edge (though Evie gets a black eye). There follows an ungentlemanly physical victory over Robert, and a second rescue of the girl. Oliver's discovery of the missing necklace in Bounce's car is a further bonus (though Evie's amused admiration is misplaced, and the garage man's suspicion could spread). In Robert's absence at Cranwell, moreover, Evie seems willing to meet Oliver at the bridge and even to permit some petting, but within strict limits and at some risk to them both. For the source of the black eye becomes dangerously clear as her plethoric father mounts guard, with his odd little wife. And Oliver is afraid to be seen with Evie anyway (a point not lost on her). The 'meeting' on the 'bridge' and the move into the bushes plot the limits of relationship, a first ironic focus on the novel's epigraph about making love. Musically too, they seem at odds, between her love of dancing and his highbrow 'passionate frustration', now fuelled as much by her as by Imogen (and overloud to his mother as well as to Dr Ewan next door). Yet the discovery that there is more to Evie than sex: a potential for music and self-improvement hampered by lack of opportunity; a longing to dance, and sing, and travel, counts for nothing to Oliver beside the salt obsession which links him with *Free Fall*'s Mountjoy and swallows everything else. Then Robert is suddenly back (and the glimpse of a delighted Evie on the back of the motorbike produces a spurt of jealousy to direct a mother's suspicion).

Initial clarity soon leads to more complex feelings and challenges, however, to both character and reader. Oliver doesn't altogether like his own elation when he learns of his rival's accident; and he soon discovers that he must try to hide his feelings from his mother. He is even more disturbed by a marked change of behaviour in Evie's parents, which must be her doing, using him as an excuse for lateness, a lightning conductor against her father's wrath. The Sergeant would not believe in any respectable relation with the doctor's son; but it is not so inconceivable that she and Oliver might be courting; and that spells danger, since his intentions are strictly dishonourable. An ironically righteous anger wells up in him at being 'used', but when he accuses her of being cheap and nasty like the Savoy Orpheans, the absurdly inadequate moral language may also challenge us. (Have we seen anything to suggest why 'It isn't like that' and why she felt she '*had to*' do what she did?) Certainly Oliver pays little attention to evidence now, in true accent, that she has genuine feelings for Bobby and an unsuspected sense of guilt; and he pays a price in her anger when he tries to 'make love' in spite of what has happened, and to claim the same rights as his rival. (Is there a truth about himself, when libidinous laughter from men outside the pub, as she passes, shows what she has continually to face?)

We can still feel sympathy when adolescent jealousy and sexual and social frustration boil over, and Oliver's fist smashes into the piano. But his 'seduction' of Evie darkens the tone. When he meets her coming out of the wooden hut that is the Babbacombes' chapel, there is something deeper than social discrimination. Not only has Oliver 'never met the Roman Catholic church outside a history book' so that to find it alive is 'like finding a diplodocus', but his response to what he does not understand is a jeering laughter that will come to seem typical. He has no idea how she could have been trying to help Robert. Instead, he demands that she help *him*, and drags her into the bushes by force (reminiscent of her father). He will not listen to her attempt to explain how 'everything's different' – if he could only see. When he thrusts his erection into her hand we can see clearly enough how he reduces her to her sexuality. (But, reading between the lines, there is also a greater challenge to us, in the implied complexity of her feelings. She does exude sexuality by nature. We know from the episode with Robert that she is no innocent, and she is sexually excited now. But there is also loathing as 'Her mouth went lopsided and instead of a smile there appeared a sneering grin, that was at once knowing and avid and contemptuous.' It will be no simple matter for a reader to deduce, between the lines, an Evie who can include the chapel, and the 'heavenly delight' at the news of Robert, but also the fatalistic mutter 'Get on with it, then.' It is of the essence of 'history', in our sense, that it demands a complex sense of character as well as a realistically observed society. But because we are put inside the consciousness of Oliver we have to sense for ourselves an Evie to whom he is blind.)

Afterwards he is peaceful and proud, impervious to the girl's sulkiness and to any sense that she may confront him with 'works' quite as 'intricate' as those the battered piano displays where the sheet music should be. He expects to overcome her sullenness and take up where they left off – but when he sees her the following evening she is surprisingly glad and excited, coming from her lesson with the wheelchair-bound neighbour who seems the only person in the town who is kind to her. What follows, however, may seem inexplicable at first reading, except for the fusion of self-hatred and sexuality we have already detected. (Is there something in the joke about Captain Wilmot threatening to beat her if her shorthand doesn't improve, together with the voice of her father from the town below, that produces both sexual excitement and the twisted face, begging Oliver not just to take, but to hurt her?) She may also be suffering pent-up frustration. For whatever reason, coitus inter-ruptus is overtaken this time by her anguished drive to orgasm, 'a moaning, private thing, full of contempt and disgust', in which the male becomes the one that is used. Afterwards they flame out at each other in fear of consequences, but there is more than that on Evie's side, and in the lopsided sneer, again, with which she mocks him. He has indeed wanted something for nothing, and she knows very well how terrified he is lest their liaison become known. 'I hate men,' she cries, but more, 'I 'ate this town – I hate it! Hate it! Hate it!' When he gets home to discover his parents' care for him – the plan to repair the piano – he bursts into tears; but for discordant reasons, none of which involve caring about Evie.

For a fortnight she avoids him, though he sees her talking in Dr Ewan's garden with the doctor's partner Dr Jones. Oliver fears what that might be about; but subsequently catches the doctor kissing her in the reception room. He wanders the lanes in search of her, but when at last they meet she has made herself up like a tart and is wholly hostile. She is not going to have a baby, but as he thanks God in sudden joy and peace, her denunciation is absolute and accurate:

'You wouldn't care if I was dead. Nobody'd care. That's all you want, just my damned body, not me. Nobody wants me, just my damned body. And I'm damned and you're damned with your cock and your cleverness ... You never loved me ... I wanted to be loved, I wanted somebody to be kind to me.'

But Oliver feels no tenderness, indeed cannot conceive of that kind of feeling for a girl from a rural slum. What she is, is 'accessible', and he waits for the moment when 'we could come to sensible terms again'. As she leans moodily on her elbow, staring at Stilbourne below, he tries to pull off her knickers – and there is a moment of shock and revelation which will finally show what her life has been – if he, and we, can read it.

Her bottom shows two sets of weals, the underlying ones seeming to have been heavily inflicted 'it may be in time with some long ocean swell', the uppermost ones more weakly; probably, thinks Oliver as 'the pieces fell into place', as the man in the wheelchair tired. Once again, faced with something emotionally incomprehensible to him, he *laughs*. But Evie is embarrassed to the depths of her being, and can only mutter, 'I was sorry for 'im.' For Oliver, an absolute gulf has opened between the 'clean' world of his parents and Imogen, and life's 'lavatory', newly revealed. Since Evie is now also terrified lest he tell her secret down there in Stilbourne, he has new powers of blackmail. (Nevertheless, what has been happening off and on since she was fifteen is not simply obscene to Evie. It is also, we might notice, 'something shymaking but good'. Once again, the challenge to the reader may be more complex than it appears at first sight.)

What neither has realized is the efficiency of Stilbourne crystal sets. The darkening 'mood' of Oliver's mother has to do both with Imogen's society wedding and with what, well able to see through a brick wall, she has realized about her son and the girl, about whom something really must be done. For Evie has dared to come to the dispensary. It seems that people feel able to talk to Oliver's father, though how far he actually listens is not quite certain. He does seem, however, to have been shocked by Evie's conviction that all men are beasts, and has assured her that he isn't, and nor is his son.

Consequences follow swiftly as his wife rushes out, slamming the door – but other townswomen also determine that Evie must go, the final straw being the trace of lipstick on Dr Jones, spotted by the sharp-eyed Mrs Dace for all her worry over her sick child. So Evie has to leave for her aunt's house in London. But before she goes she takes her revenge on Stilbourne, and Oliver, and his mother who so glitters with triumph and contempt. Evie will only sleep with Oliver now on the open hillside; and finally, in his frustration, he risks it – unaware that his father is watching through binoculars. Only now do we learn of Evie's 'hysteria', laughing and jeering, when she denounced his son to the dispenser of remedies, so that he felt he *had* to know whether it was true. And only now can we measure the attitudes of even the kindest soul in Stilbourne to the girl from the slum: the threat of contamination and disease, together with the feeling that all sex is 'wrong, wrong, wrong'. Oliver, ironically distracting himself with gypsy music, is overcome with shame; though a 'fallen' Evie seems undaunted.

Two years later they meet again, he down for the vacation and she for her father's funeral. She is very smart and has manifestly gone up in the world, just back from a trip to Sweden with her boss. Having a drink together, they put a gloss upon the 'good times' of their youth. Oliver, however, trying to match her sophistication but knowing her as little as ever, miscalculates badly when he tries to tease her about Bobby, Captain Wilmot, and Dr Jones. Her archness changes into the old impish hitting back, comparing him sexually, and loudly, with her boss. 'It all began,' she says into a suddenly silent bar, 'when you raped me . . . I didn't want you – I was only just fifteen!' She is still laughing when he hurries her outside. 'Oh – go to hell!' he shouts, just a word to him, though not to her. She also has it in her to be sorry. But when he doesn't respond, her full bitterness spills out. Will he never grow up? Never realize the abortive deathliness of the town, the snobbery of people like his mum and dad, and what it was like to grow up in a slum? She will never come back. 'So you can go on telling an' laughing, see? Telling an' laughing' – about her and her dad. Too late, Oliver begins to see that there might be 'a different picture of Evie in her lifetime struggle to be clean and sweet', not an object but a person with whom genuine relationship (and harmony) had been possible. But he still doesn't grasp that 'Dad' was no slip of her tongue, but had been, since she was fifteen, at the heart of her conflict and her trauma. (There were two sets of weals when Oliver began to laugh, and blackmail. A number of other details, going right back to our first sight of her with her father, a glimpse of love as well as fear and violence, should at last fall into place, though it is far from clear whether even the older Oliver yet understands.)

III 'THE KING OF HEARTS'

The second story is a much shorter satirical interlude, in which farce increases the comic distance. Ironies here are far more transparent. Some remain, especially towards the end, because Oliver-the-character has only grown up a little in one term at Oxford and is still in many ways as blind as he is clumsy. Yet leaving Stilbourne has helped him see it more clearly, so the gap in understanding between him and the older narrator is narrower; resulting in sharper satire. The contrast between the already trashy 'love' story put on by the town's Operatic Society – the reminiscence is of Ivor Novello – and the bitchiness of its principals, would be abundantly clear even without the novel's epigraph. The step backward this time is to the theatrical 'stills' in *Pincher Martin*, but here the displays of egotism have no metaphysical resonance, and allow a good deal of satirical laughter as the action exposes the actors more and more clearly. It is no wonder that so much time has to pass between shows for the social scar tissue to heal. For here bourgeois respectability is ripped aside to expose an underlying nastiness.

Despite his gnat-like voice, Imogen's husband has the romantic lead, and she will sing the ingénue, displacing a trained if ageing singer who has always starred before. That lady's father, the ancient Mayor, has refused the use of his parlour at the last moment so as to inflict maximum damage. The producer, a 'camp' figure, has constantly to flatter the inflamed ego of the 'King of Hearts'. (But it will not take us long to spot the explanations. It is because he is putting up the money that the Claymores are starring, though she too has neither heart nor musical talent. Evelyn De Tracy may have talent, but has seen much better days, which must be why he is in this small town on a pittance – because he needs the money.) The town's pretensions to culture or civility get devastatingly exposed, and as for the music of the heart . . .

A sharply comic performance comes from Oliver's mother who leads the tiny orchestra, nicely set off by her mute and mutinous husband. She gleams with excitement, flushed and enthusiastic about the 'romantic' music and her favourite Imogen, the Dean's daughter; and she insists on involving her son in the last performance as a gypsy violinist. (After all, he had played gypsy music endlessly, after the fiasco with Evie.) As egos begin to clash in a farcical rehearsal however, her enthusiasms pull apart, until her own ego so fuses with her desire to show off her son that she can no longer brook the Claymores, and lashes out lethally enough to stop the show were it not for the compromises found by De Tracy and Oliver.

They seem the most sympathetic characters in this story, despite the producer's weird appearance and blatant flattery, and the lad's clumsiness and self-enclosure which, together with his stagefright, make an even broader farce of the last performance. Behind the camp clothes and manner De Tracy is actually intelligent and kindly, with real insight and power of expression. For all his hidden amusement he is sensitive to Oliver's feelings and doesn't put him down, indeed guides him to see Imogen at last for the vain and insensitive woman she is. Under his influence – and a couple of strong drinks in the bar – Oliver tries to voice from the heart, however incoherently, what he has learned about Stilbourne now. Everything is 'wrong': no truth, no honesty, no sense of the transcendent, only shame about the body, and disguise, and snobbery. And as for the '*stuff* they call music' – summing up the whole irony of 'The King of Hearts' – 'It's obscene.' (He still, however, cannot apply all this to his heartlessness with Evie, though a nearness to tears suggests something stirring.) Then the irony turns unmistakably on him, as Evelyn responds by showing some truthful photographs. In one he is in a ballerina's dress and posture, in another he is supported by 'a thick young man ... they gazed deep into each other's eyes'. But for Oliver the moment is one of blank incomprehension: 'I laughed till it hurt' – a now familiar response.

In the intervals between his devastating appearances on stage, Oliver encounters an increasingly drunken stick-like figure who finally loses control of his legs (always a register of De Tracy's sufferings), and has to be put on a bus to Barchester, or wherever. But behind the clown-Evelyn, as behind the stereotype-Evie, bleakness opens up. Once again Oliver makes the Stilbourne response: seeing only the sexuality, and quite blind to the frustrated longing for feminine and physical grace, and for love, the music of the heart. But the critical edge is sharper now than in Evie's case, since this is an even bleaker and more permanent waste of a life, headed further and further downhill. Oliver's bland self-enclosure at the end, as he anticipates applause for his performance, carries a bitter charge.

IV 'BOUNCE'

The third story starts firmly in the voice of the forty-year-old Oliver who returns to Stilbourne many years later, almost by accident, and finds it modernized, prettified, photogenic – and still sterile. Through his adult eyes we seem to see clearly and without irony at first, though with a good deal of satiric bite since he lets his own feelings show now. Henry's garage and farm-machinery business has covered one side of the High Street in chromium and glass, and inside, on a lit-up dais, revolves Bounce's vintage two-seater, which (in a way) started it all. The narrator too has become a success, judging by the expensive motor which impresses Henry for the first time ever. The child in Oliver (still) is pleased, though the adult is contemptuous of how their social antennae have vibrated. He now feels he can grasp what drives Henry. 'His attitude was typical of the deep thing lying in him, the reason for it all ... the thrust not liked nor enjoyed but recognized as inevitable, the god without mercy': the drive for material success. But Bounce is dead, and it is the sentimental Welsh side of Henry that has erected the weighty memorial in the churchyard with its marble harp, and an inscription placed with exactly Henry's 'modest assurance, his sense of position, of who was entitled to do what'. But we are not to be told, yet, what it says – not until, having re-experienced the child, we are able to measure its full charge.

As Oliver sits in the churchyard, memories plunge him back into the child who took music lessons from the formidable Miss Dawlish. The story moves into flashback, but mediated now through adult understanding the child could not command; but that the adult also never knew he had. Conversely, the child's eye has a convincing vividness, empowering and authenticating what the adult perceives. Oliver can tell, now, that the violence of Bounce's father came from knowing himself a man without talent; but it is the toddler's vision of the mad old man in a highbrow fit, attacking an organ-grinder, that establishes indelibly how Bounce's life of 'music' began in discord and bullying, authenticating all the later evidence. Conversely as the child's eye takes in the dark brown gloom of Bounce's house, and – a victim of comic mis-understanding – its bleak upstairs and lavatory, we get not only his lonely fright but also a powerful experience of the desolation in which the woman lived, which the child saw without seeing, and the adult only truly sees now. (It will also take our eyes to note the significance of the photograph of the girl in the mortar-board, the pipe and cigarettes, the mannish dress.)

Then comes the child's first view of Henry, driving the taxi to the music exams in Barchester: vivid impressions of a sad-looking but mobile face, a voice with a liquid Welsh lilt, and jokes and charm. The child records innocently the effects on Bounce. (We might wonder briefly about that glycerine eye and its sharpness for an opening.) But we are then carried away by the exam fiasco; the paradox of perfect pitch accompanied by such tears and misery, and followed by music lessons supposedly for pleasure only, that remain so miserable. At least Bounce now nods off more, as bored as her pupil. The newly exciting thing is the little car Henry buys for her and the driving lessons that follow – exciting also the watchers tuning-in behind the Stilbourne curtains, a metaphor spelt out now by the narrator. Then Henry tries for a living in Stilbourne, perched in a loft above the smithy yard. There is a triangle: he polishes the car like a jewel, Bounce talks to him gruffly, through it. In his parents' gossip the boy half-hears a moral debate begin: his father sees only kindness, his mother a sprat to catch a mackerel, a lovely phrase the boy innocently repeats to Bounce herself with predictable results. About this time he notices how sphincter muscles seem to be drawing her mouth tighter – but makes no connection.

Changes come: a growing boy's bigger violin, and suddenly a Bounce who seems softer, brighter, younger, her tie replaced by frills, her yellow face 'mysteriously' feminized. But this potential (a hint of the lost youth that survived only in an elastic gait and a bouncy bosom) is rapidly dealt a double blow. The boy's incredulity shows just what the town's reaction will be; and just as suddenly, the tie is back and the mouth pursed still more. Then, out of nowhere, appear a gormless blonde and a baby: Henry's entirely unsuspected wife and child. As always, Oliver's mother speaks for Stilbourne: a superficial pity for Bounce, 'poor soul', barely concealing amusement, even 'exhilaration'. At least the narrator can feel more than that now, aware also that he 'cannot tell down what chasms of humiliation and bitterness' Bounce 'was thrown or threw herself'. The wife is also not so gormless as to move into a loft. Only a few weeks later, Bounce offers to share her house with them, much to the irritation of Oliver's mother at Bounce, and bitterness towards Henry. Sometimes now he appears in overcoat and trilby rather than the shiny blue serge and peaked cap. But what stance are we to take? How interpret Bounce's offer? Or Henry's 'glycerine' eye and rebuke, when the boy echoes his mother's attitude towards 'a dear, kind lady'?

Inevitably, strains develop. Bounce, ever more manly and gruff, may speak of 'my family' and be referred to as 'Auntie Cis', but territorial disputes lead to growing anger, and music becomes a measure of discord. Bounce's rage at the new gramophone in Oliver's house reminds us of her frustrated father; and the revelation to the youth (now) of what music can be, reveals also his teacher's musical limits – though it is not clear whether she knows them. But there is also more than one kind of frustration. We overhear not only the whining wife, but also hints of what lies at the heart of the dear kind 'aunt'; while Henry is caught in the middle. 'I got to have my kitchen!' 'No, Auntie Cis! It's not like that, at all, at all! ... But then, like you always say, you got your music.' And, dreadfully, 'All I want is for you to need me, need me!' But Henry's driving ambition also pours fuel on the fire. The yard has become a workshop now, whose noise makes teaching music impossible. This cannot go on.

So Henry takes over old Mr Dawlish's shop and cottage to turn into a proper garage, and the argument between Oliver's parents becomes heated. 'He's got what he wanted ... using her own money to re-build her own property. He'll have her last penny!' 'Young Williams works hard. She'll get her money back ... There must have been an agreement ... ' Soon after, comes the first combined harvester for hire. Meanwhile, the choice for Oliver – his new passion for music, or working for a scholarship and a successful career – becomes acute. We know what Stilbourne and even his father will say; but the measure of Bounce's bitterness is that she agrees. 'Don't be a musician ... Go into the garage business if you want to make money. As for me, I shall have to slave at music till I drop down dead.' What had begun in bullying has ended in drudgery – and she has never known a music of the heart. Meanwhile the squabbles go on, with Henry trying to hold a balance and (with bitter irony for Bounce) 'understanding' both. Till one day, suddenly, they are gone, into a new bungalow, as Oliver's mother knew would happen when Bounce was no more use to them. When Oliver goes to say goodbye just before he leaves for Oxford, what he hears in the music room is a different sound, of someone trying to learn 'how to sob her heart out' in the dark.

What follows is a road to breakdown. When he returns for the Easter vacation and comes upon the little car in a ditch in the woods, he discovers that Bounce has been staging accidents in a desperate effort to regain Henry's attention. In a convulsion of Oliver's mind, he begins at last to grasp the depth and power of her need, and the gulf between her heart and what drives Henry. There is also a contradiction between his mother's 'Money isn't every-thing' and her ambition for her son, not to mention the absence, in her giggles about Bounce, of one of the things essential to humanity that money is not. Suddenly Oliver is 'consumed with humiliation ... to think how we were all known, all food for each other, all clothed and ashamed in our clothing.' Bounce's accidents reach the courts, until she hurts someone and has her licence suspended. And then, there being no more telephone boxes, she strips herself naked except of course for a respectable hat, gloves and shoes, and paces, smiling calmly, towards Henry's business, to Oliver's incredulous horror.

For Stilbourne, this is of course a nervous breakdown, and Bounce vanishes into some 'home'. (But we might remember how Evie insisted on making sex open, and how Evelyn responded to the plea for honesty by exposing his secret too.) When she returns there is a familiar story: a post-menopausal spinster in a decaying house among cats and budgies. But what makes Bounce different is the depth of her bitterness: the irony of how Henry continues to care for her *car* ('a penance ... Henry always understands'); her confession of how in a crisis she would save a budgie rather than a human being.

We are almost ready now to read the horrible irony of Henry's 'tribute': the marble harp, the immortelles, the name of the patron saint, and above all the glycerine inscription: 'Heaven is music'.

(We had heard it before, on the lips of Bounce's father and those of Bounce herself . . .) A first measure of irony comes to Oliver as he sits beside the grave, only two yards away from 'that pathetic, horrible, unused body, with the stained frills and Chinese face'. This is another psychic 'ear test' of his response – but at first there is only revulsion and horror. In his last visit to Bounce he had sworn his little girl must never come to that, must be a fulfilled woman, wife and mother. Now he hears his own voice wrung at last into honesty: 'I never liked you! Never!' (Never 'devoted', then, any more than Henry.) Then he forces himself further. 'I was afraid of you, and so I hated you. It is as simple as that. When I heard that you were dead, I was glad.' But this is the child in him speaking. The house is being carefully demolished to extend Henry's business: it holds no terrors now, except for a trapped and dying bird which might serve as a metaphor. It is only when Oliver sits in the far corner of the overgrown garden – where Bounce must have sat in her last months gazing at the shallow, sliding river – that for the first time in the narrative he finds an adult compassion. As against the marble monument, here is Bounce's verdict on 'you always got your music' and its 'heaven': the burnt volumes, the smashed bust of Beethoven, the metronome tossed on the rubbish heap that her life has become; utterly without love, the beginning and end of the heart. Yet, back at his car with Henry, what is there to say? Irony about Henry's 'nice thought' bounces off. One can still never see through or around Henry, never tell whether there might be real feeling behind those eyes that always seem about to overflow. One *could* say, about Bounce and Stilbourne, that 'the only time she was ever calm and happy . . . they put her away until she was properly cured and unhappy again'. But suddenly, Oliver feels he could say more about the lost sound of her footsteps walking down that street; that he would give anything to lend them 'my own sound, my own flesh, my own power of choosing the future', the power of loving imagination that could get inside and recreate Bounce by giving himself. But he knows that, like Henry, he 'would never pay more than a reasonable price'.

And that brings up, very honestly, the weakness of the novel inside its achievements. It is a novel, and not three separate stories. It is bound together by the narrator and his imaginative growth; by pervasive irony albeit in differing modes; by its three kinds of 'pyramid'; and most of all by the deeply thematic congruence of its three stories of lost life. There is far more to it than appeared at the time. And yet, somehow, it doesn't satisfy, or only partially. One side of 'history', the ironic exposure of a bourgeois society, it does very well. But on the other side, the creation of complex character, it is only with Bounce that it succeeds, and then only within the limits that the story itself admits.

One trouble with the first story lies in the trickiness of irony. A reader who fails to read between the lines will simply share the blindness or blandness of the surface. But if the author behind the narrator erects too overt signals (Evie, Stilbourne, etc.), perhaps worried whether his tale is self-declaring enough, this may seem condescending. On the other hand, if the irony is made too difficult, that may annoy or at least perplex, and Golding's irony in the first story *is* testing. It takes close reading, a readiness to draw inferences, if one is to pick up all that the young Oliver can't see, and the adult narrator either can't or won't tell. But a far more damaging difficulty is with the portrait of Evie itself. Though it is essential for the irony that Oliver cannot see beyond her sexiness, the unfortunate result is that the other sides of her character can only be hinted at. It is not only Oliver who cannot tell what it is like to *be* Evie. Her 'life-long struggle to be clean and sweet' remains notional to *us*, too, hinted at rather than experienced. A glimpse of a gold cross and a girl coming out of a chapel cannot create a religious sensibility, let alone the conflict between that and her powerful sexuality. Nor can we do more than guess at the conflict of love, fear and shame in her relation with her Dad, or between pity, affection and embarrassment with Wilmot. So it is not merely to Oliver that she remains an undiscovered person, even when we see and infer things that he does not.

The second story, conversely, seems rather too simple and its farce too broad to carry much depth of feeling. Golding shows a talent for farce that had only been glimpsed before in *The Brass Butterfly*; but while he handles the stagey, indeed rather cliché material of this story well, both pointing its satire of 'Stilbourne' and making us glimpse behind the farce the bleak tragedy and waste of De Tracy's life, the narrative remains to a large extent trapped within the cliché world. It works well as an interlude between more powerful stories, but it cannot carry much weight in itself.

In the final story, however, continual interplay between the child's vision and the adult's creates a much fuller sense of depths beneath the surface. Music is a critical language and a suggestive symbolism for all that is missing: its formal properties of harmony and measure pointing up the discord in Bounce's heart, its practice revealing a hell of drudgery, frustration, loneliness. And though the ironic narrative now confesses itself unable to give itself to Bounce and so create her from the inside, we do see more of her and around her, and experience more development than with Evie. So she seems more complexly 'there' (as only one side of Evie is) though we are never unaware of the ironic limits of the view. Perhaps Bounce's eccentricity and unattractiveness make too special a case in the light of the epigraph, but there is no doubting the desolation in which the tragicomedy ends.

Moreover, as we shall see, *The Pyramid* eventually did show Golding the path forward, to both the more powerful novels that would follow.

8

DARKNESS VISIBLE

(1979)

I BURNING, BURNING, BURNING

The critical reception of *The Pyramid*, so inevitably compared with its predecessor, probably sharpened Golding's sense that the main road of his fiction still led through *The Spire*, however much he might have learned by exploring his hitherto almost unsuspected comic and ironic talent, and however difficult *The Spire* must still have seemed to get beyond. Yet surely it *was* still possible to see further and more clearly? Admittedly, the bigger novel had essentially to do with the immense difficulty of seeing whole. All its structuring and patterning had been only a preparation for one single moment of perception, at the very end. It had been necessary to exhaust all the 'languages' of the spire and to 'know' in every way, in order that Jocelin at the point of self-extinction should be able to focus its wholeness momentarily, and cry out 'Now I know nothing at all.' Only in the tentativeness of simile – 'It's like the appletree' – had it been possible to create a suggestion of something glimpsed beyond words. The tentativeness bore eloquent witness to Golding's sense of the mysteriousness of human being – fusing dark energy and bright abundance – and of the limitations of language. Nevertheless it surely had to be possible to get deeper insight, to turn glimpsing into seeing, to make darkness (and brightness) more visible?

And here the writing of *The Pyramid* proved fruitful. For might not another formal fracturing break down, once again, any *Spire*-like monolithic drive, and also help to focus a dark story and a bright story more clearly, in sharp separation this time, before attempting to bring opposite ways of seeing together, somehow, in a third story from a still different point of view? And here too progress might be sustained by taking up the challenge of an even more contemporary world than *The Pyramid*'s: both to make its darkness visible and to see whether (in those words of *The Inheritors*) it had an ending. What in the 1970s would pose the severest challenges? That most infamous photograph of the napalm-burnt Vietnamese child? The headlines about some outrage by a middle-class terrorist (like Patti Hearst or Ulrike Meinhoff?) The one kind of offender that even the liberal-minded find it hard to stomach, the pederast who keeps interfering with children and absolutely refuses to be cured? Golding had always been committed to exploring the depths where the world of social behaviour and character gives way to hidden dimensions of good and evil, joy and horror, seen most clearly in extremes – even though starting from extremes might be a high-risk strategy. So, when 'Greenfield' sets us again in the late-twentieth-century England of *The Pyramid*, still further updated 'what with the jets soughing down every minute to London airport and the monstrous continental trucks doing their best to break down the Old Bridge', author and reader must cope from the start with visions of extremity – beginning with the experience of Inferno that set the twentieth century apart from all that had gone before.

But first, what is it, to 'see'? It is a fact that twentieth-century man perpetrated 'darkness visible' in hells unimaginable to Milton – London, Dresden, Hiroshima – but in the astonishing overture of the novel Golding not only makes his readers realize Inferno, but also makes us see what he means by seeing. It must, first, be pure perception devoid of sign, all the more terrible in this case for being objective. At the height of the Blitz an area east of London's Isle of Dogs seems covered by a tent of light held up by searchlight beams. A fire-crew, helpless beside their crippled engine, gaze into a white-hot furnace where buildings had been.

The drone of the bombers was dying away. The five-mile-high tent of chalky lights had disappeared, been struck all at once, but the light of the great fire was bright as ever, brighter perhaps. Now the pink aura of it had spread. Saffron and ochre turned to blood-colour. The shivering of the white heart of the fire had quickened beyond the capacity of the eye to analyse. . . .

This is done in the purely visual terms a painter might use, though of course the context gives the objectivity of the palette an undertone of horror. Yet, re-focusing, it is out of *that* shivering glare that the 'something' which seemed to have moved turns into a naked child – the Vietnam photo recreated – whose survival is, simply, miraculous. It should not have been possible, but 'they saw him plain': the brightness on his left side that is not an effect of light; the reasons why he walks as he does; the terrible burns. The child walks out of the fire. We 'see', as no more and no less a fact than the twentieth-century inferno, an apparent miracle of survival, like the fireman under a collapsing façade who found a fourth-floor window frame fitted neatly around him. But this is as dark as it is bright, a horrible brightness, a scrap of humanity saved and maimed, a glimpse of terror and wonder – like Jocelin's at the end of *The Spire*, for we are starting where that left off. 'What had seemed impossible and therefore unreal was now a fact and clear to them all.'

But 'seeing' must here take in one dimension more. The captain of the fire crew is forced to see, 'quite clearly in a kind of inner geometry', that there was a direct connection between his moment of cowardice before he could nerve himself to go to the child's rescue, and his own survival. (Now the horror is like Pincher's).

He shut his eyes and for some sort of time saw that he was dead or felt that he was dead; and then that he was alive, only the screen that conceals the working of things had shuddered and moved ... He came, silent and filled in an extraordinary way with grief, not for the maimed child but for himself, a maimed creature whose mind had touched for once on the nature of things.

Vision, then, is a threefold process of focusing: first, and essentially, concrete perception; then through perception to insight, fusing darkness and brightness; then through insight to revelation of 'the nature of things', the existence of a terrifying field of force and design to which our normal experience is a concealing screen: through physical seeing to skrying, through skrying to revelation.

II MATTY'S BOOK

Matty's book follows that process. If vision must first come through fact it is clear why the child of the burning city must be as literal as the flames. Burnt down the left, the imaginative side of the brain, he is so literal-minded as to be almost a 'natural', a kind of idiot, not only un- but anti-symbolic. Only called 'number seven' because as a matter of fact six maimed children were admitted to hospital ahead of him, he will not be Christian-named or surnamed till later. He is so disfigured as to be undisguisably repulsive. Yet the one person in his terrible and suffering child-hood who shows him any affection brings out, instantaneously, the response of an essentially loving heart. Moreover that young nurse also realizes that 'Matty believes I bring someone with me', that behind her is an other – a perception about another dimension to life which perhaps is idiotic, and perhaps is not. Matty's experience, then, is remarkably concrete. But it is also of deep division (corresponding to the two sides of his face), and sensitive to a dimension beyond. Starting concrete, his 'gospel' becomes a deeper and deeper focusing, objectively unsentimental, and told from the outside until his thirties.

In boyhood, social trauma succeeds physical tragedy. Quite incapable himself of deception or irony, he naturally believes the 'letter' that is supposed to come from a girl from the school over the wall, and meets with horror and cruel laughter. Understanding nothing of sarcasm, he takes Mr Pedigree literally about being his treasure, keeping order, and bearing witness to wrongdoing. Again truth and a loving and protective heart bring destruction and repulse. Like the psalmist in the good book,* only literally, he casts his shoe at 'evil' (in the shape of the beautiful little boy on the fire escape outside Pedigree's room); and causes the death of Henderson and the arrest of the schoolteacher. Now he must face not only the hostility of his fellows and the familiar physical revulsion, but a traumatically shrieked-out judgement from the man he thinks his only friend: 'You horrible, horrible boy! It's all your fault!'

Yet there is no accident in the connection of love with remorse and guilt, and darkness with light. Level by level, Matty must ask deeper and deeper questions about identity and purpose. Working now at Frankleys store, one side of him still agonizes over Mr Pedigree, but the other fills with the girl among the artificial roses – and with a skrying that is not artificial, or even human at all. In the window of Goodchild's bookshop lie a parchment scrap of ancient music, a hornbook Lord's Prayer, and a skrying glass.

* Psalm 60.

Matty looked at the glass ball with a touch of approval since it did not try to say anything and was not, like the huge books, a whole store of frozen speech. It contained nothing but the sun which shone in it, far away. He approved of the sun which said nothing but lay there, brighter and brighter and purer and purer. It began to blaze as when clouds move aside. It moved as he moved but soon he did not move, could not move. It dominated without effort, a torch shone straight into his eyes, and he felt queer, not necessarily unpleasantly so, but queer all the same – unusual. He was aware too of a sense of rightness and truth and silence.

But this 'feeling of waters rising' and 'still dimension of otherness' also show 'the seamy side, where the connections are'; the balance between love and guilt; and how light, love and beauty bring out the dark deformity of the self. To questions that seem to come from nowhere in an empty church – 'Who are you? What do you want?' – come answers through tears: the Man in Black, the guilty and remorseful man who must offer up everything he wants, in penance, and can live only on the underside of the world.

So, literal as ever, Matty goes to Australia. But also out of the skrying has come a new question: no longer 'who' but 'what' am I? – a question no longer of identity but of nature. Australia's answer to his literal mind is as horrible as it may seem farcical or pathetic or even mad to us. Irony and farce return. Only between the lines of the still-objective narrative can we detect what Matty sees and how he feels, but these are no laughing matter. After he flees from the sirens of Gladstone in their house of mirrors, he loses himself in the Northern Territory – ill-omened name – and suffers a terrible revelation. The Darkness is not only in him: the Black Man springs viciously out of the desert air, crucifies, renders impotent, turns the whole sky black, a horrible showing forth of aboriginal nature. (Matty learns the facts about Harry Bummer, but is sure he sees more than they explain.) And yet a man may become a eunuch for the Kingdom of God, and in Australia Matty's learnt 'portions' of the Bible had been much concerned with vessels of sacrifice in the temple. Now his sufferings from the crucifarce point a still deeper question: not merely 'What am I?' but 'What am I *for*?'

Out of sacrifice comes prophecy – again apparently farcical: antics with pebbles and matchboxes; a clay pot and twigs which set the park on fire; a weird night-time ritual in a marsh. There is now a vast gap between the narrative and Matty's consciousness that our awareness must bridge – not helped by a modern reader's possible ignorance of the Bible, so much of which Matty knows by heart. He has found his purpose, and is telling his wordless truth with reverberant echoes of the Old Testament truthtellers who issued stern warnings to a sinful world: Elisha (beset by mocking children) denouncing the worship of Baal; Ecclesiastes warning cobblers (and readers) against folly; above all Ezekiel foretelling the destruction of Jerusalem. We begin also to glimpse the depth of feeling behind the still face. In the wilderness he enacts in silence the agony of the psalmist as the waters of affliction close over his head. He submits, shuddering, to a horrible baptism into primeval darkness and slime, but he comes through to the other shore. He not only bears witness to a light that shines on, transcending the passage through the underworld; he also proclaims the eternal glory of the wheeled Cherubim in Ezekiel and the Book of Revelation. And as he leaves Australia the essential goodness of Matty comes out unmistakably (like Lok's) when a little dust and a drop of water reveal things too deep for words – a lovingness and a grief more powerful than the condemnation Christ permitted his disciples.

He stood for a while looking up at the side of the ship. At last he looked down at his feet and appeared to be lost in thought. At last he lifted the left foot and shook it three times. He put it down. He lifted his right foot and shook it three times. He put it down. He turned round and looked at the port buildings and the low line of hills that was all a continent could muster from its inside to bid him farewell. He seemed, or would have seemed, to look through those hills at the thousands of miles over which he had travelled and at the hundreds of people that for all his care he had, if not met, at least, seen. He stared round the quay. In the lee of a bollard there was a pile of dust. *He went to it quickly, bent down, took a handful and strewed it over his shoes* [our italics].

He climbed the ladder, away from the many years he had spent in Australia, and was shown the place he had to sleep in with eleven others, though none of them had arrived. After he had stowed his one suitcase he went back up again to the deck and stood again, still, silent and staring at the continent he knew he was seeing for the last time. *A single drop of water rolled out of his good eye, found a quick way down his cheek and fell on the deck. His mouth was making little movements, but he said nothing* [our italics].

But finally, closing Matty's book like one of Golding's, a surprise ending challenges us to look again. We have seen between the lines of objective narrative how Matty embodies a New Testament as well as the Old one, and have (surely?) felt deep sympathy, despite his oddity. But suddenly we are plunged into Matty's own diary, and the challenge once more of his literalness. He may have come from seeing to skrying to vision, but can we accept his Revelation, his world of spirit – the red spirit with the 'expensive' hat – that is John of Patmos utterly divested of poetic symbolism? This Apocalyptic numerology? This cranky fundamentalism beyond even the Brethren in discarding the Bible itself and taking his Mission only from messengers of God? Matty's own words permit no figurative compromise. The world for him is literally governed by a spiritual force, a wind that roves through him, a spell that is God's. He has moved through questions of identity, nature, purpose, and now knows that the world which began for him in Inferno will end in Judgement – but the news, for him, is good, corresponding to his own capacity for forgiveness. Or else it is idiotic, Matthew's gospel; not truth of nature but the foolishness of a 'natural'. Which? There can be no ducking the question.

III SOPHY'S BOOK

Sophy's book follows the same process from seeing to skrying to revelation, but in an opposite direction. If the burnt child is first aware of himself as disfigured and only one of a number, the dark-haired little girl is aware both of her unusual prettiness and ability to charm, and of her ego and its jealousy, particularly of the ash-blonde twin sister who is able to absent herself from things, and care for nobody. Though Sophy is privileged and has everything in some ways, she cannot have what she wants most, the love of her self-centred and abstracted father. But the metaphysical nature of the story soon becomes more compelling than matters of character-conditioning or psychology, as her ecstatic 'seeing' of the dabchicks in the water-meadow begins to mutate into something darker:

They came out into the water, mother and chicks all ten on a string. They moved on with the brook and Sophy went right out into her eyes, she was nothing but seeing, seeing, seeing! It was like reaching out and laying hold with your eyes. It was like having the top part of your head drawn forward. It was a kind of absorbing, a kind of drinking, a kind of.

Darkness becomes visible in the response to brightness, a seeing that is grasping, possessive. The next day, as if the chicks and a pebble had been waiting for her, she throws it at them, somehow knowing it will hit. There is the excitement of imposing her will and power on a living creature, experiencing a force that answers and acts through her, and a 'complete satisfaction' as the stone reaches its target. Children – though usually boys – do throw stones and kill. But Sophy has 'phenomenal' intelligence and awareness of self, and before her eleventh birthday she has already conceived of herself (like Pincher) as looking out at the world from the mouth of a dark tunnel. She begins to see how that dark being can manipulate the outer little girl; begins to understand that she is alone and can belong to no one but herself. (Also, neither twin can bear being out of control.) Soon she discovers a 'weird' kind of power: that she seems able to walk through respectable people's inattention and do what she likes; that she need obey no rules but her own desires; that she may even, uncannily, be able to exert control over other people.

As she grows up, moreover, she begins to understand how inside-Sophy is connected to something happening in the world. After she and Toni have got rid of their father's latest mistress and the threat that he may marry her, Sophy finds Win's transistor radio, left behind, and hears two talks which speak directly to the dark creature. One is about how the universe is running down, the other about extrasensory perception. The first she feels she has always known. The second she mocks, because its scientific statistics miss just the dark excitation, the 'other end of the tunnel, where surely it joined on'. Now she feels not only 'a hunger and thirst after weirdness' but that 'Something pushed her, shoved her, craved'. With puberty comes a sense of new power, but the daylight beauty only makes the dark direction more visible. It is as if 'other eyes opened in the back of her head and stared into a darkness that stretched away infinitely', or as if she were an expression 'of the darkness and running down'. She explores sex with calm deliberation but the experience of intercourse, after letting herself be picked up, seems trivial. Behind vagina and womb she feels a turd working its way, and reacts with a convulsion of hate. Sex becomes at best a 'faint, ring-shaped pleasure' with her respectable Roland – until, that is, she stabs him with a penknife in a moment of anger, and experiences orgasm for the first time. The inside darkness finally joins on to the force that is running the world down to simplicity. She finds her *being*, not merely in defiance, power, or even the excitement of inflicting pain, but in being part of that destructive force.

So she stops pretending. With feckless Gerry, charmingly amoral young ex-officer and drug taker, she finds what she thinks is complete acceptance, in the permissiveness of the post-1960s. (Golding colours his own prose with a version of the argot of the period that has already dated.) She is unfazed by the discovery that he is doing occasional armed robberies for a living, with a not-too-intelligent squaddie friend who knows what it is to kill. Her only criticism is that what they do is small beer in terms of profit, risk, and excitement. The culminating plot of Sophy's book is to persuade them to do something much bigger: to kidnap some prince or millionaire's child from the public school at which Gerry's other friend Fido is the PT master (and where Matty is, also). So she sets out to seduce Fido, to see where a fire could best be started to distract attention, and to fantasize still more exciting possibilities should things go wrong afterwards, and they have to get rid of the child. To Sophy, the dark force seems obviously at work in a series of uncanny coincidences: a date that is all sevens; their meeting Fido by chance; and even the sudden reappearance of Toni, who had run away to Afghanistan, Palestine, Cuba and perhaps Russia, and turns up again just in time to be recruited, along with her resources.*

There is however no determinism: even now a dual potential remains. When they play the Rorschach game at a party and she gazes into the ink-blot, the sensation of immersion and extinction in darkness (like the child being caught in the wave) produces hysterical screaming and a dead faint. And in her last meeting with her father, which so shamingly exposes her hopeless love, and his indifference turning to hatred, we may see more in her passion than the outrage – to her – of the sexuality and grief in it. Yet it is

---

* Our view of terrorism has been transformed for ever by September 11, 2001, and a reader might now wish that Golding had concentrated on Toni's political evil rather than Sophy's psychological/metaphysical kind. Yet something pyschological (at least) must underlie terrorist murders of the innocent.

finally her commitment to the darkness, and the deadliness of her nihilism, that seem the news of Sophy's book.

Everything's running down. Unwinding. We're just – tangles. Everything is just a tangle and it slides out of itself bit by bit towards something that's simpler and simpler – and we can help it. Be a part ... *The way towards simplicity is through outrage* ... And she was there; without the transistor she was there and could hear herself or someone in the hiss and crackle and roar, the inchoate unorchestra of the lightless spaces.

Like Matty, she brings someone or something with her.

('I was speaking to – of – I was someone – .') We know there will be outrage. Presently.

IV ONE IS ONE AND ALL ALONE ...

It would seem, then, that the effect of juxtaposing Matty's book with Sophy's is a Manichaean division. Darkness has become unmistakably visible; brightness not so clear perhaps because of the oddity of its manifestation, but also obvious as soon as one looks. Yet we are aware of similarity as well as opposition. The two characters could hardly be more different: Matty repulsive, half-educated, deprived; Sophy lovely, sophisticated, privileged. He is loving, sacrificing, faithful, almost saintly (though a kind of idiot); whereas she is highly intelligent but cynical, nihilistic, sadistic, deadly. Yet these apparent opposites of 'good' and 'evil' turn out to be more alike than either is like 'ordinary humanity'. In loveless and traumatic childhoods, both long to be accepted, but will be rejected again and again. Both know themselves to be dual (the two sides of Matty's face, 'inside' and 'outside' Sophy) and are aware from childhood of forces beyond them acting through them. Both become 'seers', forcing us to see deeper and deeper into the nature and working of things; and as soon as we compare the revelations, we find them remarkably parallel, contrasting modalities of the same process of discovery. A shoe cast and a stone; a skrying glass and a transistor; a dark pool and an inkblot; the parallels are as striking as the differences. Darkness and brightness not only become visible in people, but also as dimensions of power active in the world. Both characters look forward to a final unravelling of complexity, indeed to the end of the world as we know it. They were dual, but at the end of their 'books' each seems resolved, and looks forward to the resolution of the universe. As at the end of Sammy Mountjoy's autobiography, there seems to be no bridge. Indeed, the final book of *Darkness Visible* seems at first to say just that, in several ways. 'One is one' announces its title (as in the old song), so all alone presumably, and ever more will be so.

Appropriately, the narrative is broken into several points of view now, Sim Goodchild, Matty, Sophy, Sim again, Mr Pedigree (whom we have seen at intervals, going further and further downhill) – all seeing differently. Sim even thinks of himself as a committee of discordant members, and of everyone as separated by barriers of adamant from everybody else. The new seer is sardonic and disillusioned. Youthful ideals and sentiments have given way to cynicism. As the challenge of Matty was his literalness, so anything Sim sees will have to pass the test of a scepticism which trusts in nothing but his own experience. Beliefs for him are second-class ideas; he can only truly believe in his own existence. That, moreover, tells him with certainty of the uncontrollable 'thing' inside him that compels him to hurt other people, and of the 'unruly member' of his private committee that is still active in an elderly man's sentimental memories of the lovely little Stanhope girls. So, when Edwin comes to him with excited good news of a charismatic encounter with a Man in Black, Sim inevitably reacts with the weariness of one who has heard it all before, many times; and with the mockery of a bookman for a teacher who now wants to give up language in order to find the truth.

Yet Edwin's experience – not only in but somehow through Matty's presence – was of seven words made visible: not in terms of meaning, but as sensations of shape and light in a dimension beyond the ordinary. Once again the emphasis falls on physical seeing. A vision of something*ness* depended on seeing some *thing* – for all Edwin's babble and mistakes about Matty, whom he neither remembers nor has any idea what he is looking for or why it should be secret. What breaks through Sim's scepticism, also, is no philosophical wisdom, or belief in religion or the occult, but rather two physical realizations we are made to share, albeit in words.

The first is to *see* Matty in the park as we have never seen him before, and to sense, welling through the physical realization, his overwhelming grief – and his anger, when he takes Sim's 'all this is nonsense' as directed at him and his quest. Sim also notices how Matty seems outlined against his background, so that he himself is its point, and not his history or ideas. The second, when Matty becomes a medium for Sim to see into his own palm, distinguishes seeing from the interpretation of signs, and skrying not only from charlatan fortune-telling but from any idea that significance can be read off from lines in words. Revelation comes through the act of seeing itself, and seeing whole.

The palm was exquisitely beautiful, it was made of light. It was precious and preciously inscribed with a sureness and delicacy beyond art and grounded somewhere else in absolute health ... Sim stared into the gigantic world of his own palm and saw that it was holy.

But these episodes are interwoven with others of tragi-farce. After the first, we see Pedigree's little game with the ball, hear his defiance, and then watch (through eyes that recognize what he is, but know nothing of his history at Foundlings) his tragically renewed rejection of Matty and Matty's sorrow. Edwin may think everything hangs together, but his theories sound absurd. Sim's scepticism returns when Edwin organizes what he thinks of as a kind of spiritual seance in the Stanhope girls' flat above the stables. (We shall discover that Matty, too, is thinking in ironically different terms.) Sim's hand may be transfigured when Matty looks into it – but the sordidness of the flat punctures the last romantic illusion about the girls, and as the three men hold hands around the table, Sim's itchy nose comically banishes any sense of the spiritual. Farce rules.

Yet when the absurd Edwin speaks one word into the silence there opens (in an astonishing passage) a 'speech' which is not mere word but music, vision, spirit.

There was, surely, no mere human breath that could sustain the note that spread as Sim's palm had spread before him, widened, became, or was, precious range after range beyond experience, turning itself into pain and beyond pain, taking pain and pleasure and destroying them, being, becoming. It stopped for a while with promise of what was to come. It began, continued, ceased. It had been a word. That beginning, that change of state explosive and vital had been a consonant, and the realm of gold that grew from it a vowel lasting for an aeon; and the semi-vowel of the close was not an end since there was, there could be no end but only a readjustment so that the world of spirit could hide itself again, slowly, slowly fading from sight, reluctant as a lover to go and with the ineffable promise that it would love always and if asked would always come again.

Does it matter that ordinariness returns? Or what word Edwin actually spoke? (It was probably 'joy'.) For we are concerned not with what the word 'means' but what it *is*, in being and becoming. The barriers are broken; the three 'rivals' of the old song have become one, for a moment. And if once, then why not again, in the cycle?

To plunge back into Matty's journal of this period, is of course to mark sheer difference again. When Sim heard the word and rejoiced, Matty saw evil spirits clawing at the circle – and wept. Yet the structure of vision grows the same. When he had seen into light and deformity before at Franklyns, Matty thought he had to choose. But now, to his puzzlement, the wicked deceiver Sophy offers a ring, the symbol of union. The Whore of Apocalypse torments him in a wet dream, but gives him the priceless gift of his manhood back, which turns a world of black and white to colour, and one of silence to the rejoicing of Beethoven's Seventh. And the Manichaean split is healed by seeing, beyond words, how good comes into the world *through* evil, and light and love through human deformity: 'between the word book and the word since I have been shown a great thing. It was not the spirits and it was not a vision or a dream it was an opening. I saw a portion of providence. . . .' What opens out through Matty's familiar litera-lism, from seeing to skrying to foreseeing now, pro-vidence, of joy incorporating horror, can only be glimpsed in the space between the telling and the sense of cause or consequence, wordlessly.

But when instead of Matty, Sophy comes up through the trapdoor at the next meeting, unity is called into question again. Without him, disillusion floods back. The light is either harsh or brothel-pink. There is a renewed sense of 'dust and dirt and stink'. After she leaves in a hurry, the two elderly men stumble on a hint of something perverted: the chair with its attached ropes, hidden in a cupboard. Now something more than romantic illusion is shattered: the newly granted sense of transformation and design is, too. Each is all alone again, behind a blank wall of indifference, meeting to no purpose.

Moreover we discover, as Sophy's plot goes horribly wrong, that Matty will come no more. And in the description of his terrible end – so much more terrible in imagination, as it recalls our first sight of him – the neutral narrative voice will not tell us whether he knew what he was doing, as he died in agony, on fire again. Was there the purpose of which he'd had a premonition: the kidnapper frightened off, the child able to escape? Or only frantic and accidental whirling, in wordless agony and horror re-experienced, unable this time to escape?

Sophy on the towpath, hearing a rabbit in a snare, is filled with a sense that she may be trapped, rather than purposeful and in control. But then the fire fills the night sky and she rejoices at 'an outrage, a triumph!'. Moreover, she finally sees what the 'last outrage' might be and knows herself capable of it. Passionately, convincingly, she imagines herself murdering the kidnapped child by stabbing through his genitals, the ultimate act of darkness. But her sense of cosmic force and purpose then comes apart when only Bill arrives in panic. Her plan has failed – but Gerry has escaped with Toni and her followers, and some hostages, so that Toni's plot succeeds. Sophy the user has been used, and fooled, betrayed by her lover and her sister. Once again she collapses into hysteria and oblivion. And as she picks her way back along the towpath the darkness holds no sense of cosmic Evil triumphant – only emptiness, nothing.

Then there is farce again. The TV pictures juxtapose the scenes at the airport with the lilywhite boys in their greenness holding hands round the table, as seen by the secret service surveillance camera in the stables, which had been watching out for Toni, suspected terrorist. The juxtaposition is artful – and endlessly repeated – but the pictures do not add up. All are guilty, but at the heart of darkness now 'the horror' (there is a Kurtz at the airport) is a black farce of ignorance, and of solitary confinement, each locked into a partial view. The novel could have ended there, pointing up the continual worry of Golding's that always makes ending problematic for him: how to conclude satisfactorily without seeming to claim some final certainty. In fear of pattern making, he has increasingly sought both to tell and to question the telling to the end. Here the questioning seems to have won and destroyed any possibility of unifying vision.

Or is it, as another Man in Black said, that 'we know what we are, but not what we may be'? Does what we are determine what we become? At the end Golding summons a witness. Mr Pedigree has been woven in and out of the web from the beginning, torn between his love of the bright sons of morning and his dark obsession; a helpless victim of his 'rhythm', yet neither consenting wholly to it nor willing to be cured. He, too, might kill a child in the end. Could such seamy material finally show us 'where the connections are'? Whether in the end there is darkness or light or nothing?

This means that the fiction has to let us 'know' what Pedigree experiences at the moment of his death. But what is most extraordinary about the rendering of his consciousness in those last moments is again the physicality of perception: the sun on the skin, the sea of light, and Matty coming. Indeed, only now that Matty is dead and he himself dying – like Jocelin – can he *see* Matty, see beyond the 'horrible' appearance and the question of who was at 'fault' in the death of Henderson and the martyrdom of Sebastian. Now he can also see the true nature of the name that nobody got right, though it shows the operation of the spirit blowing where it listeth: 'the extraordinarily lively nature of this gold, this wind, this wonderful light and warmth that kept Windrove moving rhythmically'. Finally he sees the Mattyness behind the 'natural' man, the love and forgiveness that was always 'popping up', always 'connected with everything else', that he had tried to throw away, but which wouldn't go. ('Who are you, Matty?') To him he cannot only speak of the hell he knows and fears, but *cry for help*.

It was at this point that Sebastian Pedigree found he was not dreaming. For the golden immediacy of the wind altered at its heart and began first to drift upwards, then swirl upwards then rush upwards round Matty. The gold grew fierce and burned. Sebastian watched in terror as the man before him was consumed, melted, vanished like a guy in a bonfire; and the face was no longer two-tone but gold as the fire and stern and everywhere there was a sense of the peacock eyes of great feathers and the smile round the lips was loving and terrible. This being drew Sebastian towards him so that the terror of the golden lips jerked a cry out of him –

'Why? Why?'

The face looming over him seemed to speak or sing but not in human speech.

'*Freedom.*'

But Pedigree who (like Sammy Mountjoy) cried for help cannot bear (like Pincher) to let go, and clutches closer to him the many-coloured ball, his life, his heart, himself. 'But the hands came in through his. They took the ball as it beat and drew it away so that the strings that bound it to him tore as he screamed. Then it was gone.'

Do we know now? Or not? We may remember what Matty wrote:

What good is not directly breathed into the world by the holy spirit must come down by and through the nature of men. I saw them, small, wizened, some of them with faces like mine, some crippled, some broken. Behind each was a spirit like the rising of the sun. It was a sight beyond joy and beyond dancing. Then a voice said to me it is the music that frays and breaks the string.

If so, man can choose, can cry for help at the last, in order not to be what he is and has been. Though the pluck at the string be a terrible death of the self, what is made is music. It is not darkness that is made visible at the end, it is brightness. One becomes one-and-all, only that, and evermore shall be so.

Yet we cannot be *told* this, in words. Words can only bring us to the point where we ourselves can 'see' for a moment something opening through them, in the space beyond them.

And Golding must still allow for those who do not see or cannot believe that the 'filthy old thing' that is our pedigree can ever be 'cured'. For both sets of readers there has to be a gap between 'book' and 'since', between the reading and the final sense of cause and consequence. It is physically there on the final page: an empty space. It rather seems as though Golding, like Aeneas, might be holding a golden bough as passport from one world to another. (*Sit mihi fas audita loqui.*) But the space must fill with each reader's vision. Some will see only emptiness after the word 'gone'.

9

RITES OF PASSAGE

(1980)

I CONTRASTS

When *Rites of Passage* came out only a year after its predecessor, the shortest gap since the earliest novels, there could hardly have been a greater and more unexpected contrast. The first impression was of instant accessibility.

Darkness Visible remains perhaps the most challenging of all Golding's books. He had indeed succeeded in extending *The Spire*'s exploration of good and evil, though it had taken ten years after *The Pyramid*. Here again, however, was a book that seemed to incorporate insights from all its predecessors: echoes of the foolish but loving innocence of Lok in *The Inheritors*, of the dark inner tunnel of Pincher and his defiance, of Sammy's choice of being in *Free Fall*, and of the dual vision of *The Spire*. All the Golding intensity was back again, too, after the lighter comedy, irony and farce of *The Pyramid*. But if the novel had proved immensely difficult to write, it was challenging enough to the reader, also, to be perhaps caviare to the general. Its exploratory imagination was apparently willing to risk the obscure, the contorted, the absurd, in order to reveal the seamy underside where the connections are. It used distorted lenses – a saintly fool, a paedophile, a terrorist – to overturn our ordinary sense of human nature and make the warp and woof more clearly visible. It was an art of extremity, and though containing several of the most wonderful passages in the whole of Golding's work, it was also willing to risk the simplistic and the slangy, and developed a deep distrust of language in seeking to lay hold of what is beyond words. One can see, moreover, why Golding refused point blank to be interviewed about the book: not only because it had been so hard to write, but also (one suspects) because it had made goodness as visible as evil, and he wanted no interview-type questioning about that. He had achieved it only by a hard-won and arduous imaginative art, that was not to be reduced to theology, theme, or summary.

So the instant accessibility of *Rites of Passage* could hardly have made a greater contrast. Not since *Lord of the Flies* had a Golding novel enjoyed such happy public recognition. Indeed part at least of its success may have come from the reassurance that the Golding of his most famous work was alive and well, and that the quarter century which separated the two books had not diminished his narrative power. There is a similar recreation of atmosphere and concrete detail, the South Sea island replaced by a ship of the line. The smell, the cramped quarters, the clanking pumps, the sand and gravel in the bilge, the constantly tilting decks, the effect of the wind in the ropes meticulously observed – the cumulative effect is to make us think not so much of vivid description as of an 'on the spot' report. This, Golding makes us feel, is just what it must have been like to have been aboard such a ship at the turn of the last century.

But the ship's surfaces provide, even more concentratedly than a small town, a model of a hierarchically structured society, and we are no less aware than in *The Pyramid* of how its inhabitants exist in the medium of social discrimination. The quarterdeck above, the gentlemen-passengers, the dividing line painted across the deck, the lower-class passengers, finally 'the people' as the crew are called: the ship as traditional literary microcosm is here specifically a class structure. The society of 'officers and gentlemen' is an extension of its counterpart on land, ever mindful of rank, courtesies, amorous strategies, and unseen paymasters. 'Below' them is the mob of sailors, crowded, noisy, dangerous when roused, and living a life as remote (to those 'above') as any native tribe. Between the two, marking the surface, is the first of the lines it is dangerous to cross. What is striking – and the 'line' is a good instance – is how effortlessly the precisely observed detail releases the wider perspective. But the structure is filled with a tissue of social assumption (effortlessly understood by English readers, foreign to Americans) that is of the very life of the book.

II EDMUND TALBOT

For the narrative is placed in the hands of young Edmund Talbot, who exists unthinkingly as the child of privilege and patronage. Godson of a powerful aristocrat, going out by his influence to take a post in the government of Australia, we are aware from the very beginning (for all his gaiety and charm) of the arrogance of Edmund's assumptions, his touchy sense of his own status and dignity, and his willingness to use the influence of his powerful relative to his own advantage. Because of this, in spite of his infringement of Standing Orders, he is able to beard the very captain on his quarterdeck. By contrast James Colley the young parson, raised by his cloth from the lower orders – also through patronage – betrays the *parvenu* in every detail of his appearance, manner and speech, and never more so than in his exaggerated respect for his social superiors. Like his counterpart in Jane Austen, Mr Collins, he is riding for a fall even before he ignorantly exposes himself to the prejudice of the Captain (who for some reason hates a parson), and reaps the social resentment Anderson has had to bottle up over the similar offence of Talbot, whom he dared not attack.

Indeed, the first phase of the novel is concerned with a very Austen-like ironic education of Edmund, who has to learn for himself the extent of his prejudice, blindness, and lack of tact, by colliding with realities that we should detect between the blithe lines of his narrative. In Miss Granham, the daughter of the Close, whose circumstances have forced her to be a governess, he meets someone whose dignity is as touchy as his own – and is rebuked. (It was a ghastly error to try to placate her by comparing her value with that of his childhood nurse.) He almost casually insults the First Lieutenant, who has confessed that he has risen from the foc'sle, by complimenting him on having learned to *imitate* a gentleman. He must learn to distinguish between the officers – Deverel, Cumbershum and Summers – on better grounds than appearance and manner. Summmers, in due course, will have to teach him the responsibilities and obligations that ought to go with rank and privilege.

But we will also become aware – as seldom in Jane Austen – of the instability of the social hierarchy, the reverberations of a wider context in which the old world of Reason and Order has to be set against an age of Revolution. The crew are turbulent. Although we do not actually see the 'crossing the line' ceremony in Talbot's narrative – our point of view being otherwise engaged at the time – it is as much to distract the crew as to express the contempt of some officers that the *parvenu* 'gentleman' is tormented as a scapegoat, humiliated and frightened in that sea ritual that seeks to appease forces rising from below the surface, and to achieve an equatorial balance. It will be in blind ignorance of such social realities that Colley then proceeds to offer, in his uniform of rank, an opportunity for further humiliation directed not only at him but also at the 'gentlemen' above him. To compare Golding's novel with Melville's *Billy Budd, Sailor* is to mark how very much more concerned with social discrimination and resentment this English novel is. One might guess from several particulars that the name of the ship could be *Britannia*.

So the 'surface' of manners and class-discrimination is no less important than in *The Pyramid*. Once again we have 'history' in our literary and imaginative terms, not mere recreation of the past but detailed observation and understanding of the workings of a society, along with complex individual characterization. Talbot puts himself vividly on the page, more so than he himself realizes much of the time. His lively style and shrewdness of observation also bring alive a notable cast of minor characters – Wheeler, the steward who knows everything and can get anything at a price, Tommy Taylor, the mischievous midshipman, and Willis the thick one, etc – though as we go on we learn to correct his mistakes and allow for characteristics he fails to see, all in the cause of greater human complexity. The earlier novel had taught Golding a great deal about an Austen-like use of irony, which is much more assured and successful now. But perhaps most remarkable of all, *The Pyramid* had shown – and *Darkness Visible* had taken further – how effective it could be to fuse the farcical with the tragic. If the theatricality of the interlude story of *The Pyramid*, for all Golding's unexpected aptitude for farce, had seemed rather too lightweight to carry any great significance, that is by no means the case here, where the whole ship is turned into a theatre, for performances which deftly fuse the ridiculous with an increasing sense of tragedy.

First comes a farce in Talbot's cabin that could be pure Restoration comedy. Having failed to find anywhere in the ship that is private enough to seduce the painted lady Zenobia, Talbot as young rake takes advantage of everybody being at the crossing-the-line ceremony – which Zenobia obligingly leaves in order to fetch a shawl – to pull her into his cabin and have his wicked will. Unfortunately a loud explosion causes an involuntary climax to the scene, holding a danger that will be fortunately averted when the young man discovers that he is by no means alone on the ship in having enjoyed her favours.

But the explosion offstage is not, as it happens, that other farce which Edmund thinks must be its explanation: the shooting of an albatross by the notorious rationalist Prettiman, in order to explode the superstition that figured in *The Ancient Mariner*. Though it will take Edmund – and therefore us too – some time to discover what all the other characters know, the blunderbuss was in fact fired by Summers to put an end to a brutal persecution that had got out of hand, playing up to the applauding crew, but which the Captain had refused to stop despite his lieutenant's protests. In the 'badger bag' – the sail half-filled with water in which 'victims' are ducked, 'shampooed' and generally ragged before King Neptune – the unfortunate Colley has been excessively ill-treated by Deverel and Cumbershum. (Deverel's brutish exultation is the first indication to Edmund that it is the high-born officer that is the oaf and Summers who is the gentleman.) Offstage, as in Greek drama, there has occurred the first determining action in a tragedy, though it does not seem really tragic yet.

The ship then becomes a theatre, and all its passengers the audience, for a second and third action which Talbot watches and recreates for us, but without understanding what he sees, and rather more interested in the aftermath of the episode with Zenobia. In priestly uniform, Colley rebukes the Captain for the insult to his cloth. Later, still in full fig, he stalks across the vestibule to rebuke the 'people'. As he vanishes into the foc'sle there is first polite clapping, and then increasingly raucous applause and hilarity. Two seamen mince across stage in Colley's surplice and mortar-board, before Colley himself appears, very drunk, almost naked, languishing on the bosom of a brawny seaman. He exclaims in joy. Then, heedless of the watching ladies, he pisses against the bulwark, before blessing the audience in the words of the Church's General Benediction. Talbot sees him later, vanishing into the loo with a sheet of paper, still smiling beatifically.

We have been watching, it seems to Talbot, scenes of increasingly vulgar farce, and his distaste is increased by the realization that the crew have aimed their parts in it at their superiors. But the farce soon mutates into something more darkly mysterious at first, and then unmistakably tragic, as Colley fails to reappear from his cabin. Moreover Summers, risking his own career, brings home to Edmund how much *he* is to blame for what has happened, and how his abuse of his position with the Captain had rebounded on the young priest and opened the door for others to abuse him. Talbot is made to see that privileges ought to carry with them a sense of responsibility, and we see the beginnings of change in the young man when, prickly about his dignity though he is, he accepts the criticism and agrees to overcome social distaste and visit Colley. Though the first visit produces no response, he is induced to make a second, during which he tries to persuade Colley that he is making too much of his disgrace.

Here we come upon the original germ of the novel: an episode recorded in Elizabeth Longford's *Life of Wellington*, when the then Colonel Wellesley led an expedition to Manila in 1797, and the young chaplain to the 33rd disgraced himself on the journey.

After only three days at sea the unfortunate clergyman got 'abominably' drunk and rushed out of his cabin stark naked among the soldiers and sailors 'talking all sorts of bawdy and ribaldry and singing scraps of the most blackguard and indecent songs'. Such was his shame on afterwards hearing of these 'irregularities' that he shut himself up and refused to eat or speak. Colonel Wellesley was informed. He instantly rowed across to Blunt's vessel and sent for him. The wretched man declined to appear. Wellesley then descended to Blunt's cabin and talked to him like a father: 'what had passed was not of the least consequence as no one would think the worse of him for the little irregularities committed in a moment of forgetfulness ... the most correct and cautious men were liable to be led astray by convivial society, and no blame ought to attach to a cursory debauch ...'

Colonel Wellesley's broad-minded and kindly attempts to 'reconcile Mr Blunt to himself' were not successful. In ten days he forced himself to die of contrition.

To Golding, 'this was so horrific that I had to invent human circumstances to make us understand how a man could die of shame'. Now, in the novel, young Talbot echoes Wellesley:

'... this is an unfortunate business but believe me, sir, you are refining too much on it. Uncontrolled drunkenness and its consequences is an experience which every man ought to have at least once in his life or how is he to understand the experience of others? ... In a day or two we shall all laugh at your comical interlude ... Depend upon it, you will soon see things differently.

There was no response. I glanced enquiringly at Summers.

'Well, Summers?'

'Mr Colley is willing himself to death.'

How *are* we to understand such a phenomenon? For Summers is right. And what is then at issue in *Rites of Passage*? Is it in fact an Austen-like novel of ironic education: how Mr Talbot went to sea and learned to know and behave better, and how Mr Colley was also made to know himself and could not cope with the knowledge? That seems a kind of truth, but a death from shame seems an excessive graduation, to say the least, and we have an uneasy feeling that the ground has shifted under us. Have we responded so readily to certain social and moral features of the book that we have been lured like Talbot into a false understanding, that it may be Golding's veiled purpose to subvert? In a rather curious way *Rites of Passage* seems to reverse the experience of being in a maze. We enter full of purpose and interest, and are delighted immediately by the precision and variety of the detail, and glimpses of prospects far and near. We expect to be taken further in. Then quite suddenly, we find ourselves on the outside. We seem somehow to have taken a wrong turn. A re-entry seems called for, and perhaps that is also part of this particular maze. To look at three scenes which are set off from the chronicle of Talbot's diary by being given Greek letters rather than consecutive numbers, is to make precisely a new start.

'ALPHA' finds Talbot seeking to overcome boredom by recording false appearances – notably the façades made up by Brocklebank and his doxies – but failing to detect the falsehood of his own judgements by appearance. He has heard of Colley's disappearance, and thinks it right and proper in such a fellow to be ashamed of having made a 'cake' of himself. Indeed, only a reaction against Captain Anderson's treatment of the man tempers his inclination to reject him 'as a human being'. Here is the dead end of the maze.

But 'BETA', when it comes, begins with 'Wrong again, Talbot! Learn another lesson, my boy!' On the surface this refers to the misfire of his attempt to blackmail the Captain (by letting him know he is keeping a diary for his godfather) into visiting Colley as Summers had wanted – only to have Anderson neatly turn his back on him. But at a deeper level it may serve also as a warning to the reader: for 'BETA' hints at a different kind of perspective. Having trapped himself into visiting Colley again, as we have seen, Talbot finds his worldly wisdom totally at a loss as Wellesley's was, utterly inadequate to reach the supine figure with his face hidden in the bedclothes and his hand clutching a ringbolt. What ails Colley is clearly more than social embarrassment and humiliation, nor will he listen to eighteenth-century Reason and Good Sense. What kind of language could reach him?

Puzzled and disturbed, Talbot suddenly recalls seeing, on his first visit, a pile of manuscript on Colley's table and goes back to fetch what he hopes may hold a clue, only to find the papers gone. After a search, however, he discovers them thrust into a narrow crack between the bunk and the ship's side. The man must have 'leapt from his bunk in some *new* agony' after Talbot had gone, and then 'in a passion of self-disgust', stuffed the papers away where he hoped nobody would find them. Edmund takes them back to his cabin in search of the illumination they must surely cast. 'Depend upon it, you will soon see things differently,' he had said to the supine figure. Now the words ironically recoil, and like Talbot, the reader awaits enlightenment. The novel seems to be turning into a detective story, working towards a solution of the twin mysteries of event and response. What *happened* to Colley in the badger bag, and (still more important) when he was hidden from sight in the foc'sle? And *why* is he trying to will himself to death? The reader has every apparent reason to share Talbot's confidence that answers are at hand.

But we are made to wait again, for before he can read the papers, he is invited to dine with the Captain. And this scene, entitled 'GAMMA', brings a quite different modulation into the novel, and begins to alter expectations.

When he arrives, elegant banter is exchanged about the Captain's 'garden': his triumph of growing plants from seed in the great cabin. There are fleeting references to Eden and the Fall; a geranium is diseased; and Anderson remarks that 'he who gardens at sea must accustom himself to loss'. The conversation is vivid, the occasion a little bizarre, and ever so faintly, the aphoristic cadence of the Captain's remark has an ominous undertone. When Summers arrives the Captain asks about Colley, and hearing that Brocklebank has had some medical training he tries to arrange for him to visit the sick man, in order to record in the log that he has had proper attention. But Brocklebank, when he comes, is drunk, and there is another scene of farce. Brocklebank is no medical man but an artist, and claims to have painted the first lithograph of Nelson's death, though he was not of course present, and had been under the impression that Nelson had died on deck.

'Brocklebank,' cried I, 'I have seen it! ... How the devil did that whole crowd of young officers contrive to be kneeling round Lord Nelson in attitudes of sorrow and devotion at the hottest moment of the action?' ...
    'You are confusing art with actuality, sir.'
    'It looked plain silly to me, sir' ...
    'And imagine, sir, Lord Nelson died below in some stinking part of the bilges, I believe, with nothing to see him by but a ship's lantern. Who in the devil is going to make a picture of that?'
    'Rembrandt perhaps.'

The passage, for all its lightness of tone, is a crucial one for understanding the novel. Though Brocklebank is a drunken fool, he does have a point. The artist may have to keep reality at 'Arm's length, sir', in order to show what he wishes us to see. We spectators also want the act of dying to have style, order, meaning – though in Brocklebank's case the selection and rearrangement are done for commercial and sentimental reasons, a tawdry theatricality. A Rembrandt would throw light into darkness with infinitely greater powers of vision, psychological understanding, and artistry. But death (not only Nelson's) is always hidden, and alone. Suddenly the whole conversation is interrupted by a knock at the door. 'One by one, we turned. Summers stood in the doorway. "Sir. I have been with Mr Colley, sir. It is my belief the man is dead."' Another man has died alone, his face to the wall, with only a lamp for company.

The news of Colley's death marks the narrative climax of the book, and what follows is an extended meditation on how (and how far) we can 'understand' that hidden event. Earlier, when he was in Colley's cabin, Talbot had leaned over the silent figure. 'It was then that I perceived without seeing – I knew, but had no real means of knowing.' It will be the aim of *Rites of Passage*, now, to find ways of perceiving and kinds of awareness that cannot have certainties of experience or evidence, and must therefore proceed by other imaginative and artistic means. It is not an aim to be fulfilled in the way that Talbot, or the reader, expected. It will not be the truth the whole truth and nothing but the truth. Indeed, it will seek to make the reader aware of what truth can be told, and what can never be.

III JAMES COLLEY

We get Talbot's response to Colley's letter before the letter itself, and find the normally self-possessed young man in a turmoil of unaccustomed feeling: pity, self-reproach, anger at the young priest's tormentors, and determination to seek justice for him. Quite gone are the social prejudice and contempt that had clearly blinded him before. We may indeed expect to change our view of things by seeing them through Colley's eyes. However, the very first sentence of his long letter to his sister undermines detective-story expectations: 'so I have drawn a veil over what have been the most trying and unedifying of my experiences'. We begin in mid-sentence, the first page or pages having gone with the drunken Colley to the loo. In fact he is merely referring to the sea-sickness which had prostrated him, like Edmund, at the start of the voyage, but the warning to the reader is there. We do get new 'documentary' evidence; but what is important is the way that it is coloured, indeed suffused, by a mind and sensibility entirely different from the one we have been inhabiting. It is not just a matter of privileged arrogance being replaced by a nervous self-abasement, nor are all of Talbot's judgements to be reversed. Colley does remind us, still, of Jane Austen's Mr Collins, especially in the references to *his* patron, and the way that obsequiousness towards social superiors can go along with pride in his own elevation to gentleman. He is immature in several ways, as well as socially inexperienced, and his judgement of people is much more fallible than Talbot's. Some of his habits of thought are as much 'stock' as some of Edmund's. But the ways in which Colley is 'a man of feeling' extend our whole sense of the life of the ship and the voyage.

After Talbot's Augustan idiom with its constant emphasis on men and manners, it comes as something of a shock to read of the sunlight 'warm and like a natural benediction'; of 'the white-flecked blue of the broad ocean'; of 'terror at the majesty of this huge engine of war'. Sense perception comes continually alive in Colley's prose, and it is above all the note of wonder, indeed of awe, that reminds us most forcibly of a dimension entirely missing from Talbot's journal. Hearing that the ship may be sailing over waters up to two miles deep, Colley writes: 'I was almost overcome with faintness. Here we are, suspended between the waters and the sky like a nut on a branch or a leaf on a pond.' Moreover, he sees the voyage as a spiritual one, a succession of trials and temptations to be overcome. He struggles to forgive his persecutors, to content himself with the limited space to which (unfamiliar with the difference between the quarterdeck and the afterdeck) he thinks he has been confined, and to find charitable reasons for the indifference of the other passengers to him and his predicament. When, at the equator, he sees in the sky at once the setting sun and the rising moon, he sees them as the scales of God. He is a Romantic. Again and again in Colley's voyage we feel the presence of Coleridge, in ways strongly contrasting with the rationalism of Prettiman. Like the Mariner blessing the water snakes, Colley looks over the side and – no longer terrified by unplumbed depths – sees the foam and the green weed and is consumed 'by a great love of all things, the sea, the ship, the sky, the gentlemen and the people and of course OUR REDEEMER above all'.

As he writes those words, however, he is about to 'go forward and rebuke these unruly but truly lovable children of OUR MAKER!', the crew.

The Man of Feeling may seem merely a fool if he misjudges their object; and strong feelings may also make him incapable of action or balance. As we re-experience the whole tragedy through Colley, we do indeed see things differently, but we also see what Colley has in common with Matty in the previous novel, and how with the best of intentions he gets things pitiably and ironically wrong. There is a strong tinge of the new boarding-schoolboy about him, in his tendency to hero-worship, in his terrified vulnerability to bullying, and in his loneliness and isolation when 'sent to Coventry'. We may also see how one kind of conscious feeling may be fused with another quite unconsciously. In Colley's wonder at the athleticism and bronzed manliness of the sailors there is the new boy's hero-worship of the First Fifteen, but there is also something he doesn't know about himself. (As we imagine Talbot reading, we can feel him taking a double hit: how ironic, as well as tawdry, his fantasy of palming Zenobia off on Colley was, as if to repeat what had happened in the Anderson family, only worse.) Moreover, when Colley's terror at the Captain's onslaught rendered him incapable of defending himself and brought on humiliating tears, it was Talbot's overheard rebuke of the midshipmen for laughing that began Colley's hero-worship of *him*. The irony deepens at each encounter. When Talbot asked for a religious service it was purely to thumb his nose at Anderson, but we now see why Colley addressed himself to the two people he mistakenly thought the most pious, to the distaste of the one he most wanted to please. The irony deepens with Talbot's excuse for not letting Colley into his cabin; and still more when Colley does visit him in his illness and smells on his unconscious breath what he thinks is the odour of sanctity. It is the combination of strong imagination, uncontrollable fear, and the parody of Judgement that make Colley's experience of the badger bag so inexplicably horrific; and Talbot's apparent kindness afterwards so 'Royal', so much 'more than ordinarily delightful' in ways which Talbot, knowing nothing of what has happened but knowing his own rather tawdry motivation, finds inexplicable too. But we can now at least understand the consummate irony of how Talbot's visit and offer of friendship must have brought the supine man off his bunk in a fresh agony of shame and self-disgust.

Yet when we come to the end of the letter we find that there is still (of course) no explanation of what happened in the foc'sle, to make Colley so determined. The letter has dramatized a way of thinking, a mode of sensibility, which takes feelings as its criteria for authentic experience, and sees the world in terms of signs. Colley does not see the world so much as see 'through' it. But what kind of sign is the ringbolt, and the supine figure clinging to it so strongly that Summers is unable to move him? In terms of evidence, the death remains a mystery.

Some explanation is still however a public necessity. A court of enquiry is set up to examine the case and identify responsibility;

especially since an informer has now made a serious allegation that *must* be investigated. Talbot is still thinking in terms of the letter: of the shame its writer must have felt at his own intemperance, and of the effect on him of 'our general indifference' – a suggestion already dangerous enough to make Summers try to shut him up. But Anderson now suspects 'that the man, helplessly drunk, suffered a criminal assault by one, or God knows how many men, and the absolute humiliation of it killed him!' The chief suspect however, the brawny Billy Rogers, who Colley had thought the handsomest of all, turns out to be as cunning as he is good-looking. Ordered to name those with tendencies to buggery, he proposes to begin with the officers – and once faced with the prospect of an unscrupulous man making allegations that cannot be disproved, and on a hanging matter at that, Anderson calls the enquiry off. The log will say that Colley died of a low fever, and no mention will be made of any informant. (We soon hear that the most likely informant, Wheeler, has disappeared – very possibly overboard.)

For the reader, of course, questions continue to coil. Surely shame at intemperance could never have been enough? On the other hand, a criminal *assault* would hardly have left Colley so beatific and joyful afterwards? Though the letter might show potential homosexuality, it also shows this as quite unconscious and innocent. Perhaps whatever happened revealed Colley's tendencies to himself, and that caused the shame? Some time later Prettiman and Miss Granham, who have surprised everybody by becoming engaged, claim to have overheard Billy Rogers boasting about having had 'a chew off a parson' – though they entirely mistake his meaning and Summers ensures that their misunderstanding continues. But it finally does become possible to guess at a process of seeming reconciliation, partying, drunken infatuation, fellatio, which is as near to an explanation of 'what happened' as it is possible to get, though it can only be guesswork.

By that time, however, Colley has been buried at sea, with two cannonballs to keep him down. And there the matter has to rest, apart from a lying letter to Colley's sister that must eventually be written, and the trail of gunpowder that Talbot's journal represents, as opposed to the much-less-than-true statement he will have to sign. The life of the vessel resumes, and soon Talbot has recovered himself. He is not insensible of what he has learned, but recognizes with his final Ampersand that life must continue, and the ship sail on. A funeral is not a closure, except to the dead man.

There is, however, one crucial piece of evidence which suggests that 'what happened' is the surface and not the essence of the death of James Colley. He has understood very little of what has happened to him already, and less of what may happen, for he is a man not of surfaces, but of essences. When he goes to rebuke the men whose demonic howling had so scared him before, he thinks of himself as the Spiritual Man confronting the world, taking on the darkness and seeking to overcome it. Against all advice he disappears into the foc'sle, only to land up in the black hole of the cabin from which he never emerges. It is not mere event or behaviour that have destroyed his life, nor is his suffering merely a matter of depression. Nobody in the Court of Enquiry into 'what happened' has thought to question the horrific irony of Colley's cry of 'Joy' – that crucial word in *Darkness Visible* too – or of the Blessing which follows. We can only hope to glimpse something of Colley's horror by imagining what he thought he had achieved, but awoke to find that he had desecrated instead. For Colley the Christian, 'the power of Grace is infinite', and the great Love he feels 'for all things' cannot fail. (Nor, in his befuddlement, did it fail, for he must have thought he had achieved in the foc'sle a triumph of reconciliation and fellowship, with those he had always thought more sympathetic than the 'gentlemen', and a first experience of 'love' with the hero of his infatuation.) For Colley the Romantic, moreover, as for Coleridge in 'Dejection', Joy is the power to make the world anew, and when *that* is destroyed, the universe turns into a wilderness – or a nightmare death-in-life such as the Mariner experienced.

To see Colley in terms of 'character' would be to find such claims exorbitant. The objection would run: here is no more than a young man who takes himself intensely seriously. Duty is too easily defined, the Almighty's will too easily accessible, judgement too easily called into play. We have, if only by way of hints and guesses, a sexual explanation for Colley's behaviour that is common enough, and hardly unforgivable. Colley seems to have no idea of God's mercy. The first comment on such a criticism, however, is that Golding himself makes it, and assigns the comfort of it to Talbot and the Captain. For them, Colley is easily categorized: a man of desperate extremes, viewing himself passionately in one way, then being forced to see himself intolerably in quite another, torn apart by contradiction and shame that can only be resolved by willing himself to die.

The judgement of Colley passed by *Rites of Passage* however, cannot be so confined. We get nearer to dimensions that open up behind the story of event by noticing how significantly he is characterized by his *language*. He exists for us, and indeed for himself, most inwardly in terms of his writing, as indeed is true of Talbot. Though the surface world of manners is no less important in some respects than in *The Pyramid*, this time Golding has taken us as it were behind Jane Austen, to oppose the world of Fielding, Smollett, and Lord Chesterfield to that of Samuel Richardson and Coleridge. Richardson's formal invention, the epistolary novel, banished the author and allowed dramatic characters to create themselves in their own voices, since 'styles differ too, as much as faces, and are indicative, generally beyond the power of disguise, of the mind of the writer'. So the letter-journals of Talbot and Colley create two vivid characters 'done' through their styles. Yet their opposition, in creating *minds*, does much more than merely oppose a late Augustan idiom of Taste, Enlightened Good Sense and Benevolence to a Romantic idiom of Feeling and Imagination. Talbot and Colley realize for us what is involved in the opposition of two modes of perceiving the nature of life itself. For Richardson, reality was ultimately private and psychological. Diderot praised him for taking a candle to the back of the cave of the mind, venturing into the depths as it were to make them visible. But Smollett and Lord Chesterfield, coming after him, used the letter as an essentially social medium again, for travellers through worlds of men and manners, and for educating a gentleman. *The assumption, ingrained in language itself, that life is essentially social, opposes the assumption, no less ingrained, that it is essentially private and psychological.* Each man in his world.

So Colley's prose is both personal and more than that: a document of Romantic Feeling and Imagination, making clear that his view of the self is also a view of the universe. The name of Coleridge, invoked both directly and obliquely, is there to indicate a map of metaphysical unity. When Colley exclaims 'Joy!', or gazes into the water and blesses 'the blue, the green, the purple, the snowy, sliding foam' we feel the presence of 'Dejection' and *The Ancient Mariner* not as literary reference to particular poems but as extensions of Colley's sensibility, giving it precision and utterance. If however (as 'Dejection' maintained) 'we receive but what we give, and in our life alone does Nature live' then the sense of desecration that has robbed Colley of all joy makes the whole world deathly. Much more than what we usually understand by 'shame' is involved. And the horrible irony of Colley's General Benediction is that it not only reverses the salvation of the Mariner, who blessed the water snakes and changed the world, but that it is also a blasphemy. What is at stake for Colley is not merely to have damaged a character, or even to have betrayed a priesthood, but to have made *all* vision monstrous, death-in-life. The silence of the journal is what Coleridge feared: that language becomes meaningless. Colley matters not as a character so much as because he cares *on that scale*.

But we cannot get into Colley's mind as he turns his back, and we are left looking at a hand enigmatically clutching a ringbolt. Language gives way to uninterpretable gesture. It could be despair – or could be a last desperate hope. The mystery that attends his death cannot be, as it is to Anderson or Talbot, a matter of witnesses, enquiries, evidence, accusations, lies, courts martial. The story is far more than that of a man who died of social or moral 'shame'. But what more he died of, what was in his mind as he died, we shall never know. Mercy? Black oblivion? There is only the shrill sound of the bosun's pipe, 'the simple sound of life mourning death' – a voice beyond language and explanation.

There have been Rites of Passage for Talbot and for Colley – but Golding's novel seeks to create one for us, artfully, that can be more encompassing than the occasion of its duration, and is a mode of survival. *His* enquiry into Colley's death uses the journals of both young men to create a sustained paradox: to describe a world so vividly that we are moved to regard it as holding the truth, and yet at the same time to make us aware how that world has been shaped, invented – a triumph of artifice. The 'ship of the line' is also a 'floating theatre'; the Captain's Orders are 'lines to be learnt'; the whole ship engages in 'theatricals'; the central action, the crossing of the line, is a double farce that becomes a tragedy. The whole novel echoes with the sound of other men's art: Melville, Conrad, Coleridge, Richardson, Chesterfield. It is a chorus of languages: no mere pastiche but a zest of invention, a linguistic energy and exuberance that openly admits what it is doing and delights in the skill. With considerable ingenuity, also, Golding provides an analogy and naturalization within the book. As Talbot self-consciously acquires 'tarpaulin', its arcane and archaic phrases make his own idiom seem natural. Golding continually heightens our awareness of the languages we live in.

The cumulative effect of this conscious artistry is to make a reader constantly aware of a structure, a dazzling surface through which a depth can be glimpsed, but – an inevitable loss in 'gardening at sea' – it can only be a glimpse. Partly this is because life must indeed go on, and the depths are dangerous. When Colley is buried, a bracketed sentence papers over the pathos: 'At these necessarily ritualistic moments of life, if you cannot use the prayer book, have recourse to Shakespeare! Nothing else will do.' And there is always a weather eye on the ship. When the 'end' of the novel comes, it is the author behind Talbot who heads it simply with an Ampersand. This is a novel which firmly resists conclusion – even though nobody at the time realized that it would become the first volume of a trilogy.* Yet the depth that has been glimpsed at the heart of the novel is dramatically defined and emphasized by the surface which encloses it. *Rites of Passage* may decline to explore the darkness at its centre or make it visible, but calls attention to it as vividly as a stage defines an open trapdoor, or a jigsaw the shape of its missing piece. For Golding, the resources of art have, this time, to be drawn upon to achieve a *strategic* 'truth', more mysterious than Talbot's, more provisional than Colley's. They have crossed the line perhaps too easily. Golding's novel is a rite which holds 'the line' itself in respect: ever mindful of the depths, but no less mindful of the human need for passage and survival.

---

* Golding himself says in his Foreword to the one-volume Sea Trilogy that the idea of further volumes came to him only 'after volume one was published'.

IV 'I'LL GIVE YOU TWO-OH' – THE RIVALS

It would seem that the two novels in tandem* which conclude his middle phase enabled Golding to express different potentials of his art more fully than had been possible in any single book. One kind of art deftly disposes scenes on the surface to define a gap; the other plunges beyond the line, over the edge, into the very depths, Rembrandt to Brocklebank (or rather, Picasso). One book is the most powerful of all his metaphysical explorations, seeming to contain and extend the whole *oeuvre* since *Lord of the Flies*: an astonishingly original work, but difficult, contorted, obscure. The other dances along, much more light, bright and sparkling, literary, linguistically inventive, the work of a craftsman and comedian who has always been around – yet the dark gap on the stage is all the more obvious for the animation and evasiveness which surround it. Perhaps – to admirers of *Darkness Visible* – the book will then seem comparatively lightweight and superficial because of its refusal to explore what it reveals, and in spite of its offering the literary pleasures of passage. But each book is weak where the other is strongest. The protagonists of *Darkness Visible* are extreme, *outré*, and when the book approaches the social world – as soon, for example, as Sophy enters the disco – the imaginative pressure drops, the language goes brittle, the interest wanes. (Who can be bothered with Gerry, let alone Fido?) Conversely, it is when we finally realize what is at stake offstage in *Rites*, which we shall never be shown, that Talbot's language and his transitory concerns can seem most superficial and escapist. Yet each book defines the nature and integrity of the other by the vividness of the contrast. Because the one is social, it must see the nature of the novel as a rite of passage, enabling worldlings to *negotiate* dark initiation and death, to cope with the monstrous that comes up from underneath, to get past the horror of the dying in the darkness and the human left all alone in a wide, wide sea. The narrative is sewn up, the cover story prepared, the ship goes on, the reader returns to the world – although, winds being what they are, the line may have to be crossed again. The other, because its concerns are ultimate, must be taken to points of no return so

* See note on p. 395 below.

that the reader, too, is taken to where ultimate questions cannot be negotiated or sailed past. One book delights in language and affirms the power of writing as a rite of passage. The other calls language in question, and strives to open up a mysterious space between words, and make what is hidden there visible, wordlessly. Each tries for a different way of being true to the paradoxes of Golding's imagination and his truth-telling urgency: how from the real and the clear, contradictions always (for him) spread and proliferate into multiplicity, opacity, mystery; but also how art must always find ways to clarify, and to suggest a deeper unity. It is the great pleasure of the old song which gives a title to this epilogue to the middle novels, that from the singular it keeps opening out into greater and greater multiplicity and suggestive-ness and growth, yet keeps us no less contracting back trium-phantly into one. But now, by giving us two—oh, almost simultaneously, Golding has achieved an extraordinary effect. It is not that we can possibly think of them as one work, for each is much too uniquely itself. Yet manifestly they deepen the focus on the same area of preoccupation by coming from such different angles. And they seem together to have liberated each to be more itself, its kind of thing, than it could have been if it had simultaneously been trying also to be the other.

And this has liberated readers too, who may have found in one or the other book more of the Golding they really like, in a purer state than usual. The reception was certainly very different. In England *Rites* instantaneously won widespread praise and a major prize; the other remained relatively unheralded, apparently un-prized. In America it was the other way round. It seems likely that the contrast, refining out elements one way and then another, will continue to divide Golding's admirers in their preferences, without preventing a common recognition of what he has achieved.

THE PAPER MEN

(1984)

I BRING ON THE CLOWNS

It was an irony (surely not lost on Golding) that his first novel after winning the Nobel Prize seemed the least likely of all his works to attract new readers, looking to see what his fiction was like. Its 'author' – drunken, womanizing, self-centred, cynical, destructive and self-destructive – is the most rebarbative of all Golding's characters, including even Pincher Martin who has a kind of heroism to offset his unpleasantness. At first glance, moreover, the book's driving force appeared to be revenge on academic critics, particularly American ones, who had plagued Golding (present company of course excepted). The mode sets out as broad farce, to which it frequently returns, albeit in darker and darker forms. The style keeps slipping into language as far removed from Golding at his most disciplined and powerful as it was possible for him, seemingly deliberately, to get: a language clichéd and quote-ridden, carelessly conversational, slangy, self-contemptuous. We know that he could write like an angel. Why on earth should he choose to write like this?

It is a much deeper irony that, for experienced Golding readers used to reading between the lines, but challenged this time to see through the paper too, *The Paper Men* should prove to be virtually the 'final' version of one kind of Golding novel, taking his vision in this unpromising but effective disguise one crucial step further than he had ever allowed us to see with him before. On pages 122–3 the book suddenly changes gear, in an astonishing fashion, and becomes a different kind of novel altogether, containing episodes as powerful as any he had written.

Wilf Barclay, a best-selling but also apparently quite reputable novelist, awakens in the early hours from a drunken stupor, wholly unable to remember the last part (or bottle or bottles) of the evening before, his fiftieth birthday. With arid early-morning clarity it dawns on him that such black holes, frequent now, are signs of alcoholism; and he is about to tackle this one by checking the empties downstairs when he hears a noise at the dustbin. A badger! Indignantly he rushes down, trying also to manage, at once, torch, air-rifle, and pyjama bottoms that keep slipping down – only to find the boring young American professor and Barclay-specialist, who has descended on him as a house-guest, rummaging through his dustbin in search of biographical data. The air-rifle goes off, the pyjama trousers finally drop and are discarded, the guest is stripped in panic to see whether there is a pellet wound. At just this nakedly compromising moment Elizabeth Barclay appears – and picks up from the floor a scrap of paper which reads 'Longing to be with you, Lucinda'. Wilf has indeed been throwing away papers from his past. Though Lucinda was an old flame and not, as it happens, his current mistress, this is the beginning of the end of his marriage. As he makes his way to the spare room the dustbin is heard to fall over again, leaving a trail of garbage and paper, paper, paper, while a bristly black and white creature makes its escape. In this novel, however, there seems to be no escape from paper for the Paper Men: the writer and the critic who badgers him.

The episode has many of the hallmarks of classic farce, of which Golding has now achieved a mastery. Indeed, Wilf often sees himself as a clown condemned to an endless sequence of dropped trousers; and Rick Tucker, the excessively hairy American who rises like an apparition from behind the dustbin 'with a strangled cry', will provide and suffer another series of humiliations. Wilf's favourite expression, 'Ha, etc', has both the cut-off barking laugh of the cynic confronting the absurd, and the sense of life as a series of absurdities too many and wearisome to spell out. The opening scene also establishes the distance required for comedy, including Wilf's distancing of himself as a central component of the farce of it all. As farce moves into satire, on how far these two literary men will go in sacrificing 'anything' (and anyone) for papery dividends, an oddity of the 'authorial' stance is how ready Wilf is to expose himself, no less than his indefatigable would-be biographer and pursuer. He refers to himself half-mockingly as self-analyst and immoralist, but there are (surely?) contradictions between the egotism of Wilf-as-character, and Wilf-as-narrator's readiness to pull his own trousers down – and also between the conceited immoralism and the peculiar undertone of self-scorn. The clown strikes attitudes, shows off, but is also watching himself doing so, and seems oddly to relish pointing up what a 'shit' and a 'bastard' he has been. Here, too, is a first explanation for some peculiarities of the style. We have a writer who we gather, and will indeed discover, can develop power as great as the author behind him, but who seems to be churning this book out in slipshod conversational haste, in his everyday voice, unwilling to stop, examine, revise. There is a tissue of what (self-mocking again) he calls 'clitches' – the sort of thing it is easy to fall into if one isn't careful – but Wilf can't be bothered to weed them out. Indeed, the stylistic equivalent of 'Ha! etc' is his habit of calling attention to his clichés, or twisting them for satiric purposes rather than simply putting a pen through them. 'A shadow passed over the professor's face (as we say in our extravagant way)' ... or (of Lucinda's passion for polaroids of herself and her sexual partner *in medias res*) 'take it home with you, a present for the wife, the kiddies, the dear old folks in whose toothless caverns marge will not melt ...' Since Wilf is a literary man, there is also a tissue of quotation: the Bible, Shakespeare, Marlowe, Jonson, Dr Johnson, Blake, Wordsworth, Keats, Shelley, Byron, Tennyson, Pater, Leslie Stephen, Ibsen, Longfellow, Churchill – some of it out of quote marks and as it were subliminal, some misquoted, much of it again sardonic or twisted: as when Rome is called 'the dung-coloured city half as old as time'. This is not only, however, appropriate to the writer. It is, significantly, though we do not understand the reason yet, a sign of writing, indeed of language, that has no respect for itself now.

Did it ever? Can we, confronted from the start with this style, believe in Wilf Barclay as an author who not only sells well, but is highly enough regarded to have become a British Council celebrity, and the subject of papers at academic conferences? (There are however satirical suggestions about both of those.) The evidence is mixed. On the one hand, his sharp-tongued wife Elizabeth regards him as having hit the jackpot and become 'popular' by mere talent and ingenuity, rather than any depth from the unconscious: a 'sacré monster' avid for fame and ready to exploit it for seduction. The way he keeps coming back to these taunts betrays a hurt that suggests at least a modicum of truth. Also, by his own confession, the first novel he dashes off during the story is a swashbuckling historical fiction he doesn't himself much value, though the film of it makes him rich. The next is an attempt to meet the charge that he is only interested in sex, and lacks a heart; but it does not go down well with the critics. On the other hand, Golding seems willing to take a risk parallel to the one he runs of having critics and common rooms merely agog with the gossipy question of who Rick 'is meant to be'. This is appropriate enough for paper men; but it devalues a serious novel when even one of Golding's most intelligent readers, Peter Green, can see it as a mere 'squib', that will backfire because of the critics' resentment at the satire on them. The parallel risk is of seeming to imply some worth in Barclay the writer by allowing some parallels with Golding himself and his books, though to treat the novel as autobiographical would be another trap for unwary paper men. Barclay tells us, just as Golding did, that his first book which made his name not long after the war seemed to write itself and was 'a one-off'. Moreover, the next two were not bad either: 'There were things, mantic moments, certainties, if you like, whole episodes that had blazed, hurt, been suffered for', which, again, Golding might have said about himself. The second, thought to be the best, as Golding rated his own second book, bears a significant title from the Bible. Moreover Wilf will confess later that the one we are reading is not 'beautifully written' in his 'usual lucid prose', though we keep on being alerted to a concern for the exact word or phrase, and to descriptions and analyses of real sensitivity. I think we may take it that Wilf could write differently, though we have yet to learn why he does not.

After the break-up of his marriage he takes up with a high-born Italian lady: a relationship which comes to grief in a comic come-uppance, because of his scepticism about the stigmata of Padre Pio and his vehement need to insist that there can be no miracles. Meanwhile Rick Tucker continues to pester Elizabeth, who has married the awful Capstone Bowers, about access to his papers. At a conference in Seville Wilf hears Rick lecturing about him and laying false claim to his friendship and authority; until seeing him actually in the audience produces another farcical disaster. The conference papers expose how academics denounce each other and what they do to literature: divorcing linguistics and scholarship from imagination; believing that wholeness can be understood by tearing it to pieces; and treating all literature as derived from other literature. After the break-up with his 'Italian chum' Wilf begins to drink heavily again, to cultivate a universal indifference to relationships, and to fill in time by driving endlessly across Europe (like Humbert Humbert across America), anaesthetizing himself in the 'milieu of the motorway in every country, its spiritual emptiness, its pretence of shifting you to another place while all the time keeping you motionless on the same concrete waste'. With still more money, from writing travel sketches for glossy magazines, he can fly instead of driving; but he shows his loneliness, and how much despite himself he misses Elizabeth, by every now and then deluding himself that he sees her in the distance. Then, ten years after first meeting Rick, he comes across him again beside the lake at Zurich, and is pursued by him and his new dolly-bird wife Mary Lou into the mountains where he has tried to escape them.

As it becomes clear that Rick is doggedly determined to become his authorized biographer, the past of both clowns opens up at a deeper level of suppressed garbage. Through drink, and an ageing man's unnerving crush on fresh young beauty, and fear lest old shames be discovered, Wilf's memories come welling up. He can no more control them than the tongue which keeps letting out bits of what he is thinking. His past is a sequence of pratfalls. Wilf the boy tumbles, emblematically, from his horse into a dung-heap. The adolescent bank clerk is given an aphrodisiac – was it? – as a joke, and has an erection that lasts and lasts. The young man has an affair with Lucinda the nymphomaniac; then falls hopelessly in love with a girl who won't have him, and bombards her with shameful and manic letters. He employs a crooked lawyer to arrange for these to be stolen back, only to discover that what he has obtained are the lovingly hoarded letters of her dull husband. Fearful of the burglary being traced to him, he flees to South America where, caught in a revolution, he first hides in terror, and then drives in such panic along a country road in the dark that he may have hit, even killed, an Indian – but he doesn't stop. Farce rules. We all have our hidden shames, but this is ridiculous! Yet behind the sequence as it darkens there glimmer reminiscences of Pincher, of Sammy, of Jocelin, of Oliver, as though Golding were painting, in broad comic brushstrokes now, a kind of epitome of his sinners who all, in Isaiah's words and their confessional echo in the Book of Common Prayer, like sheep have gone astray. We keep our comic distance, amused, but more uneasily than before.

Meanwhile Mary Lou, with her degree in bibliography and flower arrangement and a Southern accent, may be a mere dolly-bird but she has a simple honesty, which exposes the secrets of Rick the con-man: how he laid false claim to professorial rank and literary acquaintance in order to gain access to Barclay; how he took up the specialization as a career move since nobody else was 'doing' Wilf, and there was finance from a rich man who seemed to like the novels; how he has kept badgering Elizabeth (and now their daughter Emmy). Indeed he and Mary Lou have just come from researching Wilf's birthplace and visiting his home in the Downs. But when they pursue Wilf into the Swiss mountains it becomes clear just how determined Rick is, and how much he is prepared to sacrifice. He will do 'anything' to get Wilf to sign an authorization: exploiting the attraction to his wife, and even, finally, making what appears to be a direct offer of her. Wilf manages not to succumb, for (obviously and humiliatingly) she cannot feel or pretend to feel anything for him; but he is filled with rage, and determines to seek revenge by studying Rick more closely to put him in a book. The next day however, walking a mountain path with him in thick mist, a rock falls, a hand-rail gives way, and it seems that he must be eternally grateful to Rick for saving him from falling to his death. Traumatized, hating his indebtedness, and knowing that nothing but misery can come from his feeling for the girl, Wilf flees again, even more manically and drunkenly than before, but this time leaving a string of bogus forwarding addresses, to avoid being traced. All the same, it is Rick he thinks he glimpses now, in Rome, in Portugal, like some pursuing Fury.

II BEHIND THE PAPER

At this point we need to reconsider the mode of the story, for though the action is still moved on by pratfalls and humiliations, it no longer seems funny; or containable within the limits of a satire on Paper Men. There seem to be rising through the farcical surface two kinds of awareness very characteristic of Golding. The clown himself has become aware of *pattern*: how each of his humiliations has grown out of the one before, not a mere sequence but a series. There seems to be a nemesis at work, something not only growing but growing worse. 'Oh God, oh God, oh God,' Wilf thinks beside the lake, 'the process, link by link, we don't know what will come from this seed, what ghastly foliage and flowers, yet come it does, presenting us with more and more seeds, millions, until the whole of *now*, the universal Now, is nothing but irremediable result.' This is more than clown. One is reminded again, of Pincher peering into his rock, or of Jocelin looking at the twig on his boot. 'If you could only see your way . . .,' Rick breaks in, unaware of the irony of his words.

Indeed *we* should be reading between the lines by this time, aware of ironies. And what we shall see at a deeper level than before is a man constantly on the run after each impact, trying vainly to escape not just Rick but himself: his guilt and love-lessness; his refusal to take responsibility or admit obligation (the failure of the 'relative clauses' in the prose of his life); his attempts instead to black out reflection in drink, and to reduce himself 'to what would think least and feel least'. But under the satiric farce we can already see a faint outline of a different, tragic genre, in which, indeed, Rick does seem to be functioning as one of the Eumenides.

We are also newly aware of both Wilf's vulnerability and the intensity of his blind urge to self-preservation. The accident unforgettably reveals the terror of an 'animal' under threat, which 'knew beyond all question what was precious beyond everything', itself. This also sheds light backwards on the whole history of a man on the run and illuminates all sorts of details, like Wilf's unreasoning rage at being photographed without his consent, as though that, too, made him vulnerable to another's eye and power, took something away from himself. On the other hand, after humiliation, the ego obstinately reasserts itself. Beyond his fear of being the subject of a biography is a lurking self-satisfaction at being, after all, distinguished in his way; and from there is a short step to a fiction which will *show* Elizabeth, and Rick, and the billionaire Halliday, that he is bigger than was thought. 'Liking sex and being incapable of love, indeed!' He determines to extend his range, to 'deal with simple, eternal things, youth and innocence, purity and love', to write a love story in which a fictionalized self and a girl who is an idealized Mary Lou 'rode their horses through the green fields of an English country-side' – which he finds difficult to remember now. 'Calmly, perhaps even augustly, I composed my book'; but by this time we expect to be shown how little he is capable of being either of those things. Paranoia instantly returns with a letter from Elizabeth. He says that he has read it again and again because there is much to be inferred from it; but he fails to infer all the important things: why she has written it, or said what she does about Bowers, or what her not being well might mean. Instead he fastens myopically on two asides: that Rick's persistence is like that of a man from Pinkerton's, and that Halliday (Rick's billionaire patron) may be a man corrupted by power. For these are Wilf's two nightmares: to be spied on, investigated, and have his crimes detected; and to be in someone else's power. At once he is off again, around the world this time, drinking heavily, and increasingly deranged as 'the horrors' take hold. He thinks he finds evidence of Halliday's power, and traces of Rick's presence, everywhere he goes; and he so loses track of date and place that he is arrested for suspected credit-card fraud, and has to be rescued by a consular official. And so, ironically again, this loveless and paranoid drunk lands up on the island of Lesvos, where he is hailed by Johnny St John St John, a lanky gossipy homosexual engaged on a coffee-table book about burning Sappho (who destroyed herself for love).

What could be more farcical? But (one is reminded again of *The Pyramid*) the absurd 'artist', so caricaturable, is in fact a truth-teller, a revealer, not merely a gossiper about Rick and Mary Lou (who has apparently been taken over by Halliday), and the critical reception of Wilf's new novel. Johnny not only asks the right question: 'Why a man ostensibly so indifferent to society should be, if I may coin a phrase, so shit-scared of critical opinion . . .', but comes up with a more penetrating answer than any so far. Half in and half out of the conversation, Wilf broods on the horror of Halliday and Mary Lou: that purity and beauty can be bought; and on the threat to himself of Halliday's power, now by far a greater threat than Rick. He feels that part of him has been dissected out, that memories twist in his gut like worms; including memories, now, of how *he* had taken over another man's idea (or dream) for one of his books. Perhaps bits of his thoughts are spoken aloud and give Johnny hints towards a metaphor. Be that as it may, Johnny's diagnosis is that Wilf is an 'exoskeletal' (hence spineless) creature who has spent his whole life 'inventing a skeleton on the outside' to protect the soft vulnerable being within. But that is 'terrible, you see, because the worms get inside and, oh my aunt Jemima, they have the place to themselves'. Only by getting rid of the armour, and attaching himself to something other, can he find and firm himself. Religion? Sex? Adoption? Good works? Perhaps, given Wilf's record, a dog would be best. (Johnny also hints at a darker revelation: that 'Worms under the carapace isn't just human sadism. Only One Above could be as inventive as that.')

Wilf of course will have none of this ridiculous nonsense, and runs again, more out of control than ever, and rather wishing, now, for final oblivion. There is a memory, or a nightmare, about a spell in hospital, which is all mixed up with a nurse pulling red-hot worms out of cracks in his carapace, but leaving the heat inside. And so the fugitive reaches an opposite island, where in an extraordinary epiphany Golding's novel enters an altogether different dimension. There is still farce – but it is pitch black, and volcanic.

III REVELATIONS

We are (I think) on Lipari, where Wilf's first move is to stumble, under the impression that it is a seedy hotel, into one of the windowless Sicilian Houses of the Dead where corpses stand upright in the corridors, dressed to the life. Fleeing that, across a landscape of pumice and slivers of black glass, the earth begins to shake – not through the DTs however, but an eruption of the island's volcano. It is swelteringly hot under a brassy sun. Climbing a long series of steps, past an old woman knitting like one of the Fates, he enters a cathedral where he hopes it may be cooler. He has long been interested in medieval glass, though not in its meanings, regarding it as essentially a way of keeping light under control; but the glass here is modern as he had suspected, and probably donated by the Mafia. The church is darker than it should be; and there seems to be 'a complete absence of Jesus meek and mild'. It is also dangerously unstable on tremulous earth. A small piece of mosaic falls a yard in front of him – maybe another warning, he thinks, like the rock on the mountain path. The heat seems to be inside him now; and there is a strain inside his chest. As he walks towards the altar, he glances to his left:

It was in the north transept. It faced me across the whole width. It was a solid silver statue of Christ but somehow the silver looked like steel, had that frightening suggestion of blue. It was taller than I am, broad-shouldered and striding forward like an archaic Greek statue. It was crowned and its eyes were rubies or garnets or carbuncles or plain red glass that flared like the heat in my chest. Perhaps it was Christ. Perhaps they had inherited it in these parts and just changed the name and it was Pluto, the god of the Underworld, Hades, striding forward. I stood there with my mouth open and the flesh crawling over my body. I knew in one destroying instant that all my adult life I had believed in God and this knowledge was a vision of God. Fright entered the very marrow of my bones. Surrounded, swamped, confounded, all but destroyed, adrift in the universal intolerance, mouth open, screaming, bepissed and beshitten, I knew my maker and I fell down.

He wakes up in hospital, watched over by a nun. It turns out that he has had a stroke, a 'leedle estrook' in the kindly doctor's half-comic English. But strokes are not funny. The mode now seems to have changed radically, and if vision has turned into religious revelation which, for Wilf, explains and changes everything, there is naught for his comfort. 'I saw that I had been planned from the beginning. I had my place in things. It didn't matter what I had done or would do. I had been created by that ghastly intolerance in its own image.' He is already in hell, predestinately damned; struck down by the flail of justice without mercy or forgiveness. (The reminder is of Jocelin.) He laughs at the priest at his bedside because he isn't a real priest at all. There have been no real priests of Intolerance for thousands of years. The outward appearance of 'Christ' only disguises 'the steel hard *factuality* of the intolerance', 'the divine justice without mercy' that governs all: indifferently the jealous and furious Jahweh, Christ as Michelangelo's Condemner, or the King of Hell.

Suddenly much that has been puzzling about the book becomes clearer. First of all, several previous hints of where it is being written, and why it is written as it is, come together now. The frenetic efforts of the clown on the run to escape the nemesis of his predestination were bound to seem farcical to the writer who had experienced the scene we have just read. He is typing – as we read – back in his own home, though apparently without Elizabeth, and looking across the river past a pile of his journals and papers which he plans to burn, as soon as he has finished this manuscript. He has been typing all night, and it is now three in the morning, half way through both the night and his story. He had been off the liquor, but the memory of the Lipari episode has given him the jitters so much that he has taken to the bottle again, to screw himself up to writing about it. What seems most significant, however, is what we must now understand about his attitude to language, and why he has written this book as he has done. The *colpo* – Italian for 'stroke' which he 'mistakes' as *culpa*, sin – affected his ability to speak for a while, and made him say one word when he meant another. But this is not a mere mechanical malfunction in the brain to Wilf. To him, the transpositions tell truths both psychological and religious. Indeed, when he sounds mad, garbling his words, he actually feels sane for the first time, speaking the native tongue of a man in hell; and never more so than when he corrects a painfully uttered 'My – sin', into 'Not. Sin. I. am. Sin.' Sin is not a personal act, but a permanent state and identity predestined from the beginning as Calvin thought. Wilf has had, since then, to re-learn English as a foreign language, 'the one I am using now'. But now he is sure 'that ninety-nine per cent of this language is metaphor' and has 'suspicions about the odd one per cent'. No wonder that the language of this book shows such clear signs of self-contempt. There comes to the surface a worry of Golding the novelist that has been growing novel by novel since *Pincher Martin*: the fear that language may hide reality rather than reveal it. Hence the handing over of later Golding novels not only to 'unreliable narrators' but also to suspect languages, culminating in Matty's renunciation of language altogether. The deepest truths in *The Spire* and *Darkness Visible* lay in the space between words, beyond words.

At this stage of the manuscript it also becomes clear that Rick is to be its first reader and that it is *their* biography, which Rick can check the exact dates of, later.

In the aftermath of his stroke Wilf goes on suffering physically. The heat that he felt inside him, and the pain in his chest like a wire (or a violin string) being tightened, may have been physical harbingers of the stroke, but they are also appropriate to the man who feels himself to be in hell, and the stroke has not eased them, rather tuned them up. Now, everything that the biography will expose and that he had tried to cover up, hangs together with the ongoing pain. He believes that he is no longer being fooled, and if his mouth (or ours) can still twist into a kind of laugh at his predicament, it can only be a 'lopsided' kind. It is a black joke, of a sort, that he has fame, riches, and freedom to do as he likes, only to find that there is nothing to be done. But as we behold 'old Filthy Rags' – Isaiah again on man's pretence to 'righteousness' – 'wandering with the immediate awareness that old you-know-who has its eye on him no matter what', it is the blackness that comes across rather than the joke.

He seeks refuge in catatonia, but cannot keep it up. It soon strikes him, however (a classic response to Calvinist predestina-tion), that if he is damned no matter what he does, he might as well have some fun and give the 'intolerance' a smack in the eye into the bargain. He decides to 'commit': an intransitive verb governed only by the Sin of the subject, but one that he can make as double-dyed as possible and theologically witty, in revenge. Johnny thought that his only salvation lay in attaching himself to something other, be it only a dog. Wilf decides to destroy what has dogged him: Rick.

So he gets in touch again, and arranges a meeting in the same Swiss mountain hotel as before, holding out the promise of the piece of paper that means everything to Rick. But before the American arrives, there is one more pratfall to be revealed. Taking the same walk as before, but in clear air this time, Wilf discovers the ultimate con-trick and humiliation: that when he thought he was suspended over a cliff in the fog with only Rick's grasp to save him, he was in fact mere feet above an Alpine meadow. Since Rick had taken the same walk the day before, he must have known ...

Wilf's revenge will strip all disguise and pretence away. In Rick's old photograph, given celebrity pride of place over the bar, Mary Lou's glamour has vanished in the flashlight; and Wilf is seen for what he was: an ageing roué. Rick arrives, all flared pants and necklace from the decade of peace and love, but it is not long before he reveals, with a new aggression born of continual disappointment, how much he has come to hate Wilf Barclay beneath the show of respect. (Moreover, he also has been seeing things: torturing glimpses of Wilf in the distance, jeering at him, though in places Wilf has never been.) As Wilf taunts him now about Mary Lou, and Rick reveals the American contempt for Limey vowels and pretensions that he had felt from the beginning, the scene is set for a grotesque parody of 'communion' between biographer and biographee; a rite of passage by which Rick will – as in all rites of passage – be permanently changed by the experience and its revelation about himself. He has to bark like a dog, 'yap yap', and lap from a saucerful of wine to earn his piece of paper ... and he does.

This is Wilf's smack in the eye to 'the intolerance': a damned man's defiance by double-damning himself in destroying another. As he savours the way that Rick in his utter humiliation seems to shrink under his clothes, sobbing horribly 'like bone breaking up', or notes the tiny rings of salt left by the teardrops on the table with a connoisseur's eye, Wilf has become purely repulsive. He seems to have no human responsiveness any more – even to that most telling sign of deep shock when Rick (like Desdemona after being struck by her husband) goes half asleep, and yawns. He feels nothing but contempt for someone who cares so much for a piece of paper that he can do no more to hit back at his tormentor than throw the saucer in a moment of futile rage, and call him a mother-fucking bastard. It is true that the contempt is shared out. The book is to be a 'duet' to show the world what they both are, a complete exposure of both paper men and all they have been prepared to sacrifice; as well as a revenge on behalf of 'all the people spied on' by paper men, 'followed, lied about, all the people offered up to the great public' on paper. But it is clear also, in a starkly ironic double-meaning, that the 'old intolerance' may be 'getting its own back', intensifying both the damned man's sense of damnation, and the punishment of hellish pain as the 'steel string' seems to tighten through chest and head, into another seizure.

After that all sanity and connection disappear and Wilf's memory becomes a series of disconnected scenes in which experience is dreamlike or dreams continue in the day. He comes across a grave with his birthdate on it and nothing else. Followed by a hearse in the mountains, he drives up a side road and narrowly escapes a landslide. Recurrently, he dreams of desert sand where the only respite to burning feet is to dig a black hole with one's hands. But the dream continues into the daylight desert of bars and concrete through which he moves, unable to make holes, scribbling his diary on any surface he finds, and discovering that he now has permanent pains in both hands and feet – in ironic reversal of the stigmata of St Francis and Padre Pio which were the reward of saintliness. Even when awake and sober, he is forced to spend much of his time in bathrooms with his feet in water and his hands under a running tap. Through it all runs the fear of the Power of Halliday, who begins to be conflated now with God (or the Devil) and the Great Intolerance.

Then the book reaches a second climax in an extraordinary vision of the Spanish Steps, in Rome. They are as we know them to be: 'littered with dropouts, hippies, junkies, drabs, punks, nancies and lesies and students, as usual, and all of them were wearing guitars or playing them very badly or trying to sell the tin shapes they'd cut out and spread round on the stairs as necklaces or rings or earrings or noserings, there were carpets of artificial flowers and so on'. Through this Wilf staggers to his hotel room at the top – only to see through its window the church opposite, with the figure of Halliday (it seems) on its roof, able to step across and get him. Terror and excruciating chest-pain increase, until:

I suppose I slept or went into some mode of being that wasn't quite being awake or simply being mad.

You could say that I dreamed.

I was standing on the roof next door where Halliday had stood. I was looking down at the steps. There was sunlight everywhere, not the heavy light of Rome but a kind of radiance as if the sun were everywhere. I'd never noticed before, but now I saw, looking down, that the steps had the symmetrical curve of a musical instrument, guitar, cello, violin. But this harmonious shape was now embellished and interrupted everywhere by the people and the flowers and the glitter of the jewels strewn among them on the steps. All the people were young and like flowers. I found that he was standing by me on the roof of his house after all and we went down together and stood among the people with the patterns of jewels and the heaps of flowers all blazing inside and out with the radiance. Then they made music of the steps. They held hands and moved and the movement was music. I saw they were neither male nor female or perhaps they were both and it was of no importance. What mattered was the music they made. Male and female was of no importance to me, he said, taking me by the hand and leading me to one side. There were steps going down, narrow steps to a door with a drum head. We went through. I think that there was a dark, calm sea beyond it, since I have nothing to speak with but with metaphor. Also there were creatures inside the sea that sang. For the singing and the song I have no words at all.

We see once again with the visions of Matty and Sim and the dying Pedigree in *Darkness Visible*; but it is again not darkness but radiance and harmony that we experience, the seaminess of ordinary reality transfigured, in a beauty and peace behind them and beyond all language to do more than suggest. Feeling as though an unendurable boil had burst, Wilf's immediate reaction is to weep and go on weeping, but when the tears cease he becomes miraculously happy and unstressed. The pains in his hands, feet, and chest have not gone, but have become bearable and somehow on the mend. He is not interested in whether he had been dreaming or awake when he saw what he saw; nor in religious, scientific, psychiatric or philosophical 'explanations'- all abstraction. For he believes he has glimpsed 'asisness', the ultimate reality behind appearances, *given*, in an 'involuntary act of awareness'. There is no more need to run: he knows where he is going and 'the rest of the journey would simply be provided'. Simple human contacts become agreeable. But as soon as he attempts to write in the lucid prose of his novels, his writing hand hurts so much he has to stop. He is still subject to Judgement, and there is still a book to be written: not, however, in the old style and imagination which falsified but 'more hippity-hop' and thus appropriate to the seaminess he has to confess, but capable of rising to involuntary awareness of the Last Things beyond words and paper: sin, judgement, forgiveness, hell, and heaven. The book we are reading was written in the way it was written in order *not* to be literary.

IV PSYCHE AND THE ARROW

When he goes home, however, at Elizabeth's invitation (for Bowers has scarpered) there are some radical questions to be asked of his new happiness and sobriety. What difference will the Vision make to his attitude to Rick? Not much, it seems, as he tells a newly successful Johnny, with no apparent remorse, that he has 'killed' his dog. And to his wife? He finds, when he gets home, an embittered and emaciated Elizabeth in the last stages of cancer, to whom his health and happiness are unbearable, and whose summons meant only that he should have to pay something, at last. In the face of her suffering, his words of equanimity about death and the ultimate meaning of things may well deserve her terrible eldritch laughter. It seems too late for reconciliation with her or with their daughter: there can be no warm-hearted Barclay book coming to terms with the past, for 'We were about as warm-hearted as scorpions'.

When he meets Rick at his club, it is to prove the truth of Elizabeth's judgement that the two paper men have destroyed each other. The scene in the club dining-room, under the statue of Psyche which is its most valuable possession, is the climactic farce of the book and (deliberately) the unfunniest. Rick proves seriously disturbed before it begins, when Wilf finds him squatting on the floor of the lobby. The gate-crashers into the meeting, Johnny and the sculptor Gabriel, ensure that the evening gets steadily drunker. Only Wilf remains stone-cold sober, but all the more responsible for the row, indeed riot, that develops when he tells Rick that he has now decided to write the biography himself. There is irony, since he never explains that he intends it as a gift to Rick, which will enable him to make his peace with Halliday and ensure the rich man's continued benificence. But novelists should know something about human Psych-ology, and in any case the most significant thing about the statue is that Love is missing, so that Psyche seems to be looking, not at Eros, but to see what's on the menu. Wilf may have had a vision of ultimate reality, but he remains entirely lacking in human sympathy or understanding, let alone the faculty of actively caring for another human being. He seems to have no idea at all of what his change of mind will mean to Rick, after the humiliation he has put him through. Now, to the scarifyingly contemptuous laughter of Elizabeth we have to add the expression of contempt and dislike on the face of Mrs Stoney the club cashier, the morning after the riot before.

While this was happening in London, Elizabeth has died; but for Emmy's grief he has again no fatherly feeling, but only a stranger's repulsion for 'what fell from her eyes and nose'. At the wake there is another expression of contempt from a relative of Elizabeth's or friend of Bowers, though Wilf passes it off as home-counties choler. But from the young priest he tries to patronize comes something serious: a sudden brilliant crosslight on the stigmata of which he has dared to boast. The priest reminds him that there were three crosses, three sets of wounds on hands and feet. To do Wilf justice, he has never been backward in recognizing his own seaminess, and he instantly accepts the truth that he is one of the Thieves; and its consolations. 'Not for me the responsibility of goodness, the abject terror of being holy! For me the peace and security of knowing myself a thief!' He sees the wit in having, for opposite reasons, what St Francis and Christ himself had had; though it seems too late for the final ironic 'custard pie' of a thrust in the side.

But it is not too late. Wilf finishes his book with a quiet sense that aside from 'repetitions, verbals, slang, omissions, it's a fair record of the various times the clown's trousers fell down'. There remains the question of Rick, who has begged and cursed and yapped so much that he has been forbidden the house, and is now dodging about the trees outside, spying on Wilf. 'He hasn't the least idea that I have it in my power and what is more in my purpose to heal him. I'll get him his dream.' Wilf's gift will be 'all that means anything to set over against the lying stories, the partial journals, and all the rest'. But Wilf in turn seems to have no idea that his plan to burn all his collected papers in the next moment or two will precisely rob Rick of *his* dream once and for all, which was to research the whole truth, learn the whole language, understand the whole development, for himself. The book of confession has left Wilf quietly happy, perfectly calm, miraculously free. 'That's not reasonable, it's a fact. Either I have broken away from the intolerance which is impossible, or it has let me go, which is also impossible.' He feels that he has changed. He will never drink again. And 'Who knows? With intolerance backed right out of the light there is room for an uncovenanted mercy like the one that drives me to give Rick these papers ... by which those unsatisfactory phenomena' – the two paper men – 'may be eternally destroyed.'

The next second, in mid-sentence, comes the thrust to the heart, the heart which Wilf Barclay has so wholly and signally lacked: a bullet from the figure flitting vengefully through the trees with Capstone Bowers's gun. Wilf and Rick have indeed destroyed one another, but whether mercifully or not is for us to judge.

What are we to think? This 'ultimate' novel might seem to confirm – more clearly than ever before – that Golding's major concern as his work developed has not only been with evil (as some thought about *Lord of the Flies*) but also with an 'uncovenanted mercy', available to even the most repellent and destructive human beings. Nevertheless he has been as careful as ever to leave room for doubters to come to quite different conclusions.

Wilf is, of course, that *sine qua non* of the modernist novel, an unreliable narrator – few more so, since he is drunk and stressed out through most of the events he narrates. We can clearly see the possibility of different characterization: another Rick, another Mary Lou, even another Wilf, and so of different narratives. Rick is so established as a hairy clown in Wilf's mind that the clear signs of the man's intelligence and sensitivity come as a complete surprise to him; and though these can reinforce our sense of how Rick's 'paper' ambitions have corrupted the man he might have been, we have also to recognize that Wilf may have jumped to conclusions about the offer of Mary Lou, and the degree of Rick's foreknowledge in the con-trick on the mountain path, as we know he deluded himself about Rick's pursuit of him in Rome and Portugal. This applies *a fortiori* to Wilf's portrait of Mary Lou, whose instinctive honesty might suggest different readings of the episode in the Weisswald, and her break-up with Rick and employment by Halliday. Even Wilf may be more complex than the clown he determines to show us. It is clear from his continuing obsession with Elizabeth that he did love her in his fashion, and care about what she thought of him. The drunkenness and escapist running about the world may show consciousness of guilt as much as rejection of responsibility. But if we can so clearly see his unreliability as a narrator, must this not affect the credibility of his visions too? – affected as they so obviously are by alchoholism, disturbance both mental and emotional, heat and heart-trouble?

Moreover, Wilf himself is well aware of how suggestible he has always been. If the pill his rugger chums gave him – aphrodisiac, or just imagination? – could so easily turn the young bank clerk into a monstrous Priapus; and if a hypnotist could so easily make him see his own initials apparently burnt into his hand, are not the visions and the stigmata the results of the same suggestibility? It is clear that despite moral shortcomings he has a basically religious sensibility; and of course openness to suggestion (or shall we roundly say imagination) is characteristic of the novelist, as Wilf himself recognizes. But how to draw the line between the imaginative and the imaginary, especially when the 'novelist' is an alchoholic?

So Golding is careful, once again, to leave room for a quite different reading: for sceptics, and for those who may see the ending as no more than a thoroughly merited execution. But even if we were to take Wilf's visions as those of his creator, there remain two very awkward questions about them. For the radiant vision is as radically divorced from behaviour and human relationship as the horrific one; as much a matter of faith alone, excluding works and relationship. Though Wilf thinks he has changed, his no longer wanting to drink and his new calm seem insufficient when we put them beside his continued inability to feel anything for his daughter, or for Rick. Can we be happy with a vision so determinedly metaphysical *as opposed to* humane? And what about poor demented Rick – another way of making the same point, and pointing it at the novelist?

However, this may be to ignore the nature and significance of the uncovenanted mercy itself, involving also the Last Judgement of Wilf and his twin visions. For the wittiness (in Wilf's sense) of the Mercy is precisely that it pierces so emphatically to what Wilf lacks and cannot apparently develop by himself. Beside this, his visions were clearly not enough, however true. In *Lord of the Flies* we had not only to read between the lines to find the significance of the officer's language and Ralph's tears, but also to feel, through the empty paper after the last words, the need for a grief (for Simon) that is not expressed at all, but is nonetheless implied by the exclusiveness of Ralph's response. May it be that, once again, it is we who have to care about Rick (since the protagonist so manifestly does not), in the space of paper at the end, the significance of whose emptiness only we can see? Perhaps, once again, the missing piece of a jigsaw may draw the most emphatic attention to itself, though a black hole it will remain.

One does have the sense that Golding may have used the most rebarbative of all his 'authors' as a device, a kind of concealment, behind which he can hint at something always there as a possibility in all his books, and push it one step further than before, though with the greatest tentativeness and indirection. At the end of *The Inheritors* Tuami the artist turns a death weapon into an affectionate shape. At the last of *Pincher Martin* an uncovenanted mercy plays over the claws of the self locked on itself, a mercy which it is bound to see as destructive, but is actually a timeless Compassion; and compassion also speaks in gentle human tones at the very end. At the end of *Free Fall* – the missing piece beyond the contradictory visions – we find human compassion sitting where a judge had been expected, and are bidden to attend to a human truth. At the end of *The Spire* the visions of evil and soaring abundance coalesce, but their ultimate colour is rose. At the end of *Darkness Visible* it is the human lovingness of Matty that is transfigured into a Mercy both terrible and radiant to Pedigree, at the point of his death. The epigraph of *The Pyramid*, giving perspective to the three stories, is 'If thou be among people, make for thyself love, the beginning and end of the heart' – which is precisely where Wilf has failed, and we shall fail if we can respond only to his visions, powerful as they are. Golding's has always been an intensely religious imagination, though it is only in and through his creative language that it reveals itself. His worlds may seem evil, and (after Lok and until Matty) peopled by the loveless. But if this novel goes a step further than ever before in imaginative implication, allowing us to wonder, in the space beyond the last word, whether even the most repellent of human beings may receive uncovenanted Mercy-in-Judgement like the one who thieved heaven on the cross, the final pointer (or spear-point) is to the importance of the human heart – so signally lacking in the purported author, but not (I think) in the real one. All depends, however, as always, on the reader's response to the space between and beyond the words.

CLOSE QUARTERS

(1987)

I THE HISTORY CONTINUES

To come from the feverish intensity of *The Paper Men* to the expansiveness of *Close Quarters* and *Fire Down Below* is to enter a qualitatively different experience. Of course, each of Golding's previous novels had seemed remarkably different from the last one; but that was because each was powered by a new leap of compulsive imagination. These two, by contrast, are sequels – though *Rites of Passage* had appeared to be complete in itself – and they seem also to have been written without the inner pressure that drove all the others. One's first impression is of a relaxed Golding who simply liked and remained intrigued by the characters who survive at the end of *Rites*, and was still curious about what they might do and become in the rest of their journey to Australia. If it is true that *The Paper Men*, in its disguised and riskily rebarbative strategy, was a way of completing the Golding vision at its most intense, then the relaxation of the next two books is understandable. Having explored his most serious 'say' through the intensities of eleven novels, with often a great deal of angst and struggle to articulate his vision, Golding in his late seventies proposed to enjoy himself. And if, to one kind of Golding reader, the result is less challenging and compelling than Golding at his finest, there seems a fair chance that the trilogy will seem to others the most accessible and straightforwardly enjoyable of all his books. (Moreover Golding's mythic imagination is always volcanic. One can never be sure when and how it might erupt.)

There is another way of putting the difference, however. Golding can be seen to have set himself, for the first time, the challenge of writing almost *wholly* in the imaginative mode of 'history' rather than of 'myth' – in the terms we explored in Chapter 6 – whereas *Rites* had pitted them against each other. Where in mythic fiction 'characters' are human lenses through which we begin to uncover preterhuman and deep-structural truths about ourselves and our world, in 'histories' the delight and fascination is with the characters for their own sake, and with the shifting perspectives provided by their relationships and their reaction to the challenge of events. Since there is theoretically no limit to what is interesting for us to know about them, the fiction naturally becomes expansive rather than intensive – limited only by 'outside' factors of setting (Highbury, the circles of La Belle Epoch high society, Russia in peace and Napoleonic war) or defining time (deaths, marriages, the passing of an era, the end of a voyage). Starting from intimations of characters and their potential as individuals, what the novelist has to do is to imagine happenings which can elicit their inner complexities, and explore how their relationships develop and shift in response to those events. Where 'myth' depends on making us see *through* human lives, to discover a deeper dimension than we have ever seen, the rewards of history are those of recognition, at a more sensitive human level than we might ordinarily manage, of the complexity of people not unlike ourselves in situations that seem 'real' to us. Most of all, in mythic fiction the structure points to a conclusion shaped by the nature of the deep-structure it must struggle to reveal; and time is experienced as the 'kairos' (in Frank Kermode's terms) which inevitably gathers towards that conclusive revelation – whereas in history-writing the only shaping seems to be by the characters themselves as they develop chronologically, in relation to one another and to events. There is always in 'histories', moreover, an incompleteness: the sense of a story that will go on (albeit beyond our experience) after the arbitrary ending of the book.

So we begin with Edmund Talbot buying from the purser a blank volume in which to continue his journal; not of course the one that in *Rites of Passage* set two visions of the world against one another, for that is all sewn up and inaccessible now, but another one just for and mainly about himself. Colley was the Golding 'mythic' character whose death was the imaginative starting point of *Rites*, and Talbot the worldling invented to set him off, and to have his own eyes opened to dimensions unknown before. But afterwards Golding clearly retained an affectionate interest in the lordly young man, and a sense that there might still be considerable mileage in following his education further; for he is after all (at twenty-one or so) recently down from university and not much more than a boy.

II TAKEN ABACK

However, Edmund, as Golding's surrogate 'historian', soon sees that to confront a blank page is to face some problems. His own consciousness is the medium, but, where is he to look for a hero, and a story? The latter can only come from outside events; but Talbot happens to be beginning when nothing very interesting is going on, and soon finds himself writing about the weather. That will soon change. Indeed the first event, causing a lacuna between the opening section and the next, is the literal 'interruption' of a blow to the head. But Edmund will come to recognize that this second volume of his journal can have no shape *other* than that given by events. (And since the voyage is still not over when the last page of this book is written, he will also discover that there can be no conclusion either, only an arbitrary coming to an end.)

Edmund's journal, however, is Golding's novel, and when one looks back over it one can see that the shaping by outside happenings (Golding's inventions, of course) does amount to an amused and ironic structure. If the first half of *Close Quarters* had a section title, it would be 'Taken Aback'. Edmund is laid low for three days by a heavy blow to the back of his head from a flying rope, hurriedly set loose to spill the wind from a mizzen sail that threatens to pull the whole ship under. Jack Deverel's drunken irresponsibility, and the incompetence of the midshipman to whom he has left the quarterdeck, have allowed the ship almost to capsize when struck by a squall from an unexpected quarter. She rights herself only when her foremast cracks its block, topmasts come crashing down, and a furious Captain Anderson arrives to take over. The painful outcome of Edmund's attempt to help will not let us see him as heroic. What we do see, instead, is how being 'taken aback' affects him and his relationships with other people, and permanently damages the ship itself, changing the whole nature of the voyage.

One effect on Edmund (and the author behind him) is to revive the interest in language that was a feature of *Rites*. For English is profoundly metaphorical, and a huge part of the metaphoric enrichment which its users have ceased to notice has come from being a seafaring nation. Being made to realize again the original impact of 'taken aback' will be only the first of many examples of revivified sea-metaphors which habit has deadened. This, and the continual learning of 'tarpaulin' terms, is part of the geniality and expansive interest of the second and third books of the trilogy; but it also marks the contrast with the mainstream of Golding's fiction, which had become more and more sceptical about language, so that the deepest perceptions had to be hinted at beyond words. To get to close quarters with what lies behind a metaphor may, however, revive a lost apprehension.

A more significant effect is to call in question again, and more deeply, the social bases of Edmund's judgement and the pernicious effects of English class-consciousness. He had had to learn in *Rites* the implications of his own snobbish blindness to Colley, and his own responsibility (among others) for Colley's tragedy. The others notably included Dashing Jack Deverel, in the badger bag. So Edmund had already begun to measure the fallacy in his original judgement that Deverel was the most gentlemanly of the officers, and to measure also the contrast with Summers who is a good officer and a good man, but not a gentleman, having been promoted from the foc'sle. There is now no doubting Deverel's irresponsibility; but his reaction to being furiously rebuked and put under open arrest begins a process of getting to closer quarters with both him and Captain Anderson. For it soon becomes clear that Deverel the aristocrat cannot and will not accept the reversal of status which has given humiliating power over him to some Lord's 'by-blow' (brought up by a parson as we eventually learned in *Rites*) whom Deverel's father would not have at his table. This casts a revealing crosslight on the Captain's prickliness at Edmund's careless assumptions of privilege, and also on his hatred of parsons. Step by step, Deverel will become more and more manic in his attempts to challenge his captain; and we will learn to see, behind the dashing whiskers and manners, the real weakness of character which will make a stronger and stronger contrast with Summers.

As his friendship with Summers grows, Edmund confides more of his views and ambitions: calculated, and Tory of course. We learn the planned shape of a career for the elder son with an encumbered estate: apprenticeship in a colonial administration through his godfather's influence, followed by election to parliament from a rotten borough and the hope of a 'plum', then an arranged and advantageous marriage in ten years' time with a suitable girl now in the nursery. Pacing the deck with Summers his voice rises in defence of rotten boroughs and a hereditary governing class; so that we suspect there will be some kind of row before too long with the radical Mr Prettiman. Edmund is not a lord. We shall learn that his father is an uneducated squire whose wife's family is the influential one; but his *de haut en bas* behaviour has already earned him the nickname of 'Lord Talbot' on board. We will see him look down his nose at offers of friendship from little Pike, and he is quick to react to familiarities, even from Charles Summers. Only the sarcastic Miss Granham, governess though she may have been as well as daughter of a canon, is able to puncture his superior class-complacency, as she had done before. He is an unthinking patriot, with annoying assumptions of *noblesse oblige, pour encourager les autres*. It is clear that he still has a great deal to learn, even after what now seems merely the primary phase of his rites of passage. On the other hand we become aware of the narrowness of his experience. He is classically schooled and literate, but has not much more to draw on in human terms than his relationship with his younger brothers and his old nurse. And, as Miss Granham perceives in a moment of compassion, he is still not much more than a boy, expressing attitudes he has inherited and never critically examined.

By contrast, we come to appreciate even more at closer quarters the virtues of the self-made Charles Summers, the extremely competent and caring First Lieutenant; though we will also discover more signs of his social vulnerability and the sharpness of the chip on his shoulder. Deverel calls him a 'Methodist', meaning no compliment, but we had already begun to find him a good and religious man in *Rites of Passage*, and further experience confirms our impressions. As an officer, he is everything that Deverel is not; and seems to combine efficiency with humanity to an extent that also casts a crosslight on Anderson, whose reaction to emergency shows great courage and seamanship but whose humanity seems as limited as ever. Indeed we begin to discover that one of the strengths of 'history' writing, as we see deeper into the complex web of characteristics and relationships, is how characters do cast light on one another. As well as the primary comparisons and contrasts between Edmund and Charles we may begin to detect similarities as well as differences between Deverel and Edmund, and Summers and Anderson (both of whom, socially disadvantaged, must have been given a start by patronage, though we don't yet know how). And as the web spreads, and we get to closer quarters with Miss Granham, Prettiman, Pike, Oldmeadow, Bowles, Brocklebank, we also begin to see how getting to know one person often means seeing another afresh.

Having been taken aback once, it is not long before young Edmund is taken aback even more, with another two bangs to the head, and the loss of his heart altogether. The crippled ship is being borne back towards the doldrums, and in a 'wilderness of heat and mist' a sail is sighted. The chances are that it is French. (The date is 1813. Napoleon is wholly occupied in Russia and English naval supremacy is assured, hence the dispatch of an ancient warship as a kind of passenger vessel to Australia – but a single French ship is a possibility, and the newness of her sails makes it even likely, since English ships have been endlessly at sea.) Though both are becalmed, Summers explains how they will inevitably drift towards each other. They must prepare for action as best they can, with limited resources of guns and manpower. So Edmund, though taken to task by Prettiman for unthinkingly 'patriotic' attitudes, and in marked contrast with the alarm of little Pike at the danger to his family, is the first to volunteer to help man a cannon. Alas, he is far too tall and clumsy for the gun deck, and is first knocked over, hitting his head hard on the planking, and then suffers another resounding crack on the beam above when he tries to stand up. Furious at his humiliation, and with blood trickling down an ashen face, he joins the boarding party, armed with a cutlass by a Deverel who also hopes to escape from humiliation by distinguishing himself in action. But this is no O'Brien or Forester novel of heroism, though there is a moment of great drama as the other ship looms through the mist; and though Miss Granham, touched by Edmund's honest disclaimer, is inclined to give him the benefit of heroic intentions rather than clownish performance. The ship is English, and *Alcyone*'s news is of halcyon days of peace.

Peace takes some imagining after two decades of war and revolutionary change; and Edmund is politically aware enough, for all his splitting head, to reflect that too many catastrophes have occurred to allow any optimism about the good old days returning: 'it would be a sad world which our people were greeting so noisily'. With peace, too, comes indiscipline among the crew with the prospect of liberation from the navy and the press-gang, and a gloomy outlook for the officers as ship after ship has already been laid up. And with *Alcyone* come two more shocks from outside – people, not weather now – which will eventually complete the process of taking Edmund aback, and changing him for ever.

The first person to clamber over from *Alcyone* is Wheeler, Edmund's original steward, whose disappearance towards the end of *Rites* – believed drowned – was the one mystery in that book about which no evidence had come to light. Only suspicion remained: that he may have been the informer about what happened to Colley in the foc'sle, thrown overboard perhaps by Billy Rogers in revenge. Wheeler insists that he simply slipped; but then his own safety might well demand that he say so. What is even more puzzling than how he went overboard, however, is his survival after three days in the water, and the miracle of his being found in the track of the only other ship within thousands of miles. Edmund has prided himself on his rationality; though after Colley's death he also thinks himself capable of more feeling than he was aware of. The apparition of Wheeler the revenant poses a challenge to both claims.

Edmund's whole consciousness and idea of himself is however much more immediately taken aback by the other apparition from *Alcyone*. His first sight of Marion – Lady Somerset's 'prodigy' in Brocklebank pronunciation – affects him as though struck by lightning, and chases nearly everything else from his damaged head. The combination of love at first sight with concussion, suffuses four chapters with a happy kind of delirium. The two ships lashed together are festively transformed. Trunks come up from the depths and men and women don finery. There is a dinner at which Edmund meets Marion Chumley and loses his heart to that amusingly self-deprecating 'young person'. He doesn't seem to mind, now, being scoffed at for his questions at dinner about steamships, for there is the sweetness of Marion springing to his defence. (He also loses nothing from us, who know the future.) At the 'entertainment' given by the crew, the usually prickly 'Lord Talbot' hardly bristles at a jest at the expense of his broken head, for Marion calls it 'unkind'. At the ball, only Deverel's misbehaviour can cast a momentary shadow. The aping of their betters by the 'satiric dogs' of the foc'sle merely draws from Marion a sense of their gaiety and freedom that speaks volumes about the restrictions of her life: a young woman not at her own disposal, indeed the penniless protegée of a rather silly 'romantick' Lady. On the quarterdeck, for all the barriers of eighteenth-century propriety, it becomes clear that the attraction is mutual. He, who had so carefully calculated on an advantageous marriage ten years hence, declares himself ready to sacrifice his career now for the love of a poor parson's daughter. And when she has to leave the party like Cinderella, she goes as far as a young person properly can, to an admission of preference. Edmund's delirium turns to a mad determination somehow to contrive that she transfer to their ship rather than be carried off to India.

Golding meets a new challenge rather well: not only in dramatizing the intoxication of young love, but in writing a comedy of manners and conventions that can almost measure up to Jane Austen, though debarred by his choice of form from her third-person wit and irony. Instead, through Edmund's half-delirium, Golding captures the sense of a floating world, a dreaminess of self-abandon that is yet conscious of the proprieties as well as the impulse to out-manoeuvre them. There is affectionate comedy without condescension, largely because of Marion's own humour. Who would have thought that Golding, who had been accused of not being able to write about women, could have produced such charm? What is involved however is no less than a personal transformation in which we specifically measure the old 'Lord Talbot' against a new world of feeling, and summon dead Colley back into the reckoning.

For as Edmund listens to the singing of Mrs East at the entertainment, it is nothing less than a new dimension of human being that overwhelms him and makes him weep unexpected tears. It is not merely the effect of concussion, or of sympathy for the young woman who had so narrowly escaped death and now stands childlike, singing her unaccompanied song. It is something in the song itself, 'as simple as a hedge rose, yet it haunts me still'. Only the boatswain's pipe at Colley's funeral had previously called to him, as indeed Colley's journal had done, from a dimension beyond the limits of eighteenth-century rationalism. But now 'Bonny at Morn', for all its simplicity, admits him 'to halls, caverns, new palaces of feeling – how foolish and impossible! Those tears which I had been able to restrain at my introduction to a new life now fell ... They were neither tears of sorrow nor tears of joy. They were tears – and I do not know how this is possible – they were tears of *understanding*!'

Marion saves his embarrassment – and perhaps her own at having felt less – by a story against herself. *She* has been taught to sing with more artistry and tremolo, though she can recognize nature when she hears it. But when she was rebuked as a schoolgirl for an essay which unfashionably (for we are in the Romantic period now) preferred Art to Nature, it was because she had realized as a moneyless orphan that Nature had done her down, and it would have to be Art which earned her a living, as a governess presumably, should no husband turn up who is willing to take her for her own bonny self without a dowry. Behind the romance are some stern realities. Yet what Edmund and Marion are experiencing now is a quite different kind of understanding of their world, and of what makes for the integrity of themselves; an understanding that pierces through and goes beyond all socio-economic conditions and cultural arguments, let alone Lady Somerset's 'Byronism'.

In this context the comparison and contrast with Deverel is transcended even as it is being fleshed out. Edmund keeps a cool head, despite the bang on it, when Deverel demands his help in challenging Captain Anderson; and still more when Anderson in turn calls him to witness how he had avoided receiving the challenge, with perhaps a death penalty for Deverel's rashness at stake. Despite Anderson's scorn, Edmund insists on thinking out all the possible consequences before he will decide what he is prepared to do or say. It might be hard to choose between this politic caution and Deverel's madly emotional rashness. But with Marion, Edmund begins to enter a realm where caution would harm the integrity of the self, and he throws it to the wind. Conversely, the conversation he overhears between Sir Henry

Somerset and Anderson, which will end in the quiet transfer of Deverel to *Alcyone*, shows them as motivated not by justice but by a class-consciouness that bears sharply on how Anderson has treated Edmund. Their aristocratic connections gain both young men a leniency not open to the less privileged. But when Edmund declares himself to Marion he declares against class and social considerations.

Yet no considerations of any sort can prevent her from being borne away to India. If she cannot transfer to his ship, he appeals frantically to Sir Henry to allow him to join *Alcyone*; but that politic gentleman must of course refuse lest he offend the god-father, the very reason for Edmund's special treatment heretofore. Post-concussive delirium combines with grief to overwhelm the lad. A wild figure shouts 'Come back!' against the wind, then collapses for three days of helpless weeping. So much for the rational man. The Edmund who staggers from his bunk three days later, will in certain respects have changed forever.

III THE NETHER REGIONS

The second half of the novel might have been entitled 'The Nether Regions', for in it we probe much deeper below the surface: into the real condition of the ship; into certain truths about the great British Navy most shocking to Edmund's patriotic naïveté; into other characters seen at still closer quarters; and (sharpest of all) into our diarist's interior, to shed light on the consciousness of the new man.

Edmund has not been long on his feet again before he realizes a difference in the motion of the ship that is causing serious discomfort to all its passengers. Without topmasts and the full use of the foremast – and hence, for reasons of balance, of the mizzen mast also – the ship is not only moving far slower than before, but also rolling far worse. Some of the passengers, particularly the Pike children, are becoming seriously ill, and there is pressure on Edmund to act as emissary to the Captain, to persuade him to change course and make for South America. The drunkenness of the ship's carpenter, investigating the state of the planking, leads to suspicion that the ship's 'rendering like an old boot' could be much more than a humorous phrase. With timbers so old, the 'wringing' caused by the stress of the squall might be a lethal concern. Are the timbers rotten? Is the planking not merely leaking but coming apart? When Edmund goes below, into the depths he had visited once before in *Rites* – looking then for somewhere to seduce Zenobia, and now on the excuse of being of service to Deverel, who has in fact been got rid of to *Alcyone* – he discovers more than he had bargained for. Down there, Summers and the new officer Benét who was exchanged for Deverel, are arguing about whether it might be safer to try to move the chronometers to the deck above. On his way towards them in the darkness, Edmund has become horridly aware not only of the many noises that come from water seeping between old planks which have lost their oakum, but also of what appears to be a wave passing through the bilges when she pitches and rolls. Summers insists that they are pumping no more now than they did before, and that the 'wave' is no more than seepage, but is that true? As to changing course for the River Plate, he explains that it cannot be done. Back in the warm water of the doldrums, the weed on the ship's bottom has vastly increased, so that they can make very little progress. Indeed they are almost at a null point where adverse winds and currents match what they can do with limited sails. Their only hope is to edge even further south, where they may hope to pick up winds from another direction, strong enough to carry them in a great curve towards their destination. In the meantime, in the privacy of the darkness, Summers admits that the ship may sink before they get there. Two possible remedies remain: Benét proposes a drag-rope to try to remove the weed – an operation usually done only in dock or by careening in a safe shallow – and Summers proposes to truss the ship together with cables passed under the keel. To complete this dark picture of what is happening belowdecks, the ship is now 'sagging' and 'hogging' – bending downwards and upwards in the middle – as well as pitching and rolling. But crew and passengers must be kept in ignorance of the true position.

This all comes out with calm professionalism. But 'nether' truths about the navy also begin to emerge, and Edmund's naïvely patriotic notions take a jolting. Signs of rivalry between the two officers strain discipline; the new one already being favoured by the Captain at the first Lieutenant's expense. The capricious system of promotion and patronage has allowed one of the midshipmen to grow old in the service, and he has become senile on this voyage. Edmund learns that under wartime pressure this ship and many others were built too fast, and by corrupt builders who took dangerous liberties for profit. And the purser has bribed a number of sailors to ensure his own safety should things go badly wrong, for there are far too few lifeboats, and little likelihood of sentimental nonsense about women and children. The officers may need to deceive the crew now, as much as the passengers, about the true situation. Hearts of oak are not what they seem, either in the vessel or its crew.

The appalling motion of the ship becomes a test of character. The prominent passengers set up a committee to voice their complaints to the Captain, and commission Edmund to do so, much against his will. (He insists on consulting Summers first.) Prettiman is as irascible as ever, but shortly afterwards has a severe fall which banishes him from sight. On the other hand Bowles, the solicitor's clerk, behaves with unsuspected gravitas, and Old-meadow, the marine officer, will show an equally unexpected dignity later, when it turns out that he too has discovered the straits that they are in. By contrast, little Pike becomes increasingly hysterical about the condition of his children, and the irritability of his wife under stress. A marked change occurs in our perception of Miss Granham. Already in *Rites* she had threatened Edmund's social complacency several times, and her engagement to Prettiman had begun to allow the respectable governess and canon's daughter to reveal some radical opinions. Under the stress of the new circumstances, however, it is her womanliness that comes newly into focus, behind the sharpness of her manner. After the scare over *Alcyone* she shows a graciousness to Edmund we might not have expected, and she it is who tries to do something for Mrs Pike, and is snapped at for her pains. In turn, Edmund's chivalry, when faced with her distress over Prettiman, produces a response which shows how much her apparent self-control may cost her. His attempt to cheer her up with his account of his old governess is both clownish and tactless again, but the real kindness of his gift of the packet of tea brings tears of which she is ashamed, but which she cannot control. There is more in common between her and the young man than either has recognized, though their relationship will remain a blend of irritation and unwilling liking. It is not long before another attempt at chivalry brings the knowledge, as he tries to help her back to her cabin, that she is indeed womanly, and moreover isn't wearing stays. (In a wish-fulfilment dream she actually becomes conflated with Marion.)

The most revealing 'nether' exploration however, is of the rivalry between Summers and Benét, and the light this throws on the captain. Behind the professional disagreements lie significant differences of temperament and social outlook. Benét's family are émigré French aristos, and his blithe self-confidence is clearly bred into him. But because he is also scientifically educated and professional in naval matters, Anderson's response to him is quite different from his attitude to Talbot. The 'by-blow' Captain is class-conscious enough to allow the one young man privileges because of his godfather's influence, but it is done with a resentment not felt towards the other, because Benét (the exile) has had, like Anderson, to make his career professionally. Couple class-feeling with professional respect, moreover, and Anderson's contrasting attitudes towards the aristocrat officer and the one who has risen from the lower decks become intelligible. Snobbery is at its acutest where levels of disadvantage chafe one another. Add to this the charm of Benét's manner and his good looks – a factor only delicately touched on, and perhaps casting light backwards on the trial in the previous novel – and Anderson's favouritism becomes explicable, though no less potentially danger-ous. To this must also be added our growing insight into the contrast in temperament between the two lieutenants. Summers is careful (perhaps to a fault?), but Benét is blithely daring (perhaps to recklessness?), and none too respectful of the rank which means a great deal to the other, because hard-won. Given the social chip on Summers's shoulder, his jealousy (which Edmund calls 'an almost feminine weakness') is growing.

Feminine or no, it grows in Edmund too; and there too 'nether' knowledge casts revealing crosslight. For Edmund's initiation into the unaccustomed world of feeling brings irrational suffering as well as new understanding. He is beset by irrational fear that Deverel in *Alcyone* may make progress with Marion now, though her dislike had been clear enough. He then becomes even more jealous of Benét, though the whole reason for the Frenchman's transfer was his flirtation with his captain's wife. It is jealousy in fact which drives Edmund into the nether regions in search of reassurance; but when he gets it, the green-eyed monster merely changes shape. Under challenge, Benét makes it clear that Marion to him is an unformed schoolgirl. His taste is for older women. But within seconds Edmund is torturing himself with a new suspicion: that Marion's having kept watch for her patroness suggests an immoral character. Only when he summons the vivid memory of the young woman herself, her parting words, and the note from her which is at last delivered to him, does he begin to understand how depth of feeling may seize the slightest excuses for self-deception and self-torture. The contrast is with Benét's parade of poetic feeling. The comparison between the two 'bereaved' young men gathers momentum as Edmund realizes how deep feeling demands poetic language, which (prose-man that he has been) he cannot finally command. But the comic account of his attempt to draw on his classical education, and his ultimate failure to express what he feels, play off against our growing sense that with Benét it is all poetic show and little emotional depth. (One might remember Captain Benwick in *Persuasion*.) This gilded youth seems far too sunny and self-satisfied for genuine, let alone deep feeling.

Though Edmund comes off rather well from that particular comparison, the main effect of our 'nether' exploration is to establish how far he has yet to grow. As he staggers out from his three days of weeping we are vividly reminded again of how he has traded on privilege, for he continues instinctively to do so, as he imperiously summons the busy First Lieutenant. Then privilege rebounds on him as he learns why the committee of passengers has chosen him to carry their message to the Captain. Though Pike's hysteria about his children is indeed irritating, the limits of Edmund's sympathy are uncomfortably clear too, by contrast with Miss Granham. Moreover he is as irritating to Prettiman as Pike is to him. He, also, talks too much with too much facility, and listens far too little. And though his politic suggestion of going through Summers is sensible, it is also evasive, as his refusal to bear witness for Anderson had been. As he journeys into the depths, the first thing he hears is a denunciation from the gunner Askew, who had rather liked his gameness on the gun deck, but finds his lordliness distinctly unlovable. When, in the nether regions, he insists on learning the true position, he has to learn also the responsibilities of privileged knowledge. *Noblesse oblige pour encourager les autres* is much more difficult than he imagines, and not best served by glib assertions that he would not be elsewhere for a thousand pounds (or by his frequent slips of the tongue). On the other hand, though his resilience and optimism can seem foolish, he is slowly learning to be laughed at, and he does absorb the various lessons life is teaching him. Alas, by a familiar life-irony, when he does begin to care for others it comes too late. He thinks up the solution to the sufferings of Pike's children – how Nelson overcame seasickness by sleeping in a hammock rather than the captain's cot – but his previous conduct ensures that his bright idea cannot get heard. He has broken in on the Captain too often; and when he goes to see the Pikes he is shooed away by a stony-faced Miss Granham who, in her sensitivity to their and Prettiman's suffering, can only see him as an intrusion. And Summers seems too busy for once to listen – though there may be some other reason for that.

The greatest irony of all is that Edmund himself is failing altogether to listen: to a challenge which keeps confronting him in his own cabin. He is now sleeping where Colley died, having insisted on giving up his own berth for Marion, should he succeed in having her transferred. (It is tenanted now, ironically, by a Zenobia fearfully transformed by seasickness.) Edmund's initiation into a new world of feeling has brought Colley several times to mind. The devastating irony is that, blinded by obsession with Marion, and jealousy, and class-superiority, he fails to see how he is repeating exactly his responsibility for Colley's death. For Wheeler is falling apart right in front of him, but he has no eyes or ears for the steward for (or at) whom he continually shouts, and on whom he relies as much as before. He vaguely wonders why Wheeler sticks so close to him, until he learns that the man is still afraid of reprisals from the men on whom he informed. But of the greater grounds for Wheeler's growing terror he has no idea, because it never occurs to him to imagine what a servant might feel. Their first conversation makes the back of his neck prickle when Wheeler says that he *did* drown, though only after three days: 'I did – and the life in me so strong.' But all Edmund can say is that Wheeler was a lucky dog to be picked up, and Marion (and concussion) soon drive from his mind any curiosity, even, to know what the steward meant. Of all things, after his own breakdown and recovery he tries to talk to Wheeler about Marion on *Alcyone*; and it is hardly surprising that the servant should examine his face curiously 'as if the face of a man was something new and strange to him' – for Edmund's only response to *him* is to repeat how lucky he was, and that he should give thanks. 'An extraordinary shudder shook the man from head to foot. He bent his head and got out of the door without looking at me again. Certainly there was no possibility of making a confidant of him –' The irony is corrosive. Even when Wheeler openly appeals for help and understanding, Edmund fails him as badly as he had failed Colley. He comes back from his journey to the nether regions to find Wheeler cleaning his cabin for the third time that day. 'What the devil?' the young man cries. 'You are haunting me!' (Earlier, again without listening to himself, he had likened him to a ghost.) Wheeler pauses, then speaks 'in what I can only call his other voice, a voice with a curious trace of some other society in it, other places and customs. "I'm in hell, sir."' But Edmund is overcome with the stress of all he has learned below, and with seasickness, and a fit of vomiting. The moment passes in which he might have learned something of what it *means* to feel after three days in the water that you have already died inside; then to be rescued from that certainty and be forced to live again, in fear; and now to be absolutely terrified by the likelihood of having to drown again – for Wheeler is of course aware of the real situation. (His experience was that of Pip in *Moby Dick*, who lost his mind.) We know nothing yet of what he used to be,* this odd fellow who always seems to know everything; but the other country Edmund hears in his voice is predominantly a country of the mind, of suffering, isolation, and derangement, in the light of which his own troubles are trivial indeed. When drunk, Edmund condescends far enough to get from Wheeler his version of how he came to go overboard, and promises that the man can go on 'haunting' him if he will tell him the truth about what happened to Colley, though he refuses to pass this on to us. But he soon forgets his drunken agreement and, ironically, having just begun to care about Pike's children, shouts at Wheeler to get out again. But

---

* He sounds and behaves rather like an Oxford 'scout'.

this time the man's desperation is so great that he doesn't immediately obey. For:

> 'She's moving more, isn't she, sir?'
> 'You're out of your mind, Wheeler. Now be off with you!'
> 'I can't drown, sir. Not again, I can't' ...

But Edmund still thinks this is 'nonsense'. It takes the most devastating of all the crosslights to measure his lack of imagination. For in the middle of the operation to clean the weed off the ship's bottom, Brocklebank, that monster of self-absorption, who is aware of the possibility that they all may drown, actually makes Edmund summon Wheeler to describe to them, in public, 'what must have been a deuced unpleasant experience'. Oldmeadow protests, and a 'strong interior convulsion seemed to shake Wheeler from head to foot'. Edmund in sudden realization apologizes, and means to make it up to the man, in money, later. But Wheeler has vanished again. Edmund for the first time does try to imagine what might happen if the ship did sink, and is frightened into a cold sweat. But what should the human response have been that is neither Brocklebank's armoured inhumanity (or artist's curiosity), nor Edmund's equally inhumane lack of interest? And is it too late? Edmund may have entered new worlds of feeling and poetic imagination, but he has not done too well in them.

In a closing phase, the metaphoric 'nether regions' become literal and nightmarish, and distil out into episodes which raise fundamental questions about human responsibility and dignity. Edmund sleeps drunkenly through the first attempt to clear the weed off the ship's bottom with a drag-rope, which partially succeeds. But though much weed has been cleared and now can be seen floating out from the side like a carpet, when it comes to the keel itself the rope sticks. So does the narrative of the operation, interrupted by Edmund's various concerns and encounters. There seems to be a heated argument between Summers and Benét, in which the Captain again takes Benét's side in favour of trying to clear what may be a lump of coral by increased force, even wagging his finger at the young man archly, like an uncle agreeing to a jape by a favourite nephew. The men cannot however shift the obstacle by their own power, and the question arises whether the capstan should be used. Summers, to Anderson's irritation, believes that such a risk, to the keel itself, requires the Captain himself to give the order. In the argument between them that takes place out of hearing, only the word 'responsibility' comes floating across. Summers returns to the work with a stony face and the body-language 'of an anxious and angry man'. As the capstan turns, the whole ship creaks and groans. Then the drag-rope suddenly moves, and men fall over themselves because the resistance is gone. Edmund writes:

I have seen all this ... in nightmare, not once but several times, and shall do so again. In nightmare the shape is bigger and rises wholly awesome and dreadful. My dreaming spirit fears, as my waking spirit fears that one night the thing will emerge, bringing with it a load of weed that only half conceals a face ... I saw with waking eyes down by the crazily unstable waterline something like the crown of a head pushing up through the weed ... The thing rose ... it was a head or a fist or the forearm of something vast as Leviathan ... Then it slid sideways, showed a glimpse of weedy tar and timber massive as the king tree of a tithe barn, slid sideways, and disappeared.

They have pulled off a portion of the keel. But as the Captain angrily berates Summers for saying so where he can be heard, and the carpenter later assures them that he has managed to plug the hole below the waterline, Edmund is aware that the nightmare is not merely about the extent of the damage, or its bearing on the success or failure of the operation. What is nightmarish is a fear that in their blind arrogance they have called forth some spectre, some monstrous threatening force in themselves and the world, hidden below the surface of life which is all that they can see. (The scene has correspondences in many of Golding's major novels, see above p. 213) But Edmund insists that a man must proclaim 'to a world of blind force and material ... *I am a man. I am more than blind nature!*'

However the purser, standing beside him, is also a man, and one totally armoured in self-interest, caring absolutely nothing for the fate of man, woman or child outside himself. Doesn't being 'a man' have to do with responsibility, for others? But how, then, does Edmund measure up?

The answer comes swiftly. While the purser and Edmund converse, Brocklebank is muttering about the theft of something or other from his bottom drawer. We soon discover what it was.

As Edmund reaches his cabin he sees Wheeler inside, and is about to reprimand him for being there again, when there is an explosion, and the man's head disintegrates. The blunderbuss with which Prettiman had meant to shoot an albatross in *Rites*, but which Summers fired to save Colley from further humiliation, has now become the means of suicide (right in Edmund's face) for a man who has experienced 'the nightmare death-in-life', like Colley and the Ancient Mariner. For the second time Edmund has paid no attention to a tragedy happening before his very eyes. (When the blunderbuss first went off, we remember, he was copulating with Zenobia.) Miss Granham's compassion, as he faints, is like her, as we know her now, but unwittingly ironic about Edmund. 'Poor boy. He has far more sensibility than he knows.'

And yet the last of the three distillations shows that in the end she is right. For there is one more revelation *de profundis*. Once again Edmund must change cabins, but there is none to spare. Summers has to offer him a berth in the lieutenants' quarters, but to Edmund's astonishment he does so with cold dislike and some contempt. What on earth has gone wrong? The explanation is shaming to them both. As Summers's jealousy of Benét has grown into paranoia, it has seemed to him that the golden youngster has not only robbed him of his standing with his captain but has also eaten him out of Edmund's friendship and patronage. Edmund has been blind, again, to the effect his continual conversations with Benét (trying to get something out of him about Marion) have been having on his friend. There has also been a misunderstanding about what Summers understood as a promise of patronage; and Edmund is forced to explain that the only patronage he has to offer is the praise of Summers in the first journal to his godfather. There is incipient comedy in the fact that this conversation takes place with the usual leg-bending and stretching of keeping one's balance at sea. Yet deep emotions are involved. Summers feels humiliated in confessing both his jealousy and his material hopes from the friendship. But his feelings have run much deeper than Edmund's and they touch the young man with a new sense of what friendship requires. For once, he does not stand on his dignity, and misunderstandings can be cleared. Instead of pretending to 'a political and detached observation' of men and women, he not only sees deeper into his self-enclosure, and his failings (towards

Summers, Marion, and Wheeler) but is moved to tears of remorse. And for once he overcomes his lordly reserve in both offering his hand and returning his friend's warmth. Love, friendship, and responsibility for others would seem to be the criteria for growing into manhood.

Finally, Edmund's juxtaposition with the purser — who *does* regard other human beings with a political and detached observation — brings out how very different he has become. In a book which cannot have a conclusion, the underlining of this provides at least a comic postscript. The sense of disaster partly dissipates in black humour as the purser, now fearing the worst, tries unavailingly to recover the money he has lent to all and sundry. Edmund insists that he is in debt only to Wheeler's heirs, but he gives everyone the chance to have something of themselves survive in the firkin he buys from Jones, on condition that the man preserves it in his cynical scheme to save himself. Social distinctions vanish as everyone enjoys the joke at the purser's expense. For not only does the wholly anti-social man have to preserve something of everyone; but he has to agree to buy the barrel back should they live — for (says Edmund) 'I'm odd like that, you know.' The turning of his own phrase on the purser spreads all over the ship, and the joke makes Edmund suddenly popular. But the real point is that Edmund is not odd in the purser's fashion — not like *that*, at all, now, as the second volume of the trilogy comes to an end.

12

FIRE DOWN BELOW

(1989)

I TRIANGULATIONS

Slyly, Golding begins *Fire Down Below* by having Summers take Edmund way up aloft, to the main masthead from which the midshipman Willis has just been lifted, comatose from his punishment for the voyage's first disaster. Perched on this high point of vantage, we begin with a conversation that (like the lead-in to a new episode in a television series) deftly touches on the main heads of the situation so far, by way of reminder to readers of *Close Quarters* two years before, and introduction to new ones. It soon becomes clear that this final instalment of the education of Edmund Talbot will be mainly concerned with two triangular relationships: one being his involvement with the ever increasing rivalry between Summers and Benét, and the effect of this on passengers and crew; and the other some much closer encounters with Prettiman and Miss Granham, which will produce a new view of them, and a pronounced change in Edmund and his confident Tory judgements. There is also, however, a more hidden theme. Seen from up there, in the great sweep of sea and sky, wind and water, the ship shrinks to a rowboat and her inhabitants are diminished, to midgets. Up there the instability of the foremast becomes clearly visible; and Mr Smiles the sailing master's very unsmiling remark about the comatose boy, 'It is a time for dying', reverberates uneasily. *Close Quarters* was a human drama, but it ended with a ship that might well sink, and an apparition suggestive of some monstrous threat from below the surface of the ship-world, and beyond human control. Summers's cables passed under the keel may succeed in holding rotten timbers together. Benét may persuade the Captain to risk an attempt to repair the split in the foremast-shoe by scientific means, using the force in the contraction of red-hot iron. But Bowles the solicitor's clerk voices what has become a reality for them all: the reality of a 'settled dread'. And the world seen from the masthead – on this day seemingly benign – may indeed contain greater forces than human beings, be they scientists or sailing masters, can manage. We may have to judge human character from that perspective too.

At deck level once more, Edmund, for all his high spirits and confidence, remains haunted by his experiences of death and love. He proposes now, to the consternation of Summers, to move out of the wardroom and back into the cabin where Colley and Wheeler died. He says it is to preserve his future reputation. A colonial administrator must not be afraid of ghosts. But whatever the motive, it will involve facing up to the darkness of the past. On the other hand, his relations with Benét seem governed (and be-devilled) by the fact that the yellow-haired young man from *Alcyone* is his only source of information about Marion, and also, inevitably, a focus for the jealousy that always goes with sexual love.

The radical disagreement between Summers and Benét over the plan to repair the foremast-shoe divides the ship into factions. The Captain, of course, is in favour of Benét and has absolute authority. Edmund (also of course) is on the side of his friend. Our sympathies tend to be with Summers, partly because we live in Edmund's consciousness, and partly because of the first officer's caring and responsible nature. He cures Edmund's seawater itch by contriving a rainwater soaking and a change into ordinary seaman's clothes – which (Edmund thinks) may even help to cure his habitual hauteur as well. More seriously, Charles's case against experimenting in a wooden ship with white-hot iron bars shut into a huge wooden block is not merely obstructive or jealous; and his example from common experience of how a fireback may go on smouldering even when the fire is out, is a powerful one, though Benét's model persuades the Captain that this will not happen where there is limited oxygen. We also tend to react as Edmund does against the young man's cocky air of triumph, his scant respect for his superior officer, and his suspicions of deceit over the supplies of iron and charcoal. We know Summers better than that. But passengers and crew begin to take sides also. Even the mild Oldmeadow suddenly reacts against Edmund's privileged friendship with the first officer, and the judicious Bowles shows up how partisan Edmund has become.

There is also friction between Edmund and Benét that has nothing to do with the foremast. Their temperaments grate, and their 'compleyntes' of separation from those they love become competitive. Edmund's efforts to pump Benét about Marion run up against indifference to the 'schoolgirl', and Romanticism (or posturing?) about her older benefactress; whereas Benét's poeticizing leaves Edmund cold. The Englishman's pronunciation of French is to the émigré a source of amused contempt, which Edmund seems never to notice. Through the verbal fencing there does emerge a little information about those last moments when, as Edmund lay insensible, Lady Somerset contrived to throw the two notes to Benét across the gap between the separating ships – but the effect is spoilt by his infuriating deconstruction of Marion's *billet doux*, so guarded from a 'Romantick' point of view. The two young men part in irritation; and a slip of Edmund's tongue betrays his festering worry about whether Marion, in keeping watch for Benét and Lady Somerset, may have been engaged in something 'reprehensible'.

However, Bowles is right to insist that the young émigré is no fool. His ideas have already helped the ship's speed, though they also put her at risk. We ought moreover (after the comparisons of the previous volume) to remain alert to the similarities between the two young men which play against the contrasts. Both have had privileged upbringings and education, though in different cultures. Both have traded on privilege in their relations with the Captain. And – amusingly to close readers – both are so self-centred and obsessive that each only listens intermittently to what the other says. So misunderstandings and misjudgements grow, and are entrenched.

As to the second triangle, as early as the second chapter Edmund's *de haut en bas* judgement of Prettiman ('our comic philosopher') is called in question, in terms less of 'wicked' politics than simple humanity. As the wind mounts to a gale and the ship pitches steeply Edmund wakes to a cry of anguish, soon repeated, and goes to find its source: the cabin to which Prettiman has been confined since his fall in the previous volume. (We have seen and heard nothing of him ourselves since the committee meeting in the saloon.) Edmund hardly has time to see Miss Granham go to her fiancé's aid from next door before another pitch sends him cannoning – greatcoat flying open to reveal bare legs and his nightshirt – smack into Prettiman's door. Unsurprisingly he gets a rather glacial reception from a lady he respects much more than her husband-to-be. He is also driven to reflect that, comic though the man might seem, 'the comic are able to suffer as much as the rest of us'. He hears from Bowles about the emigrants' regard for Prettiman. Is there more to him than he had thought? Soon there is another débâcle with Miss Granham. Because she too has changed into seaman's garb, he tackles her for being where she has no business, just as Celia Brocklebank had mistaken him. How much of social judgement depends on appearance?

Though his pride takes yet another tumble – literally too, when he is caught off balance by another heave of the ship – he rebels against being continually misunderstood and rebuked by her. People's opinions of one another have been modified by experience on this voyage; so why should hers of him be so fixed? Smilingly (and unusually attractive in the half-light) she agrees to be 'acquainted all over again', and though he commits another near *faux pas* about her age, and she teases him about his indifference 'to where and how you fall', it looks like a fresh start. His underlying regard for her shows clearly in his pleasure at the reconciliation. Moreover, Prettiman for some reason wants to see him.

II NEW BEGINNINGS – AND COMPLEXITIES

In the next phase of the voyage new beginnings do seem possible. At last they have found the trade winds – albeit much further south than the roaring forties – and can head directly east. In the newly repainted cabin Edmund spends a wretched night; but though his original motives for being there were worldly, he does begin to come to terms with the ghosts of Colley and Wheeler and his own responsibility for their deaths. The ringbolt that Colley clutched, and the indentation in the beam where a tiny spike of metal is still lodged after Wheeler's suicide, force him to imagine something of their sufferings – 'extremes of dread and sorrow' – as he has never been able to do before. He finds himself muttering words rather like Miss Granham's as he himself lay apparently unconscious on the deck when the ship was taken aback, 'about a poor boy who had too much sensibility'; but though that was true of Colley, it had not been true of himself in relation to the two dead men. He recalls his pompous remark about sharing the lot of others 'who would one day be part of my care', a noble sentiment he had emphatically failed to live up to. He falls into the kind of black hole of which Wheeler had spoken to Webber, and finds himself in his own shame and fear clutching the ringbolt as Colley had done. At last he falls into uneasy slumber, but wakes to the sound of 'a familiar voice, choked with sobbing: "You could have saved us."' It is his own voice – through which the dead can accuse him, and he accept responsibility.

His interview with Prettiman begins to change them both. Aware now of his own 'offhand ability to spread destruction', he sits down cautiously beside the sick man and studies his pale sleeping face, so often ludicrously contorted in anger before but not at all laughable now. Indeed likenesses appear: Edmund tends to be impatient too, and irritable (as when Prettiman's mutterings recall a previous life as a clerk in Chancery and touch on a member of Edmund's family). Both have a passion for fairness beneath political differences. When at last Edmund, instead of rattling out social formulae, tries to listen, and the other to control his irritation, it comes out that Prettiman thinks he is dying, and wants to be married first. He wants Edmund as a witness who could testify to his wife's right to inherit, and also prevent any claim that the marriage could not have been consummated. He must take charge of a signed statement that the couple had had relations before marriage. If Edmund chokes off his habitual 'Good God', it is not merely because the habit irritates Prettiman. The casual blasphemy won't do for his complicated feelings. There is criticism of Prettiman's inconsistency in resorting to a 'superstitious rite' – though Edmund basically shares that view. There is horror at the man's howls of pain whenever he moves, and the stench, and the monstrous swelling beneath the bedclothes. There is unexpectedly powerful anger and revulsion at a revelation he takes to be true – responses that hint again at something sexual in his own feelings for the lady. Above all there is *sadness*. In his attraction to her, as to Marion, there is now a tincture of poison. The fresh start with the Prettimans will not be plain sailing.

When Summers suggests another new idea, that Edmund should

be rated midshipman and take the middle watch with him, his feeling for the First Lieutenant deepens into greater intimacy and respect, and gives a new gloss to the *Iliad* story of the friendship between Glaucus and Diomede to which Edmund keeps likening theirs. But we can detect here, also, the first signs of new complexity. Though Edmund does not realize at first, this is another proof of Charles's care for him, as well as his readiness to take on more himself and so diminish the stress on his fellow officers. As Summers prepares a sea-anchor against storms to come, we watch traditional seamanship that contrasts with Benét's scientific experiment. And when, on their first moonlit watch together, Charles recalls the excitement of an ex-able-seaman's first introduction to the mysteries of navigation, we also get a parable about the need for caution and practicality, as against Benét's theories of lunar navigation and the frisson he gets from risk and danger. Edmund gains a deeper sense of what it means to be a first lieutenant, constantly on duty as a ship's 'husband' concerned with every detail, but also capable of the kind of care that 'contrived much out of small things' and can make of that carefulness a 'generosity' and a 'warm ... thoughtfulness' that (though manly) remind Edmund of the old nurse who is obviously the one person in his home life who has genuinely cared for him. However, his consciousness adds the word 'pedestrian' as he thinks about that kind of care, and there is also a strong hint now that one may be too cautious. The chronometers clearly ought to have been moved a deck higher, since water has soaked them now. A better balance comes in the knowledge that Benét, more ready to take risks, was absolutely right in that case, and Summers wrong.

In the magical moonlight of that first watch, however, Edmund learns another side to his friend, in the light of which it is he that is the pedestrian one. The narrative about navigation gives, also, a sudden insight into the depths of emotion that lay (and perhaps still lie?) under the First Lieutenant's down-to-earth attitudes. This impression is confirmed by the effect of the beauty of the night, the wake glittering like diamonds, and the men quietly singing. Shyly Summers confesses how the heavens make him think of his God: 'When I consider the heavens the work of Thy fingers, the moon and stars which Thou has ordained –', but Edmund is more surprised than moved by a quotation he seems to know less well than he knows Milton. His response to religious feeling is instinctively rationalist; and though he does have some sense of poetry and mystery, now, in him these have only to do with being so much in love. There too, however, Summers is surprising. For him, it is enough to have watched Edmund and Marion dancing together, and to have seen her the next morning, 'staring through the side of our ship as if she could see what was going on inside', to dismiss the young man's dark suspicions and jealousy, and to know that she will not forget him. What this lonely man sees in women is their passivity, gentleness, impressionability, and 'most of all their passionate need to give' – which some readers may regard as showing his own feminine side, and others dismiss as sexist sentimentality. Be that as it may, it is again in sharp contrast with Edmund's eighteenth-century cynicism about female 'blue-stockings' and 'wits', and the continuing self-centredness about which Summers teases him. In the moonlight when men can say 'to a transmuted face' what they could not in the daytime it is Edmund, withdrawing so instinctively from any emotion but his own, who seems the more earthbound one.

The phase of new beginnings reaches a twin climax with the wedding, and the triumph of Benét's scientific repair. The wedding, seen through the swirl of Edmund's complex emotions, is both farcical and disturbing. The young cynic, wounded by his 'disappointment' in the first woman to give him an idea of the dignity of the sex, sees it as society's ceremony of sexual sacrifice, inevitably accompanied by innuendo – and inescapably ironic in this case, given his private 'knowledge'. Though Miss Granham wears white, there twinkle in her ears Zenobia's garnet earrings, which Edmund remembers only too well from the climax of their sordid intercourse. The bride has a bouquet of real flowers from the Captain's cabin, and Anderson appears in the splendour of his Number One rig; in both cases, Edmund believes, through the persuasions of Benét who appears like a flag lieutenant in the wake of an admiral. But, ludicrously, Anderson begins by force of habit with the first words of the funeral ceremony! And the farce concludes with Edmund having the bouquet thrust at *him*. He also has to witness the near reverence with which people crowd to press the dying man's hand. By himself afterwards, in a welter of complex emotions about the wedding and the superstitious but impossible forecast that his will be next, Edmund bursts into rather hysteric laughter – and then into disturbing and unexpected tears.

The very next day there is a flat calm, so Benét's scheme can be attempted. It is a triumphant success. Not since *The Spire* has Golding had such a chance to share his fascination with what physics can do for engineering; and as each of the great baulks that have been staying the foremast is knocked away, while the contracting metal rods scream and bang, even Edmund can feel an awe and indeed a majestic beauty at how the fissure in the six-foot cube of wood is tightly closed and the foremast drawn firmly upright again. Though he is put off by Benét's blend of condescension with scientific and poetic rapture; and burns his hand on an iron plate so hot as to make him wonder whether shortage of oxygen will indeed quell the burning that must be taking place inside the huge block, the triumph of human ingenuity has to be admitted. Unfortunately it is Summers who has to pay the price – and not only in jealousy, or even chagrin at being so publicly proved wrong. For Edmund finds his friend plunged into an abyss of gloom and anger, and utterly humiliated. The Captain, on whom any hopes of his advancement must rest, has given him a tongue-lashing, but deliberately without witnesses so there is no chance of redress or appeal. He is called 'dull' and 'superannuated'; and is to cease his 'obstruction' of a 'brilliant young officer'. Though the Captain will take no action yet, Summers is warned, furiously, to *watch his step*. Edmund's sense of fair play is outraged, and he is at last able to find his role in the Glaucus-and-Diomede symbolism of friendship where bronze armour can do in exchange for the gold of Charles's goodness to him. He promises that in addition to the tributes contained in his first diary, his very first action on landing will be to beg his godfather to use his influence to have Summers promoted captain. This would still depend on privilege, but the warmth of Edmund's friendship and sense of injustice does begin to comfort Charles and bring him to himself.

III STURM UND DRANG

The fresh beginnings, then, are climaxed by regained speed in the right direction; but for all of them there seems to have been a price in complexity and grief. With more speed they will ship more water, and have to pump more. Almost at once the wind gets up again, and seamen begin to mutter that it will get worse before it gets better. The next phase of the novel looks like being a great deal stormier in every way. Soon the wind is so strong that one cannot look into it. The waves mount higher and higher; until Edmund begins to feel that they are in a place 'for no man: for sea gods perhaps; for that great and ultimate power which surely must support the visible universe'. The 'surely' implies doubt still. But in these masses of water there is an unfanciful embodiment of his vision of some huge force rising from the sea bed like an apparition of Neptune in their Odyssey, something utterly different from the mumbo-jumbo at the equator. For a while seamanship holds the huge waves almost miraculously in check. Charles's sea-anchor is paid out astern, and from it spreads a film of oil like a path of mild silver light under which the monstrous waters, high though they may swell, do not break. There is something symbolic for the ordering of human life in that too. But as the phase of new beginnings gives way to the certainty of far worse tempests ahead, human and inhuman, it remains to be seen whether there will be enough oil on troubled waters to save them.

For human relationships begin rapidly to deteriorate under the stress of the elements. As the storm worsens, both Bowles and Edmund have moments of black depression, irritability and despair. Oldmeadow is furious with Summers when he and his men are commandeered for pumping, and quarrels with Edmund over it. Edmund reacts in fury to the news that Benét has put into effect the very idea he had had, of how to make things better for Pike's children. He remembers bitterly how Miss Granham sent him away in anger before he could tell her about it – yet in an illogical fit of jealousy seems to think that Benét has stolen it from him. What is really the matter is that she may (must?) have accepted from Benét what she would not from him. He begins to drink, then staggers out and picks a quarrel with his rival. When he calls the Frenchman a fool, hysteria mounts in both; for Edmund, in his ignorance of French, has no idea why he should seem to the other man to be insulting his name, his parents, and his nationality. (It will turn out that 'Benét' – French for simpleton, but now with an acute rather than circumflex accent for English purposes – was a surname adopted by his refugee father, as an ironic comment on his naïveté in having at first accepted the Revolution before it became the Terror which forced him to flee.) Now the young Frenchman gets angry enough to voice a normally suppressed French view of the perfidiousness and indeed loathsomeness of the English. They are shouting outside Prettiman's cabin, but even when his wife opens the door to see what is going on, they do not come to their senses, but begin to push and shove. Edmund claims that it will help if the way that Prettiman is lying is reversed, and Benét claims the same idea. Quarrelling and thrusting, they push past to do it; the Frenchman shoves once too often, and the Englishman falls on the sick man's legs. Prettiman faints with pain. His wife speaks 'in her stony, governess's voice. "You have killed him."'

As Edmund flees to his own cabin, curling up foetally like Colley, and feeling that he has fallen into a black hole like Wheeler, he seems at the nadir of his life. Emotions swirl: prayer that it should not have happened (but prayer without belief); mad ideas of punishment, and of reparation (except that the widow would probably prefer to 'buy' Benét rather than accept Edmund's hand in penitence); and continuing double standards in his mixed feelings about her premarital conduct. When he eventually staggers out into the saloon it is to face the lady herself, and the most absolute Clarissa-like denunciation. He has had no idea of the hopes of a new world that he has ruined:

I saw you come aboard with your privileges about you like a cloud of, of pinchbeck glory! Now you have trodden with your clumsy feet into a place which you do not understand and where you are not welcome. He will regard you indifferently, not as a man but as an agent of his death, as it might be a spar fallen from the mast. He will be above forgiving you. But I am not above it, sir, and I will never, never forgive you!

As she gets up, swaying, her rejection of his help this time, while revealing that she too had felt some degree of attraction before, shows that it has now turned to hatred. 'Above all, do not touch me!' It is said with venom.

In the belief that Prettiman is dying, the emigrants so crowd outside his door that they have to be forbidden the ship's waist so that the crew can do their work. This is the man he has killed. 'There is death in my hands,' he tells Charles, 'I kill people without knowing it.' Colley, Wheeler, and now this. Summers tries to restore some proportion about the degree of his responsibility: foolish, impulsive, with a physical clumsiness he will grow out of, and the man was dying anyway. Yet it is the hatred and contempt of the lady that hurt most, and Summers can give no comfort there. The best he can offer is to confess a secret which suggests that good can come out of trouble: for his own promotion from the lower deck came out of the crime of reading while on duty. But since the book was the Bible, and the Admiral who heard about it and proceeded to promote him to midshipman was a devout Christian, the parable tends rather to underline a difference.

Outbursts between men under stress get stormier. Pike has got drunk to escape his wife's contempt, and blurts out, 'I 'ate 'er. I 'ate 'er. Sodder.' But instead of inspiring sympathy, the parallel brings on a blind rage in which Edmund heaps on the little man every insult he can think of, taking out his own feelings on the nearest victim. In a few moments the judicious Bowles will vent a burst of rage on Edmund, in the same sort of displacement. Both join in manic laughter at Brocklebank: forced to vent his mephitic fartings outside his cabin but then still forbidden the bed of his Celia; who, he now confesses, is not in fact his wife, but is beginning to behave as though she looks forward to becoming his widow. But the jackass laughter is only another revelation of stress worked off on a convenient victim. And it may be the ironic parallels, as much as the disgusting old man producing his broken tooth, that become more than Edmund can stand. Outside the door, however, is the still more maddening sight of Benét in the throes of composition. From the shouting match that ensues, however, comes the realization of how Edmund has made mistake after mistake. If the Frenchman was wrong to see an insult to his name where none was intended, the poison in Edmund's suspicions about Benét's 'fornication' – in fact, merely silly romantic flirting – and hence about something 'criminal' in Marion's behaviour, is revealed to be all in his own mind. Moreover the woman in Benét's latest poem who has doffed her woman's weeds is not a naked Lady Somerset but Mrs Prettiman in her seaman's clothing; for the fickle Frenchman has transferred to her his romantic attraction to older women who remind him of his mother. Amusing to us this may be, but it infuriates Edmund. Yet as he shouts to the passing but enigmatic sailing-master 'Mr Smiles, can you hear me? We are in love with our mothers', the sarcastic 'we' may have said more (in pre-Freudian terms) than he meant to say, and his anger is fuelled by underlying dread.

In this phase of rising storms, the human barometer has risen sharply; but Edmund then awakes to a literal tempest so violent that disaster is only narrowly averted by Charles's heroism, and Edmund's too. He had sensed before that there might be forces beyond all possibility of human control, but here, now, is actual horrific experience of a world of natural power so great as to dwarf all human perspective. The waves had been monstrous before – but now the ship passes over sheer mountains of black flint, first plunging backwards down a vertical cliff as one of these passes underneath, then hanging with her bow pointing vertically down, before sliding into an abyss with no seeming likelihood of ever coming up again. The remaining sails alternately hang useless as the black cliffs cut off all air, or thunder like cannons as masts emerge from each deep ravine and sails fill explosively. When Edmund claws his way to the quarterdeck it is deserted, with only a body on the deck near the wheel to which Charles Summers perilously clings, struggling to steer by himself. Instinctively Edmund rushes to his side, and together they barely manage to prevent the ship from broaching to, and going down. It is not until later that Edmund realizes how the watch must have deserted their posts, or appreciates why the Captain appears in the waist with a pistol in his hand. Help eventually arrives; but then the terror increases with the intermittent noise of a thump and roar like waves hitting rock ... except that there is no land within thousands of miles. The mountainous waves are rearing still higher, sharpening their incline, and beginning to break and crash over themselves with a noise and a rush of air so powerful as to strike Edmund stone deaf. The oil astern is still offering some protection, but soon a seventh wave beyond all seventh waves lifts flint mountain and calming oil to the sky, and then so crashes over the whole ship that a passing seabird would see only the tops of masts above the welter of foam. Afterwards the oil-mark is fifteen feet up the mainmast, and several more sails are gone. Benét and his men work in the rigging; but has the ship not suffered a mortal blow? Almost miraculously she survives, and the sea gradually goes down, though it will take everyone – crew, soldiers, and emigrants alike – to clean off the pervasive oil so they can get about the decks in safety. Nothing can be done about the dereliction of duty which must be ignored, since the men so out-number the officers. Charles makes the best of it: 'Men, like cables, have each their breaking strain.' But the foremast has held, and even though food and fuel are running short (and the dislike between the two lieutenants remains) the sails are replaced, and cheerfulness returns at the progress they are able to make, after all the *Sturm und Drang.*

This phase of the novel ends, moreover, with two scenes that both recall and invert the twin climaxes of the previous phase. Benét triumphed there, but now suffers a comeuppance. He seems quite indifferent to the renewed fear of death which has come over the ship as, paper in hand, and with an ecstatic smile, he knocks at Mrs Prettiman's door, enters, and closes it behind him. This is too much for the passing Edmund, who rushes (delicious irony) to save the lady's reputation; but once again slips and is flung face-down by a roll of the ship before he can reach the door. He is however in time to see Benét coming out much faster than he went in, and sent flying by the next roll to fetch up with a jolt against the mizzen-mast. The smile has gone; and on the Frenchman's cheek, coming up pink through the sallow skin, Edmund glimpses the mark of a lady's hand. He taps (bravely) on her door to see that she is all right, and seems about to get a lashing too, from a virago very handsome in her rage – when her husband calls next door. Edmund waits apprehensively, as he is told to do. But from the 'dying' man's bedside comes an astonishing sound of laughter. And when she returns and summons him into her cabin after latching the door ajar (to save *his* reputation, she says), he finds instead of fierce contempt a woman divided between amusement, irritation at Benét's presumption ('a man young enough to be – a younger brother, Mr Talbot'), and a clear desire to make things up with his clumsy rival. For, extraordinarily, good *has* come out of evil. Edmund's fall onto Prettiman has acted like a modern osteopath on fracture and dislocation, and (together with the shift into a better position) has largely freed Prettiman from pain and allowed him to turn the corner towards recovery, though he is unlikely to walk properly again. Being a fair-minded woman (who can allow some merit in Benét's verses despite her crossness), she can also see, now, the good intentions behind Edmund's clumsiness. She can even admit to shame mingled with delight at her husband's recovery, for she misses the elevated consciousness that the expectation of death had brought them – and she is astonished that Edmund shows himself capable of understanding such mixed feelings, such conflict between her head and her heart. Suddenly he is someone she can talk to, and for the first time, as she talks, he sees the extent of the Prettimans' idealism. She sees her husband as a Tom Paine for the southern ocean, who meant to lead a band of reformed convicts into the outback, to found a better society in a promised land. Many tensions remain. She suspects Bowles of being a government spy, and even thinks her husband's fall may not have been accidental. (It is Edmund who had promised his powerful godfather to keep an eye on Prettiman and his printing press.) He is still cynical about their dream, and, when she is fair about Benét's contribution to their safety, he remains a partisan of Summers, for which he gets one of her backhanders: 'when your careless assumptions of privilege have been most provoking you have been rendered tolerable by your evident admiration for that worthy man.' He is also annoyed by her tone of moral authority and the way she writes him off as a boy; but his attraction to her is greater than ever, and keeps blocking his impulse to retort that someone who has behaved like a trollop has no right to be critical of him, or 'astonished' when he confesses to being an admirer. Finally annoyance wins when she is satirical about the courteously rounded Johnsonian periods in which he asks to pay his respects to Prettiman; and when she associates his pomposity with his youth. Yet reconciliation with Edmund has clearly accompanied the humbling of Benét.

And this is rapidly followed by a reconciliation with Prettiman himself. As Edmund sits again beside the sleeping man, the change for the better is obvious, though the face is still wasted and lined. Curious to see what Prettiman had been reading, Edmund leans forward to look, exclaims 'Pindar', and the man wakes. 'Had to move, didn't you? Had to speak' ... but this time the irritation is half smiling, and disappears altogether when it becomes clear that Edmund knows the Greek poet and can identify the quotation the sick man had been looking for. Here is a second bond between them. And when Edmund says he has come to 'congratulate you on your recovery and apologize for my part in it' the pomposity produces, not criticism, but a burst of delighted laughter at the unintended absurdity, in which Edmund can join. Cross-examined as to self-seeking reasons for having kept up his Greek, Edmund is about to leave in a huff, but they agree to be gentle with each other, and despite disagreement about whose attachment to his lady is the nobler, and about the social order, Prettiman appears to think that Edmund is a 'specimen' with which something can be done. Tackled as to what universals he knows at first-hand the young man says, 'I know fear. I know a friendship which would exchange gold armour for bronze. Above all, I know love.' It is a good answer, especially when it is extended by St Paul to the Corinthians. Then, asked to read to the sick man from *Candide* he sees how very deeply moved Prettiman is by the account of Eldorado, which fits his rational and Deist credo, and may be the source of his dream of a new kind of community in the Australian outback. Moreover, Edmund is able to point to the connection of the passage to Pindar's Fortunate Isles – and they become friends. There are still irritants. The young man remains sceptical of the older man's dreams, and his butting-in can still be annoying. Moreover, on the subject of the paper Prettiman entrusted to him which must be destroyed now and kept secret forever, Edmund narrowly escapes revealing that he had swallowed its fiction; which would have destroyed the nascent friendship forever. Once more, in being prepared to believe the worst against his own instinct and response, he has poisoned his own mind. But a friendship has indeed begun, and will grow steadily now. Edmund remains uncertain whether, or how far, he can share Prettiman's views; but what he soon becomes sure of is that each encounter leaves him 'with a sense of well-being, of enlightenment, of feeling that ... the universe was great and glorious' and that his adventures of the mind with the Prettimans – for she has a mind as strong and as independent – are a crown of living. He has never met anyone like them. They question all his assumptions, about the Crown, hereditary honours, the dangers of democracy, war, the family; 'indeed there were times when it seemed to me that I threw off my upbringing as a man might let armour drop around him and stand naked, defenceless, but free!' He is not quite defenceless, because each middle watch he can test their ideas against Charles's 'absolute integrity'. But there is a whole new stage now in the education of Edmund Talbot.

Unfortunately, experience of the Prettimans tends to bring out more of Charles's limitations. He has no capacity for general ideas, for 'Always his mind moved at once to the practical'. He dismisses liberty, equality and fraternity on the practical grounds that they have led to the guillotine and Napoleon. He has tested *his* ideas in the fire of his religion; but Edmund cannot share that. Set against the Prettimans Charles seems 'diminished'. For all his goodness, courage, seamanship, and practical care for others, Edmund begins to fear he might not have the intellect, leadership or vision that are needed in a captain. Putting his problem before Prettiman, he sees that he might in friendship have promised more to get Charles promoted than he either can or should perform; and he convicts himself of meanness in flinching from the thought of having a mistaken recommendation traced back to him. Moreover in the new dispute between Charles and Benét, over whether longitude can be calculated from the angle between sun and moon, even though both are moving – a dispute in which Anderson is delightedly on Benét's side – Edmund finds that Prettiman sees the difference between the officers in non-partisan terms. Summers may be all that Edmund thinks, but there are limits to his intellect, and the gap between a man 'who has a natural aptitude for the mathematics and one who has not' is 'absolute – a matter not of quantity but of quality'. Last but far from least, his friend's worry about the danger to Edmund in associating with a Jacobin atheist, who has courted the adulation of people aboard (though saying nothing that could be construed as incitement to rebellion), not only strikes Edmund as old-womanish now – though Summers reminds him of the mutinies at Spithead and the Nore – but reminds him uncomfortably of just the things he himself used to say about Prettiman's 'wicked' ideas, before he got to know him better.

He tries to make Summers understand that Prettiman is no atheist but a passionate almost mystical Platonist and Pantheist, who sees in the universe an Order, a Good and an Absolute Beauty to which it is the longing and destiny of man to conform. Even criminals can lift their heads to the stars and, opening themselves to the Fire of universal Love, be inspired to new humanity. (Hence his dream of Eldorado in Australia, which is more mystical and less rational than Voltaire's.) On moonlit watch with Charles, Edmund had himself felt something of this natural mysticism; but Summers quoting from the Psalms had not moved him as his new friend's fiery idealism and sheer charisma are able to do. Yet when the acid test comes, and Prettiman invites him to come with them, he cannot respond. As soon as he is away from Prettiman's spell, there comes over him again 'the cold, plain awareness which we call common sense'. He is an essentially political animal, his talents are for administration and governance, and for him the price of becoming a disciple of Prettiman would be 'impossibly high' – though he does want to exercise power for the good of his country, and is still chauvinist enough to believe that this would be to the benefit of the world, also.

While, then, it is what he perceives in Prettiman that helps him to see the limitations of Summers, it is the qualities he shares with Summers that make him see why he cannot finally go along with Prettiman. He is beginning to strike a balance, not absolutely, but in terms of his own nature and self-knowledge. At last he is finding himself, and where he truly stands. (Ironically, there will soon be a contest to find which can better plot the ship's position: astronomical mathematics, or practical dead reckoning – discarding one chronometer and averaging the other two. The results are almost identical. There again, Edmund will learn to see on both sides.) However it is not balancing judgement that most comes home to him now, but sadness. There is deep sadness in the silence that intensifies because Edmund can say nothing to the invitation to join the Prettimans, but must feel the full weight of their disappointment. And there is deep sadness too, in the grief of Summers at the knowledge that Edmund is growing away from him, and sadness in Edmund that he cannot deny it.

The two triangular relationships are almost fully plotted now; but the physical universe has something overwhelming to say still on its own behalf, about the insignificance of human beings and their relative attitudes and thoughts about this and that. On a middle watch with Charles which in its edginess contrasts markedly with the glamour of the first moonlit one, Edmund in his optimistic way tries to cheer up his 'sulky' friend by pointing out that they are now standing eastwards at seven knots into the dawn. Only, it isn't the dawn. It is the moon setting in mist and reflected from ice! It is not even a mere iceberg, but a continuous cliff between a hundred and two hundred feet high, and stretching as far as can be seen in both directions. They are heading straight for it. Frantically the whole crew swarm up, and every possible sail is set in the attempt to claw the ship round. The masts bend under the strain and Summers is rebuked by the Captain once more, in public earshot this time, for calling attention to the danger to the mended foremast. Moreover, they had been running before the wind; so when they turn, the sea still runs towards the ice and every wave seems to heave them sideways. As the fog parts for another moment, a huge berg breaks off the cliff, and two ship-sized pieces which must have fallen just before, leap up from the sea like salmon. Helpless, they are filled with 'horror of that neutral and indifferent but overwhelming power with which our own ridiculous wood and canvas had nothing to do ... ' A contrary wave from the falling bergs behind them washes clean over the ship, which loses its headway, while men fight the wheel and screams fill the air. This is the moment for the purser Mr Jones, in immaculate oilskins, to march to his boat with Edmund's firkin in his arms. Clearly he believes it is time to go. Indeed this total crisis is a litmus test of character. The Captain's calm, and his ghastly smile at Edmund when the fog clears again to reveal the sun shining on a mountain towering above the cliff, show his courage and command again, whatever his failures in justice or humanity. When Edmund goes to tell the Prettimans about the situation, he finds a Roman calm in both, and total commitment to each other. Prettiman wants her to leave him, but she will not hear of it. All Brocklebank can think about, however, is wanting to sleep with Celia; whereas Edmund suspects that she has her eye on *him*, in that phenomenon of the relation of deathly fear to randiness. But he is a different man from the youth who pursued Zenobia. He comes out of the crisis quite well, trying to help the others and cheer up the children with no self-conscious *noblesse oblige* any more. Benét is excited by the exhibition of the power of nature, but is also as seamanlike as Anderson and Summers. When the fog retreats to show them within a furlong of the ice, it becomes clear that they are now moving with great speed in parallel to it, in a current from south to north – as indifferent to them as the ice which is apparently stationary, though bergs still break off behind them in regular explosions. Then horror mounts as the cliff seems to rotate around them. They have begun to spin. Falling ice-blocks take off a sail, and then the front half of Jones's boat which vanishes through the rails with him and young Tommy Taylor. Suddenly the ship is going backwards faster than she had ever gone forwards, in a crisis 'beyond seamanship'. It is sheer luck that another huge ice-fall, a few thousand tons, throws them off to starboard. The ice vanishes, and they find themselves in relatively still water, turning gently.

Golding proceeds to enjoy himself, and wind down, by inventing a donnish letter – written some time later by a geographer in Edmund's old Oxbridge College – which suggests by inversion what must have happened. The don boasts (like one I remember, from Golding's old college) of having never been further than London, and seldom so far. But he points out certain facts behind Edmund's 'set of disjunct but gaudy impressions'. The cliff height, if a berg, would imply a depth of at least 700 feet, and though this is possible, such depth, vast length, and immobility rather implies solid land below the ice. Since this geographer has spent his life disproving the possibility of an Antarctic continent, he thinks it must have been a reef – but it may dawn on us that the north–south cliff could be an extremity of Antarctica. (The Antarctic Peninsula was, in fact, first sighted in 1820.)

IV CONCLUSIONS

a) Anticlimactic

With this last demonstration of the fearful powers of Nature, the action of the voyage is over. Edmund disengages himself from a fainting Celia and goes to reassure the Prettimans. The old ship sails on in weather so calm now that the days become a cruise. Pike's children play on the deck, and the night-watch is an enchantment again. Though Edmund's impression of the Prettimans' heroism remains indelible, his common sense gets stronger the nearer they get to Australia. Ideological and temperamental differences widen again, though affection remains. What means most to him, now, is an image that comes through Brocklebank's comic worry over precisely what the surgeon of *Alcyone*, fresh from examining Edmund just before the ships separated, had told him. (Of pipe, trencher, bottle, and couch, *which* had to be 'less', and which 'none'?) Between the lines of the old man's rambling story comes a picture of Marion so agonized over Edmund as to be quite careless of exposing her feelings in public. Alas, only a cobweb-thin tissue of yearnings links them now.

As the voyage draws to its close, the main problem for both diarist and novelist is anticlimax. Edmund thinks of ways in which fiction might pep his diary up, but as historian must content himself with matters of record. Proximity to their destination makes the crew more and more discontented, and shows up the emigrants' extraordinary ignorance of the nature of the continent and its inhabitants; but his own patriotism is reinforced as they move past landmarks whose English names seem a welcome. Then suddenly, on landing, their society disintegrates so quickly that there is no time for proper farewells.

Someone from the Administration arrives to bear Edmund off to his new life. In his first interview with the Deputy Governor he plucks up courage and diplomacy to plead that Summers be given command of the old ship, now to become a permanently moored guardship – only to learn that Anderson and Benét (who had refused the offer) had made the same suggestion, a backhander in their terms, before seeking passage back to England. Still, the name of Edmund's godfather and the mention of Charles's piety to an official as pious as the Governor, turn the scale once more; and Edmund sees his friend overcome by the joy of a long-cherished dream come true. For years he had kept an epaulette hidden away. But there is bathos for Edmund again, and not merely because the thing is crumpled and tarnished by having been so long in store. No: the trouble is that his friend should be *so* pleased to be made harbour master and acting-captain of 'a moored and super-annuated vessel'. It seems to place him, with finality.

Among the letters from England, moreover, comes a new placing for Edmund too, which completes the education of the erstwhile 'Lord' Talbot. In his father's 'usual ill-spelt and indeed ungrammatical hand' comes the news that his godfather is dead, and with him, all hopes of preferment through that powerful influence. From now on he will have to work his own passage. He feels dislocated, and suddenly very lonely. He misses his friends from the voyage, but those he can track down are concerned with their own affairs. In Mrs Prettiman's last words to him the whole voyage seems to shrink in significance. He has had to grow up, but so what? She bids him not to refine upon the meaning of their journey. It was 'not an Odyssey. It is no type, emblem, metaphor of the human condition. It is, or rather it *was*, what it was. A series of events.' That is a blunt definition of 'history' as opposed to 'myth'. And even if, to him – as he stares gloomily across the harbour during the party for the King's birthday – it was at least a personal *bildungsroman*, a sort of 'sorrows of Edmund', he no longer thinks himself as of obvious importance to others and has found, when he revisits the ship, that its locations of past drama are emptied of significance, now.

b) Tragic

But as he gazes across the harbour at it, there seems something odd: a mist forming around the bows where the great anchor hangs motionless. It is not mist. It is smoke. Through a telescope he sees the distant figure of Charles begin to race about in frenzied activity. Suddenly the hole in the deck where the foremast had been turns red, and flames burst through. Charles tries desperately to unmoor the hulk of the old ship from its jetty adjacent to the harbour's powder store. Slowly the burning hulk moves out on the breeze, among the anchored ships, which begin to raise sails frantically to get out of the way, as Charles beats on the old ship's bell. Then he dives into the lobby and is gone. A frozen Edmund suddenly realizes what deadly danger his friend is in, and begins to run from the Residency all the way down to the quay with its godowns, where he leaps into a ship's boat and begins to row unhandily. As the blazing hulk runs aground he is able to catch and board her. He wraps his neckcloth round his face and begins to search, but Charles is nowhere to be found. Then there is a fearful explosion almost under his feet, the whole ship opens, and a tower of flame envelops what is left of the mainmast. Edmund's hair is on fire as a voice bellows to him to jump – and Cumbershum lifts him from the water by the collar into a boat. He is badly burned, and

Charles is dead. No trace of him is ever found. At his funeral he is praised, and so is Edmund; but this cannot allay grief, or a final bleak proportioning. 'It was in the driest and emptiest of interior illuminations that I saw myself at last for what I was, and what were my scanty resources. I got up, as it were, and stood erect on naked feet. The future was hard and full. Nevertheless I girded myself and walked towards it.'

This is the final event in the ship's last voyage – and also, it would seem, in the *bildungsroman* of the sorrows of Edmund and how he grew to be a man. Golding's novel might well have ended here. But what sort of story is it, 'at last'? And what is it for a man to see himself and his 'resources' for what they are? It has clearly been a 'history', a sequence of events, with a cast of characters we have got to know in close encounter, with a mature sense now of their resemblances, differences, capacities. But will 'history', either of a group or a person, quite suffice for our final sense of human being?

For Mrs Prettiman was surely wrong? The book is not only a Pindaric of human courage, cunning and endurance. It *is* an Odyssey, fusing these with a 'mythos' of the human condition. Homer's sea story had at its heart both man's heroism, and his blindness to and indeed defiance of the powers in nature that the Greeks called gods – and so does Golding's. Far back, Summers had warned that victories over nature always have to be paid for. Without playing down its human drama, the most powerful and lasting impression the novel makes is its recreation of elemental grandeurs: the realizations of the sheer superhuman power of wind, water, ice, and fire: the fire down below which Benét causes, but Charles pays for with his life. It is against these that human friendship, rivalry, cunning, courage and justice must be seen in their final proportion.

c) Fortunate

The novel might well have ended with Edmund's response to the death of his friend: a tragedy. But, instead, there is another, happy ending, making Edmund's own story over into comedy. Insofar as the book is fictively 'historical' Golding had the right to do this. The conclusion of a series of events can go one way or the other as chance and fortune decide, and in fiction the novelist chooses those.

So *Alcyone* arrives in Sydney with the news of Bonaparte's escape from Elba, but bearing also Marion. With her not only happiness but humour and good-humour return. Golding had clearly grown fond of the seventeen-year-old girl and the opportunity she gave him both for social comedy, and for the other kind which is a function of intelligence and of a sense of proportion that can rise above circumstance and ego. No reader of the last chapters would wish them otherwise, for they are both funny and charming. Some readers, however, may feel that their undoubted arbitrariness – for Edmund's fortunes are also restored – marks again the contrast with Golding's major novels, where the vision seems so wholly organic that nothing could be other than it is. (Edmund's mother uses a bequest from his godfather to buy him into Parliament via a rotten borough, though he will join the reformers to get rid of such things.) The distinction seems valid. Yet there may also be a question of proportion: for the *Odyssey* ended happily, after all, with the restoration of love and a home-coming, after suffering. Maybe it is in the assertion of love and friendship, as well as courage, cunning and endurance *against* the superhuman powers in the world, that the true human proportion is to be found?

d) A dream – or vision?

One last twist remains, however. By way of postscript, an ageing Edmund receives a letter from Oldmeadow, who has settled in Australia on a ranch bigger than Cornwall. Having read the letter's last glimpse of the Prettimans riding away into the outback, Edmund goes for a walk on which his mind revisits all his old shipboard acquaintances, seemingly with not much emotion. But that night he has a dream; and it is with this that Golding chooses finally to conclude. Seemingly buried to his neck in the soil of Australia, the dreamer watches from ground-level as the Prettiman expedition rides past a few yards away, and on into the distance, chattering and laughing.

You would have thought from the excitement and the honey light, from the crowd that followed them, from the laughter and, yes, the singing, you would have thought that they were going to some great festival of joy, though where in the desert around them it might be found there was no telling. They were so happy! They were so excited!

Edmund does not wish it to be more than a dream, 'because if it was, then I have to start all over again in a universe quite unlike the one which is my sanity and security'. He wakes up trembling, but soon comes to himself with the thought that 'we could not all do that sort of thing. The world must be served, must it not?' Only, Mrs Prettiman had said that he 'could' come too.... But he never 'countenanced the idea'.

As always, Golding leaves space for his readers to judge for themselves. Must we go deeper than the setting of human love, friendship, intelligence and endurance against the apparently inhuman and superhuman indifference to us of the powers of nature? Does the deepest truth finally lie with Colley's and the Prettimans' *joy*? – that there is (as Coleridge thought, and lamented its loss in 'Dejection') a light, a warmth, a luminosity, a fire both down below and above, within man and suffusing the whole physical universe, that makes all things not two sides of a proportion, but one and the same? Or is that just a dream?

13

THE DOUBLE TONGUE

(1995)

I

In what turned out to be his last book, Golding is still trying new things. For the first time he writes from a woman's point of view. Also for the first time his love of Greece, and of its literature which he taught himself to read in the original, gets directly into his fiction. We find ourselves in first-century BC Aetolia, about where the port of Itea now is, across the gulf from Corinth and on the road to Delphi.

But at the beginning we have nothing to do with place, time, or point of view. Our protagonist's earliest memory has no situation and no sense of self; and it is wordless, though we can only guess at it through her words. 'Blazing light and warmth, undifferentiated and experiencing themselves': this was the child's experience of a primary reality, intensely unified and joyous, 'a kind of naked being' beyond place or time or separate ego.

Later – but soon enough – comes the baby's first sense of separation, difference, transgression. Incontinence brings indulgent laughter from mother and nurse but also a knowledge of 'reprimand', as instinctive (albeit wordless) as the baby's knowledge of anger, pain, and love. Later, the girl-child's curiosity about 'the modest slit' between her legs, which will define her throughout her life, brings punishment, still indulgent, but with it the first sense of guilt. A little later still, watching the boy next door killing ants with a primitive reed flame-thrower, comes a first fascination with power and cruelty.

So far, she might be any girl; but the next memories set this one more and more apart, however ambiguously to the narrator, clearly a much older self. She had had no idea of the ants as living things, but confronted with the death agony of fishes being burnt alive in a frying pan, many girls might have uttered her cry of horror and protest. What makes this one different is the cook's report that when he hastened to obey her and throw the fish back in the tank, they swam away unharmed. The incident is recounted, however, with a good deal of adult scepticism. Won't house slaves believe anything, no matter how unlikely? Had Zoileus perhaps thrown the fish away or hidden them, before being forced to stick to his story once it had gone from housekeeper to master and mistress? But a reputation for oddness begins to attach itself to Arieka; the 'little barbarian' whose name we hear for the first time hereabouts, with its suggestion of difference perceived from the cradle.

Her family are well to do; but she is a disappointment to them. It would seem that from the very first they had seen her as ugly, sallow and somehow other. After the episode of the fish, her conformist mother reprimands her for having drawn attention to herself as no well-bred female should do; but this keeps happening. Her elder brother amuses himself by drawing letters in the dirt for her and – before leaving to take care of family business in Sicily – encourages her to read a simplified version of the *Odyssey*. But when a visiting bard performs an episode of Homer she becomes 'exalted' and cries out, as no girl should do, with a real passion for the poem. Another oddness occurs when her touch seems to heal a sick child thrust into her arms by its anguished mother. Once again the story is partially (mostly?) discounted by the older narrating self. 'I do not think I am a healer and I am the one to know, surely?' Yet she knows also that 'We are wrapped in mysteries.' For all her scepticism a residue of the mysterious remains; and as she looks back at the girl she was, just before her first menstruation, she thinks that there can be something strange about girls at that stage of their lives. Sometimes the unattractive ones, god-blighted, unlikely ever to be loved or married, may acquire an odd compensating and furtive power to bring about their wishes. She hedges this around with so many reservations that the possibility almost vanishes. The power, if power it be, is 'furtive and dishonest, knows how to hide, how to claim, how to disguise, avoid, speak double like the snake or not at all'. It can never be proved; and there could be other explanations. After her harsh father has taken away her favourite doll and disciplined her – the first of many times – by solitary confinement on bread and water, she goes straight to where the doll had been hidden; but that might be merely instinctive knowledge of her oppressors and where they would hide it. However, one of her most embarrassing moments resists that kind of explanation. Full of pity for the treadmill donkey Pittacus in his agony of sexual frustration (her father's mare is on heat) and his enormous and painful erection, she feels consolation and love go out to him 'through my aching head and suddenly reeling mind', and he is immediately quietened. But there is a hoot of mocking laughter from the boy next door: 'He fancies you!' And the explanation of her physical condition comes with the first tap of blood on her sandal, and the rapid fleeing of her father from her state of uncleanness.

By now the story has developed a feminist dimension as well as its possibly mysterious one. Arieka is not only an unloved child, but also part of an oppressed sex, and her unusualness has to do also with her clear recognition of this fact, even as a girl. She is the daughter of a provincial aristocrat and rich landowner with a share in the ferry between Corinth and Delphi and business interests in Sicily. He is a Phocian, a member of the powerful and greedy Aetolian clan who in 334 BC had annexed Delphi and helped themselves to its vast treasures, on the pretext of needing these to fight 'just' wars to protect it. (Arieka's deadpan account of this, echoes what the child is told: exposing her family's clannishness and materialism, though there are further reasons for irony which have not yet become apparent.) There is little of Greek *civilization* about this father or his household. He seems interested only in money, and a patriarchal society allows him to be a domestic tyrant lacking affection and imagination. His wife is wholly submissive, making no protest at his harsh treatment of their daughter – in fact apparently sharing his belief that girls should be seen and heard as seldom as possible. He clearly regards the girl as mostly a nuisance, requiring periodic ritual withdrawal, and sure to be costly because of the large dowry that will be needed to take her off his hands, since she has status, but no beauty. The indictment is all the sharper because he is not a particularly cruel character for his times. Slaves are not beaten in their house, though when the boy Leptides, son and heir to the smaller estate nearby, beats the naked bottom of his pretend-slave in a childish 'game', he clearly believes that this is what masters are allowed to do. Pure gender injustice follows, for after her innocent confession Arieka is blamed and punished too, since her father holds that in such cases the female is always somehow at fault. If, then, there is irony (for us) every time Arieka addresses him as 'Honoured Father' it is to be placed at the door of a society which grades daughters and wives only a degree or two higher than the household slaves. They may not dine on couches with the men, are not educated, are not free to speak, act or travel as men are, but are supposed to remain inferior creatures chained to domesticity.

There seems to be only one back-handed advantage in being a woman, in Arieka's view. With the periodic withdrawal into untouchability comes a licence to think 'untouchable' thoughts – and our narrator confesses that as an old woman, in her eighties we now learn, she is still doing so.

One last episode with Leptides confirms and completes the estrangement from her family. At fifteen she is marriageable in society's eyes, and the sexual interest (and social envy) that were visible in the childhood 'game' bring a proposal from Leptides' family. Her parents' authority is absolute, and her father is only too anxious to get rid of her in any reasonably advantageous alliance; but the proposal fills Arieka with such horror that she tries to run away, disguised as a boy. The old woman recognizes now that this was really an anguished appeal rather than a serious attempt to reach her brother in Sicily, but it is both farcical and disastrous. The donkey Pittacus is difficult to steer because he is so used to going in circles. Suddenly she finds herself in the midst of a hunt, is bucked off, attacked by the hounds, and exposed in a state of near nakedness to Leptides and all his companions, before being rescued by a semi-stranger who flinches from her in some distaste. Leptides withdraws his proposal, to the fury of Arieka's mother who can see only the social humiliation: to be refused by such as Leptides! She seems to care nothing for her daughter's distress. Once again Arieka finds herself in solitary confinement, and the deepest disgrace of her life. Nobody will want to marry her now, even for money, after such exposure. She had shown herself a hopeful child despite her physical unattractiveness. She is brave, caring, imaginative, and intelligent, though she accuses herself of being muddled because her intelligence is not the rational and orderly, still less the philosophically educated kind, but rather a capacity for comparison, inference from experience, and imagination. Even as a child, she has also a religious temperament, an openness to Hamlet's belief that there are more things in heaven and earth than reason can account for. She has not been aware of more than a child's conventional belief in the gods that grown-ups say they believe in. But the worst of the deep depression she falls into now is the sense that even the gods are ashamed of, and will have nothing more to do with her. In her misery she has withdrawn deeper and deeper within, until only the gods remain, and she seems to see them turning their backs. Only then does she realize how stricken with grief she is to have lost them. Even the family Herm who marks the boundary of their land seems glad to be leaving. Then there is only a black void in which there is nothing but herself, and an understanding of how death might come as a relief.

But she is a resilient girl, and the demands of the body must be satisfied even when the soul seems dead. She gets up, relieves herself, begins to live again.

And at once comes an inexplicable delivery. The man who rescued her from the dogs is Ionides Peisistratides, a priest and apparently an important man in Delphi; and he comes now with an offer to take her there, to serve one of the Pythias who give voice to the world-famous oracle. There is the unusual experience, for Arieka, of being treated with kindness and consideration as he explains the arrangement, softening her father's angry interjections. She will be adopted by the Temple Foundation to whom her dowry will go (as would happen in more modern times in the making of a nun), and Ionides will become her guardian. Her mother and father clearly resent not only the expense, but also a valuation of Arieka so different from theirs, and do their best to denigrate what it will mean. Finally her father declares roundly, 'We don't want the girl any more.' But before Ionides completes a rebuke, Arieka at last finds her voice to make a far more telling one, spontaneously. For her, the prospect of leaving makes this a *wonderful* day.

II

So she leaves a home she realizes, now, that she hates and would put a curse on if she dared. Her father barely raises his eyes from his accounts, though he is amused by her ignorance of what the gold pieces are that he gives her for her dowry. Her mother coldly tells her to be 'good' (i.e. by social standards), if she can. At the last moment however Arieka stops the carriage and runs to throw her arms round the Herm, in an unloved child's paroxysm of grief and frustrated affection. By contrast, as the procession and its guards wind up the spectacular mountain road to Delphi, Ionides chatters away in very friendly fashion, all the more loquacious because she is so silent – and revealing more to us perhaps than to the girl who watches his adam's apple moving up and down but doesn't yet register, in her inexperience, some of the implications of what he says. It becomes clear to us that he is homosexual, and though a priest, not at all a religious man. Arieka will not be sweeping floors, but has been chosen as handmaiden to the junior Pythia, because of those mysterious powers as a child. But his view of these is very ambiguous. They may well, as she protests, have been 'mistakes', the more plausible (he thinks) because of her virginity and ignorance – but these will be just as useful now, as will her belief in the gods. When she flinches from the idea of having anything to do with 'that place', it may be because she is truly religious, or merely frightened, a distinction without a difference to Ionides. (Or is it that, as he admits, he will sacrifice anything for a dramatic touch, a quip, a witty paradox? And what is truth, anyway?) The only things which seem genuinely to move him are a passionate hatred of the Romans and a longing to revive the past glories of Hellas, but these strike no answering chord in Arieka who thinks his intensity about them almost deranged.

They arrive in Delphi; and the girl's essentially religious and imaginative temperament comes through the old woman's scepticism as she recalls her first impression of it: 'fresh and beautiful and deadly', the 'gods hiding everywhere but allowing themselves to be sensed, as if at any moment with a flash of light and a clap of thunder one would start into presence and purpose and power'. (How much does this differ, however, from the superstition of the mob which surrounds them, and the violent hysteria when she, in her innocence, touches a string of beads held out to her?) There follow wonderful descriptions of the Temple with is colossal statue of Apollo; and when the shutters of her new quarters are thrown back, of buildings in white stone that seemed to lift and tumble up, up rather than down, as if they were escaping the earth and flying like a storm of birds into the sky. And as my eyes became accustomed and distance deepened, I saw how the separate buildings were picked out, adorned as a woman by jewels with delicate patterns of colour which danced round architraves and capitals or glowed in the shade of colonnades. Then, beyond all and as if it held up the deep blue sky, was the precipitous wall of the Shining Rocks.

There are the wonders of her new set of apartments, and the still greater wonder of the book-room, containing all of Greek literature, even the earliest text of her beloved Homer, and Sappho, and Euripides, and ... and ... Ionides encourages her to read and read, especially the poetry, until hexameters might come almost as naturally as speech. It is hardly surprising, given the deprivations of her childhood, that she bursts into tears – though whether in sadness or joy, anxiety or fulfilment, she cannot tell.

III

When she is taken to meet the two Pythias, the spiritual contrast between them measures the distance between a 'modern' scepticism (and self-centredness) and a dying faith. The younger of the two is not only fat, indolent and painted, but clearly cynical about her supposed function. Can the girl sing? A few notes would be useful, though so would grunts and the occasional wail. When Arieka fails to understand, she calls her a 'nestling', with contempt rather than tenderness, before turning away, bored. In utter contrast the elder Pythia sits white-robed in darkness, blind, her voice a thread of sound, her face (when the shutters are opened) stripped down to the bone in extreme old age. But as she feels the girl's face her fingers are perceptive. Arieka's childhood has shown that there is a good deal of boy in her as well as girl. The old priestess also feels for her, worrying that her mouth will prove too small, and that the god will tear it. This Pythia has absolute conviction, drawn from her own experience, of the reality of Apollo and his power. (We learn later that the god 'raped' her.) Moreover she believes that his power will show itself truly again, though it would seem that Ionides is sceptical. Finally, now, Arieka learns what she is intended to become: a Pythia herself, to voice the god. She is overcome by hysteria, struggling to get away in a paroxysm of fear. But when she comes to herself the old woman tells her that there is no escape: she is already in the god's hands, and must learn to be strong enough as well as chaste. Perhaps Apollo will be merciful and not tear her mouth or take away her sight. Ionides will teach her, and he knows everything – though the Pythia cannot see round him and is unsure what he wants. But he will prepare Arieka as a good workman readies his tools, perhaps even preserving the innocence, goodness and affection the girl confirms as she fails to understand what the old woman means by a liking for 'simple country flowers'. (But does that mean keeping Arieka 'credulous'? In her new status she will have to lose her name, but is she likely to lose her questioning mind?)

As she dines with Ionides, an equal now – the first time she has ever eaten with a man, on a couch – she finds out who he actually is. He is the Chief Priest of Apollo and the most important man in Delphi. He wants the oracle to return to its original state of purity and sanctity; and Arieka in her innocence and gratitude says she 'would do anything, anything in the world to help you'. But if Apollo won't bring this about himself, there is a strong hint that his High Priest is quite ready to ventriloquize and manipulate instead. For there is great need of the god to hearten and advise against the Romans; and even though Ionides doesn't seem actually to believe in him, or the other gods, he certainly believes in that need. He has seen the destructive power of a legion in action. Our narrator, looking back, is still unsure whether he was serious about his disbelief, or merely wanting to shock, for he sang different tunes on different days. The girl is certainly shocked, but having never heard anybody express such atheism before, she cannot actually believe it – especially since he immediately admits that he is incurably flippant. Perhaps, he suggests, the awkward question of belief is not what is most important, for too much Socratic questioning can make it impossible to do what otherwise comes naturally. What is important is that if the god does exist and chooses to speak, the instrument should be ready; and also that the questions should become worthier of a god's answers than the trivia to which the oracle has had to descend in modern days. 'Of course' the gods are real, why make a meal of it?

So, paradoxically, Arieka becomes free in her commitment and enclosure, and is happy for the first time in her life. She is never alone with any man except Ionides, but she is allowed, heavily veiled, to see Delphi in his company; and allowed also to get rid of her pert and too-pretty maid from home, who is ill-behaved and reminds her every day of her own ugliness. She is trained now to project her voice, to write as well as read, and to communicate in body-language. She reads deeply and widely and gradually learns to speak in hexameters. Soon Ionides trusts her enough to show her the 'columbarium': the secret way that he communicates by carrier pigeon with other oracles, and so gains news from all over the civilized world. (But surely, asks Arieka, the god has no need to be told what is happening? – a good question, though Ionides turns it aside by quipping that Apollo does apparently need to know what the question is before he can give an answer, and so may need reminding of other things.) It seems that she may not have to become a Pythia till she is thirty; much younger than usual, but the need for reform is urgent, given the way that Delphi has been despoiled by Arieka's ancestors and appears degraded now. These days it seems to depend as much on tourism as religion. Arieka sees her first Roman,* and sees also how on both sides superficial politeness covers real dislike. Finally she pays her first visit to the Cave where Apollo fought and killed the great Earth-Python and created his own oracle, with a priestess as Pythia.

The low entry hall and side rooms, cut into the mountain, have been robbed of the treasures that used to fill them, and the gloom does nothing to evoke the sun-god, but it is nonetheless a place of terror to Arieka who can't stop her teeth from chattering, and tries to make another run for it. Ionides resorts to emotional blackmail. If she leaves she will have to return to her parents. So, gradually, she controls her fear, mixed with grief now for women who seem mere instruments for the purposes of gods and men. She even manages a laugh when told that she is brave; but there is also the first hint of self-pity as she imagines herself writhing and crying out in the god's power on the tripod: the fate of 'little Arieka whom nobody loved'. She is not much consoled by being told that the old Pythia's fear that her mouth will be torn was 'figurative'. But at

---

* This is one of the places where the work shows itself to be unfinished. Golding in his final revision would have changed this man's name from Metellus, needing that for later.

least she doesn't have to go down yet, through the dark opening, into the place of the tripod and the brazier and the crack in the rock – and the presence of the god.

Time passes. The First Lady dies of extreme age, and Arieka becomes Second-Lady-in-waiting. Though she is not yet a Pythia, gifts begin to arrive for her, and Ion explains both the prudential reasoning behind these, and how they can be turned into money like those that come to him. But Arieka's concerns remain very different. What she wants from life is what she has never had: the sense of 'home', and people to love her, and reconciliation with the gods who had deserted her. To cheer her up, Ion tells the story of Moses whose God would not let him see his face, but did allow him to hide in a crack in the rock and glimpse his back-parts. So Moses was not deserted; and maybe, Ion jokes, it will be the same for Arieka sitting above the crack in the rock of Delphi. When she protests at his flippancy, he insists that he and she can say what they like, 'and if anyone complains we can say we are inspired'. Their beliefs and sensibilities remain deeply divided – but soon the time for the Questions will arrive, to test the sceptic and the religious one alike.

IV

Unexpectedly, the Second Lady dies also, two weeks before the spring solstice. There is only one Pythia now, and Delphi hums with gossip about her and her relations with the gods (or demons, for the superstitious believe as easily in one as the other). Even in Athens there is a feeling that Apollo must have some purpose with the new young Pythia, by disposing of two predecessors in such rapid succession. Indeed, as Ion jubilantly announces, the Athenians are coming with a grand procession, a 'pomp'. The Archon will ask the first Question himself, and there will even be a performance of the play that Euripides set in Delphi, the *Ion*. But Arieka retreats into the book-room beside Perseus, the learned slave librarian with whom she has made friends, if nothing like as closely as with *her* Ion. That relationship indeed seems to her to have become almost as intimate as a marriage, though it remains wholly unsexual, given his distaste for her female body. But in his excitement, now, the gap between their beliefs becomes even more visible. While she is worrying about the source of things, reading about how the worship of Apollo replaced an older matriarchal earth-religion; he is seeking advance notice of the Archon's Question, and expects to find it out. He lets slip boastfully that he knew about the pomp before most Athenians, since it was decided only that morning. A penny drops: the purpose of the columbarium is not just gathering news but an exchange of intelligence between oracles, helping them to formulate answers in advance. Arieka is outraged at the deception of all who expect to hear the word of the god.*

V

As the time rushes nearer, Ion tries to coach her. There will be two questions from Athens, one much more important than the other; and two Romans asking which of them will rise the higher. He still has no sense of how she feels as he concocts answers. For Arieka, the gods are no less real for having turned their backs on her, and she fears that they will punish blasphemy. Ion hastily retreats. He will have no control over her when the time comes, and would be only too glad if the god did speak. The oracle must not, of course, be *rigged*, but if the god chooses to be silent, answers there must be or there will be no more oracle. He convinces himself as he goes along; but the bobbing of his adam's apple and the sad smile begin to reveal him more sharply. He is a man who lives by words – but he knows this, and part of him wishes sadly that there were more to the world than his reason sees.

We now know that Golding's novel poses the same challenge as the *Ion* of Euripides. What credit can a 'modern' and rational person give to a god or gods and their reputed dealings with mankind? As Arieka rides in the ancient ceremonial carriage, and enters the darkness of the cave, that is the real Question at issue.

The first day of the Oracle is one of the great scenes in Golding. After shawms have sounded, Ion guides Arieka down the worn steps in pitch darkness, the noise of the crowd outside sounding like surf on a beach. She can see nothing, even when in her terror

---

* Here a passage of MS is missing, and this very short section might well have been expanded in revision.

she tears off her heavy veil. Then she begins to shudder, deep into the bone, and in a convulsion falls to her knees; while from her mouth come deep yelled greetings between Apollo and Bacchus (the guardian of the shrine in the winter months), followed by 'rolling, rollicking laughter' that goes on and on, pumping out of her chest. She begs for mercy through a bloodied mouth, and in the glow of the brazier sees the 'skeletal otherworldly' form of the tripod. She crawls to it painfully, and feels herself forced to climb into the seat, sometimes wailing, but with no escape. For, she feels, it is the god who forces her and twists her again convulsively there. It is as much a rape as the sexual kind, as she defiantly alleges, shouting in her own voice 'One mouth or the other', before the rollicking laughter begins again. She says nothing when Ion first asks and then answers the question about the prospects of Julius Caesar and Metellus Cimber.* It is not Apollo's answer, nor has she given it – but what have the gods to do with such trivia?

Now she remembers that she should sprinkle laurel dust on the coals – but suddenly sees also that the safety bar, meant to protect a Pythia overcome by the fumes from falling with her face in the brazier, has not been fastened. Is that also a cruel divine joke, since (as her father said) her face would never be her fortune? But as she is seized by yet another convulsion and makes the sign to ward off her own blasphemy, she drops a whole handful of the dust into the brazier – and amid clouds of smoke she blacks out. Later she hears from Ion that dark figures appeared from the side-rooms to carry her away to her own chamber.

Ion's account is only what a sceptic would have heard: 'your two shouts first and that odd saying', then some sniggers from the crowd, and then some 'mouthing' from her. He recognized no gods – and is chiefly worried that the onlookers, who had enjoyed themselves, might have found the whole thing comic rather than holy. All he remembers from her mouthing was a disturbing mutter about 'lies and lees'. But he is scared in other ways. Young Caesar is asking too many questions, and the big Athenian Question is yet to come. Moreover the Athenians have insisted

---

* North's *Plutarch* makes 'Metellus Cimber' a leading conspirator in the assassination of Caesar, and Shakespeare follows him. A Metellus Celer became consul in 60 BC, the year after Caesar.

that the Pythia (and therefore he) must know nothing about it – and 'we can't play about with that one'. But Arieka is not playing. For her, the gods were *there* in the cave, and she deeply dislikes his contrivings. For him, only a faint chance remains that she – so 'highly recommended' – just might get an honest answer out of the god. Both are living on a knife's edge, differently.

The second day is a different kind of test: a number of questions from agonized individuals, little people, but about matters of life and death for them. Arieka compares herself to the sacrificial she-goat, a female made to 'consent' to male enforcement; but somehow she knows that the god will deal with her gently today, and in her compassion for those who suffer, she does consent. This time she calmly takes in the grotto, the creatures cast in the metal of the tripod, the curtain that hangs at the back (and presumably hides the cleft in the rock where the serpent lived and the vapour arose), and the signs of her ancestors' pillage. 'Here I am,' she says, 'ready and willing. Do your will. Are you there?' There is no reply, but in the silence she this time trickles laurel dust onto the brazier, again and again – and wakes up in her own bed. She discovers from Ion that she had spoken things beyond her knowledge: the name of a poor woman's dead daughter, and presumably a satisfactory answer to the disguised Athenian Question slipped in among the others, about which dictator to ally themselves with in order to ensure free passage for their corn through the Hellespont. Ion doesn't believe she was 'asleep'. Instead, he talks of the Second Day as if it were a theatrical performance, assumes that she put on her strangely 'numinous' voice, and makes a joke of her fear of blasphemy. She believes she understands him now:

Most of his mind was a kind of shell of opinions and brittle quips. Inside the shell was a mind made up and closed to change because it was really a prime tenet of his that he *knew*. In the shell itself were contrary opinions which he produced together with their opposites so that he was secure from having to believe in any of them. I began to see how the oracle, like Ionides, was surrounded by contradictions. Whatever lay at the centre of the oracle, that mysterious heart of it which spoke so often with riddling words so that only a suppliant who was both wise and humble could choose the right interpretation, I believed, no, I felt I *knew* there was something connected with the hidden centre of existence that lay there and sometimes spoke.

So Arieka's experience over the two days seems to suggest – like Euripides' play, for all its probings – that the gods do exist, and do care about human beings. But the third day of Questions is disillusioning. She is taken to the grotto in an ordinary cart through pouring rain, and she slips and falls on the wet stone steps. In her irritation she has sharp words with Ion. There is no crowd and only two questions to which the god has nothing to say. As Ion 'obsequiously' answers the one from a rich Corinthian, Arieka examines the curtain which shows, in archaic style, Apollo killing the great earth-snake. But is there not still something snakily double-tongued and riddling about his oracle too? And is it not curious that the hexameters recorded as the voice of the God of Poetry should so often have been inferior verse? Should we then think of the divine as always having to come through the corruption of human utterance; stained as it were by the blood of the Pythia's mouth? Or, are Ion and the oracle he is so anxious to preserve simply fraudulent? Or again, is he (as he himself claims) the one honest man who knows what he is doing? Or, yet again, can we see and live on two levels as he urges Arieka to do, with what seems a curiously modern sense of ambivalence?

Afterwards he insists that they propitiate the Corinthian who is displeased at having been relegated to the Third Day, by asking him to dinner along with a local landowner and his wife. The talk turns to secular affairs: the growing banditry in the countryside, the possibility of appealing to the Roman governor, and why the Romans should have become so powerful. Ion holds that it is fear of their neighbours that has driven them in ever widening circles of conquest and control. The man from Corinth, a Phoenician, believes that it is because they know how to combine: a hit against the Greeks. Yet is there not among younger Greeks, asks Ionides (revealing a little of his heart) the beginnings of a pan-Hellenic movement? His guests don't seem to think much of its chances, however, since most people prefer strong government and security to 'freedom', and are loyal to their city rather than any larger grouping.

VI

So Arieka embarks upon her career. With familiarity her fear goes, though a residue of awe remains. Apollo, having broken her in, seems to 'ride' her gently (when he does). She even begins to speak in hexameters. Ion stops editing her answers; and the reputation of the oracle grows again. So does her wealth. (In search of a big enough receptacle, they open an ancient chest and find Cretan Linear-B tablets which record the treasure given by Croesus more than six hundred years before.) With her success, the High Priest himself begins to change, seeming to admit now and then that there might be something in religion, and that the world might after all be stranger than people think. But gradually, though she keeps sacrificing to Apollo, Arieka's own belief becomes less and less secure as her sense of the god's presence fades. She recalls how, even as she watched the *Ion* that first spring festival, she had felt she understood the play better than Euripides. She doesn't specify, but hers would certainly be a feminist point. She would see it as Creusa's play; and no man could understand as Arieka does what it feels like to be raped by Apollo, or how it feels to have been then deserted, not just once but twice. The tension in the playwright between faith and scepticism could not be as strong as hers, who (as she writes now) has had physical experience she was sure was of the god, but has felt her belief and relationship steadily fade. Nobody could understand better, from the inside, the questions that arise from Euripides's portrayal of a riddling oracle; and amoral gods who, even if they ultimately mean well, desert us for decades and when they reappear, either don't speak the whole truth, or know less than they pretend. She remembers how her Ion, in his really cynical days – having gone even further in 'modern' scepticism and ambiguity than his Euripidean namesake – used to maintain that the old myths embody not religious but human (we would say psychological) truths. But what is the psychological truth in Arieka's case?

She broods on the illogic or superstition of people who somehow manage to separate the continuous idea of the Pythia from any individual woman or women. But what does she believe about herself? Was she ever really possessed? Or can an experience like hers in the Cave that first day be put down to hysteria, her terror having translated itself into the very experience of which she was terrified? But that theory could easily be reversed. 'Perhaps', she thinks, 'the truth of life and living lies in the strange things women' – saints or sibyls – 'do and say when they are hysterical.'

Gradually, over the passage of time, she reaches 'a dry and dusty place where unease and doubts have blown about until that wind drops and they fall in unswept heaps'. In that arid spiritual desert, if she cried out with Creusa 'O my soul, how shall I keep silent', out of their shared experience – 'He tore her. He tore my entrails and bloodied my mouth' – would there be anyone to hear her?

Ion wants her to begin entertaining guests in the off-season, to help him 'as a pigeon fancier'. She objects that none of her utterances has depended on inside information. If the oracles lack 'a certain universality' (i.e. politically), she insists that the fault lies with the questioners not Apollo. But, asks the new half-believer, cannot she compel the god, as the lovesick Simaetha in Theocritus – cruel comparison – tried to magic her lost lover back? But she cannot. Apollo may have deserted her again, but somehow she cannot treat him disrespectfully.

VII

Yet as she tries to think like a philosopher – is it we who create the gods in our need, as has apparently happened in Egypt where three older gods have been combined as 'Serapis'? – she sees her childhood experience differently. Had she *made* the gods turn their backs, so they shouldn't see her shame? Would that not imply that, even as a child, she hadn't much use for the Olympians? In sheer horror she flinches from the void again, recognizing its atheism now; and rapidly tries to talk herself back into belief. She cannot ask for help from Ion, even though he is no longer as cynical as he used to be, for she must not risk disturbing 'his tired, his ageing approach to the mystery'. And how can she ask the oracle? That would certainly be one paradox too many! It has to be the void, then; and the hexameters which come from some kind of inspiration, whether poetic or divine; and the fact that now and then the oracle has seemed to work, whether by good luck, or some flexibility of interpretation, or some of Ion's intelligence-gathering.

Moreover, as Arieka's belief has faded, so too has the flow of presents. They discover that the roof of the Pythion is also falling to pieces and will have to be replaced as a matter of great urgency, and huge cost. Though a famous architect offers his services free – despite being an atheist – because of his respect for an ancient building that dates from Mycenaean times, there is no way the Temple Foundation can meet such a cost. There will have to be a begging expedition, and Arieka, to Ion's consternation, insists on going too. The High Priest seeks advice from Athens and finds, rather to his surprise, that the Athenians are intrigued by the idea of meeting her. So they set out, leaving behind young Menesthia, who may or may not become a Pythia, to deal with any questions that may come for the god Dionysus while he is on duty in the winter months.

Arieka travels, veiled, in the Pythian carriage. She sees for the first time how it must date – albeit with many reconstructions – from before Apollo's conquest, since he does not appear in its paintings but only the Python and 'our fat Mother Gaia' the Earth-goddess. In her old home for a night, before crossing the ferry to Corinth, Arieka gains a modicum of satisfaction at her sister-in-law's fear of her. The house of their Phoenician friend is guarded by Romans, for after they burned the city it has had 'a rowdy element' hostile to them and their friends. (To Arieka's shock, Ion maintains that these rowdies are the salt of the earth, a sign of things to come.) Then they continue, accompanied by an Athenian 'pomp', to Eleusis and on to Athens.

Golding is not however interested in travelogue, even though Arieka is housed in the Parthenon. She refuses to say anything about the mysteries of Eleusis. (She does however make a typically shrewd point about the disproportion of the colossal statue of Athene when viewed from ground-level.) Rather, Golding's interest lies in placing Arieka's problem of dwindling faith in the context of Athens in the first century BC, when it was the centre of culture and intellect for Greeks and Romans alike. Here is the ultimate in progressive modern sophistication: a town that is like one great university full of professors and intellectuals, and whose society seems thoroughly liberated. The ladies dine on couches with the men, and the conversation is daring. A lady of pleasure, bursting with curiosity, dares to ask the Pythia 'what it was like';

from which an 'Athenian' conversation springs, a 'cross-talk of allusions and witty remarks' in which the gods, too, 'were bandied about'. On one occasion Ion is moved to rebuke a smart young man who teases him about making up the oracles himself: 'They come from a mouth that is pure and holy, and the god speaks through it' – which, understandably, creates a prolonged silence. The irony is not only that what the young man charges has been true, but that the one-time atheist is now speaking absolutely sincerely, as Arieka cannot but recognize.

As she listens, however, she is driven to ask how much she herself believes now, after (bleakly merciless to herself) Ion's inventions and her own; after years of remembering the 'rape', but years also of 'part-belief', searching for proof that even if there were no Olympus, the gods might still exist somewhere else or in some other mode. It is too much for her. She veils her face, not as Ion thinks as a calculated gesture, but 'in sheer shame'.

Now, in this penultimate chapter, it becomes clear how this novel has reversed Golding's procedure in most of his others. Usually we find ourselves in godless worlds, but shot through by glimpses of an otherworld of mercy, light, warmth, beauty, peace, and power – perhaps then of 'God', but experienced concretely, without creed or dogma, and always surrounded by ambiguity and alternative explanations. We have usually had to decide our reading, in the space between alternatives that the novelist always left open. But this time Golding has led up to what seemed a compelling experience of divine possession, only to shred it away gradually, fade it out, until we inhabit a recognizably atheistic or at best agnostic 'modern' world, very like our own. In no respect is it more like ours than the courtesy, the 'mild and amused warmth of respect and understanding' with which the sophisticated Athenians treat these relics of a worn-out religion, which is hardly worth attacking now, except occasionally with delicate blasphemy and teasing. High Priest and Priestess are received with respect, even sometimes a little awe, but it is always shallow at best, and more what people feel they ought to be feeling than what they really do. And though there are many 'protestations of affection', there is very little money, despite Ion's deftly calculated after-dinner appeals. He becomes distinctly bitter.

Moreover their last engagement is a disaster. This time,

processing to make a sacrifice to Dionysus, they venture outside
the upper-class circles in which they have been moving, and find
themselves amongst crowds of ordinary townspeople and slaves.
Here a kind of 'religious' feeling exists, but in the form of the mob-
hysteria that Arieka had experienced when she first entered Delphi.
'There she is,' shouts a woman, and suddenly the crowd falls into
'a foaming frenzy' and they are mobbed, in imminent danger of
being crushed to death. The guards fall to cracking heads, brutally,
but 'in a matter-of-fact way' as is necessary for police in emerg-
encies – and afterwards there are dead bodies on the ground. They
never reach the altar, but Dionysus has had his appropriate due.

Moreover, as they leave Athens for home, there is a second great
disillusionment for Ion's hopes of Hellas. They could not come to
Athens via Megara because of the eternal bickering between Greek
cities. Now, on the way back, the Eleusinian welcome has soured,
and though, this time, the Megarans give them safe-conduct, it is
not to their city but by a roundabout route to the boundary of
Corinth, which will then not allow any Megarans to cross. So
much for pan-Hellenism. They are a party of only four as they
reach their Corinthian friend's house, in a snowstorm.

There, further truths are exposed before they get back to Delphi,
though their rich Phoenician friend is as kind as ever. Indeed, when
he finds out how short they still are of the sum they need, he makes
it up himself. He also gives Arieka a cloth-of-gold dress and a
delicate gold crown. Though she cannot be persuaded to wear
them herself, when they are displayed on a hetaera even more
beautiful than the one he had brought to dinner in Delphi, Arieka
is irresistibly reminded of Helen of Troy – and in a passion of
imagination breaks out in a whole poem in hexameters. Worse
still, in a moment of vanity, she admits that the verses are her own.
Through the storm there arrives the Propraetor of Southern
Greece, a bluntly outspoken Roman conscious of his power,
who quickly lets both Pythia and High Priest know that he intends
to be obeyed on his 'patch' and that, well aware of Ion's pigeon-
fancying, he will be keeping an eye on him. Quickly, the
Corinthian distracts him with wine and the girl, and Ion with a
boy, but for Arieka the evening is spoilt. She feels left out and
jealous, 'a plain old thing whose dignity and sanctity were
disregarded among the noise and dancing and drinking and

fondling' – but when she tries to assert herself by pouring a libation, nobody takes any notice. As they bid farewell in the morning, the Roman gives Ion a blunt warning to confine himself to his religious duties. It finally dawns on Arieka that the deepest purpose of the columbarium is a nationalist conspiracy.

VIII

When they reach Delphi, still in such snow and wind that she has to walk some of the way, it is to discover that part of the roof of the Pythion has now fallen in, and that the roof of the book-room is giving way too. There is going to have to be a choice; but they both care so deeply about books that it is not at all clear which is the more important. Luckily it is the Latin rather than the Greek scrolls that are most at risk. There is also concern about Menesthia, whom they had left in charge. She is quite cheery about having given 'answers' sitting on a milking stool in the porch while they were away, able both to make herself 'feel funny' sometimes, and to tell people what she thinks they want to know – a very discomfiting parody of the oracle. But she has no religious vocation, and as the months wear by she gets more and more miserable. They have to let her go home, to a father who welcomes her, as Arieka's would never have done. Meanwhile Arieka's own powers when under the influence of the laurel dust, seem to have lessened, and the Olympians seem to have receded further and further away again. She is even unsure now, having read more, and become aware of the contradictions in the myths, who exactly the twelve are, and whether Apollo counts as one. A new Pythia-in-waiting is found, a pious girl with Egyptian connections who worships Serapis as well as Apollo, but her dour piety is off-putting, and 'If we were about the business of inventing Gods where would it end?'

Suddenly, without warning, Ion disappears. Arieka is so used to assuming he is around that she doesn't realize he is gone, until Perseus begs her pardon for having been ordered to go with him. They have travelled to what should have been a secret meeting of the chief conspirators, with passwords and all. But after they have sat for a while on a rock in the middle of nowhere waiting for the others to arrive, the Romans appear to arrest them instead, and it becomes clear that all their activities and co-conspirators have long been known. Perseus expects to be tortured but, humiliatingly, they let him go unharmed. As Ion is led away declaiming that he is in the hands of God, the officer says, 'Come sir, your Holiness, it's not as bad as that!'

Arieka has no idea what to do. Ion has given Perseus, to take to her, a curious silver key with a labris – the Cretan holy double-axe – at each end, but since she doesn't know what it is for, she puts it away. She can't ask the oracle for advice and transmit the answer to herself, but in her anxiety she is drawn to the building. There they are: the niches for the priests, the tripod, the brazier, the curtains with their embroidered images; the holiest place in Greece, in the world, she tells herself. As always, the sight of the curtains makes goose pimples rise on her skin and the rhythm of her breathing quicken, but she notices that it is the serpent trather than Apollo she is frightened of – little Arieka, still afraid of the dark. She knows, really, that the curtains have been embroidered by some flesh and blood woman, instructed to make the image of the god and the darkness he had faced. Let them hang! It is Ion she cares about, 'more than a husband, that quicksilver, quicksand, learned mountebank of the gods! I believe in him, liar, soothsayer, self-deceiver, fool, the eighth wise man –' She prays that Apollo may bring him back safe; but it is grief before a void once more.

When she gets back to the Pythion Ion is there, and she wets his feet with tears; but he is in a state of helpless rage and humiliation. (It is the secret of Roman power, Galba had told him, that it robs men of their dignity.) He curses in a frenzy, clasps his arms, and rocks back and forth, chanting his own name hypnotically, 'finding a place to hide, to draw into and away from himself, his shame the last bit of clothing to be dropped before the void, where at last there is the peace of not-god, not-man – nothingness –'

But being Ion, he cannot keep it up, cannot go on suffering the nothingness as Arieka has done, cannot indeed keep himself up. From that moment he begins to dwindle away in both mind and manliness, and though he dies only in extreme age and senility, he had really died a long time before.

The day his body dies, Arieka sits in the holy place, occupying Ion's niche, but there is nothing, no sense of him there. After this, she lets the Second Lady 'go through the motions' in her place. For herself, the oracle has died with Ion. Yet when the winter comes she goes to the grotto one last time, having realized what the silver key will fit. She pulls the curtains back and reveals a double door. 'I stood before it for a long time, but the only thought that came to me was that whatever happened it did not matter much.' So she opens the door and reveals ... solid, impenetrable mountain rock. There is no cleft where a great serpent lived whom Apollo was supposed to have slain; no prophetic vapour from the depths, whether cthonic or Olympian – just bare rock.

With exquisite irony there comes, the very next day, a letter from the Archon of Athens. The city wishes to recognize her long service as Pythia by erecting a statue on the Field of Mars. She answers – 'remembering the void' but 'feeling strangely that there was a kind of tenderness in it that I could explain to nobody' – that she does not want an image of herself, but a simple altar on which is written:

TO THE UNKNOWN GOD

IX

Scepticism, even atheism, would seem to have triumphed in the end. The inscription looks ironic, a sort of return-to-sender message: 'Not Known Here'. If there is any tenderness in the void from which the last god-fakery has vanished for Arieka, it is a tenderness of regretful memory, a last touch of sorrow for a lost faith that could not last.

And yet, the inscription is surely ambiguous? To be unknown – because unknowable? – is not necessarily to be non-existent? We may have rational ways of explaining away the curious incidents of Arieka's childhood, and a possible psychological theory about the phenomenon of 'possession' – though not, perhaps, for what her unconscious has known when in that state. But will such explanations really do for the experiences that the old woman has conveyed to us, even through the narrative filter of her sceptical old age?

There are moreover three pieces of evidence which must be brought into the final questioning. There is Arieka's first memory (which also, one gathers, comes out of Golding's own life): a primal *experience* – before words and self, and therefore self-deception – of blazing light and warmth experiencing itself together with the child: in a word, of 'God', or call it Apollo. The name hardly seems to matter, for the experience is not dependent on any creed or even 'belief'.

The second is a hidden date. If Caesar, born in 100 BC and described as a young man when he came to Delphi in the story, were, say, twenty-nine, that must have been circa 71 BC and Arieka – then sixteen – will have been born about 87 BC. She tells us in the opening chapter that she is writing the book 'in my eighties' – therefore after 6/7 BC which is thought to be the most likely date for the birth of Jesus Christ. The mythology in the *Ion* of Euripides already makes much of the descent of Creusa from the Erecthean family, born of Earth; and her rape and impregnation by Apollo is therefore, as much as the oracle itself, part of the Olympian take-over from powers of the Earth. This is even more explicit in Golding's novel. The phase of religion then centred on Olympus has now also passed, but 'God', unknown to Arieka, has already come into the world in a new revelation. Perhaps, since she is a mantic woman, the inscription she chooses for the altar, and the tenderness with which she chooses it, may be a hint from her unconscious of something *there* still, albeit unknown to sceptical intelligence.

The third piece of evidence is the altar itself which – a wonderful touch of Golding's – St Paul will see in the Field of Mars and will preach about on the Areopagus, almost sixty years after the end of this story, telling sceptical Athenians of the God who had struck him blind on the road to Damascus.

Once again, in his last work, Golding leaves the final interpretation open. He has given scepticism its head, and apparently the last word. But another reading remains open too, in his double tongue.

14

D'YOU SEE . . . ?

How do you know but ev'ry bird that cuts the airy way
Is an immense world of delight, clos'd by your senses five?
William Blake

        In such strength
    Of usurpation, in such visitings
    Of awful promise, when the light of sense
    Goes out in flashes that have shown to us
    The invisible world . . .
William Wordsworth

My task which I am trying to achieve is, by the power of the written word
to make you hear, to make you feel – it is above all to make you *see*. That
– and no more, and it is everything.

Joseph Conrad

D'you see?

Golding, constantly, in conversation

Now that Golding's work is, alas, complete, is it at all possible to
say something about how his imagination most characteristically
weaves its texture, as revealed in the detail of the writing?

In our sixth chapter we tried to suggest three different kinds of
imaginative structuring; and to argue, on the basis of the fiction
up to and including *The Spire*, that Golding's imagination had so
far tended to order itself in 'mythic' rather than 'fabulous' or
'historical' ways, though elements of both the other kinds were
always present. It is then significant that after *The Spire* there
should have been a marked movement towards 'history' in *The
Pyramid* and the Sea Trilogy (published under the title *To the
Ends of the Earth* in 1991), in tension with a mythic imagination
still powerfully present, and indeed still dominant in *Darkness
Visible* and *The Paper Men*, the two books which seem most

intent on further examining the fused duality with which *The Spire* ends.

But how does Golding's imagination work in detail? Obviously this will differ from passage to passage and novel to novel, a difference that comes out as we interpret the interrelation of texture and structure. But are there features of Golding's imagining which are like a signature, and might bear on the likelihood that his work will last?

One might begin with a passage from *Lord of the Flies* which is instantly recognizable as Golding; not one of the major episodes, but one which nobody but he could have written. Ralph, on the reefless side of the island for the first time, wanders down to the rocks:

Down here, almost on the level of the sea, you could follow with your eye the ceaseless, bulging passage of the deep sea waves. They were miles wide, apparently not breakers or the banked ridges of shallow water. They travelled the length of the island with an air of disregarding it and being set on other business; they were less a progress than a momentous rise and fall of the whole ocean. Now the sea would suck down, making cascades and waterfalls of retreating water, would sink past the rocks and plaster down the seaweed like shining hair: then, pausing, gather and rise with a roar, irresistibly swelling over point and outcrop, climbing the little cliff, sending at last an arm of surf up a gully to end a yard or so from him in fingers of spray.

Wave after wave, Ralph followed the rise and fall until something of the remoteness of the sea numbed his brain. Then gradually the almost infinite size of this water forced itself on his attention. (pp. 136–7)

In all sorts of ways, of course, this passage plays its part in the experience and interpretation of the novel as a whole: but if for a moment one takes the fragment out of the whole mosaic, one may notice, in the texture and movement of the language itself, that Golding's imagination is essentially visual, and that it is the accuracy of the seeing that is most striking, and (always) the source of its power to make us see more than we know. For as we look there wells, out of the concretely focused consciousness, something at first unconscious, but then forced on our attention. We look from down here, out there, along, and down here again, in opposite and successive movements of the eye – and then we see how they are both opposite, and one. We take in how the deep sub-

surface movement out there relates to the plastering down of the
seaweed hair right here, and conversely. The eye of Golding's
prose is always on the move, looking this way and that, full of
tensions, but progressing as Blake or Lawrence do by marrying
apparent contraries. Finally something is revealed which is at the
limits of perception, a force, a power, something 'almost infinite'.
It is a key lightly touched, and easily acceptable should we so wish
in terms of lunar gravity; but what actually and powerfully
imprints itself is the existence of dimensions, fields of force
beyond the human, which yet surge up to us and demand attention. Ralph unconsciously resists; his consciousness is so much
more at home on the apparently safe and humanizable side of the
island that this 'other' dimension numbs his brain. This is however
the only moment in the passage when we are aware of him as an
individual character. For the rest, he is pure eye. In a moment, of
course, the fiction will turn back to the boys and their relationships, but we have been asked to look out for a moment, to catch
sight of something beyond.

Here then is a first Golding signature: his fiction is primarily,
remarkably and powerfully visual. Like the Mariner, he holds us
with his glittering *eye*. But it is also characteristic of him to move
through the visual to the visionary, and to seek the relationship
between these. Yet the more we come to wonder about the nature
of his seeing – as caught in the movement of the prose itself – the
more paradoxical and distinctive it may seem. He is quite different
from Blake and Wordsworth for whom, in their different ways,
concrete visualization of ordinary experience is a barrier to vision,
and for whom therefore the eye must be cleansed or put to sleep
before the visionary can truly 'see'. But he is also quite different
from Joyce and Conrad for whom (again in different ways) there is
nothing but the eye and the object; so that it is only the visualizing
itself, the act of artistic perception charged with individual
response on the rescued fragment of experience, that can capture
the epiphanizing radiance; or 'through its movement its form and
its colour, reveal the substance of its truth'. Golding is unlike the
modernists in Blakean and Wordsworthian ways; and unlike the
Romantics in Joycean and Conradian ways; he is both intensely
'sceptical' and intensely 'religious' (so that neither word can have
its straightforward meaning); he uses the visionary against the

visual and the visual against the visionary. So what and how does Golding 'mean', by 'seeing'?

Interestingly, the eye seems equally pre-eminent in Conrad's 'before all to make you *see*' and in Wordsworth's accusations against 'the most despotic of the senses'. No mere literary critic should tangle with the argument implied here, which is ultimately metaphysical – but it seems that whether one believes the physical universe to be all there is, so that the empiric making real of that 'all' to the senses becomes particularly important against the abyss of non-being and non-meaning; or whether one suspects that the physical universe is a mask for 'something far more deeply interfused', so that a Gloucester or an Oedipus can only 'see' truly when the vile jelly is out; it is the eye above all that conditions our view of 'reality' for good or ill. In our everyday language we may say (with Nick Shales or Sim Goodchild) that we will believe only what we see for ourselves, though that may mean we may believe more, the more that an author's language makes us visualize. Or we may say that sight is nothing without insight, and may deceive like words; that it is only when the physical eye is 'made quiet' by some deeper kind of perception that we can for a moment 'see into the life of things', wordlessly. Golding's fiction, paradoxically, will insist on saying *both*.

Certainly, from the earliest impulse to create a coral island more 'real' than Ballantyne's, the function of the eye in realization was all-important. We argued for example that in the finding of the conch (pp. 2–5) physical realities came first for the author, and must remain first for his readers. Hence the glimpse of the shell in the context of salt water, brilliant fish, green weed; then the fulcrum and lever to disentangle it and bring it to the surface; then the seeing close-to, in its strange cream and rose spiral embossed by an art other than the human; and finally the harsh otherness of the noise that shatters the peace of the island and terrifies bird and beast. The conch is no mere 'symbol' but a shining *thing*, vizualized, realized, through which other meanings emerge or are destroyed as human breath comes through the spiral. The book proceeds by a series of revelations which make us see more and more in what we have seen already; but the authenticity of each step depends on that of the one before, and all are grounded in the original undoctored sense perception.

So the first function of seeing is as the cliché has it, that it is believing. Or rather, as when Sammy Mountjoy says 'I do not believe merely, I see', it is authentic precisely because it keeps at bay the idea-making, patterning mind, so that all that lies *in* the objective situation can come through. In *The Hot Gates* the author, talking learnedly about Thermopylae, sets out to climb the cliffs over which a traitor had led the Persians. He snatches his hand from a rock on which there is a lizard, he gropes and slides, he suddenly sees a snake. 'So much for the map, pored over in the lamplight of an English winter ... I stayed there, clinging to a rock until the fierce hardness of its surface close to my eye had become familiar. Suddenly the years and the reading fused with the thing. I was clinging to Greece herself.' Not the idea, the map, the mental cataract over the retina, but imagination plus the bedrock of the thing-perceived-in-itself produce the double power that can put Golding behind the eyes of Leonidas, and us behind his.

Indeed, the reverse power of the human mind to *un*realize, so that what is before the eyes is converted to image for the ego's urgency, is a potent source of evil. The end of the conch, as it shatters with Piggy, comes about because of eyes that can no longer see shining thing or boy, but only empty shell and fat-pig, which stand in the way and fuel the power-urge. In *The Inheritors* we have both the most wonderfully imagined of all Golding's fictions, because it is both the most innosensually realized, through eyes wholly un-sapient and non-egotistic, at one with what they see; and also a terrible proof of the nature of our difference, shown by our ability to understand what those innocent eyes can see but never take in. Situation after situation comes extraordinarily alive as we see through Lok's eyes; but page after page we have to decipher, between the lines, what lies behind that other kind of seeing that turns him into an image of murderous and ravenous cruelty on the rock face.

So this brings us to a first paradox in Golding. There can be no true seeing that is not primarily and simply visual, undistorted by the mind; yet concrete seeing in itself is always blind at a deeper level, because unaware of the nature of things and of ourselves. It is only we who can really see in *The Inheritors*, by focusing Lok's eyes with our own:

As he watched, one of the farther rocks began to change shape. At one side a small bump elongated then disappeared quickly. The top of the rock swelled, the hump fined off at the base and elongated again then halved its height. Then it was gone. (p. 79)

It is only when we bring to bear *our* knowledge of suspicion, fear and hostility, which take not-self for enemy and so turn looking-out into spying, that Lok's register of meaningless activity suddenly clicks into focus. We see-with-insight, of which Lok is incapable, his first glimpse of man. But it is not only a matter of human evil. There are whole dimensions of nature (water, ice, the tiger, the flux of time and change); and of language (which works by differentiation as against communal telepathy) which the People cannot enter, however nearly they approach the brink. So if the wonder of the book is to be inside Lok and Fa, and its horror to discover thereby what it is to be us, the power of its vision is always *double*, fusing sight with insight. Only we can focus Fa going over the Fall with both Lok's grief and the perspective of history. Only we can look over Tuami's shoulder at the shape of innocence-with-experience. The central action of *The Inheritors* is to see through, and into, and past that purely concrete perception which is at the same time the rock and guarantor of vision. It becomes clear why the so-called 'gimmick' endings in Golding, making one look again, are never in fact gimmicks but structural necessity.

Pincher Martin reinforces that paradox and brings to light a second one. It is above all, again, the concrete realization of the rock that holds our riveted attention and conviction – only to find out that it is radically false, 'made up', because it not only lacks but actively seeks to evade a deeper kind of insight. Pincher examines the barnacled cliff and peers into the crack, only a foot from his face (p. 125), in which is 'a terrible darkness'. Suddenly he envisages the whole rock in the water, and wonders how it can be so familiar – when he hears a loud plop from the outlying rocks. However close the imagined rock to the eye, however loud the attempts of the mind to distract itself from becoming aware of what it is doing, inexorably the surface of Pincher's seeing will split to reveal the 'terrible darkness' and the hidden reality it has been his frenzied obsession to deny, by inventing out of his own mouth a world in which his ego can go on living. Concrete perception turns inside out in a Blakean way (though in horror, not delight) when instead of being behind his eyes looking out, they become the windows of a room with reality trying to get *in*. For the Pincher self-enclosed ego, the ultimate reality is revealed as a vast world of terrible darkness, closed by the desperate inventiveness of his senses five. So, now, 'insight' has to turn metaphysical, forced to contemplate the signature at the heart of things, whether that be loving design, or black lightning destroying the self that sought to evade it by refusing to 'die'.

But (the paradoxes continue), while concrete seeing is now twice blind if it also lacks the visionary glimpse of what is preterhuman, the most visionary of all Golding's characters is the blindest of them all. Jocelin laughing with joy as the sun explodes through the stained glass, or remarking the optical illusion of the slanting pillars of sunlight in his dust-filled cathedral, cannot *see* Abraham and Isaac in the window, or that his great ship has indeed begun to go askew. So confident that the light is God the Father's, he cannot see 'sundust' either; how it is the dust that makes the sun so solidly visible, or how God (and the Beast) become visible 'through people'. Looking at the dumb man's carving of him with its 'wide blind eyes', he nods. 'It is true. At the moment of vision, the eyes see nothing.' That, for this author, is the most dangerous blindness of all. So the action of the novel is precisely to bring home to Jocelin how blind he has been to physical reality, to people, to relationships, to the nature of things, until at the very last moment of his life – cleaned of himself – he can bring the two windows of his eyes together and focus that extraordinary mysterious *thing*, the spire, in a moment of wonder and terror fused with all the languages of explanation, but going beyond them all. The whole book is a preparation for that moment of visual perception, that must be of stone before it is anything else, that must be wholly 'objective', but finally seems to hold so much in such fusion of opposites that it can only be caught in a flash by the eye and hinted in the tentativeness of simile.

So we begin to understand not only why 'seeing' in Golding is so paradoxical, sight and insight, visual and visionary, but also why he must be constantly employing one way of looking *against* the other. To the visionary, the concretely visual Golding must always say as Roger Mason does: 'Let your eye crawl down like an insect, foot by foot ... look down! See' – for only then can Jocelin take in the physical challenge and frailty of the tower, translated from idea into 'a skin of glass and stone stretched between four stone rods'. And it is not only the horrific sight of the earth stirring like grubs in the pit, or of the extra counter in the children's game far below, that tell of the tower swaying silently like a tree – the eye must focus, also, however belatedly, on the tear splash on the dubbined boot, the sprig of mistletoe, all the human as well as physical realities of the 'lesson for each height'. Only concrete seeing can peel away the cataract of the idea, the symbolizing, the religiose and egotistic delusion.

But equally, to the sceptic who believes only what he can see with his ordinary eyesight, and to the cynic who has seen it all, must be made to come home the extraordinary strangeness of things, the mystery of their beauty, and their horror. So to Sammy Mountjoy in his salt obsession, painting the nude body of his Beatrice with harsh electric lighting to make the picture sear like *Guernica*, comes the extraordinary revelation that what his brush has caught is blessedness. So to Wilf Barclay, cooling his hangover in the cathedral with its fifth-rate Mafia glass, comes the horrific revelation of the steely-silver Christ with carbuncle eyes striding towards him; a vision that overturns his view of the world. So Sim Goodchild, who could believe only in himself, sees for the first time the exquisite beauty, artistry, and well-being of his own hand, 'stared into the gigantic world of his own palm and saw that it was holy'.

This is probably the most Blakean moment in Golding: 'To see a world in a grain of sand and a heaven in a wild flower, hold infinity in the palm of your hand and eternity in an hour.' But it brings out a third paradox about seeing in Golding's fiction. Although its most powerfully imagined revelations have come from perception supercharged by intensities of wonder or of terror, so that his is an art of extremes, yet it is at its most extraordinary when ultimates are focused in the most ordinary things, and with the greatest impersonality. The tree in the General's garden in *Free Fall* (p. 45) is an experience of the ordinary become miraculous: the moon 'flowering' in a 'sanctuary of light; the 'stillest tree that ever grew' whose leaves 'floated out like a level of oil on water'; the 'ivory quiet' beyond. 'Later, I should have called the tree a cedar and passed on, but then, it was an apocalypse.' Such moments do indeed catch sight of Last Things, beyond personality ('We were eyes'): here, a sudden revelation of holy peace and beauty in ordinary reality transfigured. But there is also another kind of seeing that is no less intense, but utterly egotistic. It was there in the ego-intense seeing of Pincher, of Sammy, of Jocelin, the hint of hectic in the eye embodied in the touch of corruption in the language – for after *The Inheritors* Golding's novels are mostly 'written' by others, the language of the fiction coloured by the point of view. It is clearest of all in the episode of the dabchicks in *Darkness Visible*, as Sophy 'went right out into her eyes, she was nothing but seeing, seeing, seeing! It was like reaching out and laying hold with your eyes ... a kind of absorbing, a kind of drinking, a kind of.' (pp. 107–8) As opposed to a vision of evil this is an evil kind of seeing, that claws in unison with some force in the nature of things when Sophy finds the stone fitted to her hand, the perfect destructive arc, the fiercest satisfaction. More extraordinary still is the way that light transfiguring the ordinary may focus a judgement of the dark self. The glass ball in the bookshop window holds nothing but the sun, bright, and pure; but it blazes, as clouds move aside. 'It dominated without effort, a torch shone straight into [Matty's] eyes, and he felt queer, not necessarily unpleasantly so but queer all the same – unusual. He was aware too of a sense of rightness and truth and silence.' (p. 48) But this 'still dimension of otherness' – how much better Matty's simplicity than Edwin's language of mysticism – this revelation of golden peace, is the light against which Matty sees his own darkness, and renounces.

Golding's seeing continually courts the danger of seeming Manichaean, fracturing into separate worlds without a bridge. And yet, a final paradox, he seems as stubbornly insistent as the old song 'I'll give you one – oh' that the many not only grow out of, but must be drawn back into the one. No seeing, it seems, can be truly human that is not split, or even multiple; but none can be true unless all things are made one, if only for an instant. Grief can be a bridge. Indeed, seeing through eyes washed clean by tears is one of the deepest dimensions in Golding, because that vision differs from both innocence and guilt, which can fuse into it. As Sammy Mountjoy emerges from the 'cell' he sees the camp and its people anew, through the tears that have sprung from shameful insight into his own being. Horror fuses with release; self-awareness longs frantically to escape self; grief and terror cry out and change what cries; so that 'dead' eyes can open on new seeing. As 'huge tears' drop into the dust Sammy sees, through them, both huts and shining, both 'boxes of thin wood' and 'treasure houses full of sceptred kings', both 'dust' and a universe of 'fantastic crystals'.

I raised my dead eyes, desiring nothing, accepting all things, and giving all created things away. The paper wrappings of use and language dropped from me. Those crowded shapes extending up into the air and down into the rich earth, those deeds of far space and deep earth were aflame at the surface and daunting by right of their own natures though a day before I should have disguised them as trees. (p. 186)

This goes further than the infant Samuel's cedar tree, not only because it has admitted horror as well as wonder, but also because it goes on to insist that 'Everything is related to everything else' – though Sammy will go on worrying to the end of the book about the nature of that relation.

And yet, in hindsight, the passage won't *quite* do, though it holds the seeds of much that is to come. It seems rather too rhetorical, leaving the concrete realities too easily behind, hence not realized enough. We are told, rather than seeing and feeling for ourselves, what Sammy sees and feels. But before trying to analyse those most extraordinary later places where Golding tries more successfully, through a character, for an inclusive vision that contains all the paradoxes, and sees the infinite *in* the grain of dust, it might be as well to reprise what inclusiveness needs to be. Golding seems to have felt the need for this himself in setting out to make *Darkness Visible*, for at the beginning he clarifies the essential threefold process that he means by 'seeing'. It must always be grounded in pure sense-perception. For Golding the sceptic and modernist that is indeed before all, and everything. But what comes through that seeing is another dimension in it, and another, each providing a lens for further and deeper focusing: from seeing to insight, from insight to revelation or epiphany, but in a religious rather than a Joycean sense. Something infinite is revealed through physical seeing, and seeing into, but it is not the creation of the artist. So as Golding aims the firemen's eyes at the holocaust in *Darkness Visible* (pp. 12–13), seeing begins with the most delicate and precise discrimination of colour. White fire turns pink or blood-colored, affected by cloud or smoke. Then eyes catch movement where no movement should be. They flinch away in horror; but the captain's gaze is drawn to where the others are carefully *not* looking. Now the fire is brighter than ever; its pink aura has spread; saffron and ochre turn to blood. The shivering white heart of the fire quickens 'beyond the capacity of the eye to analyse'. It is out of that horrific glare that something condenses: the burning child, whom we 'see' first as (like the Vietnam photograph) no more and no less a fact than the inferno: a miracle of survival. But then the paradoxes mount: it is as dark as it is bright, a horrible miracle, a child saved and appallingly maimed, a terror and a wonder. Then comes yet another dimension: the connection between horror and wonder, a hidden design. The captain is forced to see still further in, to the direct link between his survival and his moment of cowardice before going to the child's rescue: he too is a maimed creature 'whose mind had touched for once on the nature of things'. So true seeing, for Golding, must focus dimension through dimension: first and essentially sense-perception; then through perception to insight, both dark and bright; finally through insight to the revelation of a field of force and design in the universe, to which our normal experience is a concealing screen – through seeing to skrying, through skrying to revelation in which all the paradoxes engage.

It is no wonder that Golding's attempts to see whole have had to become much more daring, complex and difficult in the later work, as they have sought to become more inclusive. There are also two new factors. If we compare, say, the last 'vision' of Simon, with those of Jocelin, or Pedigree, or Wilf Barclay, we find that suspicions have grown in Golding: of the falsifying power of the human ego; and hence of the deceptiveness of language itself and how it may distort reality. True vision may come only through dead eyes, through the death of the self and the discarding of the very language which had been necessary to set the vision up. Rhetoric becomes suspect. More and more the deepest feelings and visions will have to be created *in the reader*, wordlessly, in a space between and beyond the lines on the page. And this involves an increased risk that response may not come, and the vision fail.

After the horror of the series of 'seeings deeper' that began with game and have ended with Simon's death, an authorial language seems confidently to restore order. Peace and beauty seem to follow violence as calm follows storm; and as the Pacific tide comes in, Simon's body becomes part of the rhythms of the natural universe (pp. 189–90). The advancing line of phosphorescence 'bulged about the sand grains and the pebbles; it held them each in a dimple of tension, then suddenly accepted them with an inaudible syllable and moved on.' Through its granular concreteness the seeing begins to re-embody Simon's kind of inclusive vision, its acceptance of what *is*, in a larger perspective now, as we take in the fact of his disappearance. But what is, is neither beauty, peace and order, nor horror, because it is both. If the phosphorescence 'dressed Simon's coarse hair with brightness ... and the turn of his shoulder became sculptured marble', what it consists of is 'strange, moonbeam-bodied creatures with fiery eyes', the same transparencies we saw in the daylight scavenging for food 'like myriads of tiny teeth in a saw'. And if, in sudden distance and high-shot, the pull of sun, moon and tide takes Simon's body out to sea beneath 'steadfast constellations', putting man's violence into perspective, the rather scientific language reminds one also of the world's indifference to man. This is the same sea and tide that Ralph had watched on the other side of the island travelling its length 'with an air of disregarding it', and with a remoteness that numbed his brain.

The vision is concrete and universal; uses seeing to create insight and revelation; fuses opposites into inclusive acceptance. But a quick comparison with *The Inheritors* will show a difference between authorial description, however beautiful and meaningful (such as Sammy's vision through tears), and a response created in a reader by bringing one to a point where one's own vision leaps beyond the words that have brought you there, and feeling wells up powerfully within. A coldly objective anthropological eye reports the appearance and behaviour of a 'red creature' near the end of *The Inheritors*. The reader who has lived the novel inside Lok is nonplussed; cannot take in what is being described. Then, suddenly (p. 220), there is shocking awareness – actually some of the grief and love and horror that is Lok's – for suddenly one *sees* what the 'light poured down over the cheekbones' *is*, and one's own eyes may begin to prick. Only then, with indescribable disturbance, does one realize the full horror of what Lok is weeping over. The effect is indescribable because it has renounced description. It can take place only through, and then beyond the words, with the whole experience of the book to power it. We may weep for Liku as we do not weep for Simon (though there is a challenge in Ralph's tears, at the end).

In *Pincher Martin* the physical and human world will crack open to reveal the metaphysical, including Tuami's question in its metaphysical form. In *Free Fall* and *The Spire*, vision increasingly splits into such opposite ways of looking that bringing them together becomes as problematic as the books seem to have been to achieve. Golding ceases to write in his own voice; and becomes increasingly suspicious not only of pattern but of language itself. So complex and tentative is the final vision of *The Spire*; so much has to be got into its preparation, with such careful cross-reservation, that it is impossible to discuss it again properly here; but even a brief comparison with the 'end' of Simon will show up major differences in the seeing. Patterns of insight have multipled, but since each convinces, none can be exclusively true, and although we know more about Jocelin in more terms than any character in Golding thus far, it is only to exclaim by the end, with him, 'Now – I know nothing at all!' Secondly, the eye-clouding that had begun with Pincher has intensified. We live not only behind obsessed eyes, but those of a visionary blindest of all – yet Jocelin also reacts further than anyone before, in grief and self-repudiation. Well before the end his eyes have died to himself, and his final focusing comes only at the point of death. Thirdly, there is a new sense of the obliquity and transience of seeing whole. The entire structured and patterned fiction is but a preparation for a single moment of perception, caught in a flash like the kingfisher from the corner of the eye against the 'panicshot darkness'. Seeing is indeed Conrad's 'everything' – for if it fails the whole act of creation fails, and nothing is left but delusion. Yet for all its ambiguities, the ignorance that follows knowing, the transience and obliquity, the fiction seems more convinced than ever that only the 'rock' of concrete seeing will hold everything: 'our very stones cry out'. Only focusing the spire *itself* can enable 'all things to come together'. So, at the very end, split vision slides into focus, and sees the uprush of rosy-coloured substance as one thing that (for all its crookedness) can break 'all the way to infinity in cascades of exultation'. Numerous opposites fuse: the concrete and the infinite, the visual and the visionary, the divided and the one, the spiritual and the fleshly, the crooked beauty, the terror and astonishment, the falling and the soaring caught in the movements of the eye.

However – and this is the most important difference from *Lord of the Flies* – one may say these things, but they are now very clearly only signs and sayings. The vision fails unless readers 'see' for themselves; unless, as the words stop, something that can only be pointed towards does flash across the 'inward eye' of which Wordsworth spoke. Language can finally only use 'likeness', though imagination can pierce momentarily through the sign – for Golding is not in the end a modernist. Just as having seen the appletree gives Jocelin what is no more than a simile for the power of crookedness-with-blossoming-abundance he glimpses for one instant in the spire, so our seeing of the spire through words must pierce beyond where words can go – or vision fails.

The fiction plays for high stakes now, and risks losing everything. To the reader who must honestly say that he *doesn't* see, there is only a partial reply. One may test whether all the preparation has been taken in, since all is necessary for the full ambivalence and inclusiveness to work – but if comprehension does not issue in that flash which is beyond words and intellectual grasp, there is nothing more to be said. Indeed Golding has always allowed for a sceptical reading: for the real possibility of delusion in Simon, or Pincher, or Jocelin (or Matty, Pedigree, and Wilf Barclay to come); for an ending in nothing, or in ambiguity; though the imaginative pressure seems otherwise.

He then had to go further, to try to turn glimpsing into seeing, making darkness (and brightness) plainly visible; and to see-to-the-end almost past the point of death. Again the fiction had to be even more complexly divided: the rejected good and apparently triumphant evil distilled out and diametrically opposed in the stories of Matty and Sophy, then a further fracturing of points of view, and a testing to destruction of the unity that had momentarily been experienced by the lilywhite boys. Moreover Golding clearly wanted the despair that precedes the final vision to be even darker than in *The Spire*, because not confined to a single consciousness. It is not only to Sophy the nihilist that 'there is now nothing visible but darkness'. Sim feels that all are guilty, nobody can know the truth, and television screens everywhere mock his moment of deepest vision. Matty is dead, horribly on fire again, and there is no way of telling whether his death was accident or design. Or is there? For in Golding's 'mythic' view of reality, ordinary seeing is always a lens to something deeper. There can be no true seeing that does not try to tell the ultimate nature of things and ask (past death itself) whether, in those words from *The Inheritors* our darkness has an ending. And *Darkness Visible* not only goes further than *The Spire* in wanting to see where the spire is pointing; it also reorchestrates *Pincher Martin* and *Free Fall* in its concern with whether, in the end, there can be *change*. Does what we are determine what we may be? In choosing to conceive the death of Pedigree the paedophile, Golding deliberately chooses the seamiest material to uncover 'where the connections are' and to imagine his answer to whether a man may cry out and be different – whether in the end there is darkness, or light, or nothing at all.

Though Pedigree is dying, what strikes one first about the final seeing is its liveliness, grounded in the senses as always: the sun on the skin, the sea of light, the wind. There is also the now familiar insight that only with the extinction of himself can Pedigree see beyond Matty's horrible appearance into the love and forgiveness that were always there. But there is something new now: the imagining of how (as Matty had said) an immense power may operate through a deformed man – even after his death. Though Matty was a 'natural', ugly, in many ways foolish, we have known his power of loving forgiveness in the same way as we experienced the grief of Lok, not by being told about it, but by being made to create it for ourselves between seemingly unintelligible lines, as we watched (for instance) Matty taking his light through the foul depths, or shaking the dust of Australia *back* upon his shoes. But now sense experience – 'the extraordinarily lively nature of this gold, this wind, this wonderful light and warmth that kept Windrove moving, rhythmically' – gets apocalyptically heightened as we are made to see a supernatural power emerge, *through* a 'Matty' not dead but transformed, consumed away into the Spirit itself that had partially moved in him while he was alive. This Being is loving, and terrible; promises freedom, through anguish – for Pedigree who (like Sammy) had cried for help cannot bear (like Pincher) to let go, and has to have torn from him his life, his heart, himself. Do we 'see'? What Pedigree sees consumes all into itself. It costs everything, but if the power of the spirit does come into the world through human deformity, then men can cry for help at the end, and be saved from themselves. Darkness is visible to the last in the two-toned face of reality, but then the last fire burns it away into brightness. And though it is intensely painful and destructive to the ego, it is the music that frays and breaks the string.

Yet we cannot be 'told' this. Words can only bring us to the point where something either becomes 'visible' in the 'opening' between them, in the space beyond – or does not. Golding scrupulously allows for those who cannot believe that the 'filthy old thing' that is our pedigree can ever be 'cured'. For both sets of readers there has to be a gap between 'book' and 'since'; between the narrative and the final sense of cause and consequence. It is there on page 265 of *Darkness Visible*: an empty space that must fill or stay empty with each individual reader. Perhaps Golding has emerged from the underworld with a golden branch – *sit mihi fas audita loqui* – but some readers will see (as is their right) only emptiness after the last word, 'gone'.

That gap, between the telling and the seeing whole, gets a sardonic underlining in *The Paper Men*. For all its mocking of the critic, it is the writer who makes (and suffers) the most cutting comment on the very medium he uses, language itself. Any attempt at clarity in lucid prose is stigmatized, for (to the man who has seen the terror and the wonder) the hints of reality that matter only come when words displace themselves into another dimension out of the hippety-hop of argot. Both the terror glimpsed in the cathedral, and the wonderful vision that transforms every element of the concretely realized seamy material of the Spanish Steps, require modes of perception beyond speech – and finally beyond eyesight too: through light and movement to horror, or music, and then to silence. But now revelation is also not enough. Not even experience of the transforming power, not even tears and the desire for the destruction of the self, can finally open Barclay's eyes so that all things can come together. It is still paper, and words, and self, that he is concerned with at the end, so that he cannot *see* Rick. Only the last of the stigmata can strike home (as appalling mercy had done to Pedigree) to where the lack is – the love and compassion without which the visionary remains fatally self-enclosed, and that matter quite as much as seeing, and much more than words. Again, however, there is space for those who will see the ending in purely human terms: that two deformed people have destroyed each other.

We have been following a line of exploration in the later fiction from *The Spire* to *The Paper Men*. But *The Pyramid* went back to *Free Fall*, in order to develop a different, even contrary, 'historical' direction. While still driven to take further and further the kind of vision that cracked open the quotidian world, to reveal the infinite beyond, there also seems to have come home to Golding how the inclusiveness he wanted might demand a richer sense of the complexities of human character and relationships, and the ways these are affected by society. *Free Fall* had embodied an awareness that we live in two worlds: the secular one of Nick's sceptical humanism, acknowledging nothing beyond us here, but making earthly knowledge and human goodness all the more precious; and Rowena's religion which pierces beyond, in knowledge of God and Evil, but lacks Nick's human kindness. So *The Pyramid* may have involved much more than the discovery of formal ways to get beyond the monolith of *The Spire*. It may also have been a decision to pursue Nick's secular world, in a kind of Blakean or Lawrentian 'contrary' which was needed for progression and greater whole-ness. If the vision of Jocelin and Pedigree only became possible at the moment of self-extinction, it is this world that we have to *live* in – and Rick's bullet makes its lethal comment on the visionary to whom society and human relations mean nothing, and who lacks a human heart. 'Seeing', in *The Pyramid*, is differently defined, in terms of perceptiveness about society and character.

The novel so places Oliver in a subtly and sardonically observed society that it becomes very clear how it conditions him and affects his ability to see into and relate to others. Because seeing is now wholly secular and social, language comes into its own again – and it is essentially through his language that we get to know Oliver, boy, youth and man, better than he knows himself. For the novel's irony is not only social; it is also a mode of characterization. We get complex insight into the young Oliver and what he cannot see, but in Richardsonian fashion the older one also creates himself through his narrative style, and its limitations. The irony has a deeply human purpose. For as *we* are challenged to see between Oliver's lines, what begins to come into focus are the hidden people to whom their society is blind, or ill-disposed: Evie, Evelyn, Bounce. And the purpose of the seeing is to create in us the compassion that society, and even Oliver who should know and feel better, notably fail to give. 'If thou be among people make for thyself love, the beginning and end of the heart,' says the epigraph, pointing to what had been lacking also in Jocelin, and wholly lacking in Wilf – though not in Matty. The ironic art is not wholly successful in *The Pyramid* but it points toward the success of *Rites of Passage* and the Sea Trilogy.

In *Rites of Passage* two worlds, and the languages of perception appropriate to each, are set against one another. Since the narration is mainly given over to the worldly one, we see mainly as Edmund sees; but the insertion into his Journal of Colley's letter challenges that kind of seeing, and once again – only much more inwardly and powerfully than the ironic art of *The Pyramid* could manage – a hidden person is complexly created. The clash of the two accounts shows very clearly how much the worldling has to learn about seeing, and this time the irony is an education to the character almost as much as to the reader. The Colley story begins to change Edmund. Destructive snobbery and class-division begin to be overcome in him; he begins to learn compassion and responsibility. But the book not only contains rites of passage for its characters, it is itself a rite of *passage* for its readers; emphasizing how life must go on (if more perceptively now), and ways must be found to come to terms with the gap that has opened up in worldly seeing. The Colley story has made us aware of what remains missing from Edmund's vision and his language, a gap all the more visible because of the liveliness that surrounds it. But life continues after the surface has closed over the depths.

In the two further volumes the tragedy of Wheeler, another hidden person who has seen into the depths of things, continues to show up how much blindness remains in Edmund; and how much further he still has to go in learning to see better. This is also explored in humanist terms as he gains insight into the contrast between Summers and (in different ways) both Deverel and Benét; and into the Prettimans. He is taken aback by love, and the stresses of jealousy as the second book of the trilogy turns into a love story. As Edmund listens with Marion to the singing of the lass who has narrowly escaped death, and as the apparent loss of Marion prostrates him with grief and hysteria, he is plunged into a whole new dimension of the human heart. He also has to learn about the jealousy that is the other side of both friendship and love: the jealousy of Benét that overtakes both himself and Summers. But the most powerful scenes in these two volumes also open his eyes (as Ralph's were opened, in the passage from which we began) to the huge and preterhuman forces in the universe that human life skates over – until they announce themselves with terrifying force. Edmund's first vision of something rising from the depths has a long history in Golding's fiction. But its metaphor of a power, a 'god', that must rise into consciousness to bring this human Odyssey into proportion, becomes concrete, as the voyage goes on, in Golding's terrifying creation of gales and huge walls of water; the astonishing experience of the ice-continent; and the lethal fire which superficial knowingness had allowed to smoulder down below, and which causes the death of the man who had warned against such superficiality. Edmund cannot finally share the religious sensibility of Summers, or even Prettiman's ardent idealism. Our protagonist remains locked in his kind of 'enlightenment'. But at the very end, his dream of the Prettimans setting out to explore beyond the frontier of his kind of civilization, in honey light, joy and singing, while he remains earthbound, is a poignant awareness of loss and limitation. He cannot wish it more than a dream 'because if it was, then I have to start all over again in a universe quite unlike the one which is my sanity and security'. Golding has given his trilogy largely over to humanist eyes, but (as always) that kind of seeing keeps splitting open to reveal a further dimension in, and through, the concrete world we live in. Dream, or ultimate reality? The question, as always, lands in *our* laps.

What turned out to be the final novel goes even further in apparently handing over the fiction, not now to the purely human only, but to positive scepticism about the existence of a god. In a reversal of Golding's usual structure, the 'religious' kind of vision starts in the first words (mediated, as always, through concrete sense experience) and reaches its peak in the first third of the book, as the Priestess of Delphi is taken over by Apollo and speaks beyond her human knowledge. But she lives in a secular and sceptical age like our own. Her deepest relationship is with a faithless priest, for whom the oracle is essentially a political device – though his many-sided sophistication has one facet which can acknowledge, under her influence, that there *may* be something more in religion. As the novel goes on, however, the Pythia's own faith steadily diminishes, until it reaches a bedrock of disillusion by the end. She herself gives rational explanations for her experiences of strange power erupting into her world, and even taking her over. And in one sense her suggestion for a monument in Athens speaks for a world in which God is, simply, unknown. Yet the whole process is ambiguous. The chronology of the novel tells us that a new religious age has in fact begun: a new revelation, deeper than the old outworn vision, and though not known yet, very much about to be known. And are the rational explanations anything like as convincing as the experiences they try to explain away, and which the old woman's words have brought unforget- tably alive? (Similarly the real Ionides – as opposed to the pathetic creature who has died before his death – is not dead at all, but vividly alive in the pages the old woman has written.) It is of the very nature of the oracular that it should be couched in ambiguity. To each reader his reading.

Yet all can acknowledge the integrity and honesty of a writer who is very much of his age in one sense, yet differs from nearly all its authors in the power of his mythic vision, evolved out of convincing sense experience, and in his insistence on submitting it to radical challenge himself, and allowing space for readers who come to different conclusions. He might, like D. H. Lawrence, have called himself 'a passionately religious man', though (like Lawrence again) he was committed to no system, church or dogma – and his value lies in the weave of his imaginative language itself, not reducible to any 'theology' abstracted from it. He seems to have agreed with Lawrence and Blake that true vision had always to consist in, and progress through, contraries, paradoxes, and creative oppositions. If his work lasts – as surely it will – it will be because of the power and exhilaration of the *writing* and the integrity of its self-challenge. A last distinction might point, also, to a kind of humility about the nature of literary creation that could be called 'religious'. This comes out by contrast with a major writer who was a modernist in ways that Golding, for all his modernity, was not. Virginia Woolf writes, in a famous passage from her essay 'A Sketch of the Past', of

the rapture I get when in writing I seem to be discovering what belongs to what; making a scene come right; making a character come together. From this I reach what I might call a philosophy ... [that] the whole world is a work of art; that we are parts of the work of art. *Hamlet* or a Beethoven quartet is the truth about the vast mass we call the world. But there is no Shakespeare, there is no Beethoven, certainly, and emphatically there is no God; we are the words; we are the music; we are the thing itself.

By contrast, here is Golding lecturing on 'Belief and Creativity' (*A Moving Target* p. 197):

The writer watches the greatest mystery of all. It is the moment of most vital awareness, the moment of most passionate and *unsupported* conviction. It shines or cries. There is the writer, trying to grab it as it passes, as it emerges impossibly and heads to be gone. It is that twist of behaviour, that phrase, sentence, paragraph, that happening on which the writer would bet his whole fortune, stake his whole life as a *true* thing. Like God, he looks on his creation and knows what he has done. *A* truth. *An* unsupported conviction. *Like* God.

Virginia Woolf, quite certain that there is no God, is the creator of a world of words which is then self-existent, the only epiphany or 'showing forth' of things there can be for the writer, or for the reader who shares (first person plural) the joy of literary and imaginative absorption in the words and the music. For Golding the truth and joy are no less in the writing itself – but the writer's creativity is caught out of an elsewhere, from which it comes transiently, and into which it will vanish; and he speaks earlier in the essay of panic lest it escape before it can be realized. What moves into the mind and cries out to be realized is something given, shining in itself with light that is not the author's. He may be 'like God' when he captures and builds into his fictive creation such moments of illumination, but that is because he has shared for a while in God's creativity. 'We are said to be made in his image, and if we could but understand our flashes of individual

creativity we might glimpse the creativity of the Ultimate Creator!'
But, as always, Golding reveals a tentativeness; claiming only *a*
truth, a maybe, quite unlike Woolf's emphatic confidence. For all
his power, he always leaves space for other readings.

WILLIAM GOLDING

A Biographical Sketch
by Judy Carver

1911 On 19 September William Gerald Golding was born at his grandmother's house, Karenza, 47 Mount Wise, Newquay, in Cornwall. His mother Mildred (*née* Curnoe) was then aged forty. His father Alec Golding was born in 1876, the eldest of three sons of a Bristol shoemaker. Alec was a socialist and agnostic, with a firmly rationalist outlook. He became a teacher, and took a teaching job in Newquay, where he met Mildred, his landlady's daughter. He and Mildred married in January 1906 shortly after his appointment as science master at Marlborough Grammar School, where his exceptional talent for teaching was attested by the Inspectors' Reports for 1906 and 1912, and by many pupils. The Goldings' first son Jose was born in October 1906. During 1911, the Goldings took a lease of 29 The Green, Marlborough, which remained in the family until 1959. Golding spent many childhood holidays at Karenza, and became familiar with the coastline around Newquay. He also visited Kingswood near Bristol, staying with his paternal grandparents.

1916 Jose Golding went to Marlborough Grammar School.

1919 Golding was sent to a 'dame school', later described in 'Billy the Kid' (1960).*

1921–30 Golding went in his turn to Marlborough Grammar School. Like his brother, he was competitive and clever, played sports and was reasonably diligent. He was musical, as were both

---

* For a comprehensive list of William Golding's published works up to 1994, see R. A. Gekoski and P. A. Grogan, *William Golding: A Bibliography* (London: André Deutsch, 1994), referenced below as 'Gekoski'. Unless otherwise indicated below, all Golding's books are published in the UK by Faber and Faber. My acknowledgements and thanks are due to so many people and institutions that the list would be half as long as this biographical sketch. I hope to acknowledge such help in another work.

his parents. He won prizes for drawing, and was a good sprinter, as well as playing cricket, rugby, hockey and golf. Golding and his brother were good companions, often going for long walks together in the Wiltshire countryside. Golding and his father had something of a battle about the need to study Latin, as recorded in his essay, 'The Ladder and the Tree' (1960). Subsequently he came to enjoy Latin, and even to write verse in it. Home life at 29 The Green was spartan in some ways (the house was exceptionally cold and there were no electric lights upstairs until the late 1930s) but it was usually interesting. The family played a great deal of music together. Golding's father was fascinated by how things worked, and was ingenious and inventive as well as extremely knowledgeable. Among other achievements he made a radio, wiring earphones to each bedroom. The family listened avidly from the 1920s on. Golding's journal, kept sporadically from the age of sixteen to twenty, makes clear his determination to be a poet. In 1924 Jose went up to Brasenose College Oxford, to read history; he graduated in 1928 and became a teacher at a school in Grantham.

1930   Golding went to Brasenose to read Natural Sciences. A near contemporary at Brasenose was Adam Bittleston, who was a follower of Rudolf Steiner. Bittleston introduced Golding to Steiner's ideas, and the Anthroposophical movement. Golding was not convinced, but he was influenced, and the two were friends till Bittleston's death in 1989. At Oxford Golding met many other people, mostly through college or through music. He had few friends among scientists, and perhaps realised early that his choice of subject was a mistake.

1932   Golding ran into difficulties at Oxford. His sister Eileen Hogben (she was adopted by Golding's parents at the age of thirteen after her parents died; by birth she was his first cousin) remembers that during the summer of 1932 there were intense discussions between Golding and his father. Golding wished to change to English Literature. This would involve further expense (and Golding was not a frugal student). However, Alec agreed, and, characteristically, once he had taken the decision, helped his son with his new syllabus, writing out a translation of *Beowulf*, for example.

1934   Golding gained a BA honours degree (a 'good' second). During the last two years, Adam Bittleston had been encouraging Golding about his poetry. Bittleston knew an editor at Macmillan, and sent him some of Golding's poems. In the autumn, Macmillan published Golding's *Poems*, but they did not meet with great success. His future at this time seems to have been unclear to him. He lived for several months in London at 1001 Finchley Road, which at the time functioned as a centre, and chapel, of the Christian Community, a movement for religious renewal started with the help of Rudolf Steiner. Here he played the piano for assemblies, and also wrote a play about the legend of Persephone, commissioned by Bittleston and performed by members of the Community. In 1934 and probably 1935 as well, Golding also gained some theatrical training and experience, partly at the Little Theatre in Hampstead, and at a theatre in Bath.

1935–7   In the autumn of 1935 he became a teacher at Michael Hall, a Rudolf Steiner school then in Streatham, south London. This was probably another consequence of his friendship with Bittleston, who was ordained priest in the Christian Community in 1935. Golding spent two years at Michael Hall, teaching various subjects, and participating in the musical and dramatic performances at the school. But teaching was still, for him, something of a *pis aller*. In the summer of 1937, a friend asked the writer David Garnett, on Golding's behalf, if he could advise on how to make a living by writing. Garnett wrote to Golding in July, and gave him some practical advice about getting work as a reviewer. Nevertheless, in the autumn of 1937 Golding went back to Oxford to study for a teaching qualification.

1938   In January he started his teaching practice at Bishop Wordsworth's School, Salisbury, and in June passed his exams. In September, he took a post at Maidstone Grammar School. In Maidstone he also taught at the local prison, and at the school he did a great deal of music and drama, as well as cricket and rugby. His pupils remember him as a cheerful, round-faced man, energetic and quick in his movements. He helped direct a school performance of *Julius Caesar*, put on some kind of political pageant in the town, and played an active part in both the sporting and musical life of the school. He joined the Left Book Club (partly because of the opportunities it offered in drama via its Theatre Guild). Through politics, drama and his friends at the school, he became acquainted with the Brookfields, a large and interesting local family. Despite the recent death of the father of the family, and the death of the third son Norman in Spain, as a member of the International Brigade, the household was a welcoming one. Almost as soon as he met the eldest daughter, Ann, he fell in love with her, and she with him.

1939   In September, a few weeks after the declaration of war, they were married in Maidstone Registry Office, both ending previous engagements to do so.

1940   In April, Golding took up a post at Bishop Wordsworth's School. Pupils remember him working on *Julius Caesar* with them, and especially the mob scenes and the murder of Caesar. He and Ann moved into a small cottage in the village of Bowerchalke nine miles from Salisbury. At the school they made friends: in particular, a musician on the staff called John Milne, whom Golding had known slightly at Oxford, and another musician called Tony Brown. These friends were important to Golding then, and remained so, though he was always conscious of his inferiority to both of them as a musician. With Tony Brown he played more chess than with any other person; they played each other over more than thirty-five years.

   In September, the Goldings' first child, David, was born. In December Golding and John Milne both left Bishop Wordsworth's to join the Royal Navy.

1941–44   Golding's war experiences were varied. He was in the cruiser *Galatea*, leaving her a few months before she was sunk (he later said that the list of people lost in her was name after name of his friends). He served in the Atlantic both in *Galatea* and the destroyer *Orion*, and was involved in the pursuit of the *Bismarck*. In 1942 he was seconded to M.D.I, a Ministry of Defence establishment under the auspices of Lord Cherwell, and devoted to the invention and development of weapons. At M.D.I he used to carry fuses and detonators in different pockets; unsurprisingly he made a mistake, and was lucky that the resultant explosion didn't kill him. He subsequently felt he was more use on active service, and returned to sea at his own request. He crossed the Atlantic in 1943, waiting for several months in New York to bring a minesweeper back to home waters. In 1944 he commanded a rocket-launching craft in the D-Day landings, and later in the Walcheren operation in The Netherlands. These events affected him profoundly, both because of his own actions, and through witnessing the death or terrible injuries of his comrades. In an unpublished work written in the winter of 1947–8, he describes seeing a companion vessel blown up and, as he says, even worse, another one mined and sinking, when he could not turn his own ship round to save the men in the stricken one. He commented, 'These are memories to dim the sunlight.' One of Golding's brothers-in-law noticed a change in him after the war: he was less tolerant; he required more of people.

In the autumn of 1944, around the time of the Walcheren operation, Golding found time in his captain's cabin to write a kind of literary chronicle of progress so far, and he seems to have taken some sort of decision to move away from poetry. Another part of his wartime experience had been his study of Greek, and in particular his reading of Homer. Stephen Medcalf, a scholar and friend, has suggested that Golding's acquisition of Greek, and his developing knowledge of Greek literature, played a part in transforming him from a talented but minor Georgian poet into the innovatory novelist.

1945   In the early summer Golding was offered promotion and a command in the Far East. He declined, but in any case the war in the Far East soon ended. Before that, the Goldings' second and last child, Judith Diana, was born in July. In the autumn Golding returned to Bishop Wordsworth's School and civilian life.

1946   The Goldings moved to Salisbury, living in a flat owned by the city council.

1947–52   In April 1948, Golding's sister Eileen married Bill Hogben, a marine engineer. Their only child, Elizabeth Mary, was born in 1949.

During the war, Golding had learned cautiously to enjoy the sea, and to love the English coastline. In 1947 he and his wife scraped together the resources to buy and convert an old ship's lifeboat called *Seahorse*. It was during the next winter, writing his unpublished account of their family holiday in *Seahorse*, that he recalled the horrors of Walcheren and the loss of his fellow sailors. This account, and the one he wrote about the next year's holiday, were apprentice tasks for Golding, but they are quite accomplished, with consistency of tone. He wrote two novels, and submitted them to publishers, without success. In 1950 he published a poem called 'The Sea' in *Poetry Review*.

In these years after the war, Golding and his wife were both involved in amateur dramatics. Ann Golding was a talented performer. Golding, as well as acting, directed several plays, including a production of the *Alcestis* of Euripides. At school he put on several productions. His pupils remember him reading Greek plays to them, as well as material that he had written himself. He was involved in many other school activities. He and John Milne ran the Combined Cadet Force, and took boys sailing in the school whaler. He played music, sang in the school choir, and learnt the oboe because the school orchestra needed one. He ran an Archaeological Society and an Astronomy Group. He played a great deal of chess, with masters and pupils. He taught for the Workers' Educational Association, mainly about literature, but also music. By the autumn of 1952, he had begun work on a novel he called 'Strangers from Within'. He and his wife had been discussing children's books, including R. M. Ballantyne's *The Coral Island* (published in 1857). When he said to his wife that real children would not behave like those in children's books, she urged him to write about it.

1953   In January he started sending the novel to publishers. Many rejected it, until in September Golding sent it to Faber and Faber, where a new editor, Charles Monteith, picked it out of the rejects, started to read it and was gripped.

1954   In September, after some changes to the text, the novel was published as *Lord of the Flies*. It met with immediate interest and praise.

1955   *The Inheritors*, another novel of great originality and power, was published in September. It always remained Golding's favourite among his novels. This year he was made Fellow of the Royal Society of Literature.

1956   The Golding household now had a little more money, and they had already bought the first of several unreliable cars. They bought a new boat, *Wild Rose*, which had amenities like an (unreliable) engine and a lavatory. In August the Goldings set off for France with a good weather forecast but endured a fearful three-day crossing, battered by a fierce gale, which seriously endangered the boat and her crew. John Milne came to Le Havre to help them sail home after repairs.

Pincher Martin, a powerful account of the experiences after death of a drowned naval officer, was published in October. It was generally well received, though there was some controversy over the ending. Golding also contributed the story 'Envoy Extraordinary' to *Sometime, Never: three tales of the imagination* (published by Eyre and Spottiswoode); the other two stories were by John Wyndham and Mervyn Peake.

This year Golding's elder brother married a fellow teacher, Theo Parker.

1957   By now Golding had some involvement with literary life in London. He was a member of the panel of the Book Society, run by Tony Godwin of the bookshop Bumpus. He had started writing for *The Bookman* and *The Listener*, and was broadcasting. Several of his works were dramatised for radio. He was still teaching, but his headmaster took an enlightened position about giving him time off, and for six or seven years Golding was able to balance his two occupations. Some pupils and staff, however, found him distant and preoccupied.

Through contacts in London he had made several new friends who were very important to him. Wayland Young, later Lord Kennet, shared many interests with him – music, religion, literature, Wiltshire – and Golding cared a great deal for him and for his judgement. With Peter Green, another member of the Book Society panel and a distinguished Classical scholar, Golding talked much, especially about Greece and Greek literature. He also enjoyed – and would have liked to emulate – Green's wide erudition and literary gusto, as well as his fierce independence.

1958   *The Brass Butterfly*, his play, adapted from his story 'Envoy Extraordinary' and starring Alastair Sim, opened in Oxford on 24 February, toured the provinces, and then ran for a month in London. The text of the play was published in July. In June Golding became a member of the Savile Club. In the summer holiday he and his family went to sea as usual in *Wild Rose*. With them came Golding's father Alec, aged 81. The trip went well, and Golding returned his father safely to Marlborough. In the autumn Jose and Theo brought the first of their two children to Marlborough.

By the late 1950s Golding's many activities were leading to fatigue. He was finding it much more difficult than usual to write his next novel. During the autumn he and his family moved from Salisbury, having bought the somewhat enlarged cottage in Bowerchalke where they had lived in 1940. In November, Alec was diagnosed with cancer, and following an operation to remove the cancer he died suddenly of a heart attack in hospital on 12 December.

1959   Golding was much affected by his father's death, and it added to his difficulties in writing. Later he recorded that he had shed more tears over his father than he had over any other human being. He had early on rejected his father's rationalist outlook, but was profoundly influenced by Alec's scientific curiosity and zest, and by his passionate commitment to social justice. In the spring the Goldings and their children went to Italy, using some prize money Golding had won for his story 'Envoy Extraordinary'. In October the BBC did a programme about him in the 'Monitor' series, and in the same month *Free Fall* was published (it contains a character very clearly based on his father, as Golding acknowledged). Golding had to cope with some savage reviews of this book, though as a result he became good friends with an Oxford couple, Pamela and Kenneth Gravett. During this year Golding also published eight pieces in periodicals, including his short story 'The Anglo-Saxon'. In the autumn, his mother became very ill, and the lease of 29 The Green, the family home in Marlborough for nearly fifty years, was relinquished.

1960   Despite his personal struggles with writing, Golding produced many shorter works this year and was becoming well known. Gekoski lists twenty-five items in periodicals for 1960, including the autobiographical essays 'The Ladder and the Tree' and 'Billy the Kid' (both based in 29 The Green), as well as the short story 'Miss Pulkinhorn', the reviews 'Islands', 'Headmasters', and 'A Prospect of Eton', and the essay 'On the Crest of a Wave'. He was attracting the attention of critics and scholars. He met two young university lecturers, Ian Gregor and Mark Kinkead-Weekes, and a friendship resulted and flourished. There was the prospect of a film of *Lord of the Flies*.

In August Golding's mother died. She was nearly ninety, frail and with diminished faculties. She was a self-effacing figure, much wrapped up in her own imaginings, and her importance to others was not always clear to them.

1961   In April, the Goldings and their children went to Greece. The American magazine *Holiday* helped with travel expenses, and Golding wrote several articles for them. The Goldings drove across Europe and down through Yugoslavia. They arrived in Thessalonika and then followed the eastern coast of Greece down to Thermopylae (the 'Hot Gates'). They moved on to Athens and made various trips. At Marathon, Golding, telling his family the story of the battle, involuntarily gathered a small crowd of tourists around him. They went to Sounion, to the Peloponnesus, and to Delphi, then a sparse, quiet village with an astonishing and unspoilt view.

In the autumn Golding and his wife went to the USA. He had been appointed writer in residence at Hollins, a women's liberal arts college in Virginia. They spent the academic year there, making many friends and also travelling. More articles followed. Gekoski lists nineteen works in periodicals for this year, including 'Astronaut by Gaslight', 'Party of One: Thinking as a Hobby', and 'Tolstoy's Mountain'.

1962   While in America Golding worked on drafts of *The Spire*, as well as delivering the first version of his lecture 'Fable' (on *Lord of the Flies*). He also published six items in periodicals, including 'Through the Dutch Waterways' (a travel article which in draft had contained details about the wartime Walcheren operation), 'Surge and Thunder' (a review of Robert Fitzgerald's translation of *The Odyssey*), and 'The Hot Gates', his own essay on Thermopylae.

During this year, he resigned from Bishop Wordsworth's School, and became a full-time writer.

1963   In May, Peter Brook's film of *Lord of the Flies*, which had astonished and gratified Golding, was shown at Cannes. Golding and his wife visited Peter Green and his family in Greece (Green remembers him at work on *The Spire*). In August they also went to Russia on a trip organised by COMES, the European Community of Writers, in a group which included Angus Wilson, with whom they became friends. The French delegation included Jean-Paul Sartre and Simone de Beauvoir, and the Russians included Ilya Ehrenburg and Alexander Tvardovsky. A test-ban treaty was signed between the super-powers during their stay in Moscow, and politics greatly affected the literary discussions.

Golding published 'Digging for Pictures', 'Advice to a Nervous Visitor' and several other essays. He made more new friends, among them the artist Michael Ayrton and the psychologist Anthony Storr. David Cecil, the critic and literary historian, who lived a few miles away in Dorset, also became a friend.

1964   *The Spire* was published in April. It received mixed reviews, which distressed Golding, especially since he considered it one of his very best novels. In the summer all four Goldings went off to Greece. They spent nearly six weeks living next door to Peter Green and his family, in Methymna on the north coast of Lesvos.

On their return in the autumn, both the children left home, and for the first time since 1940 (apart from the stay in America) the Goldings were a couple on their own. For a few years Ann Golding had had a part-time post teaching arithmetic at a boys' school. She was excellent at her job and enjoyed it, but now she gave it up to be at home with her husband. She was always the first person to whom he turned for advice and criticism about his writing, and it was a great advantage to him to have her at home.

1965   Golding collected some of his essays and reviews in one volume. The book acquired its title, *The Hot Gates*, from the first essay, his piece on Thermopylae. The dust-jacket design was by Michael Ayrton, using his portrait studies of Golding. Also in this year, Golding's essay 'An Affection for Cathedrals' was published.

Over the years, Golding had often been criticized for his

portrayal of women, and so in the mid 1960s he wrote an (unpublished) account of his relations with women, which he called 'Men, Women & Now'. Out of this process grew his next novel, *The Pyramid*.

1966 Golding was awarded the CBE. An excerpt from *The Pyramid* was published in *Esquire*. He and Ann decided to go to sea again, and bought a beautiful Dutch sailing barge called *Tenace*. In July Kenneth Gravett died tragically, and Golding felt his death deeply.

1967 This year five of Golding's works were published in periodicals, including a review of his friend Andrew Sinclair's translation of selections from *The Greek Anthology*, and another excerpt from Golding's new novel. *The Pyramid* was published in book form in June. Like *Free Fall*, it was a novel in a modern context with a first-person narrator. Both novels contain elements of autobiography. *The Pyramid* also had mixed reviews, but Golding was learning to ignore them, making sure that those nearest him knew he did not want to be told any hurtful details.

In July, *Tenace* was run down and sunk off the Isle of Wight. Golding, his wife and their daughter, with three friends, had been making for France. The ship that hit *Tenace* rescued all on board, but Golding, already depressed by personal difficulties, was shocked and badly shaken physically, as was his wife.

1968–1970 Golding again began to find it more and more difficult to write, or to have faith in his writing. (He wrote an account of these feelings himself, and called it 'History of a Crisis'.) The situation was exacerbated by family anxieties, particularly about his children. In the absence of a new novel, he also became worried about his finances. These years were bleak in many ways, and the strain showed, partly in Golding's personal struggles with alcohol, partly in a degree of withdrawal from ordinary social life. But these factors can be overstated. He was often busy and cheerful, even if there were grim moods at times. Also, he still took pleasure in travel, in music (particularly in playing the piano), and in friendship. His friend Tony Brown had moved to Bowerchalke, and he and Golding played chess several times a week. During the 1960s Golding had made friends with

James Lovelock, the scientist, who also lived in Bowerchalke. Golding took enormous pleasure in Lovelock's ideas, and admired his innovatory imagination as well as his practical scientific ingenuity. He was pleased that his suggestion of Gaia was adopted by Lovelock as the name for his hypothesis of the earth as a self-adjusting organism.

In 1970 The University of Sussex made him an honorary D.Litt.

1971 This year improvements began in many ways, though he still struggled. His son was happier, and in January his daughter married Terrell Carver, an American and a graduate student at Oxford, as she was. Crucially, Golding himself had a book coming out in October. *The Scorpion God* reprinted 'Envoy Extraordinary' and added two new stories. Before its publication, Golding and his wife went to Italy, staying for part of the time with Wayland and Elizabeth Kennet. Golding mentioned to them his vivid dreams, and they urged him to keep a dream diary. The Goldings drove to Rome, and there he had what he called a 'great dream', which later influenced Wilf Barclay's Roman dream in *The Paper Men*. He began a careful reading of the works of C. G. Jung. Jung's ideas had always been attractive to him, and he had discussed them with Tony Brown, Anthony Storr and Michael Ayrton. In time he became less convinced of the validity of Jungian concepts, but he never lost his sense of their benevolence. From the autumn of 1971 he kept a journal, which started as a record of dreams but gradually became an account of his writing as well, and of daily tribulations: worries about the British economy, irritation with correspondents, the English climate, and his struggles with various machines (lawn mowers, chess computers, cars, cameras).

1972–9 In 1972 Golding started reviewing again, producing around twenty items over the next decade. His journal for the early and mid 70s shows his self-doubt and self-disgust (he was prone to bouts of fierce dieting, for example), but there was progress and satisfaction as well, and occasional happiness. Golding had a sharp, self-critical awareness of the ludicrous aspects of his life, and the journal gave him somewhere to confide this (he gave himself mildly derogatory nicknames). Also, his journal shows the manner in which *Darkness Visible* slowly took shape. Indeed, he started another novel – *Rites of Passage* – before *Darkness Visible* was finished. He worked on one for a few days and then reverted to the other. Unsurprisingly, under the circumstances, they are very different.

In 1974 the University of Kent made him an honorary D.Litt.

During this period he lost three of his closest friends: Michael Ayrton died in 1975, John Milne in 1976, and Tony Brown in 1977. In 1976 Ann Golding had a major operation. Nevertheless, there were good things – David was helped by his conversion to Roman Catholicism, and also the first of the Goldings' three grandsons was born in 1976, and the second in 1979. The Goldings themselves were travelling. In many cases Golding gave talks for the British Council, and at local universities. A trip to Australia was particularly good. They also had several good holidays in Italy and Yugoslavia, and in Switzerland they made friends with a Swiss scholar and linguist, Heinrich Straumann, and his wife Ursula. They also began to take more pleasure in their garden. For Golding his water garden, which he himself developed, became a preoccupation. His journal, a daily discipline but often a pleasure, gave his working day a framework, and he practised the piano energetically. Older griefs – the loss of his father, the failure to be a great poet, the regrets about *Tenace*, and the feeling of futility and sadness in some aspects of his personal life – began to recede in the presence of successful activity.

1979   *Darkness Visible* was published in October, winning the James Tait Black Memorial Prize.

1980   *Rites of Passage* was published in October, winning the Booker McConnell Prize. In November Golding was the subject of a South Bank Show television programme.

1981   In March Bill Hogben died of cancer aged fifty-nine.
In September Golding was seventy. By now he had steadied himself, had stopped worrying quite so much about money (partly because of his two new novels), and had begun to enjoy most of life again. The University of Warwick made him an honorary D.Litt.

The Goldings, following the generous example of his parents in the years before he and Ann became prosperous, had begun taking their children and grandchildren on long summer holidays. From 1978 until 1992, except for one year, the family went to France – especially Brittany – or more rarely to Spain for about a month each summer. Golding and his wife studied French and Spanish, and Golding in particular read extensively in French literature. Ann Golding took up painting; he did a number of drawings, keeping her company. They also travelled more widely, often under the auspices of the British Council. In the 80s and 90s they visited Canada, the United States, India, Japan, Mexico, Malaysia, Singapore, Burma and Egypt, as well as making many trips to parts of Europe previously unfamiliar to them, such as Austria and Czechoslovakia. Back in England Golding had begun to explore and appreciate the Wiltshire countryside from a new point of view. He took up horse riding, and thereby regained some of the experience of risk and independence which sailing had given him.

1982   *A Moving Target*, a new collection of essays and reviews, was published.

1983   In the summer both Oxford University and the Sorbonne gave Golding honorary doctorates. In October he was awarded the Nobel Prize for Literature. His pleasure was only partly dimmed by some adverse comments made about it. He was willing to believe that, while others might be worthy of the prize, he certainly was as well. His Nobel lecture gave him the opportunity to voice his concerns about environmental issues.

1984   *The Paper Men* was published in February. That spring Golding and his wife went on a trip up the Nile. In the summer the University of Bristol made him an honorary LLD.

1985   Since 1983 Golding had been kept busy by engagements arising from the Nobel Prize. Eventually he and Ann Golding found that being no more than ninety miles from London filled their lives with interviews, visitors and even sightseers. In April 1985, they moved to Tullimaar, an elegant Georgian house about six miles from Truro in Cornwall, and less than twenty miles from Golding's birthplace. He delighted in Tullimaar's connection with the diarist Francis Kilvert, with Princesse Marthe Bibesco, and – reputedly – General Eisenhower.

In July *An Egyptian Journal* was published. In the autumn of

1985 they travelled to Canada, crossing the country by train, with Golding giving lectures and readings in many places. During part of this trip Charles Monteith joined them, giving lectures as well. Then the Goldings returned to England via the United States, where their daughter and her family were spending a year in Virginia.

1986   Faber and Faber published *William Golding: The Man and his Books. A Tribute on his 75th Birthday*. Edited by John Carey, it contained tributes from many critics and fellow authors, including Ted Hughes, Seamus Heaney, Stephen Medcalf, Ian Gregor and Mark Kinkead-Weekes, as well as an illuminating interview with Golding by Carey himself, and a memoir of Golding's father by a former pupil.

1987   In January Golding's elder brother Jose died. In June *Close Quarters* was published, a sequel to *Rites of Passage*.

1988   Golding was knighted by the Queen. His daughter published a novel, and despite its mixed reception Golding was pleased and proud.

1989   *Fire Down Below*, the final novel of the Sea Trilogy, was published in March, bringing its hero Edmund Talbot to Australia. In this year, Golding's old friend Adam Bittleston died, and his son David became ill again. Golding himself began to experience some frailty, but he was still energetic.

1990   Golding reviewed *Hothouse Earth* by John Gribben, under the title 'The Earth's Revenge'. In the early spring the *Sunday Times* sent him and Ann on a cruise around South-East Asia on board the *Sea Goddess*, a luxurious cruise ship, and Golding wrote an essay about it for the *Sunday Times* called 'The Life of Lord Riley'. He also published the essay 'Two Spires' in the *Annual Report of the Friends of Salisbury Cathedral*.

1991   Golding celebrated his eightieth birthday. He revised the separate volumes of his Sea Trilogy to make a single volume, *To the Ends of the Earth*.

1992   During this year Golding worked on 'Scenes from a Life', an account of episodes in his childhood and early manhood (part of this has been published in *Areté*, Issue II, spring–summer 2000). In the summer the Goldings made a trip to Oviedo in Spain, where he was given an honorary D.Litt. by the University. Then the Goldings, together with their son David, now recovered, and their daughter, son-in-law and three grandsons (the youngest born in 1983), went to a seaside village in Galicia. Ann Golding was increasingly frail and could not walk far.

In the autumn Golding was told he had a malignant melanoma on his face, and in December, just after Christmas, it was removed.

1993   He seemed to recover well, and began work on a new novel. In February he wrote a comment, published in the *Daily Mail*, on the James Bulger child murder case. In early June his old friend Peter Green visited him, finding him as energetic as ever. The Goldings gave a party at their home on 18 June. By then he had finished two drafts of the new novel, and intended to begin a further draft after the party. However, on the morning of 19 June Golding's son-in-law, going to wake him, found he had died of heart failure. Five days later, on Midsummer's Day, he was buried in the churchyard at Bowerchalke. By that time his wife Ann had already suffered a stroke from which she never fully recovered.

In November Golding was remembered at a memorial service in Salisbury Cathedral. Wayland Kennet paid generous tribute to him and his work, and Ted Hughes read from *The Inheritors*, so that the pillars of the cathedral rang with Golding's imagined words of prayer to the goddess Oa.

1995   Ann Golding died on New Year's Day, eighteen months after her husband, and was buried beside him in the churchyard at Bowerchalke. In June, Golding's last novel, *The Double Tongue*, was published.

INDEX

References to William Golding are shortened to WG. Titles of novels by William Golding, where they appear as main headings, are printed in full with the date of publication. Names of characters from the novels are enclosed in single quotes and accompanied by italicized references to the source novel: LF (*Lord of the Flies*), TI (*The Inheritors*), PM (*Pincher Martin*), FF (*Free Fall*), TS (*The Spire*), TP (*The Pyramid*), DV (*Darkness Visible*), TPM (*The Paper Men*), RP (*Rites of Passage*), CQ (*Close Quarters*), FB (*Fire Down Below*), DT (*Double Tongue*).

plea for 'Summers' to be given
command 333
poetic failure 307
privilege and responsibilities 257,
260, 308
quarrel with 'Benét' 322–3
rated midshipman 318–19
relations with Captain 257, 262, 297,
302
rivalry with 'Benét' 307
seduction of 'Zenobia' 258–9, 304,
320
seeing without understanding 259,
263–4
social education 257, 260, 314, 329,
378
social prejudices 257, 264, 297–8, 378
spying for godfather 327
tears
at parting from 'Marion' 303, 307
at singing of 'Mrs East' 301–2,
379
of remorse 313
visits to 'Colley' in his cabin 260,
262, 263, 266
weed appears as monster rising from
depths 311, 379
see also Close Quarters; Fire Down
Below; individual characters;
Rites of Passage
'Edwin' (DV) 249, 250
cry of Joy 250–1
Man in Black 249
spiritual seance 250–1
'Elizabeth Barclay' (TPM) 275, 276
dying of cancer 288–9
pestered by 'Rick Tucker' 277, 279,
281
Emma (Jane Austen) 207
Euripides, Ion 348, 352–3
'Evelyn De Tracy' 237
sexual orientation 230–1
'Evie Babbacombe' (OE) 224
denounces 'Oliver' to his father 229
expressions of hate 227
feelings for 'Robert' 226
forced to go to London 228
growing sophistication 229
orgasm 227
parents 225
potential for music and self-
improvement 225
relationship with 'Oliver' 225, 229
relationships

with her father 228–9, 237
with 'Oliver' 225, 229
with 'Oliver''s father 228–9
revenge on Stilbourne and 'Oliver'
228–9
Roman Catholicism 226, 237
self-hatred 227
sexuality 225, 226–7, 237
visits to dispensary 228, 229
weals on bottom 228–9
wheelchair-bound neighbour 227,
228
see also 'Oliver'

'Fa' and 'Lok' (TI)
cross the deep water 72–3
drunkenness 86
fallen consciousness 81, 85
in stockade 73–80, 82
'Fa' (TI) 50, 53, 65–6, 77
death-plunge over waterfall 88, 90,
95, 97, 366
developing consciousness 80
dismembers doe 60–1
essential innocence 88
hostile images of New Men 84
invents cultivation and irrigation 54,
62–4
leadership 71
mate of 'Lok' 56
search for 'New One' 79
struggle with language 53–4, 63
watches death of 'Liku' 79
see also 'Ha'; 'Liku'; 'Lok'; 'Mal';
'New One'
'Father Adam' (TS) 175, 190–1, 192,
195–7, 199
'Father Anselm' (TS) 175–6, 186, 192–3
Fielding, Henry 269
Fire Down Below (WG 1989) 314–37,
398
Antarctica 332
arrival in Australia 333
quarrels in response to increasing
stress 322–5
storm 322–6
within the ice field 331–2
see also Close Quarters; individual
characters; Rites of Passage
Free Fall (WG 1959) 136, 138–70, 171,
204, 215–16, 222–3, 293, 373,
377–8, 391, 393–4
Becoming and Being 138–9, 141–3,

'Marlan'; New Men; 'New One'; People; 'Tanakil'
Longford, Elizabeth (*Life of Wellington*) 260
Lord of the Flies (WG 1954) 1–47, 96–7, 129, 146, 171, 188, 203, 210–11, 218, 292, 362, 388, 391

Beast 7, 11, 20, 23, 30–1, 33
  children mistake parachutist as 23
  disbelievers 20
  propitiated by offerings 26, 27–8
  'Simon' believes in internal beast 20, 23, 29, 30
child world as microcosm of adult world 22–3
conch shell
  blown by 'Jack' 25
  found 2–3, 364
  loss of meaning 40–2
  'Piggy' confronts 'Jack' with 41–2
  smashed 42, 365
  Sound of the Shell 3, 5, 7, 9–13, 19, 22, 41
  symbol of assembly 4–5, 16, 42
confrontation between tribe and 'Piggy' and 'Ralph' 41–3
evil inherent in man 28–9, 38–9
fear amongst the children 19–22, 28
first assembly 324
forest fire 12, 45
hate grown from fear 21
irresponsibility and ignorance 11–13, 18
mode of the imagination 210–11
naval officer 45–7
parachutist 22
  children identify as Beast 23, 26
  discovered and cut loose by Simon 30
  parody of death and resurrection 30
  swept away by wind 31
pig-killing chant and mime-dance 21, 25, 28, 31–3
  becoming protective ritual 34–5
  bloodlust 35
pig's head on a stick 27–9, 30, 44
rock-rolling 9, 24, 42, 44
second assembly 11, 19–21, 33, 46
signal fire 11, 12, 18, 19
storms 8, 31, 35
tension between 'Ralph', 'Jack' and 'Piggy' 8, 14, 18–19, 31, 33–4, 35
see also individual characters

Lovelock, James 394
'Lucinda' (*TPM*), ex-mistress of 'Wilf' 274, 275, 276, 278

Maidstone Grammar School 386
'Mal' (*TI*) 53, 54, 56–8, 68, 83–4
  death 56–7, 59, 77
  failing powers 57, 59, 61, 62
  funeral 50, 59
  grave desecrated by hyenas 73
  nightmare 68, 72
  struggle with language 53–4, 62
'Marion Chumley' (*CQ, FB*)
  concern over 'Edmund' 333
  first meeting with 'Edmund' 300–1
  joins 'Edmund' in Sydney 336
  love at first sight 301–3
  see also 'Edmund Talbot'
'Marlan', ruler-priest (*TI*) 76–7, 87, 93, 94
  hopelessness 114, 118
  Old Woman 123
  stealing food 77, 78
  tribal rebellion against 78–9
  see also individual characters; *Inheritors*; New Men
Marlborough Grammar School 383
'Martin, Christopher "Pincher"' (*PM*) 6, 218–19, 366–7
  actor's mask 104, 106, 109
  Adversary (Antagonist) 112–13, 116, 121
  black lightning 117, 124, 125, 127–9, 131, 134, 367
  'Campbell' 130
  cellar in childhood dreams 119, 121, 123–4, 125, 127, 133–4
  consciousness 113, 114, 115, 116, 118, 119, 129
  darkness 114, 117, 118, 119, 122, 125, 133, 134, 366–7
  death, moment of 108–9, 110, 122
  Divine Week of Creation parody 112–29
  dwarf (man-shape) 103, 115, 116, 118, 123
  eye-pain 113–15
  glass figure in jar 110–11, 112, 119, 131, 215
  greed 104–5, 106, 109
  gulls as flying reptiles 115, 118, 125
  hallucinations 116
  Heaven 123, 124, 127, 128
  hell 118, 123